After Camp

The publisher gratefully acknowledges the generous support
of the Humanities Endowment Fund of the
University of California Press Foundation.

After Camp

Portraits in Midcentury Japanese American Life and Politics

GREG ROBINSON

University of California Press

BERKELEY   LOS ANGELES   LONDON

University of California Press, one of the most distinguished university presses in the United States, enriches lives around the world by advancing scholarship in the humanities, social sciences, and natural sciences. Its activities are supported by the UC Press Foundation and by philanthropic contributions from individuals and institutions. For more information, visit www.ucpress.edu.

University of California Press
Berkeley and Los Angeles, California

University of California Press, Ltd.
London, England

© 2012 by The Regents of the University of California

Portions of Chapter 1 first appeared in Greg Robinson, "Le Projet M de Franklin Roosevelt: Construire un monde meilleur grâce à la science . . . des races," *Critique Internationale* No. 27 (May 2005), pp. 65–82. Portions of Chapters 3 and 10 first appeared as Greg Robinson, "Nisei in Gotham: Japanese Americans in Wartime New York," *Prospects: An Annual of American Cultural Studies*, Vol. 30 (2005), pp. 581–595. Chapter 4 originally appeared in somewhat different form as Greg Robinson, "Birth of a Citizen: Miné Okubo and the Politics of Symbolism," in Greg Robinson and Elena Tajima Creef, eds., *Miné Okubo: Following Her Own Road* (Seattle: University of Washington Press, 2008), pp. 149–166. Portions of Chapter 6 first appeared as Toni Robinson and Greg Robinson, "*Mendez v. Westminster*: Asian-Latino Coalition Triumphant?" *Asian Law Journal*, Vol. 10, 2 (May 2003), pp. 161–183, and in revised form as Greg Robinson and Toni Robinson, "The Limits of Interracial Coalition: *Méndez v. Westminster* Reconsidered," in Nicholas De Genova, ed., *Racial (Trans)formations: Latinos and Asians Remaking the United States* (Durham, NC: Duke University Press, 2006), pp. 93–119. Chapter 11 first appeared as Greg Robinson and Toni Robinson, "*Korematsu* and Beyond: Japanese Americans and the Origins of Strict Scrutiny," *Law & Contemporary Problems*, Vol. 68, No. 2 (Spring 2005), pp. 29–55. Portions of Chapter 12 first appeared in Greg Robinson, "Une alliance malaisée: Nisei et Africains-Américains," *Matériaux* No. 87 (Autumn 2007), pp. 49–66.

Library of Congress Cataloging-in-Publication Data

Robinson, Greg, 1966–
  After camp : portraits in midcentury Japanese American life and politics / Greg Robinson.
    p. cm.
  Includes bibliographical references and index.
  ISBN 978-0-520-27158-6 (cloth : alk. paper)
  ISBN 978-0-520-27159-3 (pbk. : alk. paper)
  1. Japanese Americans—Social conditions—20th century. 2. Japanese Americans—Politics and government—20th century. 3. Japanese Americans—Civil rights—History—20th century. 4. Japanese Americans—Evacuation and relocation, 1942–1945. 5. Cold War—Social aspects—United States. 6. Community life—United States—History—20th century. 7. United States—Social conditions—1945– 8. United States—Ethnic relations—20th century. I. Title.
  E184.J3R63 2012
  973'.04956—dc23

2011030474

To Heng Wee Tan

and in loving memory of Toni Robinson (1942–2002)

Contents

Photographs follow page 154.

	Introduction	1
PART I.	RESETTLEMENT AND NEW LIVES	
1.	Political Science? FDR, Japanese Americans, and the Postwar Dispersion of Minorities	15
2.	Forrest LaViolette: Race, Internationalism, and Assimilation	31
3.	Japantown Born and Reborn: Comparing the Resettlement Experience of Issei and Nisei in Detroit, New York, and Los Angeles	43
PART II.	THE VARIETIES OF ASSIMILATION	
4.	Birth of a Citizen: Miné Okubo and the Politics of Symbolism	69
5.	The "New Nisei" and Identity Politics	85
PART III.	INTERETHNIC POLITICS	
6.	Japanese Americans and Mexican Americans: The Limits of Interracial Collaboration	105
7.	From *Kuichi* to Comrades: Japanese American Views of Jews in the 1930s and 1940s	139

PART IV. AFRICAN AMERICAN SUPPORTERS OF JAPANESE AMERICANS, AND THE SHIFT IN NISEI VIEWS OF AFRICAN AMERICANS

8. African American Responses to the Wartime Confinement of Japanese Americans — 157

9. The Los Angeles Defender: Hugh E. Macbeth and Japanese Americans — 171

10. Crusaders in Gotham: The JACD and Interracial Activism — 183

PART V. THE RISE AND FALL OF POSTWAR COALITIONS FOR CIVIL RIGHTS

11. From *Korematsu* to *Brown*: Nisei and the Postwar Struggle for Civil Rights — 195

12. An Uneasy Alliance: Blacks and Japanese Americans, 1954–1965 — 217

Epilogue — 241

Notes — 249

Index — 303

Introduction

This book illuminates various aspects of a central but unexplored area of American history: the midcentury Japanese American experience. A vast and ever-growing literature exists, first on the entry and settlement of Japanese immigrants in the United States at the turn of the twentieth century, then on the experience of the immigrants and their American-born children during World War II.[1] Indeed, the official roundup of some 120,000 American citizens and permanent residents of Japanese ancestry on the West Coast and their subsequent confinement in government camps (often, if imprecisely, called the "Japanese American internment") represents the single most-documented subject in Asian American studies and a vital theme of popular debate. Yet the essential question "What happened afterwards?" remains all but unanswered in historical literature.[2] Such neglect is unjust, as the postwar evolution of Japanese American communities deserves extended and careful study. Excluded from the wartime economic boom and scarred psychologically by their wartime ordeal, the former camp inmates struggled to remake their lives in the years that followed, and to build new social ties and community structures. If the generation of resettlement and renewal that followed the release of inmates from camp lacks the massive drama and conflict of the wartime events, it must be accounted equally important, if not more so, in setting the course of mainland Japanese American life.[3]

This volume consists of a series of case studies, in the form of essays. They shed light on various developments relating to Japanese Americans in the aftermath of their wartime confinement, including resettlement nationwide, the mental and physical readjustment of the former inmates, and their political engagement, most notably in concert with other racialized and ethnic minority groups. In the process, I explore and test various conclusions about the nature and particularity of the postwar Japanese American experience. The bulk of the material in the collection is previously unpublished, or in a few cases has appeared only in French-language editions—the latter element a product of the author's life in Montreal, a North American city at the crossroads of anglophone and francophone scholarship. Even the fraction that has already seen print in some form has been expanded and updated to take account of new research and scholarship. The text, it will be noted, does not follow a strict chronology, but takes up in turn a set of key themes that shaped Japanese communities during the midcentury period. While the focus is on postwar events, some of the chapters begin chronologically in the prewar or wartime period in order to provide proper background and context for understanding what occurred thereafter.

This collection is not intended to be either definitive or comprehensive. Rather, the work represents something of a new departure, a broad-based investigation of a complex and largely uncovered subject, designed to provide an opening for further inquiry and more extended discussion. Like all generalizations, my exposition is limited and admits of exceptions. It is my fervent hope that the volume will help move scholars in history, political science, law, ethnic studies, and other fields to engage the primary material available on postwar Japanese Americans and fill the sizable gaps that exist in the literature.[4] My case studies are limited, and my conclusions are thus necessarily tentative. As the late historian Winthrop Jordan remarked about his audacious findings on the origins of racism, "I shall be enormously surprised—and greatly disappointed—if I am not shown to be wrong on some matters.... Some, but not *too* many."[5] I certainly make no greater claim to infallibility.

I wish here to outline the direction of the work that follows by describing briefly its central themes. The first theme that I discuss is the generational shift in the structure of group leadership, as the Issei leaders who had dominated Japanese communities in the prewar years were displaced from authority by the Nisei. The plight of the Issei after 1941 was poignant. Barred from citizenship by their adopted land, the immigrants were thereby transformed at a stroke into "enemy aliens" by the outbreak of war between the United States and Japan, and exposed to arbitrary restrictions. Virtually all community leaders were interned by the Justice Department for indeterminate periods, while the rest were confined in government camps with their families or fellow bachelors, then further humiliated by official directives barring noncitizens from community government positions. Forced to dispose of the bulk of their property at the time of removal, the Issei were generally unable to reestablish their prewar businesses and farms and were relegated to menial labor or dependent on economic support from their children. Although the 1952 McCarran-Walter Immigration Act permitted Japanese immigrants for the first time to become naturalized U.S. citizens and to vote, the Issei men who had dominated prewar group life were largely sidelined from community affairs. Conversely, the Nisei came of age in this period. Assuming community leadership posts, they worked to establish themselves in mainstream society, to acquire education and economic opportunity, and to win recognition of the group's civil rights. Nisei also concentrated on family life, marrying other Nisei (or, increasingly, taking non-Japanese spouses) and sharing in the nationwide baby boom.

The efforts of the Nisei, in turn, were shaped by a number of contingent factors. One was spatial. The mass movement of inmates out of the camps and the question of where and how they should resettle raised practical and ideological concerns among Japanese community leaders, as well as among those outside. Government leaders, anxious to avert potential racial violence by hostile West Coast whites, actively discouraged Japanese Americans from returning to their prewar homes. On the contrary, following the simplistic theory that the concentration of minorities in populated regions catalyzed prejudice, officials from President Roosevelt on down launched plans to disperse the inmates in small groups throughout the country in order to dissolve their distinctive ethnic characteristics and promote their integration. Many Japanese Americans and their sympathizers agreed that Issei and Nisei, once relocated outside the West Coast and its endemic anti-Japanese prejudice, would be accepted as equal citizens and become absorbed into the larger population.

While there was some regional variation, most visibly in the presence of official exclusion and discriminatory legislation in West Coast states and its absence elsewhere, in actual fact the experiences of those who returned to the West Coast and those who resettled elsewhere—whether in areas with existing Japanese communities or in those without—were not so dissimilar. All faced housing shortages, made worse by restrictive covenants and other exclusionary devices. As a result, Issei and Nisei were forced to crowd together into temporary lodgings or take substandard housing, often in or next to slum areas, where they came into broad contact with other nonwhite neighbors (a fact that would ultimately be of capital importance in fostering interracial contact and the formation of alliances). Meanwhile, resettlers nationwide were victimized by underemployment and job discrimination. Excluded from capital and bank loans to start businesses, they were forced to take jobs with requirements well below their educational level. As a result, both by choice and by necessity, Japanese communities were forced to band together to ensure necessary services and to work together for common goals.

In sum, the variations in the status of the community had less to do with the region of settlement than with the particular characteristics of the local community and the nature of the resettlers themselves. There was thus no inherent advantage for Issei and Nisei to resettling outside the West Coast, and the truth of this point was demonstrated by the steady reflux of Issei and Nisei to the West Coast, which by mid-1947 was once again home to the majority of the mainland ethnic population. (In marked contrast, Japanese Canadians were forbidden to resettle on the Pacific Coast until 1949, and few cared to return even after the ban was lifted.)

Part I of this volume centers on the questions of resettlement and dispersal. It opens with an essay, "Political Science?" that places the government's scheme to "distribute" Japanese Americans throughout the country in larger context by looking at the policy alongside President Franklin D. Roosevelt's parallel plans for mass postwar transportation and resettlement of Jews and other European ethnic minorities throughout the Western Hemisphere. The existence of such plans, and the president's establishment of the M Project, a secret team of social scientists, to facilitate it, underlines the eugenicist thinking that underlay the official actions in both cases.

A related chapter, this time covering the semiofficial realm, discusses the views of the sociologist Forrest LaViolette and his contribution to debates over resettlement and absorption. LaViolette, a rare non-Japanese scholar of Nikkei in both the United States and Canada who served as a "social analyst" at the Heart Mountain camp, is a paradox. On one hand, he bravely supported equal rights for Nisei and quietly organized assistance for resettlers. At the same time, he remained so heavily fixated on the urgent need to dismantle separate minority communities in order to foster equality that he hailed forcible dispersion of ethnic Japanese in both countries as a positive step for civil rights, and mass confinement as a providential means to that end. The following essay, "Japantown Born and Reborn," offers a comparative study of the experience of Japanese Americans in New York and Detroit, two cities outside the West Coast where vital Japanese resettler colonies formed, with the conditions faced by those who returned to Los Angeles, the main prewar Japanese population center. It thereby tests the official theory that Issei and Nisei, once dispersed outside the West Coast, would naturally face better conditions.

Connected with the spatial question of resettlement was the issue of assimilation and its meaning. This was not only a central social and cultural question for the Nisei but a deeply political and indeed existential matter as well. Before the war, as John Modell and others have demonstrated, Japanese communities practiced a political and economic strategy of racial accommodation.[6] Rather than directly challenging race-based exclusion, Japanese immigrant communities developed a segregated niche economy, centered on the agricultural and fishing sectors, in which ethnic-owned businesses employed the large majority of community members. At the same time, Japanese communities maintained their closest ties with Japan, through networks of consulates, business groups, and media, while large numbers of Nisei were sent to Japanese school to learn the ancestral language and culture. A significant fraction of Nisei—as many as 25 percent of the total by some estimates—were sent back to Japan for schooling. (Because of cultural differences and their lesser fluency in English, many of the Japanese-educated Nisei, the so-called Kibei, remained at a certain distance from the American-educated majority.)

If the Nisei were made conscious of their Japanese identity, they likewise attended public schools and absorbed mainstream values and popular culture, like other young Americans. What is more, the group was splintered into various cliques and factions. The Japanese American Citizens League (JACL), the largest and most visible single group of second-generations, was composed largely of young professionals who were heavily Republican in political sympathies and assimilationist in temper. The JACL restricted its membership to U.S. citizens and stressed the Americanism of the group. Liberal and intellectual Nisei were visible in Young Democrat clubs and the vernacular press. They too trumpeted their Americanism, but favored more radical political reform and nonconformity in cultural terms, embracing jazz music and modern art and literature.

The exigencies of war and mass confinement washed away prewar alignments. First, following the Japanese attack on Pearl Harbor, the Japanese consulates and schools shut their doors, and they remained closed long after the end of the conflict. Nisei found themselves in a kind of limbo, and in the altered and unfamiliar circumstances of wartime and postwar life, activists and intellectuals were impelled to rethink their group identity. Because attachment to Japan had become heavily stigmatized—all things Japanese were "rat poison," in Miné Okubo's piquant phrase—the Nisei had to define themselves, and justify their collective existence, in exclusively American terms. Nisei were warned by government officials, and by each other, that they needed to manage carefully their self-presentation to avoid seeming different or threatening. Many Nisei Americanized their names and took to heart the official instructions they received to avoid other Japanese Americans and to "assimilate" to mainstream (middle-class Anglo-American) values.

Yet the old accommodationist strategy of seeking equality solely through good citizenship had evolved. Many Nisei, as they left camp and resettled outside, were inspired both by outrage over the wartime violation of their citizenship rights and by their new acquaintance with other racialized groups to perceive themselves as a minority among other minorities. Even the reconstituted JACL, though it retained its platform of Americanization, engaged in multiethnic coalition building. In an ironic turn, the wartime events not only opened mainstream media outlets to progressive Nisei, bringing them to the fore as community spokespeople, but also placed activists such as Larry Tajiri, Mary Oyama Mittwer, and Joe Grant Masaoka into positions of community influence. They advocated "assimilation" through political action in the public sphere and pressed Nisei to speak out against white supremacy, both for themselves and for other groups, as the sign of their adaptation.

A pair of pieces in Part II define some of the contours of the debate over assimilation and identity. "Birth of a Citizen" describes the evolution of Miné Okubo's 1946 graphic memoir *Citizen 13660*, the first and arguably most incisive study of the camp experience. The text reveals how the particular context of the resettlement era shaped Okubo's narrative. In the interest of ensuring continued government support for Japanese American resettlement and their social acceptance, not only did the author shy away from direct criticism of federal government policy in her text (as against her drawings) and associated publicity material, but she and her supporters collaborated with official pro-Nisei propaganda efforts.

The second piece, "The 'New Nisei' and Identity Politics," describes the efforts of various Nisei intellectuals to set a community agenda by calling on Nisei to "assimilate." They not only failed to reach consensus on the meaning of such "assimilation" but offered widely varying understandings of their group identity and life. For Nisei writers Larry Tajiri and Ina Sugihara, assimilation meant participating as citizens in the public sphere in support of equal rights for all, and joining forces with other racial and ethnic minority groups—especially black Americans, who could provide an example of minority group cohesion and democratic struggle. Conversely, for the Canadian-born semanticist S. I. Hayakawa, himself a columnist for an African American newspaper and a devotee of jazz and black culture, assimilation meant above all acting like other Americans, eschewing all ethnic particularism, and consciously downplaying racial difference by organizing political action on an integrated basis. Thus, despite his genuine interest in promoting African Americans and his support for Japanese American relief and resettlement efforts, Hayakawa denounced the existence of separate Nisei social groups as a needless crutch.

Yet even when Nisei wished to expand beyond their own group, finding common ground with most other minorities proved an uncertain task. Despite their common history of prejudice, their coming together was by no means a straightforward or untroubled process. Part III details in particular the shifting relations of West Coast Japanese communities with their Mexican American and Jewish counterparts: their prewar background, the impact of war and incarceration on their attitudes, and their connections in the postwar years. In both cases, the evidence vividly demonstrates that if solidarity among victims of discrimination is possible, it is neither automatic nor easy to maintain. In the interaction between Japanese Americans and Mexican Americans, the social and economic strains that dominated prewar relations between the two groups on the West Coast were exacerbated by the war. Even as the Mexican government displaced its own ethnic Japanese population, the most visible representatives and media of Southern California's Mexican communities supported mass removal—in contradistinction to the position taken by representatives of the very same media chain outside the West Coast. Even the two groups' common efforts against educational segregation in the postwar years were limited by their opposing views on race and culture. Mexican American elites agreed that they had a separate group culture, based on the Spanish language, but hotly denied any racial or biological difference from whites. Japanese Americans, conversely, considered themselves a nonwhite racial group, but rejected any suggestion that they were culturally or religiously distinct. This disagreement limited the field of common action.

Meanwhile, "From *Kuichi* to Comrades," which explores Japanese American views of Jews, demonstrates how slow and painful the development of empathy can be. Jews and Buddhists formed the nation's two largest non-Christian religious populations, while the Jewish and Japanese ethnic communities shared numerous cultural similarities, including a common emphasis on education and entrepreneurship. Yet, despite lasting friendships among individuals, Japanese Americans and Jews largely failed to achieve lasting rapport on a group basis in the first half of the twentieth century. Instead, the two were competitors and *frères ennemis* of a sort: businessmen, scholars, and others from each group seemed to express envy and rivalry as much as amity for those of the other. Indeed, members of prewar West Coast

Japanese communities—in an ironic reflection of their success in absorbing mainstream cultural values—gave voice to a nasty streak of anti-Semitism, and one that was quite open in comparison to their recorded opinion of other minority groups. Nisei began to change their views over time, especially as they resettled outside the West Coast, yet the two groups did not form the same community of interest with each other that both, in their different ways, managed to achieve with African American groups.

The last part of the book, in turn, is devoted to exploring various aspects of the historically consequential and complex matter of relations between Japanese Americans and African Americans. Whereas the two groups had little contact overall before the war, the spatial and socioeconomic convergence between the two groups caused by the involuntary migration of Japanese Americans, followed by the voluntary migration of African Americans and resettlement of Issei and Nisei from the camps, laid the foundation for an entente between members of the two groups. Meanwhile, the wartime confinement of Issei and Nisei caused a disproportionate number of African American thinkers and activists to draw parallels between the condition of Japanese Americans and their own treatment, and to speak out in favor of equal rights. Such expressions of solidarity by blacks (who were placed in the unaccustomed position of supporters rather than beneficiaries of support) deeply touched Nisei activists and ushered in a series of collaborations between members of the two groups in different fields. Part IV forms a prequel in a certain sense, in that it deals with the wartime period and the special circumstances that led to intergroup alliances between blacks and Nisei. A first piece, "African American Responses to the Wartime Confinement of Japanese Americans," presents an overview of African American dissent to Executive Order 9066, outlining in the process some directions for further study. Meanwhile, "The Los Angeles Defender" (a play on the title of Chicago's African American newspaper) uncovers the outstanding, unsung efforts of Hugh E. Macbeth, a maverick Los Angeles attorney who devoted himself to defending Japanese Americans amid wartime hysteria. Macbeth's crusade combined abstract feelings of democratic principle with his personal regard for Nisei friends. Meanwhile, a short essay, "Crusaders in Gotham," traces the ways in which Japanese Americans began to respond to the sympathy and support offered by their black colleagues. What it also demonstrates is that, in spite of the goodwill between the two groups, the path to collaboration was not easy, and it suggests that a balance of social power between the two played into the success or failure of coalitions.

The two essays in Part V, taking off from the preceding part, deal with the postwar relations between Japanese Americans and African Americans, through the lens of both groups' participation in legal and political struggles for civil rights. For politics, arguably more than ideology, played a central role in the attitude of the Nisei. In Hawaii, Japanese Americans represented a significant fraction of the population and threw themselves into electoral politics following the end of the war. (As a result of Democratic Party electoral coalitions with liberals and labor unionists brokered by war veterans such as Daniel Inouye, Hawaii achieved statehood and Nisei were elected to both houses of Congress by 1962.) Mainland Japanese Americans, conversely, long lacked the voter base and political clout to seek elected office. Instead, organizations such as the JACL were forced to pursue reform goals through lobbying efforts and lawsuits.

Nisei leaders quickly realized that interracial coalition with the NAACP and other ethnic and racial minority organizations was not only morally admirable but politically wise, since as a small and powerless ethnic group Japanese Americans had little chance to realize their objectives alone. Under the influence of national secretary Mike Masaoka and his brother Joe Grant Masaoka, boss of the West Coast office, the JACL not only formed an Anti-Discrimination Committee in 1946 to press civil rights lawsuits on behalf of diverse racial groups but in 1950 became a founding member of the lobbying and information group Leadership Conference on Civil Rights, among whose members it was the only nonblack racial minority association. The coalition strategy was a success: with support from their partners, the Nisei activists not only succeeded in erasing official discrimination against Japanese aliens but simultaneously played a small though vital role in legal challenges to segregation. "From *Korematsu* to *Brown*" draws the connection between the postwar Japanese American cases, notably the 1948 Supreme Court decision *Oyama v. California*, and the epochal 1954 Supreme Court ruling *Brown v. Board of Education*.

Yet the entente between the groups never became solidly established, and soon began to peter out. In part, the intergroup coalition was a victim of its own success—within three years after the closing of the camps, the Supreme Court neutralized anti-Asian alien land laws, struck down anti-Asian fishing laws as unconstitutional, and stripped restrictive covenants of enforcement power. Japanese Americans achieved further legislative victories on their own. In 1948, the JACL secured evacuation claims legislation, providing modest reimbursement for actual losses suffered during the war.[7] Four years later, the McCarran-Walter Act opened U.S. citizenship for the first time to Japanese immigrants. These victories reinforced an already developing tendency among Japanese Americans to use self-help and accommodationist strategies to overcome discrimination, even as McCarthyism played a palpable role in their retreat from political activism.[8] Yet the splintering of the fragile black-Nisei entente also reflected the lack of solid understanding between the larger populations of the two groups, and the reality of ethnic bias that remained inside the Japanese community. "An Uneasy Alliance" is a study of the rise and decline of the alliance between Nisei and blacks. In the aftermath of *Brown* and into the 1960s, even as Nisei achieved greater social acceptance, they revealed increasing ambivalence about interracial alliances. Their hesitation broke out into internal conflict within the JACL and Nisei communities in 1963–64, in the heyday of the mass civil rights movements by African Americans.

I conclude this introduction with a heartfelt, though most inadequate, expression of gratitude to all those who made the book possible. Recently a student of mine, on reading through an acknowledgments section, asked with wonder in his voice whether an author really needed to rely on so many people in order to do a book; my answer is emphatically yes. However, in the present volume the space for such listings is limited. Therefore, since this work is in many respects a continuation of my earlier books *By Order of the President* and *A Tragedy of Democracy*, I offer a double helping of thanks to those named (and unnamed) therein, and then add a shorter list of new benefactors.

First, I appreciate greatly the institutional support I have received. A sizable portion of my research is drawn from a project on civil rights and postwar connections between Nisei and blacks that was financed by grants from the Social Science and Humanities Council of Canada, the Fonds Québécois de la Recherche sur la Société et Culture, and the American Council for Learned Societies. The Huntington Library's fellowship program and able staff made possible my research on postwar Los Angeles. The Gerald Ford Presidential Library provided support for useful research there. At Université du Québec à Montréal I received a six-month sabbatical plus a semester of research leave. I am grateful to some talented students who have done research or data entry on this project: Sébastien Bernard, Mathieu Durand, Christopher Plante, Christian Roy, and Maxime Wingender. I received support from some dedicated scholar-activists in Montreal: Dolores Chew, Frédérick Gagnon, Louis Godbout, Junichiro Koji, Paul May, Bruno Ramirez, Dolores Sandoval, Robert Schwartzwald, Shelley Tepperman and Vadney Haynes, Don Watanabe, and Dorothy Williams.

Portions of this book began life as commissioned pieces, and I thank Elena Tajima Creef, Brian Komei Dempster, Ellen Eisenberg, Nicholas De Genova, Scott Kurashige, Russell Leong, Eric Muller, Jacques Portes, Ron Richardson, and Daniel Sabbagh for setting me working—even if sometimes the original publication fell through. Niels Hooper of UC Press wins my gratitude for letting me put it all together, and for his excitement about the project.

Among the friends, witnesses, and fellow scholars who invited me to present my research to audiences, granted interviews, or shared information, I wish to recognize particularly Konomi Ara, Taunya Lovell Banks, Jane Beckwith, Ben Carton, Robert Chang, Theo Chino, Margaret Chon, Frank Chuman, Michi De Sola, Emory Elliott, Mark Elliott, Frank Emi, Peter Eisenstadt, Kathy Ferguson, Shelley Fisher Fishkin, Robert Frase, Max Friedman, Ben Hamamoto, Gerald Haslam, Alan Hayakawa, Wynne Hayakawa, Robert Hayashi, Ike Hatchimonji, Lane Ryo Hirabayashi, William Hohri, Lei Hong, Kazu Iijima, Ernest and Chizu Iiyama, Tamio Ikeda-Spiegel and Julie Azuma, Jerry Kang, Tetsuden Kashima, Nori Komorita, Lon Kurashige, Yosh and Irene Kuromiya, Emory and Ayleen Ito Lee, Cherstin Lyon, Hugh Macbeth Jr., Daryl Maeda, John M. Maki, John M. Maki Jr., Greg Marutani, Marie Masumoto, Valerie Matsumoto, Yanek Mieczkowski, Dale Minami, John Mirikitani, Frank Miyamoto, Gerri Miyazaki, Marge and Aki Morimoto, Andrew Morris, Hiroshi Motomura, Philip Tajitsu Nash, Setsuko M. Nishi, Franklin Odo, Gene Oishi, Paul Okimoto, Chizu Omori, Peggy L. Powell, Cyril Powles, Toru Saito, Yasuo and Lily Sasaki, Naoko Shibusawa, Cedrick Shimo, Amy K. Stillman, Ina Sugihara Jones, Lewis Suzuki, Guyo Tajiri, Yoshiko Tajiri, Paul Takagi, Barbara Takei, Jim and Yoshie Tanabe, Russ Tremayne, Andrew Wertheimer, Duncan R. Williams, Paul Yamada, Eric Yamamoto, Hisaye Yamamoto, Traise Yamamoto, and Marian Yoshiki Kovinick.

Kenji Taguma, editor of the *Nichi Bei Times* (now *Nichi Bei Weekly*), hired me in 2007 to serve as columnist for that historic journal. In the process my work has reached an entirely new audience and I have been able to form enduring bonds with readers and community members. I have benefited in countless ways from Kenji's warm friendship and kindness. Both Kenji and J. K. Yamamoto of the now-defunct *Hokubei Mainichi* generously permitted me access to their respective journals' back files. DENSHO, led by the magnificent Tom Ikeda, has been an exceptional force in preserving Japanese American memory, and its online archives are a primary source of material. The staff at the Japanese American National Museum have been exceedingly friendly and helpful.

Numerous kindly relatives and friends provided logistical (as well as moral) support and/or put me up during research trips: Janet Baba, Judy Baker, Ken Feinour and Shin Yamamoto, Ed Robinson and Ellen Fine, Sheila Hamanaka, Craig Howes, Kwong-Liem Karl Kwan, Christopher Legge, Michael Massing, Martha Nakagawa, Heng Gun Ngo, Paul Okimoto, Chizu Omori, Neal Plotkin and Deborah Malamud, Rick and Maki Pakola, Sydelle Postman, Katherine Quittner, Jaime Restrepo, Ian Robinson, Jocelyn Robinson, the late Lillian Robinson, Tracy Robinson, Mitziko Sawada, Rob and Louisa Snyder, Bruce and Sondra Stave, Frank Wu and Carol Izumi, Terry Yoshikawa, and Fidel Zavala and Mark Williams.

In addition to assisting with document research, Thanapat Porjit has brought sunshine into my life.

Finally, this book would not have been possible without the contributions of my beloved mother, the late Toni Robinson. In 1998, after retiring for health reasons from her law practice, in which I had worked as her legal assistant, Toni grew absorbed in my evolving research on Nisei, interminority relations, and civil rights, and eagerly read through the material I uncovered. Intrigued by her insights, I invited her to collaborate with me. She accepted on condition that our blood relationship not be publicly identified, as she did not wish to seem a scholarly interloper. We started writing together, presented as a team at academic conferences, and completed a pair of law journal articles together. In July 2002, shortly before Toni left on a vacation trip to Europe, we finished revising one of these articles for publication, and we discussed expanding the other one into a book once she returned. Sadly, Toni collapsed during the trip and died a few weeks later. The two works subsequently appeared in print and remain my most-cited articles. While I have done considerable work on my own in more recent years, this collection represents in a larger sense the book we did not get to write together; not only do its contents incorporate our two joint pieces, but the rest is equally inspired by our discussions and by Toni's generous, lively spirit.

PART I

Resettlement and New Lives

1. Political Science?

FDR, Japanese Americans, and the Postwar Dispersion of Minorities

The term *political science* usually refers to all the ways—polls, models, and statistics—that academics have used to bring scientific principles to the study of political behavior. Yet my use of these two words comes from a completely opposite direction and refers to the use of science for political purposes—an unexamined aspect of the domestic and foreign policy of President Franklin Roosevelt during the years of World War II. FDR and his advisors, believing that concentration of minority groups, especially urban-based, within established nations bred poverty and intergroup tensions, sought to alleviate conflict by scientifically planning the mass migration and absorption of unwanted groups into rural and underpopulated areas. Through the mass dispersion and assimilation of ethnic and racial minority populations, the United States would promote peace and economic growth.

My focus is divided into two distinct, though interrelated, dispersion initiatives. The first one took place within the United States. Here, during 1943–44, Roosevelt formulated plans to "distribute" incarcerated Japanese Americans in small groups throughout the country to solve the "Japanese problem." He meanwhile considered various proposals for the scattering of Jews and other immigrants. On the international side, FDR commissioned the M Project (the *M* standing for *migration*), a top-secret anthropological study by a team of scholars that eventually encompassed some six hundred reports, essays, and translations of articles on human migration and settlement. The goal of this project was to provide the president with expert advice on the possibilities for large-scale postwar relocation of millions of European refugees and members of unwanted populations to Latin America in accordance with Darwinian racial principles. The study of these interconnected programs reveals both the complexities of Franklin

Roosevelt's views of race and society and the paradoxical nature of social engineering for Issei and Nisei.[1]

Franklin Roosevelt's interest in demographics and migration developed early. As a child he noted the tensions stirred by the presence of a French Canadian minority in his grandfather's hometown of Fairhaven, Massachusetts. When he grew to manhood and moved to New York City, he was regularly exposed to nativist fears of immigrants and to the countervailing efforts of settlement workers (including his future wife, Eleanor) and other progressives to "Americanize" the newcomers. In 1920, during his unsuccessful campaign as Democratic candidate for vice president, the young FDR expressed his ideas on the subject in an interview with the daily newspaper *Brooklyn Eagle*:

> Our main trouble in the past has been that we have permitted the foreign elements to segregate in colonies. They have crowded into one district and they have brought congestion and racial prejudices to our large cities. The result is that they do not easily conform to the manners and the customs and the requirements of their new home. Now, the remedy for this should be greater distribution of aliens in various parts of the country. If we had the greater part of the foreign population of the City of New York distributed to different localities upstate we should have a far better condition. Of course, this could not be done by legislative enactment. It could only be done by inducement—if better financial conditions and better living conditions could be offered to the alien dwellers in the cities.

During the mid-1920s, when he was a private citizen, Roosevelt expressed his admiration for the Canadian government's policy of assisted settlement of European immigrants in agricultural regions: "When the individual or family in the European country applies to the Canadian agent for permission to come over he must agree to go to one of the sections of Canada which is not already too full of foreigners. If, twenty-five years ago, the United States had adopted a policy of this kind we would not have the huge foreign sections which exist in so many of our cities."[2]

Even as Roosevelt expressed interest in resettling existing urban immigrants, he articulated support for official restrictions on immigration, in ways that followed popular racist prejudices. In 1925, one year after Congress passed a restrictive immigration act that effectively banned immigration from southern and eastern Europe, Roosevelt affirmed that European immigrants should be barred "for a good many years to come" so that the United States could "digest" (i.e., assimilate and Americanize) those who had been admitted already, and he added that the government should concentrate henceforth on admitting only the most readily "assimilable" so that quick "digestion" could proceed. While Roosevelt did not specify which immigrants would meet such a standard, his language of assimilation and especially his call for "European blood of the right sort" left little doubt that he meant primarily western Europeans. Already, in 1923, , he had stated unequivocally that Japanese, like other Asians, should be excluded from both immigration and citizenship rights in order to protect America's "racial purity." In a second article in 1925, he further warned of the dangers of racial mixing:

> Anyone who has travelled in the Far East knows that the mingling of Asiatic blood with European or American blood produces, in nine cases out of ten, the most unfortunate results. . . . In this question then of Japanese exclusion from the United States, it is necessary only to advance the true reason—the undesirability of mixing the blood of the two peoples.[3]

The immediate roots of both the M Project and the plan for resettlement of Japanese Americans lie in Franklin Roosevelt's efforts to handle the question of Jewish refugees. As early as 1938, FDR commissioned Johns Hopkins University president Isaiah Bowman, who had previously advised President Woodrow Wilson at the Versailles peace conference on redrawing European frontiers, to come up with a plan for resettling Jews outside Europe without bringing them to the United States, and thus resolving the Old World's "Jewish problem" there. Bowman's idea was to disperse the Jews in small numbers—the smaller the better—in rural areas throughout the globe, so that they could live off the land and give up the commercial and banking professions that had aroused such opposition to them.[4] During the following years, Bowman and his team researched various possibilities for resettlement of Jews in Latin America and advised on the political prospects for negotiating the admission of refugees with different governments. The various plans remained generally unimplemented for a number of reasons, not the least of which was Bowman's own opposition to organizing the mass transportation of "a large foreign immigrant group" to Latin America, since it would embroil the United States in European quarrels. "Why not keep the European elements within the framework of the Old World?" he asked FDR. "Even if we do not favor migration to Latin America, but allow it, difficulties will arise."[5]

Roosevelt evidently agreed, for he took no further action along such lines during the prewar years. (His doubts could only have been confirmed by the results of the July 1938 Evian conference on refugees, which he took the initiative of organizing. Not only did the Latin American countries in attendance refuse to increase their own quotas for admission of Jewish refugees, but some actually further restricted entry.) Roosevelt nonetheless kept Bowman's initial plan in mind for later use. In particular, he began to return to the subject after December 1941, when the United States entered World War II. As the president learned of atrocities committed against the Jews and other European minorities, he began to think about the larger problem of displaced persons (DPs) and turned back to the broad lines of the Bowman plan. His concern was not simply what to do with the Jews but how to handle the several million other people throughout Europe and Asia whom the war had forced to flee their homes and who would be left stranded when the conflict ended. Roosevelt realized that this was a worldwide problem, and he firmly believed it was the responsibility of the United States, as part of its claim to world leadership, to take the lead in organizing nations around the globe to help them find new homes. Undaunted by the failure of international conferences to open doors for Jews threatened by Nazism, Roosevelt planned to negotiate agreements with Latin American states to admit displaced persons. (He rejected as politically unworkable and socially undesirable the admission of large numbers of refugees to the United States, which he did not consider an "underdeveloped country.") As Robert Strausz-Hupé, who was to help direct the M Project, later explained, "Neither strictly military nor even of immediate political importance, the [refugee] problem engaged the president's generous humanitarianism; moreover, it was likely to bear upon the future peace."[6]

In fact, FDR's interest in refugees was connected to a fundamental concern about overpopulation. In Roosevelt's view, which was shared by many social scientists of the period, the chief long-term causes of the war were population growth and overcrowding. These led to shortages and competition for scarce resources, which in turn bred the tensions that led to war. If the surplus population from densely populated regions could be resettled in sparsely populated areas, Roosevelt reasoned, these tensions would diminish. As Ladislas Farago, who was long associated with the M Project, noted:

> Roosevelt's conception of the D.P. appears unorthodox and revolutionary. He regarded the victims of the war as representing but one of . . . three groups. In the second group were the surplus populations of certain European and Asiatic countries, while the third group was made up of so-called "geopolitical problem children" whose presence in certain countries is traditionally exploited for power-political purposes. Roosevelt believed that the postwar necessity of a large-scale

resettlement of refugees would enable him to solve the interdependent problems of all three groups simultaneously.[7]

FDR's goal was to discover areas where large-scale resettlement might take place, and he sought expert help. He told his advisors that he was not interested in counsel on the political and economic questions inherent in arranging resettlement: he considered himself the supreme expert on dealing in politics. Instead, he turned to scientists who could, he believed, provide practical, nonideological, professional advice on ways to organize resettlement and to minimize the impact and friction such refugees were likely to provoke in their new homes.[8]

The president soon found a potential leader for his project. During early spring 1942, as Roosevelt began turning over in his mind the DP question, he came into contact with Dr. Ales Hrdlicka, chief anthropologist at the Smithsonian Institution. Hrdlicka was a specialist on skull measurement, which was then a common and respected aspect of anthropology. Although himself a Czech immigrant and an opponent of nativism, Hrdlicka had strong prejudices against African Americans and other racial minority groups. In a 1928 article on measuring blacks' skulls, Hrdlicka referred to the black population of Washington, D.C., as "the semi-civilized, suspicious, scattered free laborers and servants of a big city."[9] He also had a history of racial hostility toward Japanese people, which he expressed at various points throughout the 1930s.

In early 1942, Hrdlicka wrote the president to warn of his fears about the Japanese. In his letter, he informed FDR that the members of the Japanese race were innately warlike and hostile by reason of their less developed skulls, which placed them lower in evolutionary development than other "races." Roosevelt was intrigued, and he inquired about solving the "Japanese problem" through mass interbreeding. It is not entirely clear from the president's answer to Hrdlicka whether he wished to force the Japanese to interbreed with other Asian groups in order to dilute their alleged innate aggressiveness or wanted to ensure that other Asian groups interbred with superior European racial stock in order to give them a leg up against the Japanese.

Impressed with Hrdlicka's ideas on the question of reshaping the Asian Pacific population through efficient programs of racial mixing, FDR invited Hrdlicka to meet with him in late May 1942 to discuss the general problem of postwar migration. Some idea of Roosevelt's interest in planning to overcome intergroup hostility can be inferred from a letter he wrote at the time to Canadian prime minister W. L. Mackenzie King about the endemic conflicts between English Canadians and French Canadians. Canada was undergoing a crisis over conscription, which was heavily opposed by French Canadians unenthusiastic about fighting for England and empire. Roosevelt confided to Mackenzie King that joint efforts might be necessary to remove the opposition:

> All of this leads me to wonder whether by some sort of planning Canada and the United States, working toward the same end, cannot do some planning—perhaps some unwritten planning which need not even be a public policy—by which we can hasten the objective of assimilating the New England French Canadians and Canada's French Canadians into the whole of our respective bodies politic. There are, of course, many methods for doing this which depend upon local circumstances. Wider opportunities can perhaps be given to them in other parts of Canada and the U.S.; and at the same time, certain opportunities can probably be given to non–French Canadian stock to mingle more greatly with them in their own centers.
>
> In other words, after nearly two hundred years with you and after seventy-five years with us, there would seem to be no good reason for great differentials between the French population elements and the rest of the racial stocks.
>
> It is on the same basis that I am trying to work out post-war plans for the encouragement of the distribution of certain other nationalities on our large congested centers. There ought not to be such a concentration of Italians and Jews, and even of Germans as we have today in New York City. I have started my National Resources Planning Commission to work on a survey of this kind.[10]

In May 1942, FDR met with Ales Hrdlicka at the White House. The anthropologist swiftly pronounced himself willing to organize a concerted initiative to arrange postwar migration and contact according to "scientific principles of demographic movements and race mixtures." Hrdlicka suggested holding a "Pan-American Congress on Post-War Immigration," to be followed by the creation of an international migration center to coordinate policy. He no doubt recognized that this might sound unrealistic, for he then suggested as an alternative the formation of a body of experts to plan population shifts. "This body should chart the problem from the anthropological, medical, and economical points of view. It would determine the countries that will have to discharge their surplus peoples, and those that might receive them; learn by direct observation, through brief field trips, the conditions of the prospective receiving regions; and lay foundations for rational selection and direction of the migrants."[11] Hrdlicka offered to set up such a body at the Smithsonian if private foundation money could be secured. "Such a body could begin to function without delay, and begin to furnish or publish its reports within a few months."[12]

Realizing the foreign policy implications of such an action, Roosevelt immediately sent Hrdlicka's proposal to Secretary of State Cordell Hull and asked Hull to speak to him about it.[13] At the same time, Roosevelt discussed his postwar migration plans with Vice President Henry Wallace, who expressed great interest.[14] After receiving these endorsements, Roosevelt decided to proceed with the formation of what he called an "Institute of Population," and he called again on Isaiah Bowman for assistance in directing the project. Bowman explained that he was too busy to take on any more activity but agreed to lend his name to the project.[15]

Meanwhile, Roosevelt turned for administrative support to another trusted advisor, the journalist and former State Department official John Franklin Carter. Carter was the chief of a special White House political intelligence network Roosevelt had established in early 1941, which collected information on everything from experimental weapons to political conditions in Martinique. In particular, at the president's orders Carter sent a team of agents, led by Curtis B. Munson and Warren Irwin, to the western states and Hawaii during fall 1941 to inquire into the loyalty of Japanese communities. Following reports from his agents that Japanese Americans were overwhelmingly loyal—Munson estimated Nisei as "90–98% loyal" and pitifully anxious to demonstrate their patriotism—Carter had tried to organize efforts to defend Japanese communities from potential race rioting, and had lobbied Roosevelt against mass removal after Pearl Harbor.[16]

Carter agreed to act as organizer and paymaster for the migration project. However, since he had no anthropological knowledge or experience, he deputized his assistant Henry Field, an anthropologist from the Field Museum in Chicago who specialized in Near Eastern civilizations, to manage the intellectual side of the project. At the end of July 1942, Carter and Field met with Roosevelt to receive his directions, and then visited Hrdlicka. What the president wanted, Carter explained, was to bring to Washington "a small, informal committee of leading anthropologists from the United States, Mexico and Canada," who would "discuss plans for an Institute of Population and report on the ethnological problems anticipated in postwar population movements."[17] Their mission was "specifically ... to formulate agreed opinions as to problems arising out of racial admixtures and to consider the scientific principles involved in the process of miscegenation as contrasted with the opposing policies of so-called 'racialism.'"

Once this was accomplished they would "submit a report in writing for the confidential guidance of the President of the United States."[18] Carter explained that the office of the president would provide funds for travel and other expenses, and he and Field would administer the project. Hrdlicka expressed agreement with the plan. However, following the meeting Carter mentioned to Roosevelt that he had grave doubts as to Hrdlicka's suitability, and warned the president that "unless, through me, you maintain a firm grip on this agenda, he will stop at little to twist it into precisely what it should not be allowed to become: a mandate for him to impose his dogmatic anthropological convictions upon national policy."[19]

FDR replied that he appreciated Carter's concerns, but told him to go ahead anyway, commenting playfully about his goals for the project: "I know that you and Henry Field can carry out this project unofficially, exploratorially, ethnologically, racially, admixturally, miscegenationally, confidentially, and above all, budgetarily. Any person connected herewith whose name appears in the public print will suffer guillotinally."[20]

Hrdlicka soon produced a list of potential committee members—a dream team of anthropological brains. With Field's help, Carter added some new names to keep the committee from being "an Ales Hrdlicka cheering section," and to ensure the committee's unofficial nature he took out the government employees Hrdlicka had suggested. He then passed the list on to Roosevelt.[21] After looking over the plans, the president decided that a formal committee would be cumbersome and probably lead to leaks. FDR instead asked Hrdlicka to join with Bowman and Field in a committee of three, to be aided by whichever consultants the committee wished to invite. Carter transmitted the request to Hrdlicka, explaining that the committee was to address itself to the general questions of finding vacant places suitable for postwar settlement (specifically South America and Central Africa) and identifying the kinds of people who would be sent to live there. He then added some specific questions of racial eugenics personally posed by Roosevelt:

> In consideration of this problem the President wished the committee to keep especially in mind the political fact that the South American nations will insist on a base stock of their own in regions opened to settlement, that they want a "planned" melting pot with a basic "flux" of 30–40% of their own people. This base stock will naturally include a considerable admixture of Indian blood. The President wishes to be advised what will happen when various kinds of Europeans—Scandinavian, Germanic, French-Belgian, North Italian, etc.—are mixed with the South American base stock.

The memo then listed some of the specific matters that Roosevelt had gone into:

> The President specifically asked the committee also to consider such questions as the following: Is the South Italian stock—say, Sicilian—as good as the North Italian stock—say, Milanese—if given equal economic and social opportunity? Thus, in a given case, where 10,000 Italians were to be offered settlement facilities, what proportion of the 10,000 should be Northern Italians and what Southern Italians? He also pointed out that while most South American countries would be glad to admit Jewish immigration, it was on the condition that the Jewish group were not localized in the cities, that there wasn't to be "Jewish colonies," "Italian colonies," etc. How can you resettle the Jews on the land and keep them there? Historically, he pointed out, the Jews were originally an agricultural and pastoral people and the ghetto system . . . is of comparatively recent origin.

The three-man committee began slowly to set to work, but the tensions soon became unmanageable. As Carter later explained, "Hrdlicka was impossible to deal with because his whole idea was to use the government money to go down to Mexico to try to verify his theories about the migration of early American man."[22] By late fall 1942 Hrdlicka had withdrawn completely from the project.

The M Project (at first referred to as the "Bowman-Field Committee") was officially established in November 1942.[23] It was funded by allocations from the President's Special Funds.[24] Bowman again declined to serve actively, although he agreed to be an advisor and to receive a copy of all reports. Field assumed responsibility for the project. Through Archibald MacLeish, who was librarian of Congress, assistant director of the Office of War Information, and a close Roosevelt speechwriter and advisor, the M Project was offered three study rooms in the Library of Congress. MacLeish also agreed to detail Dr. Sergei Yakobson to assist. Soon Dr. Robert Strausz-Hupé and Stefan Possony—both of whom would later be Cold War foreign policy specialists, and the former an ambassador as well—came to join them. Ultimately, a project staff of approximately thirteen was built up. Many of them were Jewish refugees who joined the president's project in lieu of military service. Although the project staff did not include specialists in all fields, they were able to draw on the talent of numerous researchers within the government because of their powerful sponsor. In addition, Sripati Chandrasekhar, a graduate student at New York University, was recruited as a special expert on demography and population transfers in Asia. (Chandrasekhar would later return to India and become minister of health and family planning under Indira Gandhi, in which role he would arouse controversy for his forthright advocacy of voluntary sterilization and other means of "correcting" overpopulation.)

By mid-1943, the M Project was issuing reports almost on a daily basis. In Field's words, the task was to prepare "world-wide studies on areas with surplus population, their racial and religious composition, and their nationals' potential skill and adaptability as emigrants." M Project staffers drafted studies of previous settlement attempts and of immigration laws of potential settler countries, as well as reports, translations, lectures, and memoranda on a wide variety of topics, including maize in Siberia, animal husbandry and the development of the paper industry in British Guiana, soils of San Carlos and Valencia, Venezuela, and the American Jewish Committee's detailed studies of eastern European Jews and Jewish colonies in Saskatchewan, Argentina, and other places.

Roosevelt remained informed about and interested in the M Project, although he had no direct contact with the staffers and did not issue further agenda items for M Project studies, apart from allegedly commissioning special reports on the status of Jews and minorities in the Soviet Union for ammunition prior to his meeting with Soviet leader Joseph Stalin at Teheran. In October 1943, he invited Field to visit him at Shangri-La, the presidential retreat in Maryland (later known as Camp David), and encouraged him to continue the M Project. The resettlement of millions of refugees, according to FDR, "was not only desirable from a humanitarian standpoint, but essential from a military point of view as well . . . For the discontented can and will cause trouble, serious trouble."[25] Field would later claim that Roosevelt envisioned a wide network of irrigation canals to enable Europeans to resettle in the deserts of North Africa, as well as a project to use desalinated Mediterranean seawater to make North Africa the granary of Europe. Although he was aware that such a proposal (and a similar one to resettle Asians in Australia) would be tremendously expensive, he declared they were worthwhile in averting further wars.

Even as Roosevelt continued to receive reports from the M Project staff, he turned his attention to the domestic scene. In addition to asking the National Resources Planning Commission to come up with ideas for the distribution of Jews, Germans, and Italians, the president did some of his own canvassing on the question. In May 1943, Vice President Wallace reported in his diary that the president had spoken at length on the possibility of scattering Jews to avoid conflict. "The President consulted his neighbors in Marietta County, Georgia [the location of FDR's home at Warm Springs] and at Hyde Park, asking whether they would agree to have four or five Jewish families resettle in their respective regions. He claimed that the local population would have no objection if there were no more than that."[26] In a fictionalized dialogue, John Franklin Carter summed up Roosevelt's rationale for forcing assimilation: "It's only human nature for people to want others to conform to their standards. The Jews are a race apart, a religion apart . . . a special group inside every other nation. Such separations have always caused suspicion and trouble."[27]

Meanwhile, the question of Japanese Americans drew his attention. In the weeks after Roosevelt signed Executive Order 9066, the army prepared to remove some 112,000 people of Japanese ancestry from their homes. Roosevelt and his advisors seem to have given little thought at first to the long-term disposition of the inmates. On the contrary, they declined to assist a number of different projects submitted by Nisei leaders such as James Sakamoto, Hi Korematsu, and Fred Wada for voluntary relocation by groups of Japanese Americans and mass colonization of western farmland. Nonetheless, as plans for removal proceeded and a newly created civilian agency, the War Relocation Authority (WRA), began constructing camps in the interior for involuntary mass confinement, the president and various officials began to consider possibilities for permanent resettlement elsewhere. On July 7, 1942, Secretary of War Henry L. Stimson wrote the president to warn him that California governor Culbert Olson, whom he facetiously referred to as "that great patriot," had inquired whether Japanese Americans could be released from confinement to work as cheap labor during the autumn harvest. Stimson added scornfully that the same Californians who were so "hell-bent" on having the army rush "the Japanese" out should not be permitted to change their minds when it suited them. Instead, Stimson proposed going on with "our permanent relocation of the evacuees," which he termed "the permanent settlement of a great national problem."[28]

Once the Japanese Americans were moved into the camps, government authorities gradually developed a "leave clearance" system to permit those adjudged "loyal" to leave the camps and resettle in small groups outside the Pacific coast, which remained closed to Japanese Americans. Thus, a fraction of the inmates departed during 1943 and 1944. Within the government there were various discussions and exchanges of opinion with regard to the desirability of permanent dispersal outside the West Coast. For example, in April 1943, following a visit to the Gila River camp, First Lady Eleanor Roosevelt told the press, "I hope that as they go out, both after the war and during it, the [Japanese Americans] will go out in small groups to different communities scattered throughout the land. [Like] many people in this country [they] have lived at a concentrated point, in communities within a community, so to speak, a condition which has tended to delay their assimilation into the American society."[29] FDR himself told a Chinese American White House visitor, Hung Wai Ching, during spring 1943 that he favored resettlement of Japanese Americans nationwide and "felt that they should be spread around the country. [He] mentioned about Hyde Park" (i.e., his discussions with neighbors about resettlement of small groups). According to Ching's cryptic notes, FDR likewise proposed mass intermarriage of Japanese and the creation of a "Neo-Hawaiian" race," in view of the "success of Chinese mixture with others," and referred to a "Smithsonian anthropologist" (presumably Hrdlicka) as support for his ideas.[30]

All the same, there was little concrete planning, either in the White House or elsewhere in the bureaucracy, of means to encourage dispersion. Rather, the president and his advisors assumed, with good reason, that most Japanese Americans would seek to resettle in their prewar locations once released. FDR publicly pledged in September 1943 to permit the camp inmates to go back to their homes once the military situation made it possible, and even altered the draft of an official statement to excise language implying that Japanese Americans would not be able to return to the West Coast in due course.[31]

In spring 1944 the matter came to a head, as White House officials reached consensus that there was no threat to security that would justify further exclusion of Japanese Americans from the West Coast. Interior Secretary Harold Ickes, who was responsible for the WRA, called for the immediate opening of the camps. However, in the face of concerns over potential violence against returning inmates, mixed with election-year political considerations, the president demurred. Instead of having Japanese Americans "dumped" in California, he proposed gradual release and piecemeal relocation of the camp inmates in areas such as Hyde Park. "He stated that by personal inquiry he had reached the conclusion that quite a few could be distributed in Dutchess County and that if the same could be done all over the country it would take care of all."[32] On June 2, Ickes wrote FDR to plead with him to revoke immediately the order excluding Japanese Americans from the Pacific coast. He explained that in the absence of military necessity there was "no basis in law or equity" for the ban, and added that exclusion interfered with resettlement elsewhere by stigmatizing inmates as disloyal. Ickes warned that the "retention" of the Internees in the camps would be "a blot upon the history of this country."[33]

Roosevelt replied on June 12 that he opposed a "sudden" revocation of exclusion. Rather, "for the sake of internal quiet," his plan was to avoid doing anything "drastic or sudden." He proposed a gradualist approach, involving several steps:

> (a) Seeing, with great discretion, how many Japanese families would be acceptable to public opinion in definite localities on the West Coast, (b) Seeking to extend greatly the distribution of other families in many parts of the United States. I have been talking to a number of people from the Coast and they are all in agreement that the Coast would be willing to receive back a portion of the Japanese who were formerly there—nothing sudden and not in too great quantities at any one time.

Roosevelt added that he had concluded from discussions with people in the East, Midwest, and South that inmates, "one or two families to each county as a start," should be "distributed" around the rest of the country. "Dissemination and distribution constitute a great method of avoiding public outcry." He asked Ickes to proceed with that plan "for a while at least."[34]

While Roosevelt's advocacy of "distribution" was clearly attributable in good part to political expediency, as well a genuine desire to avoid conflict on the West Coast, he also sincerely believed in the benefits of dispersion, and tried to push it along by asking for updates on resettlement in the weeks that followed. He consulted Assistant Secretary of War John McCloy and General Charles H. Bonesteel, the West Coast defense commander, about schemes for "dissemination" of Japanese Americans throughout the country. A skeptical Bonesteel remarked, "The President seemed to feel that there should be no difficulty in accomplishing a solution of the problem whereby one or two Japanese families would be placed in each of several thousand small communities throughout the nation. He went into detail in showing how the plan would work in his own county."[35] Even after the November 1944 election, when Roosevelt at last gave his consent to preparations for lifting exclusion and opening the West Coast to return by Japanese Americans, he continued to favor dispersion. In a press conference on November 21, 1944, Roosevelt hailed the progress the government had made in "scattering" Japanese Americans through the country. "In the Hudson River valley or in western Joe-gia [Georgia] probably half a dozen or a dozen families could be scattered around on farms and worked into the community."[36]

Franklin Roosevelt did not have a chance to implement plans for mass dispersal before his death in April 1945, shortly before V-E Day. The M Project never extended beyond the planning stage. After Roosevelt's death the M Project was ordered continued for several months by President Truman, and by the end of 1945 it had produced 665 studies, making up ninety-six volumes. However, Truman did not have the same faith in planned migration as Roosevelt had had, and he did not act on the studies. Truman did ultimately evince interest in using the M Project data to promote wise disbursement of aid money under his Point IV Program for economic and technical assistance for development of Third World areas, and in 1949 he asked that each regional director be sent the papers on the relevant area. However, Point IV was a small, limited program, and the information was by then long out of date. It is interesting to speculate on the uses FDR would have made of the M Project studies. As Carter stated, "Of course, if Roosevelt had lived, maybe something could have been done, but Roosevelt did not live." Instead, all the tremendous labor involved in the M Project came to naught, although Robert Strausz-Hupé insisted dubiously, "I do not believe our labors were entirely in vain. Only a few of the migrants of World War II vintage have been settled upon homes or on the land. Yet some were. These would have suffered greater hardships had it not been for better planning based upon the research of [our] geographers, agronomists, anthropologists, sociologists, and experts in legislation on immigration."[37]

Meanwhile, the president's plans for domestic "distribution" of Japanese Americans remained equally unrealized. Once the West Coast reopened to Japanese Americans in January 1945, camp inmates began to return to their prewar home regions in large numbers, and even those who moved outside the West Coast tended (with various exceptions) to congregate together in large urban colonies. Officials offered financial support for those settling outside the West but recognized the futility of trying to interfere with the constitutional right of citizens to settle where they pleased.

It is as well that no such program was implemented, as it would have been not only tyrannical but also probably flawed.[38] One powerful indication of the limitations of such an enterprise is the official program to resettle Indochinese refugees during the mid-1970s, the first occasion after World War II that the government attempted a conscious policy of dispersal and absorption of an ethnic/racial group. Although the government had previously created the Refugee Relief Program in the 1950s to aid European and Cuban refugees and had sought assistance from religious and charitable organizations for aid in resettlement, the case of the Indochina refugees represented a race-conscious remedy in which dispersion was the favored tool to promote assimilation and overcome racial hostility. Following the fall of Saigon in April 1975, President Gerald R. Ford signed the Indochina Migration and Refugee Assistance Act. Under this law, the White House undertook a humanitarian operation to absorb and assist some 135,000 refugees from Vietnam, most of whom were military or government officials of the deposed South Vietnamese regime, plus 5,000 more refugees from Cambodia. In a notable case of public-private partnership, the White House and State Department put together a network of religious, ethnic, and progressive organizations, from Catholic charities to Ukrainian aid organizations and Chinese community groups, to sponsor the refugees. The Ford administration set up refugee camps at military bases, most notably Camp Pendleton in California, and arranged for the release of family groups from government custody once they had received offers of sponsorship. At the same time, in an unconscious echo of wartime policy, Ford administration officials insisted on the dispersion of the refugees in small family groups outside the West Coast as a condition of their release from the refugee camps. The government's strategy of dispersal—even blocking the collective resettlement of family groups beyond immediate family members—was based on hindering the growth of ethnic communities in order to avert a "Vietnamese problem." As in the case of the Japanese Americans, the goal was to ease the adjustment of the migrants and lessen prejudice against them in their new homes

It is difficult to measure whether any such dispersal strategy would have done much to dilute mass hostility toward Indochinese refugees in the wake of the Vietnam War. In any case, the punitive and ethnocentric nature of the policy undercut its purposes, and the policy was a radical failure on its own terms. Most of the refugees who had agreed to be dispersed soon undertook a second resettlement into ethnic enclaves (many on the West Coast) alongside friends and relatives, and a generation later the ethnic Vietnamese population in the United States remains concentrated in a few centers.

To conclude briefly, the lesson of Roosevelt's "political science" is that racial bias and eugenicist thinking can influence government policy in many ways, even—perhaps especially—when racial thinking bears the imprint of scientific expertise and is cloaked in humanitarian purpose. FDR and his advisors launched a visionary scheme through which they undertook to use scientific expertise to help guarantee a peaceful and stable future for the world. They genuinely believed that by shifting populations and deliberately remaking the racial composition of entire regions, they could lessen international tension and promote peace and economic growth. Yet what underlay this progressive goal was the reshaping of demographic patterns in accordance with Social Darwinist racial principles, which had already been called into serious question by Franz Boas and others, and which are outmoded and even shocking by current standards. While we are no doubt fortunate that none of the more radical elements of the M

Project was ever put into effect, we should nonetheless remember that the project *was* designed (and funded to the tune of $180,000) to be used in a serious way. At the same time, the case of the Japanese Americans demonstrates the persistence of the dubious belief that destruction of ethnic communities will ensure assimilation and social harmony (the suffering of the Japanese Canadians, who were stripped of their property during the war, barred from the West Coast, and scattered throughout the nation, calls this thesis sharply into question). We must be wary of all attempts, however well meant, to redraw human population distribution patterns, for it is as easy to stigmatize so-called racial characteristics as to valorize them.

2. Forrest LaViolette

Race, Internationalism, and Assimilation

The career and complex views of Forrest Emmanuel LaViolette provide a special window into the question of Japanese American (and Canadian) resettlement and assimilation. LaViolette, a University of Chicago–trained sociologist engaged in research on Japanese Americans and cultural values, became a lecturer at the University of Washington in the late 1930s. Even as he conducted his research, he was welcomed into the Japanese community, and achieved an unusual measure of integration for a non-Japanese. After being hired as professor of sociology at McGill University in Montreal in 1940, LaViolette further distinguished himself as a scholar of Japanese Canadians and defender of their citizenship rights. During World War II, he returned to the United States and volunteered for service as a social analyst at the Heart Mountain camps. LaViolette's dedication to action for racial equality in the public sphere, which made him stand out among his colleagues, poses important questions about the role of outside "interpreters" in struggles against discrimination. At the same time, his belief in assimilation at all costs, which led him to welcome mass dispersion and resettlement of ethnic Japanese citizens and residents, and his subsequent withdrawal from Japanese North American connections are puzzling and deserve scrutiny.

Little is known about LaViolette's early life. He was born on January 9, 1904, in Devil's Lake, North Dakota. His father, John Emmanuel LaViolette, who was of mixed English and French-Canadian ancestry, grew up in Montreal. His mother, Isabella, was an immigrant from Scotland. His older brother was Dr. Wesley La Violette, later a noted composer and teacher of jazz in Los Angeles.[1] Forrest moved to Spokane, Washington, as a baby. In 1918, he moved to Portland, Oregon. After completing a year of high school, he enrolled at the Oregon Institute of Technology in Portland. After receiving a radio certificate in 1920, he joined the merchant marine as a radio operator on ocean liners. During this period, he sailed around coastal Washington, Alaska, and British Columbia, interacted with native peoples, and made at least four trips to the Far East, including Japan.[2] After giving up his seafaring and returning to Portland, he graduated from Franklin High School, then enrolled for a year at Willamette University in Salem. He then spent three years as an executive for Montgomery & Co. In the end, he decided on a scholarly career, and in 1930 he enrolled at Reed College in Portland.[3] At first LaViolette was interested primarily in anthropology. His senior thesis, written in 1933 under the direction of P. K. Roest, a professor of sociology, was entitled "Japanese Nationalism: A Social Study."[4] LaViolette then enrolled at the University of Chicago in sociology. His original concentration was in social anthropology, and it was primarily as an anthropologist that he wrote his M.A. thesis, submitted in 1935, and entitled "Some Problems Relating to the Concept of Culture."

Over the following two years, as LaViolette completed the coursework for his doctorate and began to think about how to structure his doctoral project, he realized he was attracted more by sociology and by American society. At that time, under the leadership of Robert Park plus such stalwarts as Louis Wirth and Robert Redfield, the University of Chicago's Sociology Department was the brain center of race relations research in the United States. In particular, Park and his colleagues had undertaken a series of studies of minorities, notably "oriental Americans." LaViolette thus began to turn his attention to the experience of Asians in the United States and to accumulate research for a doctoral thesis covering the "problem dealing with assimilation of the American-born Japanese." While exactly why he chose to concentrate on Asian Americans is unknown, doubtless his decision reflected both his own West Coast roots and the influence of his professors.

In fall 1936, LaViolette was appointed to an instructorship in sociology at the University of Washington (where he was joined soon after by his wife, Vera). He was dissatisfied with traditional research methods and strove to include himself among Japanese American communities to absorb his subject firsthand. LaViolette was drawn to Shotaro Frank Miyamoto, a Nisei graduate student in sociology eight years his junior. He relied on Miyamoto not only for professional discussions and insights into Japanese American life but also for introductions to others in the community, of which Miyamoto was a native. Miyamoto later affirmed that LaViolette was an enthusiast whose highly intuitive and spontaneous thinking and frankly unstructured method complemented his own more formalized and systematic approach.⁵ The two men became such close collaborators that LaViolette invited Miyamoto to share a house with him and his wife. The unorthodox living and professional arrangement persisted for some three years and worked to the advantage of all concerned—by 1939, LaViolette had completed his dissertation, while Miyamoto had written a long essay, "Social Solidarity Among the Japanese in Seattle," the first scholarly article by a Nisei social scientist.⁶ Meanwhile, the LaViolettes hired a Nisei undergraduate, Michi Yasumura, to join the household as an au pair, although Vera LaViolette continued to do much of the actual work of caring for Forrest (whose ulcer required him to eat a limited diet; Yasumura recalled that he used to throw parties and buy all the food he could not eat to have the pleasure of seeing others devour it).⁷

Frank Miyamoto and Michi Yasumura meanwhile introduced LaViolette to James Sakamoto, editor of the Seattle-based Nisei newspaper *Japanese American Courier*.⁸ LaViolette soon became a semiregular contributor—the only non-Japanese to be so honored. His columns reflected the assimilationist views and antiracist vision of chief editor Sakamoto.⁹ In summer 1938, LaViolette published serially in its pages his first "scholarly article"—the text of a manifesto he had delivered before the National Conference on Social Work on the citizenship activities of American-born Japanese. In the speech LaViolette stated that the task was fundamentally one of applying social science knowledge to the service of race and cultural pluralism. "Our nation's problem," he stated, "is no longer that of the melting pot, but of the symphony orchestra."¹⁰ He described in detail the social structure of Japanese communities, and examined the various restrictive immigration laws, job discrimination, and social stigma they faced.¹¹ In order to prepare for the inevitable crisis that would ensue in Japanese communities as family units broke down, LaViolette urged the government to abolish unequal laws and fund social service organizations (on the model of the National Urban League) to aid the development of a mature political consciousness among young Nisei.¹²

LaViolette completed his dissertation, "Types of Adjustment Among Second-Generation Japanese," early in 1939. In it, he analyzed the development of Nisei society and its impact on character. As in his *Japanese American Courier* articles, LaViolette suggested that external factors would determine progress toward the ultimate (and desirable) goal of complete absorption of Japanese Americans into the larger society. He concluded that the acceptance and social integration of the Nisei was a complex matter, since it was not simply an interracial problem, like that of the Negro, but also an international one, as a function of the larger relationship between the United States and Japan and American hostility toward Japan's foreign relations.[13] In an article summarizing his findings, LaViolette noted that Japanese Americans strongly distanced themselves from the Japanese culture of their parents and were not welcome in Japan (those who went to Japan for education, he explained, had experiences that were "usually not satisfactory"), and so were ripe for absorption into America. He added that Japanese Americans were as individualistic as other Americans and likely would not turn into a "racial bloc" like the Negroes. Conversely, he made clear that the Nisei, given an opportunity to prove themselves, would be completely loyal to the United States in case of war with Japan. "If the Japanese of the second generation are given an opportunity there is no question where their loyalty and patriotism would place them, either in peace or war.... This loyalty to the United States was shown clearly in Hawaii when the question of boycott came up."[14] Once the dissertation was accepted, LaViolette began on the work of transforming it into a book. However, because of the looming war situation and the widespread suspicion of Japanese Americans, two different publishers who had previously agreed to publish each cancelled his book contract.[15]

In fall 1940, LaViolette was hired as assistant professor of sociology at McGill University in Montreal. Once settled in his ancestral French Canadian homeland, he was able to make use of his French-language fluency (in tribute to his roots, LaViolette would thereafter sometimes sign his name using the more French "La Violette"). He also declared himself attracted to the job because he could continue his studies of Native communities on the Pacific coast of Canada. Montreal newspapers reporting his arrival described him as an expert on "the yellow peril," adding that in addition to his five years of study of Japanese on the Pacific coast, he had already visited the Vancouver area in order to make preliminary studies of the "Japanese problem" in British Columbia as well. LaViolette warned that a Pacific war would be deadly for those communities:

> The United States is not sufficiently involved for that country to start a war with Japan [but] Japan might readily provoke a quarrel whose proportions could attain war. The Japanese on the Western coast [are] placed in an embarrassing position. They are not wanted back in overpopulated Japan, where, if they visit, they are more ostracized than by Americans on this continent. The Nipponese here cannot escape westernization. Native Japanese detect this easily and shun the visitors.[16]

He expanded on these warnings in summer 1941 in a long article, "The American-Born Japanese and the World Crisis," which, like his previous contributions, was based on a paper delivered at a professional conference. In his text, LaViolette pointed out that the growing war climate between Japan and the United States was forcing Japanese Americans to choose sides more clearly, a process that could also clarify the marginal position the Nisei held in both American and Japanese communities by making American nationalism more salient in determining the actions of Japanese Americans than family sentiment toward Japan. "This means that individuals are now more fully committed to being Americans. It means a more definite incorporation into the American social system."[17] However, LaViolette was well aware of the threats to the community that still loomed in case of war, and he was prophetic on the potential consequences:

> By Japanese novelists the second generation has been portrayed as a tragic character, neither fully Japanese nor accepted by Americans but yet expected to fight for America. Rumors have it that the *nisei* would be the first to be sent to the front; others say they will be sent to concentration camps. One *nisei* told the writer that he was "fattening" himself up for the "long lean days behind barb wire."[18]

LaViolette was midway through his second year of teaching at McGill when the United States and Canada went to war with Japan. Although military service was out of the question, as he was nearly thirty-eight, overweight, and medically unfit because of his ulcer, he drew from his youthful radio training and volunteered his services teaching evening radio physics classes to the Royal Canadian Air Force in addition to his regular duties. In marked contrast to this patriotic activism, LaViolette remained startlingly disconnected from the removal of 113,000 West Coast Japanese Americans and 22,000 Japanese Canadians from their homes during 1942 and their confinement in government camps in the interior of their respective countries. Despite his predictions of harsh consequences for Japanese Americans if war broke out in the Pacific, he remained publicly silent as pressure mounted on the Pacific coast of the United States and Canada during spring 1942 for mass action against their ethnic Japanese populations. LaViolette did not join the tiny group of liberal academics who publicly protested mass removal or formed Fair Play Committees. While he corresponded with numerous Nisei friends from Seattle, there is little record that he offered them financial or logistical assistance. (Frank Miyamoto, hired by University of California sociologist Dorothy Swaine Thomas as a "community analyst" for the Japanese Evacuation Research Study, spent the early war years in the Tule Lake camp.)[19]

Nor, however, did LaViolette line up immediately in support of the government, either with supportive public comment or with assistance to the War Relocation Authority, the civil agency created to operate the Japanese American camps. Although the WRA was desperate to recruit social scientists with experience among Japanese Americans to be camp administrators and community analysts (so much so that John Embree was named the WRA's chief reports officer largely on the basis of his having written "Suye Mura," a short anthropological study of a village in Japan), LaViolette evidently either was not asked to join the WRA or refused, for he remained in Montreal throughout 1942. In contrast, in May 1943 LaViolette took a leave from McGill and entered the Heart Mountain Relocation Center. Over the following six months, he served there as an administrator and community analyst for the WRA (LaViolette also took a collection of stark photographs of the camp's guard towers and facilities). He clearly saw his role as one of an intermediary, trusted by both sides, between the camp administration and the Japanese "residents," someone who could facilitate communication and community stability. He noted in one of his first memos:

> It may not be obvious but I think we can see utility in the assumption that the Japanese community is tending to reconstruct itself somewhat along old lines. It should be helpful if we look to see what is likely to be missing due to certain limitations. In pre-evacuation days there were certain white functionaries who represented one of the few points of accommodation between the white and Japanese. . . . In spite of what we do, it is rather evident that the process of reconstruction is under way and that stability is coming, Here I think community analysts will be vital [in such accommodation]. First, we shall have to more and more make use of, cooperate with, these reconstructed and emerging patterns.[20]

LaViolette added that he hoped to train schoolteachers and others to fit that role. "It is my guess that we should plan seminars for [schoolteachers] in which we would educate them about the Japanese, about the world in which we live, and also take then into a more active part of WRA program."[21] Given his emphasis on education, he was outraged when he discovered that Japanese American schoolteachers were being issued only restrictive teaching certificates by the Wyoming state school board, with the result that they were forbidden to teach elsewhere in the state following resettlement. "Obviously, this is discrimination," LaViolette fumed. "But it is the same sort of discrimination which had such a large part in determining the entire evacuation. [However,] there is no evidence that the WRA is partner to this discriminatory action."[22]

During his residence at Heart Mountain, LaViolette spent much of his time meeting with inmates and compiling reports on inmate opinion. His goal was to encourage Japanese Americans to make plans to resettle outside camp. During this period, the WRA undertook the large-scale segregation of those the government adjudged "disloyal" (based on a hastily designed and egregious "loyalty questionnaire") in a separate high-security camp at Tule Lake, and established procedures for granting "leave permits" (a politically expedient form of parole) so that those the government adjudged to be "loyal" could leave camp. LaViolette's chief contribution to the process was a confidential statistical study of those who had given negative or unsatisfactory answers to the questionnaire. His conclusion was that many Nisei acted from confusion, a result of being forced into a stark choice between family demands (the views of parents in prewar Japanese communities being law) and the instructions of the government. To his credit, LaViolette dismissed the influence of pro-Axis agitators, on whom other WRA officials had placed blame for the "wrong" answers by Nisei on the questionnaire. On the other hand, his writings also ignored the very real and swelling protest against confinement that had already led dissident inmates to form the Heart Mountain Fair Play Committee and would climax the following spring in its organized campaign of resistance to conscription.[23]

LaViolette left Heart Mountain in December 1943. His public comments after his departure reveal an odd (and mendacious) defensiveness. In an interview he gave to the *Toronto Globe and Mail*, he stated, "Conditions are now so good in relocation centers that there are practically no grievances." Food conditions were "highly satisfactory, and in every other respect the evacuees are carefully looked after." The barracks, he contended, "have been constructed to provide adequate shelter during even the most extreme weather conditions."[24] At the end of 1944, he published a review of Carey McWilliams's book *Prejudice*. LaViolette lauded McWilliams's book as a study of the irrationality of American social organization. However, he minimized McWilliams's description of the treatment of Japanese Americans as a particularly "un-American" phenomenon, and his strictures against West Coast whites, by saying that violent attacks of one kind or another on minority groups, particularly racial minority groups, were a long-standing feature of American history. Nowhere in his review did LaViolette even mention the central point of McWilliams's book: that Issei and Nisei were being confined en masse in camps. Instead he underlined the government's effort to atone for the "American wrongs" of evacuation by its concentration on assimilating Japanese Americans, which he contrasted positively with the "slower way of reconstruction" prevailing in Canada.[25]

His mental block about discussing the camps was thrown into even sharper relief the following year when the Canadian Institute of International Affairs brought out LaViolette's book *Americans of Japanese Ancestry: A Study of Assimilation in the American Community*, adapted from his Ph.D. dissertation. More than five years had passed since it had originally been submitted for publication. Since that time, the situation of Japanese Americans and their communities had been completely transformed by the wartime camp experience, and LaViolette had ample opportunity, in an afterword if not in revisions, to discuss the impact of camp life on Japanese Americans and assimilation. Yet he remained silent—ominously so—about the wartime experience, and concentrated entirely on the prewar community. He thereby forfeited his chance to present an up-to-date analysis of Japanese American society.

How do we explain this enormous gap, even indifference, in LaViolette's approach to the official treatment of Japanese Americans, a subject that had previously energized him, and his failure to help those who had been his main friends? I think that a large part has to do with LaViolette's extreme focus on assimilation by any means. As noted, he had lauded in his review of the Carey McWilliams book the efforts of the United States government to bring about the absorption of the Japanese minority. Similarly, a generation later, he wrote that "one would be inclined to suppose that in spite of adversity, the assimilation of the children of Japanese immigrants was accelerated and facilitated by the war against Japan."[26] LaViolette's attitude also seems to have reflected a patriotic defensiveness about the government and its role. "Already [removal] is defined as a major failure in American ideals," he complained in early 1946, "although there are aspects of the program that could support claims for major successes."[27] Here he softened his position slightly in later years, and was willing to admit that the "momentous and egregious" evacuation, fueled by West Coast prejudices, had been "our greatest action in abridging civil liberties since the founding of the Republic."[28] Nevertheless, he continued to deny that the camps themselves had been prisons—in some cases, LaViolette remained unable to actually mention the fact that "evacuation" even led to confinement. In 1971, LaViolette wrote in a book review that his goal was to give the *coup de grâce* to the idea that the Relocation Centers were concentration camps as some have called them. The Washington office and Center administrators quickly came to appreciate the social psychological personal expressions of evacuees coping with the facts of evacuation, public opinion and national policy [and worked] correcting the errors of the democratic process . . . while continuing to fight a major war.[29]

LaViolette's caution in confronting and evaluating the wartime experience of Japanese Canadians resembled his position on the Japanese Americans. During spring 1942, as politicians and pressure groups in British Columbia made the case for mass removal of the ethnic Japanese population on the Canadian West Coast, LaViolette did not intervene. In July 1942, LaViolette finally broke his silence by publishing a short account of the situation for the liberal Asian studies journal *Far Eastern Survey*, which he ultimately followed up with a sequel two years afterward.[30] Both were largely factual articles on the history of anti-Japanese prejudice in British Columbia. In them, the author ascribed the federal government's decision to issue the Orders-in-Council exiling Japanese Canadians from the Pacific coast not to racism but to legitimate military factors. In the same way, LaViolette refused in his twin articles to pronounce on the harsh operation of the "settlements" for Japanese Canadians. Instead, he described the state of affairs for the larger community and underlined various unsolved questions of resettlement and readaptation. As with Japanese Americans, the progress of assimilation was his exclusive focus. Thus, he concluded that mass migration away from the prejudices of the West Coast was a positive step, as it might speed postwar assimilation of Canadian Nisei, even if he expressed limited concern for the individuals involved: "Military necessity may have dictated evacuation in part, but provincial rights, the rising level of race prejudice, and the marginal economic position of the evacuees are barriers to a thorough-going solution of Canada's Japanese problem."[31]

LaViolette followed two years later with another article for the same publication in which he updated the situation. As before, he refused to offer any judgment on official policy, even Ottawa's cruel confiscation and sale of the property of Japanese Canadians, who were then forced to use the proceeds to pay for their confinement. This policy left those already victimized by persecution financially destitute. The most the author would do was to present it as an unsettled question: "The government looks upon liquidation as good administration. The Japanese look upon it as a breach of faith. They suspect the government has given way to political and economic pressure groups. Available evidence does not indicate conclusively the factors on which the decision was based."[32] After touring the confinement sites in British Columbia, LaViolette remarked positively in a lecture that the Canadian confinement experience had gone much more smoothly and had been less expensive than the American program, but he remained silent on the mass despoiling of property that had made it possible.[33]

In the last days of World War II, LaViolette expanded his wartime articles into a pamphlet for the Canadian Institute of International Affairs. He then in turn expanded the pamphlet into the prize-winning book *The Canadian Japanese and World War II*, which was published in 1948.[34] The book recounted the story of mass removal in Canada and the steps through which Japanese Canadians had resettled and rebuilt their communities. The work was the first to approach in detail the social and psychological effects of evacuation on the ethnic Japanese community in Canada. Once more, though, the author declined to make recommendations for government action in support of the rights of Japanese Canadians.[35] Although critics were unanimous in praising LaViolette's detailed and judicious presentation of the record of the wartime events, Tomatsu Shibutani, himself a former inmate, perceptively remarked that he was disappointed by LaViolette's failure to examine how the program appeared from the point of view of those affected.[36]

Paradoxically, given his neutral stance on Ottawa's wartime policy on ethnic Japanese, LaViolette emerged during the wartime and postwar years as a major supporter of Japanese Canadians and their citizenship rights. He started by welcoming Nisei students such as Kim Nakashima to McGill and supervising their work.[37] When in 1944 McGill became the first Canadian university to officially bar students of Japanese ancestry, LaViolette helped guide the protests by students and community activists that led to the successful repeal of the policy the following year. While he made no public comment against the policy—no doubt he felt constrained by his position—he privately organized students and helped gain publicity for their efforts. Meanwhile, as early as February 1945 LaViolette gave a well-publicized public lecture in which he claimed that the government's seizure of the property of Japanese Canadians was "open to criticism" and had done more than anything else to arouse racial hostility on an international scale.[38] He asked whether Canadians intended "to try to keep in Canada people who feel that this is their home, or . . . to send to Japan people who are Canadian citizens, among them young people who can neither speak nor write the Japanese language."[39] Shortly after, he termed mass removal a "complete defeat" for the efforts of Japanese Canadians to assimilate, and noted that community members, despite surface acceptance, remained inwardly hostile.[40] Yet in an article that explored the movement for total deportation of Canadian citizens, he declared against all evidence that the initial willingness of Issei and Nisei to go to Japan was due more to prewar prejudice in British Columbia than to the Canadian government's wartime confinement and impoverishment of ethnic Japanese.[41] The following year, LaViolette helped form the Montreal Committee on Canadian Citizenship to oppose government deportation policies. (Again, presumably because of his professional position, LaViolette did not officially join the committee, and he was careful to leave his name off its public manifestos). The committee was successful in finding jobs and housing for Nisei migrants and in challenging the government's policy of involuntary mass postwar deportation of Japanese Canadians.[42]

In 1949, LaViolette accepted the chairmanship of a joint department of sociology and anthropology at Tulane University. During his years at Tulane, he pursued projects on diverse aspects of race relations, including urbanization in South America, Nazi war crimes against Jews, and housing for minorities.[43] His most significant contribution was the 1961 book *The Struggle for Survival*, on the adaptation of First Nations in British Columbia. After retiring from Tulane in 1967 he served as visiting professor at the University of Toronto, and later at the University of Guelph. In 1973, he returned to Portland, Oregon, with his wife, where he died on September 28, 1989. Over the last forty years of his life, LaViolette maintained an almost total public silence on the question of Japanese Americans and Japanese Canadians, After 1949 he largely ceased to publish research on either group, although in a series of brief book reviews he made a limited attempt to engage the new scholarship on government actions during World War II. Curiously, he made no public comment in support of the redress movement that grew up in both countries in the 1970s and 1980s. Whether his turning his attention to other projects following his return to the United States in 1949–50 was based on a sense that he had completed his work or on the feeling of being stymied by the complexity of the problem is impossible to know.

To conclude, what can we make of the contributions of Forrest LaViolette? An unorthodox academic in his research and career trajectory, he nonetheless held to a strict objectivity in his writing. His approach aroused strong disagreement among later scholars. Ann Gomer Sunahara criticized his impersonality as false objectivity.

When Forrest E. LaViolette wrote ... in the 1940s, wartime censorship hindered his efforts. In addition, as a sociologist LaViolette was primarily interested in the exile of Japanese Canadians as a social phenomenon, one that paralleled a similar exile of Japanese Americans. Accordingly, he accepted the explanation of the government of the day—that it had merely responded to a mistaken but overwhelming surge of public opinion in British Columbia. LaViolette was unable—or lacked the interest—to determine how that surge of public opinion materialized, or how it came to be translated into the repressive policies applied to the innocent Japanese.[44]

On the other hand, Rolf Knight credited LaViolette with putting racial issues on the table amid a hostile postwar climate:

> In retrospect, the era was the golden age for obscurantist social science and retailored history. ... Whole fields of enquiry had been silenced by self-imposed taboos and it became bad form even to mention whole classes of events. When a book like Forrest LaViolette's ... arose in class discussion it was sniffily dismissed as unscholarly—meaning that it stuck its nose into a topic which then had been expunged.[45]

What is more difficult to understand is why LaViolette was such a weak reed in the defense of Japanese North Americans against official race-based wartime exclusion and discrimination. On one hand, he was clearly supportive of Japanese Americans and gladly joined in community life. Believing that he could help the Nisei by giving them guidance so that they could more easily be absorbed into mainstream society, he was a generous mentor and friend. In the prewar years, he also took their side, recommending to those in the larger society that they foster assimilation of minorities to bring an end to racial prejudice. Yet out of his interest in the abstract question of resettlement, and perhaps also his fear of alienating orthodox academics by political activism that could appear to slant his work, he remained aloof from overt political activity, despite his behind-the-scenes presence in the fight to protect Japanese Canadians from postwar deportation. Worse, he remained an outspoken apologist for official confinement of ethnic Japanese, even as concerned citizens in both nations deplored the wartime policy and the former inmates campaigned for reparations. Still, both for its qualities and for its ambivalences, LaViolette's work merits further study.

3. Japantown Born and Reborn

Comparing the Resettlement Experience of Issei and Nisei in Detroit, New York, and Los Angeles

The Japanese bombing of Pearl Harbor in December 1941 and the unleashing of World War II in the Pacific wiped out the thriving Japanese communities on the Pacific coast of the United States. In the weeks that followed the onset of war, military officials on the West Coast became increasingly terrified of a Japanese invasion. They proceeded to single out the region's Japanese American population as potential spies and saboteurs on the basis of their ancestry, and called for the mass "evacuation" of both Issei and Nisei from the West Coast.[1] The movement was further fomented and abetted by white nativist organizations and agricultural and commercial groups, who saw an opportunity to rid themselves of their long-despised economic competitors, and by opportunistic politicians. The fact that there was no documented case of any disloyal activity by any person of Japanese ancestry on the West Coast, and that two-thirds of the community's members, the Nisei, were American citizens did not ease the fears of their panicked neighbors. Rather, as West Coast defense commander General John DeWitt stated, the very absence of evidence only proved that a concentrated campaign of subversion had been prepared for the future. Anyway, DeWitt insisted, it was impossible to tell a loyal Japanese American from a disloyal one. "A Jap is a Jap," he told his War Department superiors, Assistant Secretary of War John McCloy and Secretary of War Henry L. Stimson. McCloy and Stimson soon overcame their initial doubts about the necessity and constitutionality of mass removal of Japanese Americans, and brought the matter into the White House.[2]

In response to the pressure from the military and West Coast political leaders, President Franklin D. Roosevelt (who had his own prejudices against ethnic Japanese) signed Executive Order 9066 on February 19, 1942. Under authority of this order, the army forcibly expelled all residents of Japanese ancestry from the West Coast during the months that followed. In the process, the vast majority of families lost their property or were forced to sell it at fire sale prices. Once removed from their homes, the Japanese Americans were placed in a network of "Assembly Centers," stockades in disused fairgrounds and racetracks where the Japanese Americans were housed in converted horse stalls and animal pens and treated by army administrators as prisoners. After several weeks or months, they were then transported under guard to a network of ten government-run "relocation centers" in remote desert areas or swamplands in the interior, where they sweltered in summer and often froze in winter. The inmates lived in hastily constructed tar-paper barracks, one room to a family. Health and sanitary facilities in the camps, particularly at the outset, were primitive. The War Relocation Authority, the government agency created to supervise the camps, deliberately kept food and salaries for all inmate workers at levels below that of the lowest-paid American soldier.[3]

Although War Department chiefs privately conceded as early as 1943 that there was no military necessity for continued confinement of the mass of the inmates, West Coast military commanders, under pressure from anti-Japanese American politicians and media barons, long refused to reopen the excluded areas to people of Japanese ancestry. Furthermore, the government's mass removal policy convinced important elements of public opinion nationwide that the inmates represented a danger. There was therefore significant opposition to resettlement, and no strong wave of sentiment in their favor.

The WRA gradually developed a parole system of sorts, to permit inmates to leave camp without mobilizing hostile public opinion against them. After filling out a compulsory "loyalty questionnaire" and being adjudged "loyal" by a joint military board, individuals were eligible to obtain "leave permits" to resettle outside the West Coast excluded area. The process remained slow and cumbersome—not only did candidates have to have offers of jobs and housing, but the WRA had to ensure that local public opinion was favorable to entry of Japanese Americans. The majority of Japanese Americans, unable to return home and unwilling or unable to resettle elsewhere, remained confined in the camps for the balance of the war. Nevertheless, approximately one-fourth of the confined Issei and Nisei did gain official permission to leave camp during these years and settle outside the West Coast. This first wave of resettlers was composed mostly of Nisei in their late teens or twenties who left camp to join the military or take up outside employment. In addition, a group of

Nisei college students were authorized to take up scholarships at colleges east of the Rocky Mountains under the auspices of a newly created private welfare agency, the National Japanese American Student Relocation Council.[4] As these pioneers put down roots in their new communities, they were joined by siblings and friends, and in some cases parents and other relatives. The largest populations remained in the Mountain West or moved to the industrial cities of the East and Midwest. Chicago, in particular, became a population center: from a prewar community of some 400, the Windy City's ethnic Japanese population reached 20,000 by 1945–46, while an estimated 25,000 took up at least temporary residence during those years. The WRA was responsible for finding jobs and advocating for the newcomers, a task that was taken over by private church and local welfare groups after the dissolution of the agency in mid-1946.[5]

The West Coast remained closed to Japanese Americans (apart from soldiers and some other minor exceptions) until the end of 1944, when the Supreme Court ruled in *Ex parte Endo* that the government had no authority to hold a concededly loyal citizen without charge. In response, the army lifted its blanket exclusion orders in January 1945, although it substituted thousands of individual exclusion orders for inmates it suspected. Almost immediately, most of the remaining camp inmates began to return to the West Coast despite the efforts of the WRA, which feared violent backlash from white racists, to use various administrative devices to slow the flow of such return. Though resettlement east of the Rockies did continue at a slower pace, by mid-1947 the majority of the mainland ethnic Japanese population was once again settled on the Pacific coast. As those who had first moved east out of camp returned to their former homes the Japanese populations of the Midwest and East Coast began to decline, although significant pockets remained east of the Rockies, especially in the large cities.

Whatever their destination, the former camp inmates attempted to rebuild their lives under difficult and trying circumstances.[6] Despoiled of most of their property during removal and psychologically scarred by their unjust confinement, they entered their new communities with little in the way of resources. Despite the wartime economic boom, they experienced widespread poverty and economic discrimination. In the prewar era, Issei and Nisei were largely self-employed in agriculture or as small shopkeepers, or worked for family businesses. Forced during removal to give up their shops and the land they owned or leased, most were unable to resume their former positions. Even those with significant educational or professional experience were forced to work for white families as gardeners or domestic servants, or to take low-status and menial-labor jobs.[7] Unlike the prewar era, though, numerous Nisei, notably veterans, ultimately managed to secure jobs outside the community as teachers, corporate employees, and civil servants. By 1960, the median income of Japanese Americans exceeded the national average.

Housing was an equally difficult problem. Japanese Americans were confronted by shortages made worse by poverty and widespread racial discrimination, especially on the West Coast. Most Issei and Nisei, unable to resume their former leases or to borrow money to buy land, were forced to resettle in urban areas. There officials charged with aiding resettlers attempted to steer the newcomers, especially single Nisei, into taking domestic service positions, since they would thereby be provided board. Those with the means to buy homes and hotels opened space for lodgers. For others, community groups formed hostels to ease the housing problem. However, none of these efforts could begin to absorb all the newcomers. Instead, thousands of resettlers in cities such as San Diego, Chicago, Cleveland, Los Angeles, and San Jose were forced into substandard housing, generally in or alongside black and Latino neighborhoods. Ultimately, greater prosperity plus the decline of restrictive covenants led masses of Nisei to migrate to suburbs and more affluent districts.

Although the resettlers were warned by the WRA and the FBI to fit in as much as possible and to promise to stay away from other Japanese Americans on leaving camp, they were brought together into Japanese enclaves both by internal factors such as religious observance or the desire for community and by external factors such as ethnic-based hostility and exclusion by whites. During the resettlement period, Japanese Americans took up some of their old community institutions and also developed new ones.[8] While the Japanese consulates that had anchored the prewar Little Tokyos remained shuttered, Japanese Buddhist temples and Christian churches reopened their doors in large numbers, and business groups mushroomed. Outside the West Coast, community hostels and interracial organizations such as the YMCA served as main recreational centers, providing libraries and game rooms for social events. The Japanese American Citizens League, although resented by many former inmates for its wartime policy of collaboration, was left as the sole ethnic organization of any size in the postwar years, and large numbers of Nisei joined newly constituted or reformed JACL chapters (Issei were not accepted as members until several years later). In addition to political advocacy, JACL chapters organized social events, dinners, and sports leagues—especially basketball and bowling, the two unofficial Nisei national pastimes.

A main focus of community attention was journalism. Within months after the opening of the camps a series of newspapers, predominantly Japanese-language but with greater or lesser amounts of English content, started up operations. Los Angeles's bilingual prewar dailies *Rafu Shimpo* and *Kashu Mainichi* resumed publication, and soon afterward San Francisco's prewar *Nichi Bei Shimbun* and *Shin Sekai* morphed into a pair of new weekly journals, *Nichi Bei Times* and *Hokubei Mainichi*. Resettlers in the Mountain West were served by a trio of small-scale newspapers that had continued to publish during the war, Salt Lake City's *Utah Nippo* and the Denver-based *Colorado Times* and *Rockii Shimpo*. In New York a new journal, *Hokubei Shimpo*, took pride of place. The ethnic newspaper that attained the highest local circulation was the *Chicago Shimpo*, whose progressive political outlook, in both its Japanese and English sections, attracted large-scale community attention (both positive and negative). During these same years, a set of all-English weekly newspapers started up, including *Crossroads* in Los Angeles, *Northwest Times* in Seattle, *Progressive News* in San Francisco, and *Nisei Weekender* in New York City, though most soon folded. In addition, *Nisei Vue*, a short-lived glossy quarterly magazine, started life in 1947. It was succeeded by *Scene*, which had a longer run (1950–57). The premier Nisei publication was the *Pacific Citizen*, organ of the JACL, which was published under the dynamic editorship of Larry Tajiri. Although the *Pacific Citizen* lost the near-monopoly of the Japanese American press that it had enjoyed during the war, it remained a forum for news and opinion on a nationwide scale.

One clear area of division between the West Coast and the rest of the country was the level of race-based harassment and bias. To be sure, Nisei in many areas faced insults or were refused service in stores, and job discrimination was widespread throughout the country. However, both anecdotal evidence and records testify to more widespread patterns of ethnic-based hostility and exclusion by West Coast whites, which remained unchanged into the postwar period. There were thirty-eight documented instances of terrorism against resettlers in California over the months that followed the opening of the West Coast, including sabotage of equipment, torching of barns, and shots fired into houses. Local WRA officials were forced into action in support of returnees. They lobbied newspapers to offer positive coverage of Issei and Nisei, protested harassment and violence, and looked into allegations of racial discrimination.

Furthermore, unlike in the rest of the country, the ugly climate on the West Coast was reflected in official policy. State public assistance bodies generally refused to fund or direct the absorption and adjustment of the resettlers. Instead, local WRA offices, which lacked staff and funding for such tasks, were forced to take up the burden of organizing private charity. Washington State governor Mon Wallgren maintained that Japanese Americans were not welcome in his state.[9] In contrast, California governor Earl Warren called for full and positive public compliance with the return of Japanese Americans to their old homes once the army lifted exclusion. Yet, as will be noted more fully later in this volume, Warren also signed various discriminatory legislative measures designed to discourage Issei and Nisei from returning. In 1943 the California legislature allocated funds for escheat suits to enforce the long-dormant Alien Land Act against Japanese immigrants "ineligible to citizenship" and take away the property they had acquired. The legislature meanwhile enacted a new law forbidding all Japanese immigrants to hold fishing licenses.

Despite these overall national and regional patterns, there were significant variations in the experience of resettlers in individual cities throughout the country. A close review of the progress of resettlement reveals both surprising similarities and differences, all of which complicate easy distinctions between resettlement on the West Coast and that outside. By way of illustration, let us compare Japanese American resettlement in three key urban areas, Detroit, New York, and Los Angeles. While very divergent politically and economically, each of these three areas served as a regional economic center, and each underwent important demographic shifts during World War II, including massive in-migration by southern white and African American war workers. All three, notably, were scarred by large-scale rioting and interracial conflict during summer 1943.

The initial resettlement of Japanese Americans from the camps to the Detroit area followed in its outlines the larger patterns of migration. Just over 3,000 Issei and Nisei moved to Michigan directly from camp during the war years, of whom a large majority settled in the greater Detroit area. (In addition, 534 Japanese Americans moved to Ann Arbor, home of the University of Michigan, where a military language school was created.) More specifically, WRA records list 1,007 Japanese Americans who took up residence within Detroit's city limits during 1943–44, making it the fifth-largest center of resettlement nationwide after Chicago, Denver, New York, and Cleveland. Of this total, almost 90 percent (899) were Nisei.

Once West Coast exclusion was lifted, migration slowed drastically. Individual Issei and family groups predominated among postwar migrants—Issei accounted for 186 of the 456 newcomers to the city between January 1, 1945, and spring 1946.[10]

In addition to those arrivals listed by the WRA, the city's midcentury ethnic Japanese population was swelled by the arrival of various former camp inmates who had initially resettled elsewhere (and thus did not appear on resettlement registers). For example, Fred Korematsu, who unsuccessfully challenged the constitutionality of mass removal in the U.S. Supreme Court case *Korematsu v. United States*, originally resettled out of camp in Salt Lake City, but then moved to Detroit in 1944 to join his older brother Hi Korematsu. Furthermore, some Nisei who had not been confined in camp decided to make Detroit their home. The architect Minoru Yamasaki, future designer of the World Trade Center, who had spent the war years in New York, was hired in 1945 as chief of design for the architectural firm of Smith Hinchman & Grylls, and took up residence in Detroit. Another transplanted New Yorker, sociologist T. Scott Miyakawa, entered the area in 1944 after he was hired as a visiting lecturer at the University of Michigan. At the same time, a small colony of Japanese Canadians who had suffered official removal from Canada's west coast resettled in Windsor, Ontario, where they interacted with the nearby Detroit community.

In the vast majority of cases, the Japanese American newcomers had never previously lived in or even visited Detroit (whose prewar Japanese population was limited to a few dozen individuals—103 as of the 1930 census). Those who settled in outlying rural areas were almost exclusively employed in farm labor. Inside the city the newcomers took up all sorts of jobs. A large percentage of Issei of both sexes worked as domestics or gardeners; Nisei women also found work as stenographers and secretaries, and Nisei men were also employed as dishwashers in city restaurants and as blue-collar workers in the city's dominant automobile industry and allied trades. The Ford Motor Company, which had hired Issei engineers since the 1910s and was traditionally known for friendliness to African American labor, became a major employer of Nisei resettlers, as did the Chrysler Corporation. Kustu Ishimaru and Gilbert Kurihara worked as auto mechanics in garages, while Bill Kitamura was employed by the Detroit Street Railway. Other big employers of Nisei labor included the Briggs Manufacturing Company, the Essex Wire Company, Gar Wood Industries, and the Ex-cell-o Company. Groups of younger Nisei attended college or studied in trade schools. Wayne University welcomed a number of Nisei students—including a class of fifteen cadet nurses preparing for military duty. Grace Hospital engaged a pair of Nisei physicians as residents. A half-dozen Nisei beauticians graduated from the Dermaway University of Hair and Beauty Culture in mid-1945.[11]

As time passed, a wider spectrum of skilled and salesclerk jobs opened up. By 1945, Frank Doi was hired as a dental lab technician, Grace Fujii was employed as a hospital social worker, George Kawamoto ran a photography studio, and Roy Setsuda was hired as an interior decorator. Others found public sector positions: Marie Doi was employed as a relocation officer by the WRA's Detroit office, while Roku Yasui worked for the city's Postwar Planning Division, and Jane Togasaki worked for the Michigan State Health Department. A few Japanese Americans went into business for themselves. Mr. and Mrs. Masujiro Ishioka, an Issei couple, operated an apartment house on Cass Avenue. Mr. and Mrs. Anthony Yasutake started a dry goods store in the suburb of Royal Oak. The most popular Nisei small business (capitalizing on popular stereotypes of Asian labor) was the laundry. George Akamine, Mas Hashimoto, and Tom and Jimmie Tagami and their families each opened cleaning establishments in Detroit. Few resettlers were able to establish themselves in management or white-collar positions, although the community was served by a group of medical professionals such as dentists Kiyoshi Sonoda and Mark Kanda and optometrist John Koyama.

As in other cities, the task of aiding the absorption and adjustment of the resettlers was taken up by a coalition of the local WRA office with private church and welfare groups. As early as mid-1942, WRA resettlement director Thomas Holland and George Rundquist of the Protestant Council of Churches organized a Detroit Resettlement Committee under the lead of the Reverend Father James McCormick to help locate housing and jobs for the resettlers. In September 1943 (following the lead of Rev. T. T. Brumbaugh, a former missionary in Japan) the Detroit Council of Churches established its own United Ministry to Resettlers. The Council invited Rev. Shigeo Tanabe, a Nisei pastor from Washington State, to operate the ministry. In 1945, after the WRA announced plans to wind up its operations, local civil leaders formed the Detroit Committee to Aid Resettlers of Japanese Ancestry, which operated approximately through the end of 1947. Under the auspices of the United Ministry to Resettlers, Tanabe established Fellowship House, a Nisei hostel, at 130 East Grand Boulevard. The WRA subsequently opened a family hostel at 3915 Trumbull in July 1945 under the auspices of the Buddhist Church of Detroit. Rev. and Mrs. Shawshew Sakow were the hostel's managers. In addition to serving as temporary housing for the resettlers, the hostels served as recreational centers, providing libraries and game rooms where the newcomers joined together for social events. In addition, a Nisei committee formed at the International Institute in 1944. It arranged biweekly dances and ping-pong nights to encourage sociability. Young Nisei joined baseball teams, and a Nisei basketball club participated in an interstate tournament. As in other places, the most popular Nisei sport was bowling—in 1945 an entire Detroit-area Nisei bowling league was formed. In mid-1946 a Detroit chapter of the JACL formed, under the leadership of Peter Fujioka.[12]

Permanent housing remained the most troublesome item on the resettlement aid agenda—as a report of the Detroit Relocation Committee put it, "Housing was the 'nightmare' of all newcomers to the city."[13] The wartime economic boom had brought such a huge influx of war workers, primarily African Americans and white southerners, that local housing stock was completely inadequate to contain them. (So explosive was the housing shortage that the opening of a public housing project for African Americans, the Sojourner Truth Homes, in spring 1942 had touched off mass demonstrations and threats of violence by mobs of local whites who insisted that they should be assigned the homes.) Community activists directed their attention to solving the housing problem. Jack Shimoda, a Japanese American businessman who had lived in Detroit during the prewar era, purchased a boardinghouse on Forest Avenue, which was filled with new arrivals. A number of resettlers obtained long-term housing at the city's YMCA, which also hired a cadre of Nisei workers. Nevertheless, in the end, many Japanese Americans were obliged to settle in decrepit housing in or adjacent to the city's African American neighborhoods, as white areas were all but inaccessible.

The question of discrimination was a complex one. Detroit was notorious in prewar years as a center of Ku Klux Klan and white supremacist activity, with right-wing leader Gerald L. K. Smith and the anti-Semitic "radio priest" Father Charles Coughlin as the movement's most visible figures. During the war, existing racial tensions between blacks and whites had been exacerbated by rapid population shifts, which led to overcrowding and shortages of transportation, schools, and housing. These tensions exploded into violent confrontation in June 1943, when fights at the city's Belle Isle resort area ignited a large-scale racial riot. The riot lasted three days, claiming thirty lives (twenty-five of them African Americans), and gave rise to lasting tensions. That said, according to various accounts, Nisei in Detroit felt welcomed. For example, *Pacific Citizen* columnist Dale Oka, who resettled in Detroit in June 1943, stated that he was initially wary of how he would be accepted, but was soon put at ease:

The reception accorded me since my advent to this area has surpassed my most optimistic hopes. Perhaps I belong to that fortunate few who found their relocation paths strewn with flowers of welcome instead of thorns. But I prefer to believe that the great majority of us have discovered their new lives to be similarly pleasant and encouraging.[14]

Liberal and religious groups in the city mobilized to aid Japanese Americans. As noted, the Detroit Council of Churches (which as early as spring 1942 had passed an official resolution deploring mass evacuation and calling for rapid loyalty hearings for Japanese Americans) took a leading role in aiding resettlers and in advocating for their rights. Public opinion, as reflected in media accounts, was overwhelmingly positive. The *Detroit News* editorialized in 1944, "There are now numbers of Japanese here, migrants from the Pacific coast, whose records have been sifted and who should be regarded and treated as loyal friends in the war against Japan."[15] The following year, the *Detroit Free Press* ran a positive article on the approximately 2,000 Japanese Americans, whom it termed "all American citizens who speak our own language," living in Detroit. The article featured an interview with Mrs. Terry Koyama, who praised the treatment she had received in Detroit and expressed optimism about her future: "The dispersal was good because we used to live too close together on the West Coast, anyway. Now we're more spread out and we have a better chance—without the old prejudices."[16]

Still, both anecdotal evidence and the records of the WRA's Detroit office, which was responsible for finding jobs and advocating for the newcomers, testify to widespread patterns of discrimination. When the Yoshiki family left camp for Detroit in 1944, one family member who traveled ahead to find housing called a local hotel to reserve a room. When he appeared at the hotel, however, the hotel's owners—shocked to discover that Mr. Yoshiki was Japanese and not Polish, as they had assumed from his name—refused him lodging.[17] Educational discrimination was also palpable in the Detroit area. At the outset of war, administrators at the University of Michigan made a confidential decision to limit admission of Nisei students to a quota of twenty-seven per year, spread among the university's different faculties. When challenged on its discriminatory policy, the university denied that it had established any quota, and defended its policy on the pretext that the FBI and army refused to grant clearances (a transparent falsehood in view of the fact that the Military Intelligence Service language school was on campus, housing Nisei students and instructors, and that the university simultaneously hired more than 200 Nisei employees to take up menial-labor jobs on its grounds). Even after all government controls over Nisei students were abandoned in fall 1944, the university maintained its discriminatory policy.[18]

Employers and labor unionists also were mixed in their reactions to Japanese Americans. The local chapter of the AFL-affiliated Teamsters Union (following national policy) was extremely hostile to Nisei and refused to allow them to join the union or to support their employment in the trucking industry. The leadership of the CIO was supportive—United Auto Workers leader Walter Reuther even joined a delegation to ask the Detroit Housing Commission to open public housing to Japanese Americans—but local activists were often recalcitrant. In Ann Arbor, the CIO refused to accept Japanese Americans in a factory producing defense material. Similarly, in April 1944, Tom Nakamura, a resettler from Jerome, was hired by the Palmer Company, a Detroit war plant. When he appeared for work, employees staged a walkout to protest the hiring of a Nisei. Although swift action by the local Fair Employment Practices Committee and local CIO officials limited the action to a single day and ensured Nakamura's continued employment, the incident revealed the existence of widespread, if subtle, currents of anti-Nisei sentiment.[19]

The experience of Issei and Nisei in New York forms an interesting contrast with that of their Michigan counterparts. The community in Detroit, created as a result of the wartime migration, was close-knit and composed mainly of industrial and other blue-collar laborers. In contrast, the experience of resettlers in New York City during the 1940s reflects the larger narrative of the city's distinctive Nikkei (ethnic Japanese) community. Like the larger city itself, the Big Apple's Nikkei population was notable as early as the nineteenth century for its demographic and occupational diversity, a culture of cosmopolitanism, and political and artistic effervescence. In stark contrast to its Pacific coast counterparts, the New York community was also marked by lack of group cohesion and a readiness to absorb transients and new arrivals. Both these salient characteristics—cosmopolitanism and political/artistic self-assertion—were accentuated with the coming of World War II.

It is impossible to properly understand the wartime development of New York's ethnic Japanese population without a sense of the community's history. To summarize very briefly, the first Japanese immigrants arrived in the New York area during the late 1800s, and by 1920 the local Japanese community had swelled to 5,000–6000 people. While this represented only a tiny fraction of the city's population, it was enough to make New York's Nikkei community the fifth-largest in the nation. However, this community, unlike its counterparts on the West Coast and Hawaii, was not composed of farm workers or fishermen, but included merchants, domestics, office workers (many of whom worked for Japanese firms), and industrial laborers—notably shipyard workers.[20] Even after the 1924 Nationalities Act cut off immigration from Japan and the city's Nikkei population contracted, Japanese citizens—consular officials, businessmen, ministers, students, and artists—continued to arrive as temporary residents, and sometimes for extended stays.

In addition, throughout the prewar decades New York gained renown as a center for ethnic Japanese intellectuals, artists, and performers. The city was home at various times to such internationally known figures as scientists Hideyo Noguchi and Jokichi Takamine; writers Yone Noguchi and Sadakichi Hartmann; dancer Michio Ito; soprano Hizi Koyke; and painters Yasuo Kuniyoshi, Eitaro Ishigaki, Chuzo Tamotsu, and Hideo Noda.[21] Columbia University attracted a range of Japanese students, even as authors Roy Akagi (director of the nationally based Japanese Student Christian Association), Etsu Sugimoto, and Bunji Omura taught there. During the 1930s the community was also graced by the presence of dissidents from Japan such as Toru Matsumoto, Jack Shirai, Taro and Mitsu Yashima (Jun and Mimosa Iwamatsu), and Haru Matsui (Ayako Ishigaki), who found refuge in the city and built networks of friends and political supporters.[22]

Nikkei communities in New York reflected the city's cosmopolitan flavor. Unlike on the West Coast, Issei faced no alien land laws or restrictive covenants. Affluent Japanese migrated away from the city center. (The 1921 *New York Japanese Address Book* lists a dozen suburbs on Long Island and Westchester County with Japanese residents.) Furthermore, New York society lacked the laws against intermarriage and many of the sexual stigmas that marked the West Coast. According to one community survey in the mid-1930s, at least one-third and possibly as many as half of community members married non-Japanese spouses.[23] In turn, relatively few of New York's Issei residents brought their Japanese families to live with them. Thus, in addition to being the only Nikkei community of any size east of the Pacific coast, New York's was the only one in the nation where most residents were Japanese aliens and not their Nisei offspring.

Although a few Nisei who subsequently achieved fame were raised in the New York region, such as activists Bill Kochiyama and Toshi Ohta Seeger and photographer Yoichi Okamoto, the city's Nisei population grew largely through internal migration. During the 1920s and 1930s educated Nisei from other parts of the country settled in New York, where they could more easily express their talents. Prominent among these were sculptor Isamu Noguchi, sociologist T. Scott Miyakawa, lawyer George Yamaoka, photographer Toge Fujihira, architect Minoru Yamasaki, activist Tokie Slocum, and journalists Larry Tajiri and Tooru Kanazawa. In addition, the city was home during the 1930s to a set of early Nisei book authors: memoirist Kathleen Tamagawa, novelist Kay Karl Endow (Karl Nakagawa), and poets Kimi Gengo and Kikuko Miyakawa.[24]

The city's Japanese population was enriched by a number of social and financial institutions founded early in the century, including the Nippon Club (1905), the Japanese American Association (1907), and a series of newspapers, climaxing with the *Nyokyu Shimpo* newspaper (1911; a separate English-language journal, the *Japanese American Review*, was spun off in 1939). The community was likewise served by Christian churches and missions, starting with the Japanese Christian Institute (1899), plus the New York Buddhist Church, founded by Rev. Hozen Seki in 1938.[25] These organizations were operated in large part by employees of Japanese firms doing business in New York, with assistance from the Manhattan-based Japanese consulate, and tended to be conservative and pro-Japan in their viewpoint. They were counterbalanced by organizations founded by left-leaning Issei artists and intellectuals. Under the leadership of the pioneering Marxist Sen Katayama, leftist New Yorkers founded the Japanese Socialist (later Japanese Communist) Group in America in 1919, and the Nihonjin Rodosha Kurabu (Japanese Workers Club) a decade later.[26]

In the months before Pearl Harbor, as American boycotts stalled Japanese commerce and war clouds loomed, many of the businessmen and consular officials who were the mainstay of the community returned to Japan. Once war was declared, the FBI rounded up several hundred remaining Japanese diplomatic officials, merchants, and community leaders, who were interned at Ellis Island. The New York branches of Japanese firms shut their doors, even as masses of ethnic Japanese were fired from their jobs by non-Japanese employers, throwing the community into difficult economic straits. Meanwhile, a curfew, travel restrictions, and limits on bank withdrawals were imposed on the Issei as enemy aliens. The community's two newspapers, the *Nichi-Bei jihō* and its English-language offshoot, *The Japanese American Review*, were closed. While some of those interned were later released, their community leadership had by then passed away to a left-leaning antifascist group, the Japanese American Committee for Democracy. The JACD produced a monthly newsletter and community surveys, found jobs for dismissed Japanese workers, and sponsored forums and demonstrations in favor of victory over Japan. (On the JACD, see Chapter 10 in this volume.)

Still, New York was formally unaffected by Executive Order 9066, and with the emptying out of the West Coast, the city became the largest "free" Nikkei community on the United States mainland. As the war went on, former West Coast residents released from the camps began to arrive, and the city's ethnic Japanese population swelled. At least 1,000 migrants resettled in New York during 1943–44, and they continued to arrive in even greater numbers during 1945 and 1946. As a result, the city's Japanese population grew from barely 2,000 in mid-1942 to about three times that number in 1946–47. The Japanese Americans who resettled in New York during 1943–1944 were almost entirely Nisei (at least 70 percent), while anecdotal evidence from the WRA's New York office indicates that a large number of the perhaps 1,500 migrants who moved to New York in 1945–46 were families and individual Issei.[27]

As with Detroit, in the vast majority of cases the resettlers had never previously lived in New York, and most had never even visited. Moreover, because New York was so distant from the camps, the new arrivals had usually spent an initial resettlement period elsewhere, and therefore were comparatively more affluent and adjusted to life "outside." Although the newcomers held all sorts of jobs, a large percentage of Issei worked as domestics or gardeners. Nisei men also took jobs as dishwashers in city restaurants, as hotel bellhops, as laundry workers, or as hospital staffers. Women worked as nurses, stenographers, and secretaries. As time passed and more jobs opened up, Nisei took jobs as salesclerks, service workers, and skilled laborers. Groups of younger Nisei attended college at Columbia, New York University, and the city's four public colleges (the future CUNY system), as well as denominational colleges, business schools, and trade schools—there were even seventeen Nisei girls studying at the Traphagan fashion school. Nevertheless, in contrast to other resettlement areas, numerous newcomers—Nisei and even some Issei—were able to open their own businesses, including grocery stores, restaurants, and machine repair shops.[28]

The newcomers also tended to congregate together residentially. The WRA opened a hostel in Brooklyn Heights in mid-1944, and a few hundred resettlers lived there during its two-year existence. Others settled in the Manhattan Hostel, opened by the Community Church and the New York Unitarian Service Committee in fall 1945. Even after they left their temporary quarters, many resettlers found permanent housing in two small Japanese American enclaves. One was located on the West Side around 106th–110th Streets, near the Japanese American Methodist Church, an area that one wit soon dubbed the "umeboshi [pickled plum] district." A second group moved into Inwood, near Manhattan's northern tip, where another Japanese American church set up operations.[29] Unlike Detroit and the West Coast, however, the newcomers did not generally face restrictive covenants barring them from all-white districts. Though the skyrocketing price of housing made more affluent neighborhoods generally unaffordable, relatively few Issei and Nisei took up residence in African American areas such as Harlem or the South Bronx.

Again, as with Detroit, the question of discrimination is complex. According to various accounts, New York was the first place the West Coast refugees were not made to feel different because of their Japanese ancestry. One woman later stated that the city breathed liberation: "I became a free person for the first time."[30] At the same time, an eloquent letter from an army major to the WRA scored the unjust treatment of the newcomers:

> It is unbelievable that people of Japanese ancestry are finding a happy haven in New York City. Japanese businessmen and workers interviewed must be making statements which they THINK they should, if they say that everything is sweet and serene—that they are entirely comfortable and happy here. That is definitely not the word that passes between them.... This is brought to my attention almost daily by a fifty-nine year old Japanese cook in my employ in New York City. He has been in this country thirty-nine years.... Whenever he goes along the street he is pointed at by adults and children who indicate that he is probably a spy. When he goes into public places, nearby people engage in loud and disturbing conversation which is not directed at him but which he is supposed to hear. HE is not writing to other Japanese friends suggesting that they come here.[31]

There was some official as well as unofficial discrimination. New York City mayor Fiorello La Guardia was openly hostile to Japanese Americans (although he made a generous public endorsement after Pearl Harbor of the loyalty of a local Issei, New York Philharmonic xylophonist Yoichi Hiraoka). La Guardia refused to protect Japanese Americans faced with being fired from city jobs or to permit others to be hired, although he was willing to experiment with hiring fifty Japanese Americans for "hospital helper" positions to reduce a desperate hospital worker shortage. In April 1944, when the WRA announced its plans to open its Brooklyn hostel, La Guardia publicly denounced the project and asserted that resettled internees were not welcome to enter New York. Not only did they threaten the city's security, he insisted dubiously, but their presence would spark riots among the city's Chinese population.[32]

The records of the WRA's New York office, which was responsible for finding jobs and housing for the newcomers, also testify to a widespread pattern of job discrimination. For example, a letter asking the A&P grocery store chain to consider hiring Nisei was met with a cold rebuff: "The question of placement of American Japanese citizens with our company has been discussed and it was decided we could hardly consider employing them at this time because of public reaction to such a move."[33] In late September 1943, two Nisei, Kenji Ota and Hideo Tanaka, were sent by the WRA to interview for welding jobs with a New York company that maintained a shipyard in Camden, New Jersey. Although the company assured the WRA their need for welders was desperate, Ota and Tanaka were forced to wait until several weeks after their initial interview to hear from the company. They then were summoned for a second interview. This time they were interviewed by a uniformed army officer, who proceeded to ask them a set of extraordinarily irrelevant and insulting questions, such as whether they were fluent in Japanese and whether they hoped Japan would win the war. WRA officers were so outraged by these harassing tactics that they made an official complaint and had the two Nisei provide affidavits testifying to their experience.[34] After 1945, when New York State passed the Ives-Quinn bill, the first state fair employment practices legislation, job discrimination became more subtle and somewhat less widespread.

Still, even if resettlement in New York in many ways resembled that in other cities, the city was remarkable for the unusually rapid adjustment of the migrants. The reasons for this are twofold. First, whereas ethnic Japanese communities in other cities were too small or too insecure and wary of newcomers to offer them substantial aid, New York had a long-existing, self-confident Japanese community, with restaurants, churches, and grocery stores to serve the newcomers. In addition, the Japanese population in this most rootless of cities had always been heavily young, educated, and transient, so there was less suspicion of outsiders and sojourners than elsewhere. The second reason is that New York, a historic center of settlement houses and charity work, was much better equipped than most cities with non-Japanese agencies to serve the immediate needs of the resettlers and get them on their feet. Beginning in mid-1942, the Protestant Welfare Council assigned one of its specialists to locate jobs and housing for Japanese Americans so that they could leave the camps, while the American Baptist Home Mission Society dispatched workers to greet and look after the newcomers. The Federal Council of Churches of Christ in America hired Rev. Toru Matsumoto to head their Committee on Resettlement of Japanese Americans in order to coordinate efforts. With aid from the WRA, a coalition of religious groups formed the New York City Advisory Committee on Japanese Americans in May 1943, and organized a conference on resettlement. In 1945 the WRA and the fledgling New York chapter of the JACL came together to organize the Japanese American Coordinating Committee of New York City. After the WRA announced plans to cease operations, the Greater New York Citizens Committee for Japanese-Americans formed in November 1945, under the leadership of George Yamaoka (who shortly thereafter left for Tokyo to join the war crimes team) and Robert Benjamin.

At the same time, New York's Japanese resettlers passed more easily into the city's intellectual and artistic mainstream. New York was certainly not without racism—the 1943 Harlem riot had baldly demonstrated racial tensions and the impact of discrimination—and the newcomers did face various forms of exclusion, as noted. Still, the cosmopolitan tradition of the city gave them a major assist. Almost immediately, art galleries and museums featured shows with Japanese American artists, while a select group of Issei and Nisei found employment in the creative arts: Robert Kuwahara created a daily syndicated comic strip, *Miki*; Yuriko Amemiya danced with Martha Graham and on Broadway; Ruby Yoshino toured as a concert singer; and Michi Nishiura became a costume designer. (Miné Okubo, as will be detailed in Chapter 4, made a career as an author/illustrator.) A constellation of visual artists, including such figures as Henry Sugimoto, Hideo Date, Hisako Hibi, Lewis Suzuki, and Hideo Kobashigawa, took up long-term residence in the city. Conversely, even if they faced difficulties with housing and employment, the character of the newcomers made their social adjustment easier. Unlike in other regions, the migrants were not primarily farmers with little experience of urban life. Rather, like their predecessors during the 1930s, the Nisei who chose to resettle in New York were educated, articulate, and wide-ranging in their interests and associations. A number of them, including Ernest Iiyama, Chiye Mori, Tak and Kazu Iijima, Dyke Miyagawa, Kenny Murase, Joe Oyama, Eddie Shimano, Ina Sugihara, and Nori Ikeda Lafferty, had been active during the prewar Popular Front years in political and activist groups along the West Coast (notably the Los Angeles and Bay Area Nisei Democrats clubs). Others, such as James Nakamura, Shuji Fujii, Carl Kondo, Bob Kuwahara, and Miné Okubo, were writers and artists who had staffed prewar and/or camp newspapers. They were able to parlay their experience into leadership roles in community institutions, most notably the Japanese American Committee for Democracy, in the process acting as liaisons between the WRA, social welfare organizations, and pro-immigrant groups such as the Common Council for American Unity and the American Committee for the Protection of the Foreign Born.

It is impossible to do justice in a brief sketch to the wide diversity of experiences of the thousands of Japanese Americans who migrated to Los Angeles after camp, but a summary view reveals that their circumstances were in some ways quite distinct from their counterparts in either Detroit or New York. First, the scale and timing of their entry and adjustment were very different. Because the West Coast did not even begin to open its doors until late 1944 and the WRA discouraged mass return, resettlement in Southern California was primarily a postwar process. However, the movement, once started, became a flood: by mid-1947 there were 28,000 people of Japanese ancestry in Los Angeles County (as compared with 37,000 before removal), making it the largest ethnic Japanese population on the continent.[35] Unlike in the other cities, the returnees were by no means the first Japanese Americans ever seen in the Los Angeles area: many were returning to areas where they had lived before the war, and in various cases resuming their prewar occupations or business ventures. By the same token, in returning home, they lacked the sense of exile or temporary residence that was felt by a large fraction of those who resettled in the East and Midwest.

That said, as in Detroit and New York, many resettlers in Los Angeles were newcomers. Large numbers of migrants who had lived in rural areas before the war now crowded into the city limits: Issei who had long resided in ethnic enclaves but had been unable to reclaim their property now settled in mixed areas where they were surrounded by non-Japanese neighbors. Nisei who had grown up largely among Japanese Americans, and then had been confined in all-Japanese camps during the war, now faced head-on the difficulties of living as a minority group. Even native Angelenos were often unable to return to their previous residences. In particular, the large prewar Japanese colony that had grown up around the canneries on Terminal Island in San Pedro had been, as one newspaper article described it, "the very pulse of prewar Japanese concentration around Los Angeles."[36] It had been wiped out in February 1942, when the navy had taken over the island and expelled its Japanese residents on forty-eight hours' notice. The island remained a naval installation after the war's end, and its population was forced to disperse, though a significant hub of fishermen and naval workers relocated to nearby Long Beach.

If the returnees held the advantage of familiarity with their surroundings, they also had a long-entrenched pattern of prejudice, newly inflamed by wartime passions, to combat. Public attitudes in Los Angeles were decidedly mixed, and the level of overall anti-Japanese prejudice is hard to quantify.[37] Still, various controversies reveal the extent of tension and bias. In late summer 1944, through the efforts of the Pasadena-based fair play group Friends of the American Way, Esther Takei enrolled at Pasadena Junior College (today's Pasadena Community College), thus becoming the first Nisei since Pearl Harbor to be admitted to a Pacific coast college. A group of twenty local whites, supported by the California American Legion, campaigned publicly to exclude her. However, the college's faculty and student councils voted unanimously to accept Takei, and the Pasadena Board of Education announced that it had no power to refuse her, with the result that she was registered.[38] Soon after, when the celebrated chemist Dr. Linus Pauling of the California Institute of Technology hired a Nisei gardener, the exterior of his Pasadena home was vandalized with signs calling him "Jap lover," while a Japanese flag was painted on the house.[39]

The city's public stance on the resettlers was ambivalent at best. Mayor Fletcher Bowron, who had been a primary instigator of mass confinement and who had called in 1943 for all Nisei to be stripped of their American citizenship, made a public about-face. In January 1945, he announced that all returnees would be welcomed back to the city with their rights ensured, and he made a symbolic journey to Union Station to greet an initial group of returnees personally.[40] After a meeting with Bowron in September 1946, Mike Masaoka warmly praised the city under his administration as "the white spot of the country as far as unpleasant incidents connected with our return to our former homes is concerned."[41] Nonetheless, in January 1946, L.A. county manager Wayne Allen caused a widespread anti-Japanese backlash when he made a fraudulent public statement that 4,000 Japanese Americans were on the county relief rolls. In fact, this figure included not only the fewer than 1,000 individuals actually receiving relief funds (almost all of whom were elderly Issei barred by discriminatory state laws from receiving old-age assistance) but more than 3,000 Issei and Nisei families in emergency public housing whom the county manager imputed would all ultimately become a public charge. The *Los Angeles Times* quickly chimed in with a complaint that Japanese Americans were refusing employment offers, and pressed unemployed workers to take jobs as citrus pickers. The Hearst-owned *Los Angeles Herald-Express* proclaimed editorially that idle Japanese American men should be put to work on road labor or public projects and "shipped back to Japan" if they refused to take such jobs.[42]

At the same time, securing housing was a contested and fraught process for the returnees. As in Detroit, the war had brought about a huge migration of war workers, who had taken up all available stock. In particular, there was an influx of African Americans from the South, whose arrival rapidly doubled the size of the region's black community. As a result of discrimination by white landlords as well as the overall housing shortage, many of the black migrants had no choice but to settle in the emptied Little Tokyo district (redubbed "Bronzeville"), which took on many characteristics of a slum area: overcrowding, crime, and poor public services. Meanwhile, as in Detroit, tensions over housing and recreation led to racial rioting in summer 1943, when invading white servicemen targeted blacks and Mexican Americans for assault in the so-called zoot suit riots.

As Japanese Americans began to return from the camps, the West Coast press voiced real fear of conflict between the returnees and the African Americans and others who would resist being displaced—fears that were further fanned by unscrupulous whites as a pretext for further exclusion.[43] Then in February 1945, Rev. Julius Goldwater, a Buddhist priest who was the guardian of the Honjuwani Temple, prepared to restore the temple building to its Nikkei worshipers. He obtained an eviction order to remove a black Baptist congregation that had taken over space in the building previously leased by other parties.[44] The dispute threatened to explode intergroup relations. As a result, leaders of the WRA, the NAACP, and other groups met to try to resolve further disputes over property. Gradually, Issei and Nisei landlords resumed their residence and reopened their businesses. Prewar hotels were transformed into rooming houses for returnee families. Meanwhile, other previous area residents doubled up or sought temporary housing while they waited for the leases on their properties to expire.

Again, as in Detroit, finding housing was largely impossible due to restrictive covenants in all-white areas, plus alien land legislation. In 1947, the Los Angeles Citizens' Housing Council organized a conference of more than a hundred organizations, which unanimously passed a resolution against restrictive covenants, and called for suspension of the Alien Land Act against the families of Nisei veterans.[45] Nevertheless, a majority of the city's landscape remained closed to Japanese owners and tenants. The largest fraction of returnees moved into housing, much of it substandard, in East Los Angeles's Hollenbeck Heights and Boyle Heights areas. This area, formerly a racially mixed area with a large Jewish population, was in the process of losing its non-Latino population. Some returnees found housing on North Broadway near Chinatown, or in Jefferson Park, while a new enclave formed in Sawtelle.[46] A large fraction of returnees took up residence alongside black neighbors in Watts. In the years after restrictive covenants were declared unconstitutional by the U.S. Supreme Court in 1948, the largest fraction of the city's ethnic Japanese population moved into suburban Gardena.

Meanwhile, an estimated 4,000 Japanese Americans were forced into temporary housing. A network of hotels was set up by private groups. For example, the American Friends Service Committee and the Presbyterian Church in the United States established the Evergreen Hostel in a former school for Mexican American girls on Evergreen Avenue. The WRA petitioned the city to open thirty housing centers but was authorized to create only five. In the end, the WRA and the Federal Public Housing Authority (FPHA) hastily set up temporary housing centers in former army barracks, mixed with trailers, in sites in Hawthorne, El Segundo, and Lomita.[47] In fall 1945, the Winona emergency housing project, made up of a group of converted trailers, was established by the FPHA in Burbank, and 1,300 Japanese Americans resettled there. After several months, a portion of the Winona residents found private housing, while others were moved to the camps with barracks. However, more than 500 of the residents were unable to find other housing. In March 1946, they were informed that the project was to be cleared, and some residents were expelled to other facilities. After protests by residents, they were permitted to stay on, and the majority ultimately purchased their trailers and moved off in them. The final group of 350 were relocated to a trailer camp leased by local Nisei in November 1947.[48]

Employment was another area in which Japanese American returnees had a particularly difficult experience. As in New York, part of the difficulty was due to official discrimination in city hiring. In January 1945 the County Board of Supervisors voted to bar Japanese Americans from civil service positions until at least ninety days after the end of the war, although its members admitted they had no legal basis for discrimination against those seeking the return of their jobs.[49] The Church Federation of Los Angeles protested the refusal of the county to employ Nisei, but the policy stood. In April 1945, the Board of Supervisors turned down Dr. Masako Kusayanagi's request to return immediately from leave to her job at General Hospital. Though there was a vital physician shortage, the County Board of Charities insisted that Dr. Kusayanagi (despite her three years of service as an accredited physician at two different WRA camps) was still to be deemed a student in residency, the level she had attained at the time of removal, and reported that all positions at that level were filled.[50] When Amy Nomi applied for a job at L.A. County Hospital in September she was turned away on the excuse of the board's decision. After Dorothy Okura placed first on her civil service exam as social worker with the County Board of Charities, the board claimed the privilege to hire the second-place finisher.[51] Other public sector agencies were also touched by bias. A Los Angeles post office gained widespread attention when it refused to rehire a former Nisei employee who was a decorated war veteran, though other post offices, and the Board of Education, hired Nisei clerical workers.[52] Still, as outrageous as such legal bias was, it served merely as a continuation of the notorious employment bars that had existed in prewar years, when only a few dozen Nisei had held civil service positions.[53]

The situation was scarcely better in the private sector. Throughout the postwar years, there were various reports of private discrimination. Although one industrialist with a cannery on Terminal Island had promised in early 1945 to employ 100 returnees, few office and factory employers rushed to open places for the returnees. An aluminum company that had hired a Nisei employee was forced to discharge him following a hate strike by other employees.[54] Once again, this did not represent a large-scale shift from prewar patterns of exclusion. The difference is that before the war, employment was available inside the community. Over the first half of the twentieth century, masses of Issei were able to use savings and community mutual aid funds to establish independent small businesses. Their Nisei descendants, despite a high average level of educational achievement, were all but unemployable in mainstream firms. Thus, apart from a small minority who secured executive positions working for Japanese firms, the Nisei were able to support themselves and their families by working for family or community-based enterprises (for which they were generally overqualified) or opening their own businesses. After the war, in contrast, Issei and Nisei found financing of new businesses unavailable, and there were no Japanese firms to take up the slack. Occupational downward mobility, at least in the short term, was the rule for Nisei as well as Issei. Former store owners were reduced to working as domestic servants, while truck farmers and market directors found work as gardeners and handymen. Astoundingly, while less than 20 percent of Japanese American workers in Los Angeles region were employed by whites before the war, the total rose to approximately 70 percent afterward.[55]

To an even greater extent than in other cites, Issei and Nisei were thrown back on themselves and forced to join into ethnic-specific groups to respond to the difficulties facing them. A network of JACL chapters formed in the different Nisei enclaves, and Nisei veterans' groups attracted numerous community members. Postwar Los Angeles boasted two daily Japanese newspapers, as the prewar journals *Rafu Shimpo* and *Kashu Mainichi* resumed daily publication, while the progressive English-language weekly *Crossroads* debuted in 1948. By the same token, even more than in New York—and in marked contrast to Detroit—the resettlers in Los Angeles engaged with African Americans in daily life and community action, especially in Little Tokyo/Bronzeville. The center of interracial unity was Pilgrim House, a settlement house opened for African Americans in the vacated Japanese Union Church in 1943 and headed by Rev. Charles Kingsley. Kingsley took the lead in welcoming Issei and Nisei resettlers. Pilgrim House provided returnees with day care, athletic facilities, and crafts classes. Its Common Ground committee, headed by volunteer worker Samuel Ishikawa, helped resolve conflicts between Japanese Americans, blacks, and Chicanos.[56] Nisei activists responded in kind. Mary Oyama Mittwer crusaded for interracialism and denounced Nisei bigotry against other groups in her *Rafu Shimpo* column, "New World A-Coming." Hisaye Yamamoto, hired as a columnist by the African American *Los Angeles Tribune* newspaper to serve as a bridge between the two communities, joined Wakako Yamuchi and other activists in founding a Los Angeles chapter of the Congress of Racial Equality, and in 1947–48 the two organized a series of intergroup sit-ins and picket lines to desegregate the Bullock's department store lunchroom and the Bimini Baths, a swimming resort.

Still, Hisaye Yamamoto and other writers complained that relations between the two groups in Little Tokyo/Bronzeville continued to "stink." Discrimination by Issei shop owners and pressure from Nisei who sought to displace black residents led to resentment.[57] The ethnic Japanese press complained of a "Negro crime wave" in Little Tokyo/Bronzeville during 1946–47, and a merchants' group hired a pair of Nisei ex-GIs as security guards.[58] In March 1947 a community meeting was organized by G. Raymond Booth, executive director of the Council for Civic Unity, and Rev. Kingsley in an effort to resolve the strained relations between the two communities. Various speakers, including W. E. B. Du Bois, called for conflict resolution and tolerance.[59] Improvement was slow, though, and barely six months later the Union Church ordered Pilgrim House to vacate the premises. Stripped of a permanent residence, it folded not long after.

In sum, the process of resettlement and readaptation of Japanese Americans took shape in rather distinct forms and at varying speeds in different areas. A comparative view suggests that while conditions on the West Coast were more unfriendly to the migrants, generally speaking, the ability of the newcomers to find acceptable employment and housing was also influenced by other factors, such as the size of the resettler population and the existence of social welfare agencies to advocate for the migrants. In addition, various similarities between Detroit and Los Angeles in the first period of resettlement suggest that the presence of large wartime migrant populations in any city, and rising ethnic tensions that accompanied the strain on municipal facilities, may have had as much to do with the treatment of Issei and Nisei as did historic bias toward Japanese Americans.

Japanese American resettlers in New York, like those elsewhere, faced many difficulties. Yet Issei as well as Nisei there, inspired by the city's cosmopolitan spirit, were used to living and working unrestricted by discrimination, and to dealing with other citizens on an equal basis. This attitude of openness may have sowed the seeds for a more rapid and successful adjustment by the small but disproportionately intellectual-minded and artistic group of Nisei who resettled there than either their counterparts in Detroit or Southern California were able to achieve. However, the relatively small size of the New York community, and the lack of ostentatious discrimination, also meant that there was little force holding the community together, especially after 1948.

PART II

The Varieties of Assimilation

4. Birth of a Citizen

Miné Okubo and the Politics of Symbolism

Citizen 13660, Miné Okubo's illustrated memoir of her personal experience during the wartime removal and incarceration of Japanese Americans, is a masterpiece of ambiguity. Like many works of art and literature by African Americans, *Citizen 13660* has often been assimilated by latter-day critics into the protest tradition.[1] These critics make much of Okubo's trickster nature and her use of double-sided combinations of words and images as weapons of resistance. Pointing to the disjunction between the narrative and Okubo's accompanying drawings, they contend that beneath the text's apparently clear (and supposedly inoffensive) surface narrative lurk various subversive and radical messages awaiting decryption by the attentive reader. For example, Pamela Stennes Wright finds that Okubo employs two narrative strategies throughout her book—an overt narrative that documents the story of a loyal American citizen who "must come to an understanding of her evacuation and internment" plus a covert narrative that suggests the injustices of official policy by depicting the massive disruption it wreaked on Japanese Americans.[2] "The genius of Okubo's book," Elena Tajima Creef adds, "is the unusual combination of visual and literary narrative that allows her to tell both stories . . . [pairing] its provocative, and subversive, use of the autobiographical 'I' . . . with the observational power of the artist's 'eye.' "[3]

Even though I find the various critical explorations of subversive currents in Okubo's work engaging, they tend to privilege a rather recondite subtextual reading as *the* essential version. Worse, they focus so single-mindedly on locating resistance and agency as to obscure some of the complexity of the work.[4] The emphasis on Okubo's perceived resistance risks drawing attention away from the circumstances in which her work was created, as well as her own original intentions. These are not simply matters of academic interest. The project that was to become *Citizen 13660* evolved within the specific political context of the wartime and immediate postwar period, as Japanese Americans began to leave the camps and resettle throughout the United States. Okubo's work was promoted by the War Relocation Authority, the government agency responsible for running the camps, and by its liberal allies outside of government as part of a larger program of assimilation and absorption that they designed for the Nisei. She collaborated in this operation, not only in her choice of illustrations for the book and in the brief texts she wrote to accompany them but also in her various public statements characterizing herself as a writer and fixing the meaning of her narrative. In sum, the conscious meaning that Okubo applied to the text and the critical readings it received at the time of its initial appearance deserve central consideration if the work is to be properly understood.

An examination of the gestation of *Citizen 13660* reveals the self-consciousness of Okubo's creation and how and why certain meanings became attached to it. Tracing the evolution of *Citizen 13660* requires a certain attentiveness. For her own reasons, Okubo tended to deny the intentionality that was a feature of her output more or less from the beginning. In the publicity for her book when it was first published during the 1940s, she stated that the illustrations in *Citizen 13660* grew out of sketches she did throughout her confinement in order to document the story of camp life for her friends in Europe and the United States.[5] She continued in later life to affirm that she had intended the illustrations as a private gift for "my many friends who faithfully sent letters and packages to let us know we were not forgotten," and only afterward thought of turning them into a public project.[6] Only when the work was republished in 1983, in the heyday of the redress period, did Okubo reveal that her illustrations "were intended for exhibition purposes" from the first.[7] Even then, however, she remained silent regarding the particular stages and modifications through which the project evolved.

In fact, Okubo seems to have begun transforming her drawings into exhibition material by late 1942, not long after she left the Tanforan Assembly Center and arrived at the Topaz camp—or even earlier, if we are to believe a letter that University of California vice president Monroe Deutsch sent Okubo at the time that *Citizen 13660* was published: "You have done exactly what you said you would when you were in my office prior to the evacuation period—you kept your sense of humor and portrayed the amusing incidents in your life at Tanforan and Topaz."[8] In any case, Okubo's first effort to show her images of camp life publicly was through her submission of two drawings to the spring 1943 show of the San Francisco Art Association at the San Francisco Museum of Art (today known as SF-MOMA), where she had frequently displayed her work in prewar years.[9] It is impossible to be certain as to when Okubo conceived of sending out art on the camps for display, but it can be assumed that it was well before the show actually opened. Whether or not the show's curators specially vetted her contribution in advance, it certainly would have been standard practice for them to ask artists to send in their drawings enough ahead of time to allow for the mounting of the show. Furthermore, Okubo very likely would have done all she could to get her work in extra early, given the uncertainties of wartime mail service from Topaz.

The San Francisco Museum show opened in March 1943. Okubo's camp art drew special attention for both its style and its subject matter, and "On Guard," a study of two camp guards, won the Artist Fund Prize. Both of Okubo's works received special praise from a critic in the magazine *California Art and Architecture*:

> Two entries of Miné Okubo, one of which was given the Artist Fund Prize [deal with the war]. ["On Guard"] is a fine monumental drawing of two sentries guarding a Japanese Internment camp, done solidly as a mural, in black and white tempera on paper. The two soldiers with their guns on a hilltop make a bold and strong design against the small bare barracks of the distant camp. *Evacuees*, done in the same medium and style, is a similar muralesque treatment of a Japanese family struggling with the problems of baggage and removal. Both of these drawings have a simple rich pattern of blacks and grays that is very fine.[10]

On March 21, 1943, the *San Francisco Chronicle*'s Sunday supplement *This World* included a reproduction of "On Guard." Such attention, especially from the West Coast press, lent Okubo special visibility among supporters of Japanese Americans. A school lesson plan that a Quaker group brought out shortly afterward in an effort to help raise public consciousness (to use a term unknown in the period) about the plight of Japanese Americans singled out Okubo for attention:

> Miné Okubo is another artist who will some day be well-known as the others. She was given a traveling scholarship for her fine work and spent time in Europe studying art. She returned to the University of California to learn that she had been offered another year of study in Italy, but could not return to that country because of the beginning of the war.[11]

Meanwhile, the positive response to Okubo's drawing led the editors of the *San Francisco Chronicle* (a liberal newspaper whose editor, Chester

72 / *The Varieties of Assimilation*

Rowell, had opposed evacuation) to commission further illustrations from the artist. Okubo obliged by sending a set of camp sketches. These, along with Okubo's brief commentary, were published in *This World* at the end of August 1943 as "An Evacuee's Hopes and Memories." In a prefatory note, the editors of the magazine explained that Okubo's "debut as a writer was accidental—her explanatory notes with her sketches were so much more THIS WORLD simply incorporated them into an article." At the same time, the magazine undertook "to document her objectivity" by interpolating with Okubo's text a number of quotations from a speech that Dillon S. Myer, director of the War Relocation Authority, had made earlier at San Francisco's Commonwealth Club.

As a result of Myer's comments being interpolated with Okubo's observations, her article bore the appearance of an officially sponsored publication. Of course, even without the symbolic imprimatur of the WRA, Okubo's readers would have understood that she was speaking from confinement and was thus subject to official censorship. Although Okubo doubtless felt limited in what she could say, her text does not reveal particular reticence or sugarcoating:

> The train trip from Tanforan to Topaz was a nightmare. It was the first train trip for many of us and we were excited, but many were sad to leave California and the Bay region. To most of the people, to this day, the world is only as large as from San Francisco to Tanforan to Topaz. Buses were waiting for us at Delta to take us to Topaz. Seventeen miles of alfalfa farms and greasewood were what we saw. Some people cried on seeing the utter desolation of the camp. Fine alkaline dust hovered over it like San Francisco fog.[12]

The appearance of Okubo's sketches in *This World* occurred at an essential turning point in the history of incarceration. During summer 1943 the WRA completed its program segregation of confined Japanese Americans into groups it adjudged "loyal" and "disloyal." With segregation completed—at a high cost to thousands of inmates who were further arbitrarily displaced, and with the "no-no boys" confined in a high-security center at Tule Lake, California—the issue of winding down all the other camps became paramount. On September 14, 1943, just sixteen days after Okubo's article was published, the White House presented Congress with a report on Japanese Americans. In his transmittal letter, President Franklin D. Roosevelt stated that with the successful completion of segregation, the WRA could now redouble its efforts to resettle outside the camps those Japanese Americans "whose loyalty to this country has remained unshaken throughout the hardships of the evacuation." In particular, Roosevelt promised that the Japanese Americans could return to the West Coast "as soon as the military situation will make such restoration feasible."[13]

This presidential pledge helped mobilize the WRA, which had been badly buffeted by hostile press campaigns and congressional investigations, to refocus its attention on a task it had already undertaken on a small scale: planning resettlement. It also capped the gradual transformation the agency's mission had undergone during 1943 from constructing and managing camps in which to confine the excluded Japanese to the opening of regional resettlement offices and scouting out of areas for resettlement so that they could leave camp. This new mission did not consist simply of finding sponsors who would provide Nisei with jobs or education, or of helping migrants find housing.[14] Rather, it amounted to implementing an overall quasi-official policy of dispersion of ethnic Japanese throughout the United States, and facilitating their absorption into the larger population.

The WRA, the War Department, the White House (notably First Lady Eleanor Roosevelt), and liberal and "fair play" groups—along with many Japanese Americans—broadly agreed that, by retarding assimilation and/or restricting economic opportunity, the prewar ghettoization of Japanese Americans in "Little Tokyos" had helped inspire the hostility that led to evacuation. Therefore, despite their continuing conflicts over the justice of removal and the morality of the government's operation of the camps, these disparate groups joined forces to facilitate the scattering of the Japanese American population across the rest of the country. This, they believed, would be the best solution to the "Japanese problem" as it had existed on the West Coast, and would ensure that the tragedy of removal would never recur. WRA director Dillon Myer expressed a widely held view when he claimed in 1946 that, on the whole, the Nisei were actually better off in the long run for their confinement experience and diaspora, since they could now establish themselves on an equal basis with other Americans.[15] As harsh and punitive as the destruction of ethnic Japanese communities may sound to present-day ears, these Americans—including many Japanese Americans, and not just the JACL—looked upon the relocation process as a providential opportunity for the Nisei to enter the larger society and ensure that the tragedy of removal would never recur.[16]

Government officials realized early that the key to opening the doors of the camps and ensuring the success of mass dispersal and resettlement lay in remaking the public image of the Nisei so as to reduce white suspicion and hostility toward Japanese Americans—a phenomenon for which the removal itself was largely responsible. Thus, although public relations figured only distantly, if at all, in the WRA's charter and initial mandate, the agency gradually shifted its program as the war proceeded. WRA staffers teamed up with colleagues from the Office of War Information (OWI) to produce an enormous pile of propaganda for public consumption, focusing jointly on the achievements of the WRA and on the loyalty and American character of the inmates.[17] WRA efforts included informational pamphlets, documentary films, and speaking tours by WRA director Myer, former U.S. ambassador to Japan Joseph Grew, and Ben Kuroki, a Nisei war hero. The WRA and OWI also exerted pressure on publishers and film producers to promote responsible media images of Japanese Americans and avoid hostile depictions.[18]

Liberal groups outside the government, especially those opposed to incarceration, gladly collaborated with the government's media campaign. Some of them may well have privately deplored the WRA's heavy-handed management of the Nisei's public image and suppression of internal dissent—certainly many supporters of Japanese Americans with experience of the camps considered the official picture excessively rosy—but they obviously felt that it was in the interest of all to downplay their differences in light of the enormous public opposition to Japanese Americans.

It is not clear whether government censors ever vetted Miné Okubo's drawings or text before the piece was placed in *This World*. It is reasonable to assume as much, though, given the wartime restrictions on inmates and the interpolation of Dillon Myer's words into the text. Such review was in any case common practice. When Eleanor Roosevelt drafted an article in support of the Nisei for *Collier's* magazine, "A Challenge to American Sportsmanship," she first submitted her draft text to Myer for comment.

In any event, the positive reception Okubo's article received would have placed her squarely within the WRA's sights. In January 1944, barely four months after its appearance, Okubo was able to leave camp and relocate to New York.[19] According to her later testimony, she was solicited by the editors of *Fortune* magazine to illustrate their upcoming issue on Japan—although, as she explained, she had never been to Japan—and her release providentially followed: "I was planning on staying in camp. I didn't have any money and at least I was being fed. Then I got a telegram from *Fortune* magazine. I had always thought that if you are patient enough, the gods would answer your prayers. So I left for New York."[20]

There is no reason to doubt the basic truth of this story, which was recounted in publicity materials produced at the time. Yet it glosses over the degree of official cooperation required for such a move. Even ignoring the question of whether the government recommended Okubo to *Fortune*, it is unimaginable that government officials would not have been consulted. Moreover, the WRA's leave clearance procedure was cumbersome and time-consuming—even Interior Secretary Harold Ickes was forced to wait for some eight months during 1942–43 before he could obtain release and transportation for a pair of Japanese American laborers for his farm.[21] Although the WRA later streamlined its leave clearance operations somewhat, it remained an elaborate process. Okubo's remarkably rapid release therefore bespeaks official assistance, particularly since WRA officials would have been well aware of the nature of her future employment.

Okubo's *Fortune* sketches appeared in the magazine's April 1944 issue, alongside illustrations by two New York–based Issei artists, Yasuo Kuniyoshi and Taro Yashima (Jun Iwamatsu). Okubo later claimed that when she arrived in New York and showed her sketches of the camp experience to *Fortune*'s editors, who knew nothing of the camps, they decided to do an additional piece on Japanese Americans in the special issue, with her sketches as illustrations, and then urged Okubo to collect the sketches into a full-length book.[22] Again, Okubo's account may accurately reflect her own experience as far as it goes. Still, as undeniably powerful as her illustrations are, it is unlikely that they played as solitary a role in *Fortune*'s decision making as she contended. Even assuming that *Fortune*'s editors had not previously thought to devote any coverage to the plight of Japanese Americans—an implausible notion given the circumstances of the magazine's recruitment of Okubo—the final (unsigned) *Fortune* article contained significant data on resettlement and other aspects of the government's policy that were available chiefly from official sources. This fact, along with the substantially pro-government tone of the article—it was extremely mild in its criticism of the WRA, even in its discussion of the injustice of segregation and of the operations of the Tule Lake isolation camp—strongly suggests that there was some official assistance backstage in its preparation.[23]

In the months that followed the appearance of the *Fortune* article, Okubo displayed a selection of the *Fortune* artwork at the San Francisco Museum of Art. Meanwhile, she worked on adapting the sketches into a full-length manuscript, which she evidently completed by March 1945.[24] Even as she supported herself by working as a freelance artist, she continued to publicize her work on the camps.[25] *The New York Times* printed three of her camp sketches alongside a review of her friend Carey McWilliams's book *Prejudice*, listing them as "drawings of life in an internment camp made on the spot by Mine Okubo, artist, who after two years of internment is now working in New York City."[26] Some months later, the

Times published another Okubo drawing, this time alongside a review of a book by Alexander Leighton.

At some point during these months, Okubo made the acquaintance of M. Margaret Anderson, co-director of the Common Council for American Unity, an organization dedicated to defending the rights of ethnic and racial minority groups, and editor in chief of its quarterly journal *Common Ground*. A warm friendship soon emerged between the two women. Anderson became Okubo's greatest patron and supporter, and Okubo in turn entrusted Anderson with the management of her career.[27]

Anderson was not a newcomer to the "Japanese problem." She had been interested in the condition of Japanese Americans even before Pearl Harbor, and she was a forthright opponent of evacuation. Once the removal became a fait accompli, she lobbied the WRA and other government agencies to take action against unjust treatment of the inmates, and organized efforts to aid the Nisei—notably by scheduling a planning meeting in March 1943 that drew 120 people. Anderson also opened the pages of *Common Ground* to a range of Nisei writers, including Asami Kawachi, George Morimitsu, Mary Oyama, and Larry Tajiri. In early 1943 she hired journalist Eddie Shimano as editorial assistant so that he could leave camp.[28]

Anderson's efforts to help Japanese Americans were centered on her strong belief in the necessity of prioritizing resettlement. In "Get the Evacuees Out!," an editorial she published in *Common Ground*, Anderson stated flatly that resettlement of Japanese Americans out of the government camps and their "assimilation into the American scene" was a pressing task for all Americans. "If we cannot solve so small and tidy a problem as the dispersal resettlement and assimilation of 110,000 people of Japanese descent within our borders, what hope is there for our own 13,000,000 Negroes and for the great masses of the people of the world who look hungrily to us for moral leadership?"[29] Anderson was not starry-eyed about the obstacles the newcomers faced. However, she felt that once resettled, Japanese Americans had in their own hands the capacity not only to foster their own absorption but also to help the overall cause of equality. Her views are exemplified in a letter she wrote to Socialist Party leader Norman Thomas in late 1943:

> I think there's a serious danger in the growing Nisei tendency to regard democracy as something entirely outside themselves—something that failed and will have to remedy its failures—the remedy to come to them as something of a gift package, not something they have to work for. For the final good of the group, I think they

have got to see that they must get out of the centers and fight with us for democracy.[30]

It was therefore in conjunction with her primary interest in fostering Japanese American resettlement that Anderson took up Okubo's case. She threw herself into trying to persuade publishers to take on Okubo's manuscript. Meanwhile, she sponsored a large show of Okubo's camp artwork, which opened at the council's offices in March 1945. Anderson's goal was both to advance her protégée's career and to strike a larger theme of racial tolerance. She carefully managed the construction of messages that the exhibit and Okubo embodied. Significantly, in her letter of invitation to the opening, Anderson underlined the human interest of the work and downplayed the injustice of the government's continuing policy:

> Caught in the evacuation of all Japanese Americans from the West Coast in the Spring of 1942, Miss Okubo made some 1,500 to 2,000 sketches of this episode in American history. . . . She has since developed some of these into finished paintings; others she has made into a series of drawings which tell the terrific story of evacuation with honesty, objectivity, and humor. . . . The United States has rarely produced a documentary record of any episode in its history to equal Miss Okubo's, and we wish to draw wide attention to this visit.[31]

Anderson received significant official cooperation with her project. WRA photographers visited the opening and shot several pictures of a smiling Okubo in front of her pictures—the quintessence of successful readjustment—for their documentary series on resettlement. Similarly, the WRA's April 1945 report listed Okubo's exhibit (which had moved by then to the New School for Social Research) as a highlight of its Area Public Relations program.[32]

Okubo readily went along with the line elaborated by Anderson and the WRA. In an interview with the *New York Herald Tribune* published soon after the exhibition opened, Okubo strained to emphasize the positive side of the experience and the creative adjustment of the Japanese Americans.[33] "When we arrived there . . . the camp was only half-finished. It was a real pioneering life. We built all the community services ourselves—schools, churches, canteens, even a police department." Okubo stated that she had received letters while at camp from friends in Europe, telling her how lucky she was to be in the United States. "At the time it seemed strange . . . but at that, I guess I was lucky."[34]

In mid-1945, with the blessing of the WRA, the Common Council for American Unity sponsored a West Coast tour of the Okubo exhibition, "in an effort to create better understanding of the Japanese Americans and their problems."[35] The exhibition's first stop was at Gump's department store in San Francisco, where it was jointly sponsored by the International Institute and a group of liberal civic leaders.[36] It then moved to Oakland. While the show was widely and respectfully reviewed, one anonymous (presumably white) critic commented acerbically on both the establishment backing for the show and its sanitized views of Japanese Americans:

> This picture is at Mills [College], and it is the best imaginable commentary on the whole cockeyed situation that existed with reference to the Nisei during the war. You may be sure that no inmate of Dachau ever won a prize in a Leipzig annual during his confinement. Some of Miss Okubo's designs and stylizations are interesting, but the show is valuable mainly as a document record of an episode in the history of a group which was, apparently, quite as Americanized and quite as good-natured in adversity as any of the Kelly-Kaplan-Caruso combinations which traditionally symbolize the people of this country.[37]

After its run in the Bay Area, the show moved to Los Angeles, and then to Seattle.[38] The WRA closely followed Okubo's progress and reviewed the associated publicity. "In reporting an exhibit of paintings by Mine Okubo at the Seattle Art Museum," one internal memo reported, "*Time* magazine used a photograph of a painting taken by us some time previously at an exhibit of Miss Okubo's work under the auspices of the Common Council for American Unity which provided a print to *Time* for use in the story."[39] In fact, Okubo gained such a "respectable" image from her show that in early 1946 *Glamour* magazine selected her to be among of a set of Nisei women whom the magazine wished to feature in brief biographical sketches.[40]

Meanwhile, Columbia University Press agreed to publish Okubo's manuscript. Although one later study of Okubo credited Nobuo Kitagaki, a fellow artist from *Trek*, with introducing Okubo to Columbia editor Harold Lasky, it seems likely that Anderson, with her various connections, played a decisive role.[41] Certainly it was Anderson who proudly wrote *Pacific Citizen* editor Larry Tajiri in January 1946 to give him the first news of the upcoming book publication, and who invited him to sell the work through the newspaper.[42]

Citizen 13660 was published in September 1946. Okubo would later refer to the work as a "personal documentary"—since the Japanese Americans had not (at first) been allowed cameras in camp, she stated, she had taken on the task of illustrating the inmates' day-to-day existence through her sketches.[43] However, in contrast to the approach taken by classic documentary photographers such as Walker Evans and Dorothea Lange, or even Ansel Adams's study of Japanese Americans, *Born Free and Equal*, Okubo's strategy was precisely *not* to seem detached or distanced from any part of the experience she chronicled. Rather, she presented herself as an eyewitness of camp life, and placed her self-portrait in virtually all of the pictures. In its final form of first-person narrative and self-portrayal in sketches, *Citizen 13660* thereby, whether intentionally or not, evoked Taro Yashima's well-regarded 1943 book *The New Sun*, an illustrated narrative of the author's experience in a Japanese prison.[44]

In any case, both the text and illustrations for *Citizen 13660* bore the mark of the book's wartime publication. Although Okubo's work was not subject to official censorship, it was written and accepted for publication at a time when Japanese Americans were leaving the camps and trying to reestablish themselves in mainstream U.S. society. It was of central importance to Okubo to humanize herself and other Nisei, in order to underline their acceptability as new neighbors to a largely Caucasian audience. Thus, while Okubo's work described the tragedy of mass incarceration, her narrative strategy was to portray the camp experience primarily as an absurd, humorous predicament that the Japanese Americans faced and overcame. As she commented in a text accompanying publication:

> As I look back, I recall that the humiliation and the shock of the first few days seemed to prepare us for our camp existence. The confinement itself resulted in our living like the early Western pioneers, including all the hardships of trying to build a community complete with houses, schools, churches, and a jail. Many of the discomforts of camp life were forgotten in this activity. Everyone pitched in.[45]

Okubo transmitted this message through both her comments in the text and by her use of a comic-book-like drawing style (almost fifty years before Art Spiegelman's *Maus*) to portray camp life. For example, on one page, Okubo remarks, "We had to make friends with the wild creatures in the camp, especially the spiders, mice and rats, because they outnumbered us." Similarly, alongside a sketch of an adult flying a tiny kite, she notes, "Kite-making and flying was not limited to the youngsters."[46] In one picture Okubo shows an Issei man threatened by a gang of pro-Japan inmates, but she undercuts the menace of the actual situation by including in the drawing an image of herself sticking out her tongue at the attackers.[47] This is confinement—and hence confinement narrative—as picaresque adventure.

The book's prevalent tone is droll and sad—certainly not angry or bitter—and it is at times almost nostalgic. The volume ends with Okubo's departure from Topaz:

> I looked at the crowd at the gate. Only the very old or very young were left. Here I was, alone, with no family responsibilities, and yet fear had chained me to the camp. I thought, "My God! How do they expect those poor people to leave the one place they can call home!" I swallowed a lump in my throat as I waved good-by to them.
>
> I entered the bus. As soon as all the passengers had been accounted for, we were on our way. I relived momentarily the sorrows and joys of my whole evacuation experience, until the barracks faded away into the distance. There was only the desert now. My thoughts shifted from the past to the future.[48]

This approaches the confinement narrative as elegy.

Okubo candidly addressed her narrative strategy and her emphasis on resettlement in her own public comments on the book around the time of publication. "The important part of the evacuation begins where CITIZEN 13660 ends. Since the close of the War Relocation Centers in February of this year [1946], resettlement of the evacuees for the main part has been successful, but there have been many heartaches and hardships which each individual and all families had to suffer." Although she deplored the tremendous difficulties of the Issei mothers and fathers who had worked to build a future for their children and had ended up losing everything, she expressed hope for a better future for the Nisei. "Evacuation on the other hand has opened the eyes of the younger generation. By relocating and settling in different parts of the country and by meeting new groups of people they are finding that one can be happy beyond the walls of the 'Little Tokyos' to which many often turned in the past for protection and peace of mind."[49]

In accordance with this underlying goal, the book's publicity was carefully orchestrated. Nowhere in the promotional material released by Columbia University Press was the government or the WRA attacked for their policy, and the sufferings of Japanese Americans under official rule were downplayed. On the contrary, the book received the WRA's seal of approval. Director Dillon Myer contributed a blurb directed at West Coast bigots: "[Okubo] tells her story not with rancor but with quiet eloquence. The book is a reproof to those who would malign any racial minority, and it should help to forestall any future mass movements of the type she portrays." M. M. Tozier, former WRA Reports Division chief, added his own admiring assessment, in which he revealed his astonishing lack of direct contact with the inmates and their experience:

> By an unusually happy combination of pictures and text, Miné Okubo has succeeded in giving the reader a strong sense of participation in the

evacuation and relocation center experience. She makes you feel that this actually happened, that it might have happened to you, and that it should never happen again. After reading this book, I felt that I knew for the first time what camp life looked like, smelled like, and felt like to the evacuated people.[50]

The book's reviewers concurred. Dozens of critics in national newspapers and magazines spoke warmly of the wit and pathos Okubo had brought to her study of Japanese American survival and adjustment to difficult circumstances, and lauded the lack of bitterness she displayed. These reviewers did not suggest that the government or the army had been primarily responsible for the incarceration of Japanese Americans or for the tragic consequences of the loyalty questionnaire and segregation policy. Rather, like Okubo, they blamed the hysteria on West Coast bigots. M. Margaret Anderson (in what today would no doubt be considered unethical behavior) reviewed her protégée's book for the *New York Times*, in a piece called "Concentration Camp Boarders, Strictly American Plan": "Anti-Oriental prejudice, always profitable to certain groups, was fanned by the emotions of war into a hysteria that finally led the Federal government into acceptance of racial discrimination as an instrument of national policy."[51] Staying firmly on message, she added, "The drawings reveal a two-way process at work, the gradual demoralization of a group where family ties had ceased to matter under the system of mass living and mass feeding, and the resourcefulness and resilience of these fellow-Americans who tried desperately to turn negative living into something positive." *Christian Herald* reviewer Daniel A. Poling added, "Humor and pathos, both of which are at times profound, season the volume from cover to cover. I personally visited these centers. . . . What I found there is dramatically confirmed in this timely but also timeless volume."[52]

One outstanding exception to this trend among mainstream reviewers was the sociologist and race relations specialist Alfred McClung Lee. Writing in the *Saturday Review*, he praised in forthright terms the book's drawings and its "calm and considerate prose" for revealing the fascist persecution of minorities in America:

> Miné Okubo, like those Negro Americans whom the devastation of race riots or lynching has just missed, does not need to speculate [about fascism]. . . . Of course American concentration camps were not like Buchenwald. None of the Japanese-Americans was used for medical experimentation or converted into soap. But to be taken from one's home by force because of an accident of ancestry, to have one's family torn apart, and to be treated in a free land as a prisoner—these

are enough to make one wonder, as Negros have also pondered, about the security of democratic rights.[53]

Ironically, apart from Lee, the most critical stand toward the government among Okubo's readers was taken by Harold Ickes, former secretary of the interior, who had overseen the WRA in its last years. Ickes wrote in his syndicated column that *Citizen 13660* gave a clear account of the horrendous wartime treatment of Japanese in the United States. "As a member of President Roosevelt's administration I saw the United States Army give way to mass hysteria over the Japanese." Ickes described how army officials, who had not taken precautionary measures on the mainland, lost their cool, and in response to self-interested public clamor began rounding up Japanese Americans indiscriminately and sending them to concentration camps in the desert. "We gave the fancy name of 'relocation centers' to the dust bowls, but they were concentration camps nonetheless, although not as bad as Dachau or Buchenwald."[54] Yet even Ickes strongly praised the WRA for helping Japanese Americans, and congratulated President Roosevelt on his appointment of Dillon Myer.

The Japanese American press, which had devoted extensive coverage to Okubo's show and other achievements, was less unanimously positive about her book. Margaret Anderson remarked sadly to Larry Tajiri that Okubo's Nisei critics did not realize "the whole impact of the book which made its point with consummate skill," a description that speaks volumes.[55] On one hand, Marion Tajiri, writing in the *Pacific Citizen*, noted with satisfaction, "The book has captured all the bumbling and fumbling of the early evacuation days, all the pathos and humor that arose from the paradox of citizens interned."[56] A reviewer in the Japanese-language New York newspaper *Hokubei Shimpo* added that Okubo had powerfully illustrated the difficulties of life in camp, and enthused over her humorous depiction of Issei whose faces resembled Ukiyo-e prints.[57] However, two radical New York–based English-language journals, the *Nisei Weekender* and the Japanese American Committee for Democracy *Newsletter*, berated Okubo for soft-pedaling the hardships of evacuation and its impact on the inmates. Mary Ikeda, a former inmate, commented in the latter, "Despite the comprehensive drawings and text material, however, we feel that too much was left unsaid."[58]

Perhaps in response, Alice M. Togo, another former inmate, snapped that even if Okubo's text did not directly address the ethics of removal and the damage to the inmates, her images certainly did: "[Her] sketches suggest that Miss Okubo was not unaware of the social processes operating in the camps and of their effects on individuals. She draws no conclusions for her reader, but any thoughtful person examining her drawings of the disorganized classrooms, the crowded living quarters which offer no privacy, and the institutionalized mess halls can form his own judgment."[59] Similarly, in a review in the *American Journal of Sociology*, sociologist Setsuko Matsunaga Nishi, who had been confined in Santa Anita, perceptively summed up both Okubo's goal and the constraints on her:

> Because the book is entertaining, *Citizen 13660* will undoubtedly serve an important propaganda function to a public that would perhaps be more comfortable to forget the treatment of Japanese-Americans during the war. For all but the most careful reader, the very facile nature of the book detracts from the deep subjective meaning of the drawings. If the reader were to verbalize the significance of some of the illustrations, he might be surprised at the bitter irony. It seems unlikely that the author intended to be funny. . . . What is not evident to most readers is the disillusioning torment that evacuation meant.[60]

In the years after *Citizen 13660* was first published, Okubo pursued her independent art career, which she subsidized for a time with freelance book and magazine illustration work (including illustrations for *Common Ground* until that magazine's demise in 1949–50). She preferred not to focus on her camp experience in her later work, although she was generous in sharing her story with interviewers, most famously as part of the 1965 CBS television documentary *The Nisei: The Pride and the Shame*. Nevertheless, she was impatient over being identified primarily as a Nisei rather than as an artist. "I have enough headaches of my own," she said in one interview. "I don't have to worry about race. I'm an individual."[61]

Although Okubo always insisted that she was not bitter about her wartime experience, she became far more outspoken in later years about the trials she had undergone, even as public sentiment regarding the camp experience changed dramatically. Okubo was active in the Japanese American redress movement of the late 1970s and 1980s and joined in protests. Roger Daniels has pointed out that Okubo also shifted her language during these years. Whereas in the original edition of *Citizen*, Okubo had spoken of "evacuees" and "relocation centers," by the 1980s she was using the terms "internment camp" and "internee."[62] Similarly, in her 1983 introduction to the book, Okubo asserts that "there were untold hardships, sadness, and misery" in the camps; this contrasts with her original version of thirty-seven years earlier, in which, as previously noted, she described her experience more neutrally as a mixture of "joys and sorrows."[63]

How then should we understand *Citizen 13660* and the political messages its author meant to deliver at the time of its creation? It is fair to wonder how willingly Okubo played the part of model citizen and how much of that role was forced on her by circumstance. The evidence is mixed. On one hand, she remained proud of her work on *Citizen 13660* in later years, and she was especially gratified by the letters she continued to receive about it from readers from around the world. Further, when she testified before the Commission on Wartime Relocation and Evacuation of Civilians she offered the book as testimony.[64] On the other hand, Okubo later described herself as having been "very green" at the time she emerged from camp, and she referred obliquely to the restrictive field of discourse in which she felt able to operate in 1946.[65] "It was still too early. Everything that was Japanese was still rat poison so the book became a souvenir for [former inmates]."[66] Clearly, the burden of diluting mass anti-Japanese American hostility at that moment of resettlement was at least as stifling in its way as any officially derived censorship, and its impact on the author was telling. Okubo may not have been simply referring to her camp experience when she remarked in an interview shortly after the book's release, "You had to work hard to keep yourself going, and to keep from thinking."[67]

In sum, Miné Okubo's original text and illustrations for *Citizen 13660* were consciously arranged and publicized to respond to a particular historical moment, the exodus from camp. Although the immediate crisis of resettlement soon faded, the work remained and remains no less powerful in the changed political context of later decades. Perhaps the true greatness of Okubo's work of art can be judged by its power to transcend a particular agenda, even one in which the author was complicit, and to deliver many varied, and sometimes contradictory, meanings.

5. The "New Nisei" and Identity Politics

The mass removal and incarceration of Japanese Americans by the United States government during World War II brutalized its victims not only by stripping away their civil rights and causing them to lose most of their possessions but also by upsetting their psychological equilibrium. Before the war, the vast majority of Japanese Americans on the American continent lived on the West Coast, where they built close-knit ethnic communities around Japanese schools, churches, and sports teams. Large cities also boasted Japanese-language or bilingual newspapers, holiday processions, self-help groups, and ethnic associations. The U.S. government's policy of forcible removal smashed Japanese communities, while the mass incarceration of their residents without charge or proof of guilt subverted the camp inmates' ethnic identity and solidarity, leading to widespread trauma and interpersonal conflict within the camps.

As the war went on, the government began to permit Japanese Americans to leave the camps and resettle in communities elsewhere, first outside the Pacific coast, later nationwide. The newcomers labored, amid unfamiliar and at times hostile surroundings, to rebuild their shattered lives and community structures. At the same time, the Nisei undergoing resettlement faced particular pressure, both from government agencies such as the War Relocation Authority (WRA) and from within their own communities, to "assimilate" in order to avoid being perceived as foreign or threatening. For many, that meant removing the most obvious signs of their racial and ethnic difference, such as speaking Japanese, using Asian first names, or wearing folk costumes. For others, that meant socializing with non-Asians and avoiding all-Nisei circles, although by and large they did not—and could not—totally avoid associating with other Japanese Americans. In the process, the Nisei were forced to wrestle with fundamental questions of identity and community development: Was it possible to be American and Japanese? Was the assimilation prescribed by the government possible, or even desirable? Could the Nisei express a group identity that would be free of stigma?

In this period of initial reconstruction and uncertainty, a group of Nisei writers in their twenties or early thirties, including Sam Hohri, Bill Hosokawa, Miné Okubo, Mary Oyama [Mittwer], Eddie Shimano, Ina Sugihara, and Larry Tajiri, emerged as spokespeople for the Nisei to the wider society, as well as counselors inside the community. They were part of a group of intellectuals that had been at the center of Nisei journalism and artistic life on the West Coast before the war. However, during those years they remained fairly marginal within the ethnic community, which was dominated by Issei and by conservative Nisei businessmen, and they were all but unknown outside it. It was mass confinement, paradoxically, that opened up a mainstream public forum for them. The public debate over the government's actions, combined with the efforts of the WRA to publicize the inmates positively so as to ease mass resettlement, made the condition of Japanese Americans a matter of public interest and gave the West Coast Nisei their first, limited access to mainstream media. Their writings appeared in mass-market periodicals such as *Liberty, Fortune,* and the *Saturday Review,* liberal journals such as the *Nation,* the *New Republic,* and *Common Ground,* religious publications such as *Commonweal, Christian Century,* and the *Christian Science Monitor,* and the daily secular press (including African American journals). Through these media, the Nisei writers were able both to address a diverse audience on the state of Japanese Americans in the wake of confinement and to speak to other Japanese Americans about the shape of their community in the post-camp future.

Although the Nisei writers had diverse experiences, certain common themes do appear in their writings. They all denounced the injustice of mass confinement and deplored conditions in the camps. Yet they generally represented the government's policy of resettling "loyal" Nisei as a positive step toward destroying the subordinate status of Japanese Americans. As Eddie Shimano noted, "The hope is in resettlement.... Such dispersal resettlement, I am convinced, will go far to effect speedily and drastically, with surgical thoroughness and surgical disregard for sentiment, the integration of the Japanese into American life."[1] They each expressed the hope that Japanese Americans, wherever they resettled, would embrace assimilation and shed their defensive ghetto mentality. Nevertheless, they did not simply propose blending quietly into white society, as the government recommended. Rather, they insisted in different degrees that it was the duty of the Japanese Americans, especially after their confinement experience, to engage with the larger society and participate in the public sphere. As Mary Oyama commented in 1943, "Until now the Nisei was not very social[ly] conscious, but the tremendous experience of evacuation and all its attendant ramifications is generally forcing him to realize his particular relation to society as a whole."[2]

Conversely, the Nisei writers disagreed on a number of points, most notably whether to advise return to the West Coast or advocate permanent residence outside. Ina Sugihara insisted that progress was possible only if the Nisei remained dispersed and on the East Coast. In an article for the Catholic magazine *Commonweal* (rather melodramatically entitled "I Don't Want to Go Back") she insisted that even if the Nisei had a perfect constitutional right to return to the West Coast, if they did so in large numbers it would not only spark discrimination against them by white racists but also ruin their chances for advancement by placing them at odds with other minorities:

> If Japanese Americans return in large numbers to Los Angeles's international ghetto, it will be the center of multiple discrimination and "bigger and better" riots. No one will know who is directly at fault, but tighter restrictions in the rest of the community against all minority groups will crowd them into an extremely limited territory, and lack of privacy, together with the search for a scapegoat, will cause bloodshed.[3]

In response, Sam Hohri urged the Nisei to return to the West Coast, despite threats of violence from white racists, in order to take part in fighting discrimination: "California is regarded by many who have been anticipating the days after the war as a crucial area, the main street frontage in this era now beginning. It would seem to me that the Nisei would want to be on this exciting scene and participate in shaping the fabric of civilization." More important, California itself had changed. "Caucasians are working with Negroes and Mexicans, Catholics with Jews and Protestants, cooperating in the conviction that if world peace is to be attained, understanding must begin at home."[4] Hohri put it in more pointed form to a Nisei audience:

> The night riding terrorists of the West Coast would like to spread the miasma of the South to the West. In choosing to stay away and avoid this unpleasantness, there is the danger of reverting to isolation. . . . if the terrorists succeed in intimidating the Nisei . . . their success will validly encourage and incite them to depress others—the Negroes, the Mexicans, other Orientals, Jews.[5]

Interestingly, of all the individuals who spoke in the non-Japanese press on behalf of the Nisei, the writers who expressed the most expansive vision of Japanese American identity were Larry Tajiri and Ina Sugihara, who were the only two figures from the West Coast group who were never confined in the camps. Tajiri and Sugihara insisted that Japanese Americans were a racial minority group, and as such, they could achieve first-class citizenship only by opposing all forms of discrimination and joining with other groups to fight for equality. What is particularly striking about Tajiri and Sugahara's work is the deep sense of identification they felt with African Americans as social outsiders. Their determined advocacy of alliance between Nisei and African Americans was not only a way to end anti-Japanese discrimination but also a strategy for the Nisei to learn from an established minority how to develop a cohesive and unique group identity.

Larry Tajiri, born in Los Angeles in 1914, worked as a journalist and editor during the 1930s for a number of Pacific coast Japanese American newspapers, notably the San Francisco *Nichi Bei*. During these years, he was active in literary and political circles, and helped organize the progressive Nisei Democrats group in Oakland. In 1940, he and his wife, Guyo, moved to New York, where he was hired as a correspondent for the *Asahi* chain of Japanese newspapers. Unemployed after Pearl Harbor, Tajiri returned to the West Coast, where he joined with Isamu Noguchi and a circle of others in forming an activist group, the Nisei Writers and Artists Mobilization for Democracy, which labored unsuccessfully to forestall mass evacuation. In March 1942, Tajiri was recruited by JACL president Saburo Kido to move to Salt Lake City, where the organization had taken refuge, and assume direction of the *Pacific Citizen*, its monthly newsletter. Since West Coast Japanese American newspapers were being shut down, Tajiri and his wife decided to launch the *Pacific Citizen* as a weekly (later biweekly) vernacular newspaper, and they served as editors and sole employees. In June 1942 the Tajiris began to put out an eight-page edition, composed of reprints of press commentary on Japanese Americans from across the nation plus features and editorials mainly written by themselves. Despite a limited circulation and funding, they soon transformed the *Pacific Citizen* into a forum for community opinion.[6]

Meanwhile, in spite of his demanding assignment, Tajiri corresponded with numerous friends and sympathizers, seeking to draw public attention to the plight of the Nisei, and nurtured contacts with outside editors. In early 1943, Pearl S. Buck, the most prominent national supporter of the rights of Japanese Americans, commissioned him to write a piece for *Asia*, the magazine she and her husband, Richard Walsh, edited. Tajiri's article

"Democracy Corrects Its Own Mistakes" appeared in the April 1943 issue. The text described the demoralizing effect of life in the camps and championed the WRA's policy of resettlement.

Tajiri ended his essay by positing resettlement as a test of democracy. The Nisei faced the challenge of dispersing and achieving "successful rehabilitation" in their new surroundings in order to prove that the United States could survive as a multiracial society. Meanwhile, Americans at large had the task of ending discrimination against the Nisei in order to persuade the nation's nonwhite wartime allies of its sincere support for worldwide freedom and to promote assimilation by all minorities at home. Tajiri directly associated the cause of the Nisei with that of other racial groups.

> Thoughtful men among other racial minorities recognize that unconstitutional, undemocratic procedures against any one minority can prove the opening wedge for such action against all other minorities. . . . And always it can be held as a threat against the full realization of their basic rights for the Negro, the Chinese, the Filipino, the Mexican-American and other victims of marginal democracy.[7]

Following the appearance of Tajiri's article in *Asia*, he was asked by Margaret Anderson, editor of *Common Ground*, a liberal quarterly devoted to championing the rights of ethnic and racial minorities, to draft a more extended piece on the future of the Nisei. Tajiri's essay "Farewell to Little Tokyo" appeared in the magazine's winter 1944 issue. Despite its title, the article was not in the least elegiac. Rejecting the notion of the old West Coast Japanese communities as sites of ethnic belonging, the author asserted that the existence of the prewar Little Tokyos, however understandable from a psychological or economic point of view, had fostered the development of an unhealthy racial consciousness that stunted Japanese American growth.

> As I see it, whether they settle permanently away from their former areas of residence on the West Coast or return eventually to the farms and homes they left behind, the [Japanese Americans] will have to become assimilated or become virtual pariahs. For the Little Tokyos have been shattered and—I hope—will not be put together again.[8]

Despite his rhetorical support for assimilation, Tajiri did not suggest that Japanese Americans give up their ethnic identity. Rather, he drew an implicit but essential distinction between positive and negative racial consciousness. A negative racial consciousness meant withdrawal and self-hatred. A positive racial consciousness, on the other hand, meant that the

Nisei could use their own experience as a minority group to understand the dynamics of racial discrimination on a macroscopic level and contribute to opening up society:

> To bring about assimilation, I believe it is both a necessity and an obligation for the evacuees to align themselves, wherever they go in their post-evacuation world, with the progressive forces within American society and with the mass movement of all marginal groups toward the full realization of the American dream.... [T]he racial nature of evacuation developed a recognition among many Japanese Americans that they were inescapably relegated to a place on the color wheel of America, that their problem was basically one of color and part of the unfinished racial business of democracy.[9]

Thus, Tajiri concluded that joining with members of other groups to oppose discrimination was not only strategically wise for the Nisei but fundamental to their complete absorption into a democratic community.

Tajiri's thesis was both extended and put into practice by Ina Sugihara. Sugihara, born in 1919, grew up in a small town in Colorado, and later moved to Long Beach, California. She stated later that she was scouted for a scholarship at UCLA but was rejected because she wanted to be a lawyer, a profession considered inappropriate for an Asian girl, rather than a nurse, as the grantors intended. Instead, after attending junior college she moved to Oakland and enrolled at the University of California, Berkeley. While at college she also attended labor schools. She likewise became friends with members of the pioneering political group Oakland Nisei Young Democrats, and attended meetings of the club. Unable to get a job in industry due to racial prejudice, she became a cook and housekeeper before being hired as an assistant by Ernest Besig, an attorney with the Northern California branch of the American Civil Liberties Union. In spring 1942, with Besig's help, she was hired by John Thomas of the American Baptist Home Mission Society. She thereby was able to migrate "voluntarily" to New York and avoid confinement in the WRA camps. Sugihara subsequently took a job with the Protestant Welfare Council's Human Relations Division, and worked with the Federal Council of Churches. As part of her work, she wrote articles and press releases for the Religious News Service.[10]

After the prejudice she had experienced in California, Sugihara enjoyed the cosmopolitan climate of New York. Soon after settling in the city, she grew acquainted with Socialist Party leader Norman Thomas, the only national political figure to oppose mass removal of Japanese Americans. Her talks with Thomas, building on her own experience, inspired her to join the Socialists and to throw herself into civil rights organizing in both the Nisei and black communities. Under the influence of Thomas, Sugihara developed a series of civil rights institutes at the New School, and soon afterward she helped form the New York branch of the Gandhian nonviolent civil rights group Congress of Racial Equality (CORE), founded the previous year in Chicago. CORE's director James Farmer (whom Sugihara and a boyfriend put up in their apartment for several months following Farmer's divorce) later marveled at the fierce intelligence and lively humor with which she confronted bigots.[11] In 1944, Sugihara led organizers in founding a New York branch of the JACL. (The new branch, the first east of the Rockies, was also the organization's first interracial chapter. Its operations were funded in part by contributions from African American columnist George Schuyler.)

As a JACL stalwart and contributor to the *Pacific Citizen*, Sugihara presumably knew of Tajiri's editorial stand, though it is not clear if she was familiar with his outside writings. In any case, she clearly was in agreement with his ideas on assimilation and activism. Even before the war, Sugihara had spoken publicly in favor of the assimilation of Nisei, and during the war she toured New York State to advocate aid for resettlement.

Meanwhile, secure in her New York environment, Sugihara concentrated on multigroup coalition building. In 1945–46, Sugihara and the New York JACL mobilized to lobby for congressional reauthorization of the Fair Employment Practices Committee (FEPC), the antidiscrimination watchdog committee that President Franklin Roosevelt had created with Executive Order 8802 in June 1941. Since the FEPC operated only under a wartime executive authority and was bitterly opposed by southern leaders in Congress, civil rights advocates rightly feared that it would disappear following the end of the war. As part of the struggle, Sugihara joined forces with the leaders of the NAACP, who invited her to contribute a piece on the FEPC to the association's organ, the *Crisis*.

"Our Stake in a Permanent FEPC" appeared in the January 1945 issue. Following a brief exposition on the history and work of the FEPC, Sugihara detailed some of its successes. In particular, referring obliquely to the government's mistreatment of Japanese Americans, she not too gently reminded her African American readers that they were not the only group in need of redress:

> Perhaps the most notable accomplishments of the FEPC is its successful handling of cases involving Japanese Americans through a maze of other government agencies, necessarily and unnecessarily involved, [and in the face of] war hysteria, hidden circumstances and personalities, and other factors not found in the usual cases.[12]

Still, Sugihara's point was not to privilege Japanese Americans over blacks as victims of discrimination. Rather, she argued that it was in the direct interest of both groups to fight for the FEPC. Although the FEPC had been generally handicapped by lack of authority and interference from its opponents, she admitted, and was far from ideal, it represented a considerable advance. Beyond the positive actions it took, she claimed, the agency helped foster coalitions between groups.

> One of [the FEPC's] most important functions has been to prove to people, some of whom were previously concerned over the welfare of one community group or another, that the fate of each minority depends upon the extent of justice given all other groups. . . . it eliminates the practice of discrimination as such and makes for better treatment for all, just as inequality crosses group boundaries and becomes a cancer in the lives of all of us.[13]

Sugihara was under no illusions that legislation or executive actions for civil rights would resolve the problem of discrimination. Rather, their value lay in heightening the consciousness of minority groups about their fundamental interdependence, and creating the unity necessary for fighting discrimination.

Meanwhile, in accord with her philosophy, Sugihara helped bring Nisei and black activists together again. As will be discussed further in Chapter 11, in March 1947 she attended a conference called by the NAACP on legal strategies to fight restrictive covenants, including taking the issue to the U.S. Supreme Court. Sugihara contacted the JACL's Anti-Discrimination Committee and arranged for the organization to submit a supporting brief. Later that year, she convened a meeting of civil rights and church groups in support of *Takahashi v. California Fish and Game Commission*, the JACL's Supreme Court challenge to anti-Issei discrimination, and she helped persuade NAACP counsel Thurgood Marshall to submit a brief.

Although they expressed views that were fairly common in the postwar climate, Larry Tajiri and Ina Sugihara found themselves increasingly marginalized in the Nisei community after the resettlement period. In 1952, Tajiri left the *Pacific Citizen*, in part due to pressure from conservative JACL leaders who opposed his liberal politics and independent management style. He spent his later years as the *Denver Post*'s drama critic, dying in 1965. Despite the respect she inspired inside and outside the community, Ina Sugihara likewise found herself increasingly marginalized during the postwar years. In particular, in the early 1950s Sugihara married an African American, Willis Jones. She later stated that she and her husband were made to feel uncomfortable within a Japanese American community she considered intolerant of blacks. In later years, she worked for Texaco, lived in African American areas in Queens, New York, and supported open housing. In 1977, the couple moved White Plains, New York, where Willis Jones died in 1982. Ina Sugihara Jones retired shortly afterward and lived in White Plains until her death in 2004.

Like other 1940s Nisei writers, Larry Tajiri and Ina Sugihara were articulate exponents of a viewpoint that creatively linked a mature ethnic consciousness with civic engagement and the struggle for democracy. Their writings, simultaneously pitched to the Nisei community and to the society at large, pushed assimilation as central to a reformed Japanese American identity, but proposed a form of assimilation based on Japanese Americans engaging with the larger society and joining with other groups against discrimination, most notably against African Americans.

Their ideas on assimilation were both reinforced and opposed by a contrasting Nisei voice, that of S. I. Hayakawa. Although he first achieved fame as a semanticist and best-selling author, Hayakawa remains known chiefly for his tenure as president of San Francisco State University at the end of the 1960s, during which time his opposition to student protesters won him nationwide attention, and for his subsequent election to the U.S. Senate on the Republican ticket in 1976. Yet if the story of S. I. Hayakawa's public career is familiar, his earlier career and ideas deserve closer scrutiny.[14]

Samuel Ichiyé Hayakawa was born not in the United States but in Vancouver, British Columbia, where he was the oldest of four children. Hayakawa's father had immigrated from Japan to San Francisco at the dawn of the twentieth century, returned to Japan, then settled with his wife in Canada. There he worked as a labor contractor and journalist for a local Japanese newspaper before opening a struggling import-export business. The family migrated across Canada during his youth, and he grew up in Cranbrook, British Columbia, Calgary, and Winnipeg. In Winnipeg, the Hayakawas were the only Japanese family in a Scottish and Jewish immigrant neighborhood (Hayakawa later was renowned for sporting a tam o'shanter, in tribute to his Scots associations). In 1926–27, around the time that Hayakawa received his B.A. from the University of Manitoba, the family split up. Both parents and two younger sisters moved to Japan, where the elder Hayakawa became a wealthy businessman. S.I. and a brother moved to Montreal with an uncle, where the young Hayakawa earned a master's degree at McGill University.[15]

In 1929 Hayakawa left Canada and enrolled at the University of Wisconsin, where he was so studious that friends gave him the nickname

"Don," which stuck with him thereafter. Hayakawa also wrote verse, and several of his poems and articles appeared in *Poetry* magazine over the next years. He cut a dashing figure at Wisconsin. One roommate, Robert Frase, later recalled how he sold Hayakawa, who loved motorcycles, his bike upon graduation. Hayakawa then gave him a lift to commencement, with the two of them scooting through campus in cap and gown.[16] Meanwhile, Hayakawa met and soon married a white woman, Margedant Peters. In 1935, following completion of a thesis on the poet and essayist Oliver Wendell Holmes, he received his doctorate.[17] After graduation, Hayakawa traveled to Montreal, where his brother had established himself as a businessman. He intended to remain in Canada but could not find work. Therefore, he returned to Wisconsin, took a job lecturing on English literature in the university's extension division, and contributed to *The Middle English Dictionary*. Because of his educational credentials, he was selected by the Japanese Canadian Citizens League as part of a four-person delegation that visited Ottawa in May 1936 to lobby unsuccessfully for voting rights for Nisei in British Columbia.[18]

Around this time, Hayakawa was invited (one might say summoned) by his parents to visit them. He recounted his visit to his ancestral homeland in a two-part article published in *Asia* magazine in March-April 1937. In the two pieces, Hayakawa presented his "discovery" of Japan, in the process expounding his own self-image. He opened by explaining that he felt completely American: "If I had ever been a foreigner in the United States, it had been because of the British element in my education. As a matter of fact, I had never really felt a foreigner in the United States. A Canadian, after all, in spite of a difference in allegiance, is more than half American from the beginning." Conversely, before his visit, he knew much more of British than of Japanese culture—for example, while he knew most of the words and music to Gilbert and Sullivan's *The Mikado*, he was pretty vague on the Forty-Seven Ronin. Once he arrived, he also had great trouble communicating with his family. While his father spoke fluent English, he could converse with his mother only in a mixture of Japanese baby talk and literary English. Worse, his youngest sister, who had returned to Japan at the age of five, had felt such pressure not to be "different" in Japan that she had blocked out all her English.[19]

Hayakawa's comparison of American democracy and Japanese feudalism was alternately humorous and poignant. For example, he described how he had been welcomed on his arrival and given generous presents by a deputation of his father's employees. Conversely, his father put on formal visiting clothes and stayed up half the night with the family of a deceased employee to pay his respects. While Hayakawa pronounced himself fascinated by Japanese civilization, which he was anxious to study, and by "the achievements of Japanese ethical and esthetic discipline," he felt uneasy in Japan. He was a teacher, Hayakawa said, and the teacher in Japan was only secondarily a seeker after truth; primarily he was an instrument for inculcating national greatness. He was too American, too much the skeptic and empiricist, to survive in the close-knit confines of Japan. Even before the Japanese invasion of China, Hayakawa clearly sensed the approach of militarism.[20]

In 1939, S. I. Hayakawa was named professor of English at the Armour (now Illinois) Institute of Technology, and he moved to Chicago. He meanwhile became attracted by Alfred Korzybski's ideas on general semantics. Korzybski argued for systems of thinking and language that reflected the fluid nature of reality. Hayakawa sought to popularize Korzybski's epistemological theories by means of a textbook, and in 1939 he released the first version of *Language in Action*, first with a small Chicago press, then with a more prestigious New York firm. Hayakawa was fascinated by the idea, as he put it, of "an examination of language as a preliminary to an examination of the problems stated in language." The book attracted such attention for its lucid and entertaining style that it was taken up by a major New York publisher. In December 1941, just before Pearl Harbor, the book was honored by being named a selection of the Book-of-the-Month Club, ensuring large sales. It was to go through numerous editions and make its author known nationwide.[21]

The largest part of his interest in general semantics was its emphasis on environmental factors over heredity, and the resistance of reality to fixed Aristotelian categories of "truth." Instead, in the tradition of the American pragmatists, he considered understanding as growing out of human interaction. Meanwhile, in the shadow of fascism, he grew increasingly conscious of the dangers of propaganda and racial hatred, and how people substituted facile stereotyping for thought. He concluded from his examination of fascism that ethnic chauvinism and ghettoization invited social division, while participation in democratic society promoted positive communication and equality.

Hayakawa's concerns led him in conflicting directions. On one hand, he deplored discrimination and was willing to participate in struggles for civil rights, in the name of furthering democracy. Nevertheless, he rejected all forms of ethnic particularism as reinforcing interpersonal barriers, and instead favored multigroup action on a nonracial basis for economic democracy. For example, he was active in the organization of consumers' cooperatives and cooperative housing—his wife, Margedant, edited the *Chicago Co-operative News*. He remained self-consciously cosmopolitan. In particular, because of his passionate love of jazz—on which he later claimed a somewhat spurious expertise—he became a familiar figure in Chicago's African American communities (and as a jazz pianist at café society parties). While it is too easy to read Hayakawa's interest in assimilation and distance from Japanese communities as simply a product of his rootless and itinerant youth, family and psychological factors as well as intellectual ones undoubtedly contributed.

Hayakawa's principles were tested during Word War II by the removal of West Coast Japanese Americans. While Executive Order 9066 represented exactly the kind of racist and undemocratic action that he deplored, he was wary of anything resembling special pleading for his own group. His response was twofold. First, he quietly assisted resettlement efforts, so that Nisei could leave camp and enter the larger society. In 1942, Hayakawa was contacted by his old Wisconsin roommate Robert Frase, who had been recruited to join the WRA by director Dillon Myer. In part through knowing Hayakawa, Frase was convinced that Japanese Americans were loyal, and he and his supervisor Tom Holland opposed confinement and lobbied Myer to authorize immediate resettlement. When Frase visited Chicago to establish a resettlement office there, Hayakawa hosted him at his house and advised him on securing jobs and housing for resettlers.[22]

In November 1942 Hayakawa joined the African American *Chicago Defender* as a weekly columnist, and he continued his column until January 1947. While he surely appreciated that the newspaper's editors hired him partly as an expression of solidarity with Nisei, he refused to speak solely as a Japanese American. Rather, he maintained a stance of objectivity. When he sporadically, and reluctantly, addressed issues of confinement or anti-Japanese discrimination, he did so within a larger context of promoting American democracy. Ironically, as C. K. Doreski has noted, poet Langston Hughes was more critical in his *Defender* column of government treatment of Japanese Americans than Hayakawa was. Conversely, Hayakawa was forthright in his criticism of racism against blacks in his *Defender* column and in his lectures on race relations.[23]

Hayakawa's relations with Japanese communities remained uneasy through the postwar years. During this period, due in part to the efforts of WRA employment supervisor Robert Frase, Hayakawa's friend and former roommate from Wisconsin, Chicago became the focal point of Japanese American resettlement. Most of its ethnic Japanese newcomers—a population that reached some 20,000 by 1946—were forced by discrimination and the housing shortage, as well as their impoverished state, to squeeze into slums and racially changing neighborhoods and to take menial, low-paying jobs.[24]

Hayakawa was genuinely sympathetic to Nisei victimized by discrimination and official prejudice. However, his powerful faith in assimilation and resistance to ethnic particularism led to clashes. Sociologist Setsuko Matsunaga Nishi recalled that when she asked Hayakawa to serve on the advisory board of the Chicago Resettlers Committee, which was trying to open housing and find jobs for Japanese Americans, Hayakawa was resistant and scornfully responded, "Why do you want to pull me back? Can't I just be a model of what a person of Japanese ancestry can achieve by assimilating?" He reluctantly agreed to serve, and made a large financial contribution. (He may have been impressed by Nishi's own involvement in African American circles, or by the fact that the board already boasted such prominent Chicagoans as department store magnate Marshall Field and U.S. Steel president Edward L. Ryerson.) Because of his agreement with its platform of assimilation and multiracial civil rights, Hayakawa bent principle regarding opposition to ethnic organizations and joined the JACL.[25]

During the postwar years, Hayakawa became a well-known figure as an educator and semanticist. In 1950 he was hired by the University of Chicago. He likewise served as editor of the professional linguistics journal *Etc*. Hayakawa remained an advocate of liberal society. At the height of McCarthyism, he made a courageous statement publicly condemning the actions of the House Un-American Activities Committee as a violation of the rights of free speech and free association. These same concerns led Hayakawa to reverse his position. In summer 1952, he publicly denounced the JACL's support for the McCarran-Walter Immigration Act. The act, a product of Cold War xenophobia and exaggerated concerns over "security," gave the government new powers to strip naturalized U.S. citizens of their citizenship and to exclude or deport aliens suspected of subversive tendencies. At the same time, however, the act overturned the exclusion of Japanese immigrants (albeit in token numbers, within existing discriminatory national origins quotas) and granted naturalization rights to Issei. Because these were the two primary goals of the JACL, the organization's leaders reluctantly gave the larger bill their support, and helped lobby Congress to override President Harry Truman's veto of the bill. In letters to the Nisei press, Hayakawa accused the JACL of supporting a "heartless," repressive bill and putting their own interest ahead of all those who would be damaged by the law. "To secure the rights to naturalization of Issei at the cost of all the questionable and illiberal features of the McCarran-Walter Bill appears to be an act of unpardonable shortsightedness or cynical opportunism."[26] Hayakawa therefore announced that he would no longer contribute to the Chicago JACL's Anti-Discrimination Committee. "I am afraid the Anti-Discrimination Committee has not lived up to its name. It has purchased the removal of one small discrimination at the cost of legalizing the continuance of many other forms of discrimination, and the creation of a number of and second generation citizens of all ancestries." He was not alone in his opposition: journalist Togo Tanaka and others had already condemned the JACL's actions.[27] Still, it represented an impressive statement of principle, especially since Hayakawa himself stood to gain from the legislation. Though Hayakawa was a Canadian citizen, he was barred from U.S. naturalization because of his Japanese ancestry. It was only after passage of McCarran-Walter that he was able to become an American citizen himself.

In 1955, Hayakawa was appointed professor of English at San Francisco State University. He soon after waded into controversy once again by denouncing the formation of Japanese student organizations. When invited to address CINO, a Nisei student group, Hayakawa publicly declined and proclaimed that Nisei social organizations should cease to exist. Since social discrimination had disappeared, for all practical purposes, the only remaining barriers were in the minds of Nisei, and in view of this, separate organizations were "social crutches" that were not only useless but crippling. "We shall learn to walk as free men and women among equals in a democratic society when, and only when, we throw away the crutches."[28] Hayakawa explained that when he was young, he was repeatedly steered by friends and academic advisors toward Japanese subject matter, but preferred to study other topics that interested him more. In an odd reversal, he concluded with an implicit admission that discrimination still existed, but continued to refute its importance: "The tragedy of being of a minority group is to let one's minority group obsession govern one's entire life—and not merely one's housing or other social detail."[29]

Debate ensured within Japanese American communities—and also in Japanese Canadian ones—over Hayakawa's statements. Letter writers expressed admiration for Hayakawa's successful assimilation and acknowledged that Nisei should concentrate on being good citizens and not close themselves off, but they insisted that Hayakawa's position was far too sweeping and his tone condescending.[30] As Larry Tajiri pointed out, as long as racial discrimination on campus, such as in fraternities, targeted Japanese Americans, they could not give up their own organizations.[31]

Hayakawa was invited to address CINO once more the following year, and again declined. He thereafter distanced himself from Japanese communities for a generation.

In 1968–69, a "Third World" coalition of students at San Francisco State University launched a strike, demanding ethnic studies programs and protesting the Vietnam War. When the college's president resigned, Hayakawa accepted the post, and became notable for his outspoken opposition to the strikers: on one occasion he even ripped out the wires from their sound truck at a demonstration. His relations with the community remained tenuous. Once Hayakawa became president of San Francisco State University, he attended community meetings, and then was invited to address the Southwest District Council of the JACL. The invitations caused great division within the community, and his appearances were picketed.[32]

Upon retiring from academia in 1973, Hayakawa became a newspaper columnist, then parlayed his newfound popularity with conservatives into a successful campaign for the U.S. Senate on the Republican ticket in 1976. With this victory, Hayakawa became the first—and so far only—senator of East Asian ancestry from a mainland state, and at seventy among the oldest freshman senators ever elected. (Once in office he was widely caricatured as "Sleeping Sam," after an incident where he fell asleep on the Senate floor.) During his single term in office, he aroused the ire of Japanese Americans when in a speech before the JACL he forcefully opposed official apologies and redress for wartime incarceration, and expressed his conviction that the Nisei were better off for the experience. (Hayakawa's remarks stung his audience even more because he had never been confined in a WRA camp.)[33] After leaving the Senate, Hayakawa became a consultant on East Asian relations. He sparked further liberal outrage by cofounding U.S. English, a lobbying group dedicated to making English the official language of the United States.

Nevertheless, on two occasions in later years he joined forces with progressive community members for libertarian purposes, though both times the interventions carried his own individual mark. In August 1963, at the time of the March on Washington, Hayakawa delivered a widely publicized lecture on the "Negro problem" in which he expressed his sympathy for African Americans and asserted that the way the nation handled the civil rights question would determine its place in the world. He called for a number of special public-private measures to ensure equality, including initiatives by labor unions and businesses to recruit minorities, the end of segregation in public accommodations, and incentive bonuses to attract talented teachers to schools for the underprivileged. His advocacy of special government recruitment efforts prefigured the creation of affirmative action programs and magnet schools.[34] At a time when the JACL was paralyzed by debate over Rev. Martin Luther King Jr.'s invitation to attend the March on Washington, this was a controversial position among Nisei. He rejected the argument, pressed by conservatives, that blacks should improve their situation by their own efforts, and that Nisei would jeopardize relations with white allies by supporting equality for all Americans.[35] Although Hayakawa had not delivered the lecture to a Japanese American audience, the progressive newspaper *New York Nichibei* requested permission to serialize extracts from it, with the goal of winning further Nisei support for civil rights. Despite his opposition to separate organizations, he agreed to the publication.

The other occasion on which Hayakawa joined the Japanese American community was in his strong support for Iva Toguri d'Aquino. Toguri had been arrested after World War II and convicted of treason for having broadcast for Japan as "Tokyo Rose." In the mid-1970s, even as Japanese Americans undertook the movement for redress for their confinement, investigators discovered that Toguri had been convicted based on perjured testimony, amid postwar hysteria. A campaign grew up to win an official pardon for her from President Gerald Ford. In 1976 Hayakawa was recruited by his longtime friend Clifford Uyeda, the leader of the pardon movement, to lend his support. He responded with a pair of articles in his syndicated newspaper column examining the case. Hayakawa noted that the reason Toguri had been indicted for treason, unlike other women who broadcast over Japanese radio during World War II, was that she had refused to renounce her American citizenship, even under duress. He insisted that such unshakable loyalty deserved reward, not blame.[36] In addition to his columns, Hayakawa telephoned the White House to lobby Ford administration officials. The pressure, especially from a newly elected Republican senator, may well have helped. Ford issued the pardon on January 19, 1977, one day before leaving office.[37]

Despite his unparalleled political rise, S. I. Hayakawa has been largely excluded from American history, and not just that of Japanese Americans. Part of this is no doubt because of his contrarian style, as well as his shift to right-wing politics and the expressed bigotry of his later years. For example, he spoke in favor of mass internment of Iranian Americans during the Iranian hostage crisis in 1979–80. Meanwhile, he called himself "deeply, deeply, deeply offended by homosexuality," and endorsed a measure that would have barred gays and lesbians from teaching in public schools.[38] Still, his complex thinking and courageous, if often extreme, attachment to principle provide useful counterpoint to simplistic arguments that assimilation implies conformism. Rather, Hayakawa stands as a monument to self-creation and social mobility.

PART III

Interethnic Politics

6. Japanese Americans and Mexican Americans

The Limits of Interracial Collaboration

INTRODUCTION

Historians have begun in recent years to look past limited views of race in American history as a series of interactions between individual minorities (generally African Americans) and the white majority. The study of connections between racialized groups—that is, those considered as "other" than white and subjected to discrimination on that basis—and how they view each other is a fruitful avenue for looking at the workings of society. The interplay between Mexican Americans and Japanese Americans in Southern California during the 1940s provides a particularly revealing window into the complexities of such relations. Although both of these communities were victimized by racial exclusion, violence, and economic discrimination, and their members joined together at various times in movements for fair housing, equal employment opportunity, and integrated schools, their members expressed jealousy, disdain, and mistrust toward each other. What is particularly meaningful to study are the changes in relations between these groups that were inspired by World War II, and how their subsequent interactions remained marked by tension and conflict as well as solidarity.

A prime example of both the promise and limitations of intergroup coalition between the two is the 1946–47 federal court case *Méndez v. Westminster School District of Orange County*.[1] The *Méndez* case, which put an end to the exclusion of Mexican American children from "white" schools in Southern California, is a bellwether event in the history of equal rights in the United States. Not only did the court's decision represent a major advance for Mexican Americans in their quest for equality, but it also led directly to the repeal of all school segregation laws in California, which had been up until then the largest state to maintain separate schools for minority populations. The *Méndez* case can thus be seen as the first victory in the postwar legal struggle against segregation in primary education that climaxed with the Supreme Court's epochal ruling in *Brown v. Board of Education* in 1954. *Méndez* has been enshrined both in popular memory and in historiography as a precursor of *Brown*, a challenge to racial discrimination by minority group representatives.[2] In keeping with this view, the numerous historical exhibits, articles, lectures, and commemorations featuring the *Méndez* case have tended to highlight the participation as amicus curiae of civil rights organizations such as the National Association for the Advancement of Colored People (NAACP)—notably the involvement of NAACP chief counsel Thurgood Marshall—and to a lesser extent the JACL, together with the League of United Latin American Citizens (LULAC). The result is that they portray the case as a golden moment of intergroup unity among Latinos, Asian Americans, and African Americans. A notable illustration of the tendency to view *Méndez* as a landmark of (inter)racial struggle is the work of historian Ronald Takaki, whose "multicultural history of America in World War II" provides the following commentary on the case:

> The Mexican-American struggle for justice expanded [after World War II] to the right to equal education. In the 1946 case of *Méndez v. Westminster School District of Orange County*, the U.S. Circuit Court of Southern California declared that the segregation of Mexican children violated their right to equal protection of the law guaranteed to them under the Fourteenth Amendment and therefore was unconstitutional. To support the *Méndez* case, amicus curiae briefs were filed by the American Jewish Congress, the National Association for the Advancement of Colored People, and the Japanese American Citizens League. Together, they won a victory over prejudice in education.[3]

This is all inspiring, and for many people it is clearly empowering. However, it is important to guard against romanticizing the *Méndez* decision as the product of a united front of minority groups. In actual fact, what the events of *Méndez*, and the larger context of interactions between Japanese Americans and Mexican Americans, reveal most strongly are the tensions and complexities present in partnerships against discrimination among minority groups, and the contingent nature of their self-identification as racial or ethnic minorities. The goals of the groups involved in *Méndez* were divergent and even contradictory, and the participants adopted differing legal strategies to support their respective goals. The racial factor, which ostensibly united them, was at the center of their dispute. The final court decision, and the nature of the "victory" won by the minority groups, was laced with ambiguity and irony.

PREWAR RELATIONS BETWEEN JAPANESE AMERICANS
AND MEXICAN AMERICANS

For both Japanese Americans and Mexican Americans in California, the roots of the postwar years and the *Méndez* case can be found in the Immigration Act of 1924, which severely restricted European immigration to the United States and completely barred immigration from Japan. In the years following passage of the act, ethnic Japanese (Nikkei) communities in California, home to some 70 percent of mainland Japanese Americans, remained stigmatized by nativist prejudice. Issei immigrants were forbidden to own agricultural land or become naturalized citizens, while their native-born Nisei children, although U.S. citizens, were subjected to widespread economic discrimination and antimiscegenation laws. In a few areas, notably the districts of Florin and Walnut Grove near Sacramento, Nisei children were required by law to attend separate "oriental" public schools, although Nisei schoolchildren in Los Angeles, which then as now housed the largest Japanese American colony in the United States, with some 30,000 people, attended integrated schools.[4]

Japanese American communities divided over the response to such discrimination. Issei continued to favor close ties with Japan, and large numbers sent their children back to their old homeland to be educated. The Japanese consulates in West Coast cities such as Los Angeles served as both institutional hubs and centers of community organization, especially for protest against discrimination. However, a handful of Nisei organizations challenged their elders for dominance in Japanese communities. Chief among these groups was the JACL, founded in 1930. The JACL restricted its membership to American citizens, and its leaders advocated a platform of Americanization, including exclusive loyalty to the United States and protest against anti-Japanese discrimination through the defense of citizenship rights. JACL leaders strenuously rejected any suggestion that their Japanese ancestry made them in any way different from other Americans.

Meanwhile, immigration from the Americas, especially Mexico, remained unrestricted throughout the 1920s. During the years that followed 1924, waves of Mexicans were drawn or recruited to work in the United States, notably in California, whose population of Mexican ancestry more than tripled. During the Depression years, the Mexican American population of Southern California continued to grow—although much more slowly—despite the imposition of immigration restrictions and the deportation of tens of thousands or hundreds of thousands of Mexicans and Mexican American citizens as supposedly "illegal" aliens. The vast majority of the new immigrants settled in Southern California. Most took up jobs in agricultural areas, where local farmers (whites as well as some Japanese Americans) sought laborers to pick their crops.[5] Others settled in urban areas, with Los Angeles ranking as the largest—the 1940 U.S. Census counted 219,000 people of Mexican ancestry in Los Angeles area, of whom 65,000 were Mexican-born.[6]

The expansion of the Mexican American population was matched by a heightening of barriers of inequality against them. Although Mexican Americans, unlike Asian Americans, were not targeted by race-based legislation such as antimiscegenation statutes, they were nonetheless forced to live in segregated barrios and sometimes excluded by local ordinance or custom from public facilities such as swimming pools and stores.[7] Mexican Americans were frequently placed in separate and markedly inferior "Mexican" schools.[8] Significantly, although California law did not list children of Mexican ancestry as a group that could be segregated, white educators and school psychologists in Southern California believed Mexican American children to be inferior and thus in need of "Americanization"—that is, assimilation to United States values and customs—more than a traditional academic education. They also used linguistic differences as a pretext for segregation.

Mexican American groups tried repeatedly to contest such discrimination. As with Japanese Americans, Mexican consulates were at the center of such community organization, and operated to defend the rights of Mexican nationals and their children. In 1931, parents of Mexican American children in Lemon Grove, with aid from the Mexican consulate in San Diego, brought legal action and won a writ of mandate from the Superior Court in California admitting the children to the "white" school.[9] However, the ruling in the Lemon Grove case did not seem to have set a precedent for other school districts, and Mexican Americans in the Los Angeles area continued to attend segregated schools. Similarly, in nearby Orange County, where Mexican American children accounted for 25 percent of the school population, some 70 percent were attending predominantly segregated elementary schools by 1934.[10] In contrast, the entire ethnic Japanese population of Orange County by 1940 was only 1,855, and the small fraction of Nisei children in the student population attended "white" schools.[11]

Like Japanese Americans, Mexican Americans went back and forth between identification with their home country and claiming equal rights based on their American citizenship. The leading citizens' group was LULAC. Founded in Texas at the end of the 1920s, LULAC was an organization headed by young lawyers and middle-class professionals who favored "Americanization." Like the JACL, its membership was restricted to citizens of the United States. During the 1930s, LULAC instituted legal action challenging the placement of Mexican Americans in segregated schools in Texas, with mixed results.[12] In 1941, two Mexican American families in Los Angeles County's Ranchito school district whose children had been barred from the district's new elementary school and forced to attend an older school in another district filed suit with help from LULAC. In order to illustrate the injustice of the segregation, they pointed to the fact that Nisei students in the district enrolled freely in the new school.[13] The suit failed—Superior Court judge Emmet Wilson ruled that the school board had the power to assign children as it saw fit, and declared the placement of Nisei children irrelevant.

During these years, Japanese Americans and Mexican Americans were often thrown together into close contact. There were overlapping enclaves all along the border in such locations as San Diego–Tijuana and Brownsville-Matamoros. A Columbia University geography professor noted that the adjoining cities of Calexico, California, and Mexicali, Mexico, housed transiting populations. While he claimed that all the stores, even Mexican-owned ones, were located in Calexico, he added with some exaggeration, "Mexicali is chiefly peopled by Japanese and Chinese who cannot be admitted to the United States." A large number of Japanese landowners were expelled from the Mexicali region by the Mexican government in 1937.[14]

There was also contact on a more troubled and unequal basis. In the rich farmlands of California such as the Imperial Valley, Mexican immigrant laborers toiled alongside Japanese immigrant farmhands on white-owned farms, even as small Issei farmers leasing land from whites employed Mexican American and Japanese American men (and, more rarely, women) as a source of cheap labor. As historians such as Gilbert Gonzalez and Tomas Almaguer have shown, class conflicts between members of the two groups often played out along ethnic and national lines. A classic case is the El Monte Berry Strike of 1933, where Mexican American and Japanese American workers struck after their wages were reduced by a Japanese American farmers' cooperative, under pressure from white landowners. The growers resisted and sometimes brought in Nisei as strikebreakers, aggravating the bad feelings between the two groups. The Mexican consulate took charge of advocating for the strikers and, ignoring Japanese American workers, called for a boycott of Japanese stores. The ethnic Japanese press, including the English-language pages run by the Nisei, opposed the strikers as radicals.[15]

At the same time, there was significant interaction in Pacific Coast cities such as San Francisco and Los Angeles between the pockets of Nisei and Chicano residents. In these cities, where poverty and restrictive racial covenants effectively kept nonwhites confined in particular districts, a number of Issei settled in homes alongside Latinos (and African Americans) in areas such as Boyle Heights and Little Tokyo. Japanese-operated groceries and restaurants served a mixed clientele. Nisei children attended school and joined in street life and sporting activities with their neighbors.[16] Nisei and Chicano music enthusiasts frequented jazz clubs, while musicians on the West Coast regularly played together in interracial groups. For example, Sak "Francisco" Yamashita, a Nisei from Alameda, was a drummer and vocalist with the Cervantes Mexican orchestra during the late 1930s, playing Mexican jazz.[17] Although the prewar Japanese American press was sometimes condescending in its reports on Mexican Americans as welfare dependent, newspapers prominently featured the Ranchito school case. Nisei columnist Tad Uyeno stated: "We cannot view with apathy any unjust and discriminatory regulations imposed upon the minority racial elements in this country.... Children of Latin descent must not be segregated in separate schools. Let's be sure we stand united to defend equality for all people."[18]

EFFECTS OF WORLD WAR II

The Mexican American Community

The Second World War was a defining moment for Southern California's Mexican American community, though in a different way than for Japanese Americans. By 1940, the majority of the ethnic Mexicans in the United States were American citizens, and they came of age during the war years. Nationwide, as many as 350,000 Mexican Americans, of whom Californians were a significant fraction, served in the armed forces. As was true for the Nisei, the distinguished military service record of Mexican American GIs bolstered the community's self-confidence and sharpened its awareness of unequal treatment for its members.[19] Meanwhile, as a result of wartime labor shortages, tens of thousands of Mexican American workers were hired for jobs in U.S. shipyards and other war industries—17,000 in the Los Angeles shipyards alone by 1944.[20]

Mexican Americans and Japanese Removal

Mexican American communities were also touched by the government's removal of Japanese Americans. Because the Mexican American population was so large—Mexicans were by far California's largest minority group by 1941—and varied, it is impossible to speak of a single community attitude, particularly in the absence of any definite institutional community response. The reactions of a few outstanding individuals were recorded. Ralph Lazo, a young man of mixed Mexican and Irish extraction, was incensed that his Nisei classmates were forced into camps, and he chose to accompany his friends into incarceration at Manzanar, where he remained for two years. The future war hero Guy Gabaldon, who was taken in by a Japanese American family as a child, wrote to his foster family and visited them in camp. Gilbert Sanchez, a teenager in Boyle Heights during the war, remembered his sense of outrage over the removal of Japanese Americans, and he later offered vocal support to the movement for redress.[21] There were also less positive attitudes. Future congressman Edward Roybal later recalled being a student and attending a mass meeting about the roundup. According to Roybal, he was "the only one who stood up to oppose this drastic action, warning the people they would regret this terrible thing of wartime hysteria." Roybal added that he "was booed, hissed, and had so much debris thrown his way that he had to leave the hall."[22] Actor Leo Carrillo, a member of an old *Californio* family who was famous for his role in the film/television series *The Cisco Kid*, may have helped fuel popular prejudice with his public letter of January 6, 1942. In the letter, he termed West Coast Japanese Americans a "menace" and called for their mass removal inland.

LA OPINIÓN COVERS EVACUATION

The shifting and discordant attitudes of Mexican Americans toward the removal and incarceration of Japanese Americans during 1942 were displayed in force through the coverage of the events by the Spanish-language press, the community's most visible and arguably most influential center of opinion. In particular, there was a marked division in the coverage of events by two sister newspapers, the Texas-based daily *La Prensa* and the Los Angeles daily *La Opinión*. *La Prensa*, founded in 1913 by a youthful Mexican immigrant, Ignacio Lozano, was designed as the voice of "Mexico Afuera" (that is, the Mexican diaspora). *La Prensa* provided an episodic but sympathetic account of Japanese Americans. Such was not the case of *La Opinión*, which offered a comprehensive and largely anti-Japanese American account of removal. *La Opinión*, founded by Lozano in 1926 as a satellite of his earlier newspaper, had by 1930 reached an official circulation figure of 25,000, exceeding that of *La Prensa*, and it continued to expand throughout the Depression years. Although both journals were primarily Mexican newspapers, whose reporting stressed news from Mexico and only slowly began to cover community affairs, they remained a major force in the lives of Mexican Americans. That said, while *La Prensa* frequently took up the defense of the rights of Mexican immigrants and their children, *La Opinión* was a more conservative journal that spoke primarily for various elites within the ethnic population and remained closely connected to the local Mexican consulate. While its editors also denounced discrimination against people of Mexican origin, its editorial line promoted assimilation and denounced oppositional figures such as *pachucos* as gang members and thugs.

One striking aspect of the coverage of removal in *La Prensa* is the division between its own reporters, who were generally favorable to a persecuted minority, and the comments of outside non-Latino columnists (whose dispatches were translated from English). Its coverage began on January 11 with a brief note stating that an American-born Japanese had launched a campaign to raise $50,000 with the goal of buying an antiaircraft cannon for the American government.[23] Soon after, an article listed all the "alien" groups that had written President Roosevelt to express their support for the war effort, including the Hawaiian-Japanese Civic Association and the Anti-Axis Committee of the JACL.[24] Two weeks later, *La Prensa* reported that alien enemies had been barred from certain restricted areas. Although it repeated various expressed anti-Japanese comments, it made clear that these were the opinions of Californians, not accepted fact:

> Among the plans suggested by the County Board of Los Angeles is that all Japanese residing in California less than 50 miles from the Mexican border or from the ocean be transferred to sugar beet fields in the Rocky Mountains. This proposal includes all persons of Japanese blood, whether American citizens or not. In whatever case, [the Board] agreed, something must be done, not only because there exist possibilities or probabilities of sabotage, but also to avoid the racial war with which California is threatened, inasmuch as approximately 150 Japanese have been assassinated by Filipinos in the Imperial Valley and San Joaquin valley. This information was provided by State officer William D. Cecil.[25]

Moreover, as if to underline their own skepticism, a week later, in the wake of Executive Order 9066, the journal published a long dispatch from New York extolling the model Americanism of the Japanese Americans. It offered "demonstrable proof" that more than nine-tenths of the ethnic Japanese population were loyal. The author reminded readers that more than 2,500 Nisei were serving in the U.S. armed forces, and added that Issei and Nisei had accepted with good grace the special burdens already placed on them:

> When Japanese shops in New York were closed, their owners, like the rest of the 600 Japanese in the city, laid the blame on the militarist party in their country. "I would rather go to a concentration camp in America than to return to Japan," says one member of the Japanese colony, summarizing the majority sentiment among his compatriots. In Los Angeles, where almost all the 23,321 Japanese of Little Tokyo previously opposed aid to China, the Nippons proclaim insistently today "We are with America!" And the Japanese businesses of California display signs like the following: "Property of an American Citizen" or "I am an American and I'm proud of it!"[26]

The article concluded that if other American countries could expect similar loyalty from their Japanese populations, it would be useful to start a Free Japan movement (on the model of the Free French).[27] In this same mode, a final positive article appeared two weeks later. *La Prensa* reported that a group of Nisei soldiers at Camp Roberts were contributing to the war effort by teaching their white comrades martial arts. Meanwhile, Private Yoshio Nakazawa was instructing his colleagues in the rudiments of Japanese language. "In this way, he and his fellow Japanese Americans in our army are helping the United States prepare to fight more effectively against Japanese militarism."[28]

La Prensa thereafter published only a handful of articles from outside correspondents. In late March Stanton Delaplane, a columnist for the *San Francisco Chronicle*, reported on the deathly fear that Californians felt of ethnic Japanese among them—which he said exceeded their fear of all of Japan. He asserted (rather inaccurately) that they were moving inland to sugar beet farms, and provided further misinformation on the nature of the restrictions imposed on them: "They all must move 100 miles inland. Another zone was created 100 miles inland, where there are numerous restrictions on their movements. The violation of any of the innumerable list of laws regarding movements is an automatic ticket to a concentration camp for the entire duration of the war."[29] A month later, a British correspondent, Joseph Kalmer, relying on baseless reports from the West Coast press, charged that the Japanese Americans were a fifth column: "It is possible that the hundreds of Japanese who federal agents detained in California, Oregon, Washington, Arizona and elsewhere were originally innocent laundrymen or truck farmers, but in their houses were discovered firearms, munitions in large quantities. Dynamite, swastika and Japanese flags, cameras, shortwave transmitters, signal lamps, maps, code books etc. This is not so innocent, we must say."[30] Despite this airing of suspicion, *La Prensa* did not call for mass action against Japanese Americans, nor even see fit to provide any news that West Coast Japanese Americans had actually been removed from their homes and confined until the end of October, when the editors ran a story on the camp at Manzanar.[31]

If *La Prensa*, as mentioned, paid only limited attention to events, *La Opinión*'s pages echoed the saturation coverage, much of it distorted, by the mainstream West Coast press. Its accounts began rather later than *La Prensa*'s and ignored the positive stories its sister publication had carried, even those from the West Coast. Instead, its coverage began with the announcement on January 27, 1942, that the Navy Department had decided to evacuate the 3,000 Japanese Americans inhabiting Terminal Island in Los Angeles Harbor. Two days later, upon the release of the Robert Commission's official investigatory report on Pearl Harbor, which spoke of prewar Japanese espionage activities (though without making any actual charge of complicity by Issei and Nisei), *La Opinión* reported that a movement had begun to remove Japanese from the coast to the interior of the country. It presented the evacuation as a necessary precaution, "to prevent enemy aliens from committing acts of sabotage or espionage."[32] In support of this assertion, it cited one "Yasuchi Sakamoto, a Japanese born in California who is the Secretary of the Japanese Fishermen's Association of Southern California," as agreeing with "the movement that is being organized to concentrate all Japanese in a camp in the interior of the United States." According to Sakamoto, "If I was an American citizen of the white race, living presently in Japan, I would not expect that they would permit me to reside near national defense installations."[33]

Despite its approval of a *limpia*—"cleaning up"—of the coast, the newspaper expressed sympathy with the ordinary people whose lives were affected. An article dated February 3 recounted a police raid on Issei enemy aliens at Terminal Island. The 500 aliens arrested, the newspaper explained, would be granted hearings, and those who were not released would be given the option of remaining interned in a camp for the entire duration of the war or leaving the United States:

The time that it took for the Nippons to be apprehended was filled with drama: because there were many cases such as that of Mrs. Saito, who could not hold back her tears at the sight of the police taking her husband away. In another case a child opened the door, the detectives asked for the head of the family, he responded that he was asleep, and the representatives of the authorities said that they would wake him and wait there until he had dressed and breakfasted and was ready.[34]

The next day, the newspaper underlined the powerlessness of those arrested in the headline: "All they can say is 'Shakatagani'" (*shikataganai*, the editors explained, was the equivalent of the Spanish phrase *que le vamos a hacer*).[35]

Meanwhile, as if to balance its coverage, *La Opinión* ran a positive front-page story on a Nisei doctor, Tsutayo Ichioka. It described her as the "wife of Dr. Toshio Ichioka, well known in our community," who "following a voyage to the east of the county, where she studied and practiced in the most famous hospitals," was opening a new office.[36] (Perhaps not coincidentally, the Drs. Ichioka, who ran a clinic open to poor Hispanic and other patients, continued to advertise regularly in the pages of *La Opinión* until they were forced to close their office in May.)

In the crucial two weeks that followed, pressure began to mount from army officials and political leaders in California for removal of all Japanese Americans, whether enemy aliens or American citizens. The pressure brought the issue into the White House and led President Franklin Roosevelt to approve mass removal, signing Executive Order 9066 on February 19. During those two weeks, *La Opinión* did not express enormous concern with the situation in California. It reported three times on the removal of residents on Terminal Island and ran an article a few days later on a raid of Shinto priests in which "pro-Japanese propaganda" was confiscated.[37] It also recounted the February 7 speech in which Los Angeles mayor Fletcher Bowron had accused Japanese Americans of making the city a center of sabotage and called for mass removal.[38] On February 21, it reported the arrest of more than 100 aliens in Orange County, and noted that the mayor of Long Beach and the Southern California League of Cities were urging the immediate evacuation of all Japanese, even those native-born or naturalized (forgetting there were virtually no such naturalized citizens). The newspaper reported as fact an official press statement from the league claiming that a rice paper parachute with two small electric batteries connected to a lamp had been discovered in Anaheim, while a fantasy Japanese lantern with matching candle had been located on the roof of a building that housed various Orange County offices. There were no photos or proof adduced to support these fantastic stories.[39]

However, during this crucial period the editors focused their attention not only on events in California but also on the asserted Japanese invasion threat and the menace of local Japanese subversion elsewhere. On February 9, *La Opinión* discussed the danger represented by the 50,000 Japanese residents in Peru. Four days later, the paper ran a news service story quoting Mitchell Hepburn, premier of Ontario, Canada, who predicted that Japan's navy would invade Canada within three months: "We are facing 1020 million land-hungry Asians," Hepburn stated, "who, united under a possible realignment of nations, are being positioned under the able direction of the Japanese."[40]

The center of the coverage was the perceived threat to Mexico. Ironically, however, the Mexican government's decision to expel Mexican Japanese from the Pacific coast went unrecorded by the newspaper. First, during the first weeks of 1942, raids were carried out on Japanese communities in Mexico City. Numerous Issei were arrested without charge and sent to an internment camp at Perote. Meanwhile, on January 5, 1942, Mexico's federal government issued an order for all residents of Japanese ancestry in Baja California to leave the state. Some 2,800 Mexican Japanese, including the bulk of landowners in the Mexicali region, were forced to fill out "voluntary relocation applications" and move at least 100 miles from the coastal area at their own expense. They were given only ten days to settle their affairs, and only a few of their Mexican wives and mixed-race children were permitted to stay. Their homes and businesses, including the rich cotton plantations, were taken over by local Mexicans, with no compensation offered.[41] Ultimately 80 percent of Japanese Mexicans were forced to remove themselves to Mexico City or Guadalajara. By the time that *La Opinión* began its coverage of Mexican Japanese on February 2, the largest communities had been destroyed. *La Opinión* noted that Japanese workers in Mexican industries were being fired from their jobs, and two days later that 5,000 aliens had been told to register with the government. On February 14, a banner headline told of a declaration by the Union of Mexican Railroad Workers in Guadalajara and Sinaloa, saying that they had obtained trustworthy information on the precise dates for a planned Japanese invasion of Mexico, preparatory to an attack on the United States. The article spoke of the danger of subversive aliens in the area:

> The activities of fifth columnists will be to blow up bridges and destroy roads, to prevent help from arriving from the United States. . . . The

document urges the concentration of all Germans, Italians and Japanese living in the western part of the country into camps to be established in Yucatan or near the American border, where they can be closely watched.[42]

When General Garay, the chief of staff of Mexico's army, responded that the declaration represented nothing but "morbid fantasies [and] unfounded alarms," *La Opinión* published an editorial scolding him for taking threats too lightly; it asserted that if Japan conquered Oceania and Hawaii, an attack on Mexico would be next, since the U.S. coast was too well defended.[43]

La Opinión's coverage of the Japanese "problem" in Mexico ceased entirely in mid-March, after Mexico announced the removal of the remaining Japanese residents of its Pacific Coast states. Unlike the press inside Mexico, it did not include any coverage of the caravans that Japanese Mexicans formed to travel to Mexico City and Guadalajara, or the great hardships experienced by these refugees, who had lost their property and been forced to resettle in new and unknown areas with no government assistance. It is naturally impossible to know what was in the minds of *La Opinión*'s editors. However, the sudden cutoff suggests that they were less absorbed than they claimed about the Japanese invasion menace, once it was no longer needed as a pretext for removing Issei and Nisei. Furthermore, the resounding silence of *La Opinión* on the fate of the Japanese Mexicans suggests either that they were indifferent to the plight of the refugees or that they were advised by the Mexican officials responsible for expulsion not to arouse sympathy for them.

In notable contrast, from mid-March through early May 1942 there were articles about Japanese Americans on approximately a daily basis, plus photographs and wire service dispatches. Part of the coverage was devoted to continuous stories of raids and arrests of suspicious individuals, but most of it told of the opening of a concentration camp (as the newspaper repeatedly and unashamedly referred to it) at Manzanar and the transporting of the Japanese Americans to it, as well as the temporary housing at the Santa Anita racetrack for those awaiting removal inland. Three continuing themes dominated *La Opinión*'s coverage: the guilt of the Japanese Americans and the justice of the government's actions, their good treatment by the government and their approval of incarceration, and the impact on Mexican Americans. While the historian can once again only speculate, it seems logical to conclude that the cutoff of news on Japanese Mexicans and the switch to large-scale coverage of the "evacuation" of

Japanese American districts were connected. The tone of the coverage, moreover, strongly suggests that *La Opinión* was motivated to defend arbitrary official treatment of Japanese Americans at least in part by its connections to Mexican officials and its desire not to criticize the Mexican government's parallel actions toward Issei and Nisei.

Whatever the case, the first visible comment on Japanese Americans in the wake of Executive Order 9066 came on March 19, with the running of a photo under the headline "Evacuation of Foreigners." The photo's caption read, "Mrs. Alice Tatsuni of San Francisco California, one of the aliens affected."[44] On March 25, a translated reprint of a wire service story noted that a thousand Japanese had been transferred to Manzanar, and it (falsely) described them as "victims of the fifth columnists of Pearl Harbor. Since their race was made worthy of suspicion by the revelation of defense secrets in Hawaii to the Japanese Navy, so began the exile of all persons of Japanese race on the Pacific Coast, for the duration of the war."[45]

A week later, *La Opinión* published the same article by *San Francisco Chronicle* columnist Stanton Delaplane that had appeared in *La Prensa*. The version in *La Opinión* explicitly linked the removal of Japanese Americans and that of Japanese Mexicans. After claiming that there were 200,000 enemy aliens on the coast "including Nisei and sansei" (thereby not only confounding citizens and aliens but also nearly doubling the actual figure), he affirmed that they all needed to be moved because they were a source of great danger, as was proved by their conduct:

> Mexico is also cleaning its coastline of Japanese as well as its border with the United States. There is no doubt that the sheep must be separated from the goats. Civil Liberties are respected as much as possible, and once they are suspended they [the Japanese] hardly represent a danger.[46]

Another central theme in *La Opinión*'s coverage was the fine treatment offered the Japanese Americans and their cooperation. Its editors, it is true, carried in early March a story of a Nisei, Richard Suenaga, who was rushed to the hospital after he tried to kill himself, saying in a note, "I do not want to be sent to any concentration camp in which I will be treated like a foreigner." Nevertheless, the newspaper's dominant tone was extremely positive about what it called the "adventure" of evacuation, and its editors underlined the excitement of those being removed. For example, in its account of the first "caravan" of Japanese Americans to Manzanar (which did not mention the armed guards, closed overheated trains, or lack of bathroom facilities experienced by the travelers), the newspaper waxed lyrical:

The Japanese, among whom are also those born in the United States, lent all their cooperation to the authorities to ease their mobilization, and some of them showed their enthusiasm for this adventure of going to colonize a "Little Tokyo" in the heart of the mountains of Owens Valley.... Each group of 10 automobiles goes under the direction of a Japanese leader under the orders of military authorities, and for each 250 voyagers goes a Japanese doctor. One of these, Dr. George Kawaichi, commented while leaving, "This is a very good step for all those affected. I believe that the Japanese will live happily in their new residence."[47]

La Opinión rang a more complex, if overall positive, note in a pair of columns in May. In the first, it described the departure for camp of a convoy of 1,500 Japanese, whom it described as "aliens and North American subjects by the fact of being born here," and the farewell offered by groups from the Methodist Church, to which many Issei and Nisei belonged:

> If it had not been for the police authorities intervening to hurry up the exit of the automobiles, the leaving of this group would have seemed like a Sunday excursion.... As they went, the expatriates did not utter even a sole complaint, which gave cause for both rejoicing and worry to Reverend Miller, pastor of the Methodist Universal Church, who well knows that behind the jubilation of those leaving for Manzanar burns distress over the goods they are abandoning.[48]

A week later *La Opinión* covered the departure of the last Japanese Americans from the Los Angeles area. In its coverage, it tacitly revealed the mendacious, or at least partial, nature of its previous article:

> In a contrast to the sad parting of the first groups of Japanese evacuated from this zone, a spirit of joy prevailed yesterday in Pasadena Station where 1,000 Japanese from the districts of Pasadena, Glendale and Foothill boarded trains that will take them to concentration centers in Pomona and Tulare.[49]

On April 11, *La Opinión* ran an extended news-service column on Manzanar, entitled "An Example of Democracy Is the Concentration of Nippons in the Owens Valley Camp," that made the "assembly center" sound like a holiday camp:

> The American way in Owens Valley is very different, to a high degree, from the methods of the dictators of interning enemy aliens behind strands of barbed wire, or to drive them like cattle into brigades of forced labor. The American way is the Owens Valley in the State of California.... An area of 6000 acres of land in Owens Valley will be the temporary home of no less than 10000 Japanese. Work will be

given to all residents. Some of them will be assigned to agricultural labor, others will pack fruits and vegetables. A third group will make furniture for the apartments.

It is up to the project to maintain an extensive recreation program, based on baseball and other sports, and filmmaking.

A primary and secondary school will be established, and there will be Sunday religious services for those who wish to attend.

The entire responsibility for the maintaining of order inside the Owens Valley center will be in the hands of the residents themselves. They will establish a set of rules, including that whoever leaves the colony will not be readmitted.[50]

La Opinión also expressed approval of the "assembly center" at Santa Anita. In April it cited "Colonel Earl [sic] R. Bendetsen, deputy head Chief of Staff of the Wartime Civil and Military Administration, who denounced the false rumors circulating to the effect that the conditions of the evacuees at Santa Anita are 'undesirable.'" *La Opinión* clearly agreed with Bendetsen. In a caption for a pair of photos some weeks later, it described the idyllic life of the inmates at Santa Anita, with shots of children playing and housewives drying bedsheets:

Very different from the Nazi concentration camps, where alien enemies are tortured, and go hungry until they die at the hands of their executioners, is the life led by the 18500 Japanese in the Santa Anita concentration camp. Accommodated in wooden houses on the grounds of the beautiful Santa Anita racetrack, the Nippons and their families live like at home.[51]

One consuming interest of *La Opinión* in its coverage was in what the removal of Japanese Americans could mean for Mexican Americans. One of the newspaper's first pieces after February 19 noted that Andley Harris, a Los Angeles geophysical analyst, had proposed to Mayor Bowron that Mexican field workers be granted financial aid to establish themselves in California and replace the Japanese in the vegetable fields.[52] In April, the newspaper commented that Karl Bendetsen had insisted that Japanese Americans be removed as soon as possible, and that it would not be possible to await the 1942 harvest.

Bendetsen's declaration came at the same time that it became easier for thousands of Mexicans, Filipinos, and other aliens of non-enemy nations to obtain government loans to acquire the lands of the Japanese.... The officers of the WCCA tell us that 4173 farms, with 157,755 acres, have been handed over to new owners, who have obtained loans amounting to more than $1,000,000. There are still some 2000 farms which are still to change hands. Currently more than

5200 farmers have presented their applications to obtain the Japanese lands. Included in this group are various Mexicans.

The opportunities are numerous, and they offer enormous profits to members of our group.[53]

A rare editorial the same day encapsulated the newspaper editors' gratification that Japanese American laborers, whom *La Opinión* called enemies of the nation, had been removed, as this would open up opportunities for the Chicanos:

> The conversion of Mexican farm workers (who today expend their efforts in the creation of riches for actual or potential enemies of the United States) into small landowners or leaseholders with the absolute right to the fruit of their efforts, would bring about a new and essential way of life to the masses of our laborers residing in the country. It is to be hoped that this opportunity that is now being presented to the majority of Mexicans will be properly taken advantage of, and that it will signal a praiseworthy elevation in their life style as well as the possibility of achieving economic independence.[54]

In sum, the coverage of Japanese American removal in *La Opinión* revealed a fundamental incoherence, or perhaps ambivalence. On one hand, the numerous scare stories, which resembled those in the mainstream press, revealed the editors' fears of Japanese infiltration on the American continent. Indeed, unlike most mainstream (Anglo) newspapers, the journal extended its coverage beyond national borders and connected the threat of ethnic Japanese in the United States with that of those in Mexico. In regard to both countries (and, in one case, Canada as well), its editors uncritically passed on unfounded stories of Japanese invasion threats or sabotage. In keeping with this posture, throughout its coverage *La Opinión* never questioned the constitutionality of Executive Order 9066 or the wisdom of mass removal. No doubt in part because they were dependent on official handouts for news, its editors were led to accept the official characterization of Japanese Americans as alternately dangerous and happy with confinement; indeed, the editors did their best to portray the camps as well equipped and friendly and Japanese Americans as excited and happy with their lot. At the same time, its editors did express sympathy for individuals, and a certain regret for the emptying out of Little Tokyo.

Still, the nature of *La Opinión*'s coverage, especially when set against that of *La Prensa*, suggests that its editors were motivated not only by (dual) patriotism or fear of the Japanese military but also by greed and land hunger, mixed with a wish to settle old scores with Japanese Americans. *La Prensa* long insisted on the loyalty of Japanese Americans and did not address the idea of Mexican Americans taking over their properties. In contrast, the prejudices of the Los Angeles journal's editors clearly showed through in spots. For example, unlike its Texas counterpart, *La Opinión* did not distinguish between Japanese immigrants and U.S.-born citizens of Japanese ancestry. All the same, in one feature article, "Little Tokyo Is Dead," a columnist expressed genuine feelings of sorrow:

> As for the relations between Mexicans and Japanese in this country, where our workers are concerned there is enough material for a large book, especially in regard to the Japanese who are leaving. The traditional "mom-and-pop" store . . . will pass for a long time into history, leaving behind a void in the soul of our people, since many of them speak Spanish, especially the children. And this may surprise you, reader, but reciprocity obliges us to note that many Mexicans, especially in the border regions, speak Japanese.[55]

AFTER REMOVAL
Wartime Prejudice Against Mexican Americans

In the end, the mass removal of Japanese Americans so warmly promoted by *La Opinión* bore only limited fruit for Mexican Americans in California. Mexican farm workers were in fact able to acquire or operate a small percentage of the abandoned lands; more visibly, the agricultural labor shortage in California caused the federal government to develop the Bracero Program, which brought hundreds of thousands of poor laborers from northern Mexico to work in the fields of California and the Southwest, often under exploitative conditions. As a result, the Mexican American population swelled. On the other hand, the Mexican community, in its turn, was exposed to outbreaks of wartime bigotry. Writer Carey McWilliams later opined that white Californians, having succeeded in getting rid of the hated Japanese Americans, were fortified in their prejudice and turned on Mexican Americans as new scapegoats for their frustrations.

In August 1942, after José Díaz, a young Mexican American, was found dead on a road in Sleepy Lagoon, on the outskirts of Los Angeles, detectives instituted mass arrests of Mexican Americans. Twenty of these arrestees were subsequently brought to trial, in an atmosphere marked by baseless newspaper stories of a "Mexican" crime wave and a presiding judge later found by a higher court to have been biased against the defendants. Although no proof was ever presented that Diaz had been murdered, let alone by any of those charged, twelve of the defendants were found guilty of murder and eight of lesser offenses by an all-Anglo jury.[56] In June 1943, following a long campaign of sensationalist stories in the popular Hearst press about the depredations of Mexican American gang members in "zoot suits," white Anglo soldiers and sailors went on a rampage, seizing young Mexican American (plus some African American and Filipino) *pachucos*, beating them, and stripping them of their clothing. Local police then arrested the victims.[57]

In response to these events, Mexican American activists from groups such as the Spanish-Speaking People's Congress and the Coordinating Council for Latin-American Youth sought to combat discrimination and lessen ethnic tensions through lobbying and public education campaigns and by forging coalitions with Anglo liberals, and especially with African Americans. For example, Charlotta Bass, editor of the black newspaper *California Eagle*, organized the Sleepy Lagoon Defense Committee.[58] Japanese Americans from Los Angeles also expressed support for Mexican Americans and denounced the verdict. A group of Japanese American schoolchildren at Manzanar, learning of the case in their social studies class, collected $10, which they contributed to the Sleepy Lagoon Defense Fund. An editorial in the camp newspaper warmly, if somewhat condescendingly, commented: "The maladjusted, socially ostracized, misunderstood group of 219,000 Mexican Americans in Los Angeles had lived in what social investigators had repeatedly described as disadvantaged areas. The authorities ignored this until the war broke out and the murder in August 1942 forced attention on this group."[59]

Postwar Differences Between Japanese Americans and Mexican Americans

The post–Pearl Harbor internment of influential Issei community leaders and the subsequent overall stigmatization of the Issei in the camps as "enemy aliens" left the Nisei with the chief responsibility for leading and representing the Japanese American community. The JACL, partly as a result of its (still-controversial) decision to cooperate with the federal government in executing the removal and confinement of Japanese Americans, emerged during the war years as the dominant Nisei voice, and it dominated the political life of the entire community afterward. Yet the JACL perceptibly shifted its platform at this time. While it became, if anything, even more committed than before the war to its Americanization program, the injustice of the government's wartime actions against the Japanese Americans, coupled with the spectacular military record of Japanese American GIs, made the JACL especially impatient to secure full citizenship rights for Nisei and eliminate further discrimination.[60] Under the leadership of counsel A. L. Wirin, a white Jewish Los Angeles lawyer, and his law partner, JACL president Saburo Kido, the JACL instituted lawsuits challenging California's Alien Land Act and its discriminatory commercial fishing laws.[61] Furthermore, in contrast to the pre–World War II era, Japanese Americans became active in interracial organizing. JACL leaders such as Larry Tajiri and Mike Masaoka and Japanese American newspapers such as the *Pacific Citizen*, the *Colorado Times*, and the *Utah Nippo* urged the Nisei to recognize that they were a minority group with the same problems as other racial and ethnic minorities, and that it was in their own self-interest to support civil rights for all. In July 1946, the JACL established a defense fund for civil rights litigation, including cases involving other minorities.[62] Significantly, a March 1947 *Pacific Citizen* article prominently reported a speech by Tets Kushida, the newly elected president of the organization's St. Louis chapter, in which he remarked that the JACL must work equally for the benefit of all minority groups. "An attack on one is an attack on all. We must be realistic and face facts. As long as we are a minority, we will have minority problems, and we must fight discrimination wherever it exists."[63]

The various Mexican American groups also grew more assertive in fighting for integration and defending civil rights following their wartime experience. As before World War II, a major vehicle of activism was LULAC. Along with the Coordinating Council for Latin-American Youth and the Federation of Hispanic American Voters, LULAC encouraged Mexican American parents in El Monte to demand educational equality for their children, and formed a lobbying campaign to persuade the California Assembly to repeal school segregation laws.[64] The *New York Times* reported that the Riverside school district abandoned its long-standing custom of segregated schools for African Americans and Mexican Americans in late 1946 under threat of a lawsuit by representatives of the latter group.[65]

However, Mexican American leaders chose to distance themselves from the nascent interracial coalitions and did not join in the multigroup legal struggle against "whites-only" restrictive housing covenants during the first postwar years. On the contrary, some Mexican Americans continued to reside in housing covered by such covenants. In February 1945, Superior Court judge Alfred E. Paonessa dismissed a suit by property owners in El Monte who sought to prevent Nellie Garcia from occupying property covered by a covenant barring occupancy by those of the "African and Asian race" and by "those of the Mexican race." At the request of David Marcus, Garcia's attorney, Paonessa ruled that no cause of action applied in the case since there was no "Mexican race."[66] Furthermore, LULAC and the other organizations did not coordinate their lobbying efforts against educational segregation with the JACL or the NAACP, even though Japanese Americans were still formally subject to separate schools under California law and many black children were required by local school districts to attend segregated schools.

Mexican American leaders, although they favored English over Spanish and supported assimilation, celebrated their Spanish-speaking heritage and ancestral culture. They nonetheless insisted that Mexicans were white.[67] They may have been fearful that associating with racial minority groups might lead to their being categorized as nonwhite and subjected to racial discrimination. Historian Mario Garcia has noted, for example, that the leaders of the Coordinating Council for Latin-American Youth rejected any suggestion that Mexican Americans were a "minority" and explicitly distanced themselves from African Americans:

> Fearing that any attempt to classify Mexicans as people of color might subject them to "legal" forms of discrimination and segregation, the Council rejected any implication that Mexicans were not white. The Council's insistence that Mexicans were white also appears to have stemmed from the historic ambivalence and insecurity of Mexicans on both sides of the border concerning their racial status. These feelings often led to a denial of possessing Indian blood.
>
> Council members . . . drew distinctions between Mexican Americans and Afro Americans as a way of trying to avoid the stigma of racial inferiority imposed on blacks. . . . [They] focused on ethnic rather than racial discrimination . . . [and] insisted that Mexicans were white and hence no different from other ethnic groups such as the Irish, Italians or Germans.[68]

In brief, then, Japanese Americans, who rejected any question of cultural specificity attached to their group heritage, nonetheless predominantly saw themselves as a racial minority, and sought to ally with other nonwhite groups. In contrast, Mexican Americans, who expressed pride in their distinctive ethnic and cultural legacy, conceived of themselves as white and refused interracial solidarity. Historian Neil Foley has commented that Mexican American leaders recognized that their citizenship rights depended on being able to claim that they were white:

> As whites of a different culture and color than most Anglo whites, many middle-class Mexicans learned early on that hostility to the idea of "social equality" for African Americans went right to the core of what constituted whiteness in the U.S. Whether or not they brought

with them from Mexico racial prejudice against blacks—and certainly many Mexicans did—middle-class Mexican leaders throughout the 1930s, 40s, and 50s went to great lengths to dissociate themselves socially, culturally, and politically from the early struggles of African Americans to achieve full citizenship rights in America.[69]

THE *MÉNDEZ* CASE

Origins

In September 1944, Gonzalo Méndez, a Mexican-born tenant farmer who had moved during the war to the town of Westminster in Orange County and settled on the property of an incarcerated Japanese American family, attempted to enroll his children at Westminster's "white" school, the 17th Street Elementary School.[70] School authorities refused to admit the children and ordered them enrolled in Hoover Elementary, the local "Mexican" school. Méndez joined forces with members of the Latin American Organization, a group of Latino World War II veterans in nearby Santa Ana angered over the segregation of their children. In March 1945, Méndez, William Guzman, Frank Palomino, Thomas Estrada, and Lorenzo Ramirez brought a lawsuit on behalf of their children and the 5,000 other children of "Mexican and Latin descent" in the four school districts of Orange County with segregated schools, seeking to challenge the discriminatory policy. Méndez and his co-complainants hired Los Angeles attorney David Marcus, who had previously defended Nellie Garcia in the restrictive covenant case against her, to represent them.

Marcus filed a petition alleging that the school districts' maintenance of separate schools deprived the petitioners of the educational benefits enjoyed by "white" or "Anglo" children solely because of their Mexican or Latin descent. It thus constituted arbitrary discrimination in violation of the due process and equal protection clauses of the Fourteenth Amendment to the United States Constitution and should be enjoined.[71] In their answer, the defendants claimed that the separation of pupils was practiced for the sole purpose of instructing the children of Mexican descent in the English language and was in their best interest.

Argument

The *Méndez* case was heard in late 1945 by senior district judge Paul J. McCormick of the federal district court in Los Angeles. The defendants aggressively moved to have the action dismissed for lack of subject matter jurisdiction. They argued that the lawsuit raised no federal issue, since education was exclusively a state matter, and that the school districts were governed under state law. The judge denied the motion and set the case down for trial. At the trial, David Marcus called as witnesses a number of educational and social science experts who testified that the segregation of Mexican American children as practiced by the defendants was both contrary to modern educational understanding and injurious to its victims. The petitioners also introduced evidence that directly contradicted the school boards' claims that segregation was necessitated by the alleged English-language deficiencies of the supposedly Spanish-speaking "Mexican" children.

Defense attorney Joel Ogle countered that the Supreme Court had long since settled in *Plessy v. Ferguson* (1896) that "separate but equal" racially segregated facilities were constitutional. Ogle introduced evidence showing that the physical facilities, teachers, and curricula afforded the Mexican American children were equal or even superior to those available to the Anglo children.

The Question of Race

During the trial, Marcus and Ogle entered into a crucial stipulation that race was not an issue in the case. The defendant school districts had initially argued that Mexican American children were not members of the white race, in connection with the argument that their segregation should be upheld under the precedent of *Plessy*. However, after one school official testified that the segregation was a necessary result of the inferiority of the Mexican American children to white children, and another spoke of the segregation as being based on the "social problem" created by the presence of the Mexican Americans, Ogle changed course.[72] Realizing that he had more to lose by presenting a policy based on open bigotry than from conceding that Mexican Americans were white, he agreed to stipulate that there was no question as to racial difference or racial segregation in the case. He thereafter defended the segregation solely as a rational response to the Mexican American children's alleged lack of proficiency in English.[73] Marcus and his clients, meanwhile, were well aware of the "social value of whiteness" and the potential detriment to Mexican Americans of being classed as a nonwhite "race."[74] Accordingly, they too agreed to the stipulation that the segregation of Mexican Americans was *not* a matter of racial discrimination.

The Lower Court Ruling

On February 18, 1946, Judge McCormick ruled in favor of the petitioners, finding that the school districts' actions violated their rights under both the Fourteenth Amendment to the U.S. Constitution and California state law. His decision took a powerful swipe at the constitutionality of race- or ancestry-based public school segregation. Such segregation, McCormick stated, hindered the Mexican American children from developing "a common cultural attitude ... which is imperative for the perpetuation of American institutions and ideals" and harmed them by "foster[ing] antagonisms in the children and suggest[ing] inferiority among them where none exists."[75] McCormick thus directly anticipated the language of future chief justice Earl Warren (then governor of California) eight years later in *Brown v. Board of Education*.[76] Moreover, Judge McCormick dared mention "social equality," a term (often associated with racial intermarriage) that was the bugaboo of segregationists:

> The equal protection of the laws ... is not provided by furnishing in separate schools the same technical facilities, text books and courses of instruction to students of Mexican ancestry that are available to the other public school children regardless of their ancestry. A paramount requisite in the American system of public education is social equality.[77]

Although Judge McCormick recognized that English-language deficiency was the only tenable ground on which segregation could be defended, he nevertheless found that it was not the true basis for the defendants' practices. The evidence showed, in fact, that the children were actually segregated on the basis of their "Mexican" or "Latinized" names, and in some cases their appearance. Damningly, Judge McCormick characterized the defendants' methods of determining language knowledge as "illusory." Such testing of children as was done to determine their English proficiency, he found, was "generally hasty, superficial and not reliable."[78] Further, while any English-deficient Mexican American children who were starting school could reasonably be segregated by classroom for special instruction for a short time, the defendant school districts maintained entirely separate schools for all Mexican American students through the sixth grade, and in two instances through the eighth grade—far longer than could possibly be justified by any alleged language deficiency. Indeed, "Spanish-speaking" children in "Mexican" schools were actually held back in learning English by their lack of exposure to its use.[79] Rather, he stated, it was clear that the defendants singled out Mexican American children as a class for segregation solely on the basis of their ancestry, a practice forbidden by the Education Law of California and a distinction "recently" declared by the United States Supreme Court to be "odious" and "utterly inconsistent with American tradition and ideals."[80]

THE *MÉNDEZ* APPEAL
Appellate Briefs and Arguments

Almost immediately after McCormick issued his judgment, the defendants filed an appeal with the Court of Appeals for the Ninth Circuit. Ogle argued that given McCormick's ruling that defendants' segregation practices were irreconcilable with California law, those practices could not be considered "state action" under the Fourteenth Amendment, so the federal courts had no jurisdiction over the case. Thus he effectively conceded that the policy was illegal, but claimed that this was a matter for the state courts to decide. David Marcus (joined by appellate attorney William Strong) emphasized Judge McCormick's finding that the defendants' discrimination was harmful to petitioners, as well as his conclusion that Mexican Americans were not a group for whom a school district could establish segregated schools under state law.[81] Although he noted McCormick's finding that segregated schools were unconstitutional, his argument rested primarily on the fact that Mexican Americans were not listed as a group that could be segregated. Similarly, during oral argument, Marcus rejected race as an issue:

> Marcus said there was no real racial question in this case, because Latins are Caucasians. But this, he went on, makes the discrimination even more dangerous; if condoned by the courts it could lead to discrimination on the ground of nationality, religion and social or economic position in all parts of the country.[82]

Public Comment

Even before oral argument was held, the case had begun to attract nationwide attention. Judge McCormick's ruling, with its departure from the courts' habitual dependence on physical equality of facilities, was widely commented upon in media reports and law journals.[83] The *New York Times* commented that *Méndez* was a "guinea pig case" on the issue of segregated schools and was being closely watched by representatives of other minority groups, and the *San Francisco Chronicle* called the case "one of the most important ever to come under Federal jurisdiction in this area."[84]

Writer/activist Carey McWilliams, reporting on the case for the *Nation*, added that if *Mendez* went to the U.S. Supreme Court, it could "sound the death knell of Jim Crow in education."[85] McWilliams asserted that the exclusion of race as an issue in the case was actually advantageous, because it meant that the courts could examine the effects of separate schools on children without their attention being diverted by arguments about racial difference: "With the 'racial issue' not directly involved, the court will be compelled to examine the social and educational consequences of segregated schools in a realistic manner." McWilliams also underlined the historic and multigroup nature of struggles against segregated schools in California by referring to the suit filed in federal court by President Theodore Roosevelt in 1907 to halt the San Francisco school board from segregating Japanese public school children.[86] The American Jewish Congress, hoping to arouse public interest in the case, financed the distribution of numerous reprints of McWilliams's article.

The Amicus Curiae Briefs

The widespread press coverage reflected the widespread belief that the *Méndez* case would set an important legal precedent. As a result, a number of different ethnic and political organizations moved to submit amici curiae briefs in support of the Mexican Americans. The briefs varied widely in their legal reasoning and in their strategies, but all differed significantly from those advanced by Marcus. The most powerful was that of the American Jewish Congress, which was drafted by African American lawyer Pauli Murray. It asked the Court of Appeals to overturn segregated schools as a violation not only of Fourteenth Amendment equal protection guarantees but also of federal government treaty obligations under the United Nations Charter. It urged the court to reject the *Plessy v. Ferguson* "separate but equal" standard. The brief asserted that segregation by official action of a group considered "inferior" according to prevailing community standards was "a humiliating and discriminatory denial of equality" to that group even if physical facilities were equal to those of the "better" group.[87] Another striking appellate amicus brief was filed by the attorney general of the state of California, Robert Kenny, who wished to maintain his reputation as a strong defender of the rights of minorities. Kenny likewise insisted that §§8003 and 8004 of the state's Educational Code violated the Fourteenth Amendment. Moreover, he cannily argued, even assuming that those school segregation laws were constitutional, the defendants' segregation practices were prohibited by the sections of the California Education Code that mandated free and universal admission of all children to the state's single standardized public school system. Nor did persons of Mexican descent fall into the single exception to that mandate by being expressly listed in the Education Code as a group for whom separate schools could be established.[88]

The JACL's Intervention

The JACL and NAACP also intervened on the side of Méndez. A. L. Wirin clearly felt that a straightforward attack on §§8003 and 8004 of the State Education Code was necessary. Ten days after *Méndez* was argued in the district court, the *Utah Nippo* reported that Wirin's firm had commenced a separate action, sponsored by the ACLU and the JACL, that directly challenged the constitutionality of the two statutes. The named plaintiff in that suit was Takao Aratani, a third-generation Japanese American and the son of a recently discharged Nisei GI. The complaint alleged that since the young Aratani and all other Japanese American schoolchildren in California (none of whom were in fact attending separate schools) could be removed at any time to segregated schools, they were being unconstitutionally discriminated against solely because of their race. The JACL suit infuriated Attorney General Robert Kenny. Perhaps as a result, just days later the Wirin firm withdrew the complaint, stating that the immediate purpose of the suit had already been achieved inasmuch as Kenny's amicus brief in the *Méndez* case had declared that the statutes in question were unconstitutional.[89]

Instead, Wirin and Kido sought and received permission from JACL leaders to place the organization's name on the joint amicus brief that Wirin and Kido had prepared on behalf of the Southern California ACLU, and which was submitted in the name of the ACLU and the National Lawyers Guild's Los Angeles chapter.[90] Although the JACL had never before intervened in a civil rights lawsuit involving other minority groups, Wirin and Kido were well aware that the symbolic presence of the Japanese Americans—just months after the end of their wartime ordeal—would be a potent signal to the court of the importance of the *Méndez* case and of the potential consequences of upholding inequality. The final brief listed the JACL, with A. L. Wirin and Saburo Kido "of counsel," as a participating organization.

As in their aborted lawsuit, Wirin and Kido went straight at the segregation clauses in the brief. While Marcus's primary contention was that the segregation of Mexican American children was unlawful because Mexican Americans were not listed as one of the named groups for whom separate schools could be created under the very explicit California school segregation statutes, Wirin and Kido argued that the school segregation laws—which continued to stigmatize Japanese Americans—were themselves unlawful and should be voided. Taking off from the NAACP brief (which Loren Miller had previously shared with Wirin), they began their argument by asserting that segregation on the basis of ancestry violated the Fourteenth Amendment. They contended that the amendment's equal protection clause protected citizens, aliens, and "all minorities, whether racial or religious, as well as Negro, for whom it was originally designed," and made void any law that discriminated against one of those groups unless there was a reasonable basis for singling that group out.[91] Wirin and Kido then referred to a second wartime case involving Japanese Americans, *Korematsu v. United States*, in which the Supreme Court had declared that "racial antagonism" could never justify restriction of civil rights. Using somewhat convoluted logic, they argued that such a declaration was authority for the proposition that the Constitution also forbade discrimination solely by reason of ancestry or national origin, and that it thereby protected Mexican Americans.[92] Wirin and Kido were careful to exclude any further mention of racial discrimination in their brief; instead, they thereafter focused exclusively on the unlawfulness of "arbitrary" discrimination due to ancestry or national origin, or to what the brief called in the case of Méndez and the others "the accident of birth, that of Mexican or Latin descent."[93] Wirin and Kido maintained that the Constitution forbade any law that singled out such a class without any reasonable basis:

> If appellants can justify discrimination on the basis of ancestry only, then who can tell what minority group will be next on the road to persecution. If we learned one lesson from the horrors of Nazism, it is that no minority group, and in fact, no person is safe, once the State, through its instrumentalities, can arbitrarily discriminate against any person or group.[94]

In addition to drafting the brief, Wirin participated in oral argument on behalf of the JACL, the only group other than the parties to actually present its case before the court.[95] During his presentation, Wirin affirmed that Orange County's school segregation policy unquestionably violated civil rights.[96]

The NAACP Brief

Although the Wirin/Kido brief took the position that racial segregation was unconstitutional, it did not directly attack the *Plessy* "separate but equal" doctrine. NAACP chief counsel Thurgood Marshall, for his part, was not at all sanguine about the actual possibilities of an attack on the constitutionality of Jim Crow, and preferred to build up a record of cases interpreting equality within separation. In a discussion of *Méndez* and other school segregation cases, Marshall wrote a colleague, "Frankly, and confidentially, and just between the two of us, there is serious doubt in the minds of most of us as to the timing for an all-out attack on segregation per se in the present United States Supreme Court."[97] However, the final NAACP brief nonetheless made a straightforward attack on the California segregation statutes. Drafted by Robert Carter and submitted in the names of Carter, Marshall, and Loren Miller (the latter added because he was the only one of the three admitted to practice before the Ninth Circuit), the NAACP brief amounted to what Richard Kluger later called a "dry run" for the association's subsequent briefs in its Supreme Court challenges to Jim Crow schools.[98]

The NAACP brief addressed the issue in *Méndez* as if it were a case of segregation based on race. Indeed, it radically conflated race, color, and national origin as equally protected categories on the basis of which the Fourteenth Amendment forbade discrimination. It argued that all distinctions based solely on "race and color" violated the Fourteenth Amendment. (Somewhat inconsistently, the brief referred to individuals of Mexican and Latin descent as "persons of this particular racial lineage," yet also spoke of the non–Mexican American children as being "purportedly of the white or Anglo-Saxon race.")[99] The NAACP brief further pointed to three of the wartime Japanese American "internment" cases as authorities for the proposition that, even though the Fourteenth Amendment and the rigorous standards embodied in its equal protection clause applied only to state governments, the fundamental concepts of due process embodied in the Fifth Amendment barred even the national government from making distinctions based on race or color except in extraordinary circumstances such as a war emergency. Seeking to persuade the appellate court that it was not required by *Plessy* to uphold "separate but equal" racially segregated schools, the NAACP argued that *Plessy* was not controlling on the *Méndez* case since *Plessy* had dealt only with railroads and was inapplicable to public education. Indeed, the NAACP asked the court to reject *Plessy* altogether, calling it "a departure from the main current of constitutional law" and a product of its time that was no longer "good law."[100] Instead, the NAACP stated, the court should uphold the trial court and strike down public school segregation since "such discrimination contravenes our constitutional requirements."[101]

Analysis of Differences Between the Briefs

Because their interests and agendas were disparate, the approaches and legal arguments employed by the attorneys for Méndez, the JACL, and the NAACP all differed widely. The Mexican Americans, who were not listed in the state's school segregation laws but were de facto enrolled in separate schools, primarily argued that the establishment of segregated "Mexican" public schools for their children was not only unauthorized by state law but forbidden by it. (When one of the judges, Clifton Matthews, suggested during oral argument that segregation was a long-standing practice, Marcus countered that for Mexican Americans it was in fact "recent.") The constitutionality of school segregation laws in general, and racial segregation in particular, occupied a very secondary place in their arguments on the appeal. Although they accepted the participation of other minority organizations such as the JACL and NAACP, they did not request it.[102] Rather, they sought in both their appellate brief and appellate argument to avoid any suggestion of a racial difference between themselves and the defendants. Conversely, the California school segregation law explicitly targeted "Japanese" children, although by 1946 all separate "Asian" schools had been eliminated. The JACL's primary goal was to strike at any law that singled out a group for disparate treatment solely on account of race, ancestry, or national origin, which it maintained were all equally prohibited classifications under the Fourteenth Amendment. This position was presented in even more radical terms in the NAACP brief, which not only contended that the disparate treatment of any group on the basis of race, color, national origin, ancestry, or "racial lineage" was forbidden by the Constitution except in highly specialized circumstances but also invited the court to hold the long-established "separate but equal" *Plessy* doctrine inapplicable to public school segregation, if not completely outdated and void. Curiously, although both the JACL and NAACP briefs cited the U.S. Supreme Court's opinion in *Korematsu*—a case that had reached the Supreme Court after the Ninth Circuit asked it for guidance on deciding the central issues—neither organization attempted to invoke the principle of strict scrutiny, which the Supreme Court had just begun to formulate in *Korematsu* and which paved the way for the Supreme Court's epochal 1954 *Brown v. Board of Education* decision.

The Appellate Court's Decision

The Court of Appeals issued its decision on April 14, 1947 (a corrected version followed that August). Although the Ninth Circuit unanimously upheld Judge McCormick's judgment and injunction, it clearly retreated from the judge's ringing denunciation of segregation. Focusing on narrow legal issues, the court declared that California's omission of Mexicans from its statutory list of groups whose children could be placed in segregated schools required it to hold that defendants' segregation practices were entirely without legal authorization and incompatible with California law.[103] Furthermore, in language that decisively rejected the expansive JACL and NAACP positions, the appellate court summarily declined to answer the question of whether the state could constitutionally establish segregated schools for children on the basis of either race or ancestry provided equal facilities were afforded the segregated group. Instead, the court declared:

> There is argument in two of the amicus curiae briefs that we should strike out independently on the whole question of segregation. . . . [J]udges must ever be on their guard lest they rationalize outright legislation under the too free use of the power to interpret. We are not tempted by [that] siren [song]. . . . [W]e are of the opinion that the segregation cases do not rule the instant case and that is reason enough for not responding to the argument that we should consider them.[104]

The court observed that all the cases cited by the defendants that had upheld the constitutionality of "separate but equal" facilities involved segregation of people of different races, or what it termed "children of parents belonging to one or another of the great races of mankind."[105] The Court then noted the lack of scientific support for making racial distinctions, stating:

> Somewhat empirically, it used to be taught that mankind was made up of white, brown, yellow, black, and red men. Such divisional designation has little or no adherents among anthropologists or ethnic scientists. A more scholarly nomenclature is Caucasoid, Mongoloid, and Negroid, yet this is unsatisfactory, as an attempt to collectively sort all mankind into distinct groups.[106]

Following this reasoning, and also noting that the parties had stipulated that there was no race segregation issue in the case, the court concluded that Mexicans were not a separate race from whites. Nowhere in California law, declared the court, was there any suggestion that segregation could be made "within one of the 'great races.'" Without statutory or constitutional authority for the placement of such children in segregated schools based on their ancestry, it could not lawfully be done. The question of whether laws permitting or mandating the public school segregation of children of African or Asian ancestry—that is, members of the other "great races"—were or were not constitutional thereby remained unanswered until the 1954 decision in *Brown v. Board of Education* (which, notably, did not cite *Méndez* as a precedent). The court's reasoning was extended in a concurring opinion by Judge William Denman, who had previously issued vituperative dissents in the *Hirabayashi* and *Korematsu* cases. Although Denman also avoided discussion of the constitutionality of "separate but equal" facilities for racial minorities, he warned that if "the vicious principle" were permitted, it could easily extend to Italians, Greeks, Jews, or other "white" ethnics. In addition, Denman proclaimed that the school district officials who had brazenly admitted in their brief that their actions violated California law should be arrested forthwith.[107]

THE AFTERMATH OF *MÉNDEZ*

Despite the overly dry and legalistic language the Court of Appeals employed in its *Méndez* decision and the narrow and restrictive reading it gave to the issue of segregation, the case set off a legal chain reaction of importance. Its first result was to provide ammunition for the liberals in the California legislature who had already sought to overturn the school segregation laws as outdated and prejudicial. Less than two months after the initial appellate court ruling, the legislature, encouraged by Attorney General Kenny, voted decisively to repeal §§8003 and 8004 of the State Education Code. Governor Earl Warren, who as chief justice of the United States would later write the companion Supreme Court opinions in the cases of *Brown v. Board of Education* and *Bolling v. Sharpe*, signed the repeal into law. The case also provided a precedent for striking down the exclusion of Mexican Americans from public facilities in other states. Several weeks after the *Méndez* victory, LULAC activists brought a lawsuit in federal court in Texas, where state laws mandated segregation of Mexican Americans, to end such segregation. In the 1948 case of *Delgado vs. Bastrop Independent School District*, school segregation in Texas was overturned.[108] The *Méndez* and *Delgado* decisions, in turn, gave rise to a trend of court cases challenging the exclusion of Mexican Americans as "other whites" in different areas of public life. This legal campaign climaxed in the case of *Hernández v. State of Texas*, decided by the U.S. Supreme Court just weeks before the justices announced their *Brown v. Board of Education* decision. In *Hernández*, the Court ruled that under the Fourteenth Amendment Mexican Americans could not constitutionally be segregated on the basis of their ancestry. Thus, almost eight years later, the

Supreme Court finally endorsed by the doctrine initially enunciated by Judge McCormick and passed over by the Ninth Circuit Court of Appeals.[109]

In the months that followed, some of the major figures in *Méndez* reunited for a new struggle against school segregation in southern California. The NAACP, represented by Loren Miller, and the Alianza Hispano-Americano, represented by Ralph Estrada and A. L. Wirin, sponsored a joint lawsuit against officials in the El Centro school district, who had long maintained a policy of segregating both African American and Mexican American students and who had instituted a discriminatory school transfer policy in the wake of *Brown* to evade desegregation. Following a defeat in the lower court, in summer 1955 the case of *Romero v. Weakley* was heard before the Ninth Circuit Court of Appeals. In support of the appellants, the JACL (represented by Frank Chuman), ACLU, American Jewish Congress, and Congress of Industrial Organizations (represented by JACL attorney Fred Okrand) collaborated on an amicus brief that referred prominently to both the *Brown* and *Méndez* cases. In October 1955, the court struck down the policy, applying the logic of *Hernandez* to school segregation.[110]

CONCLUSION

In the years following *Méndez*, Latino political organization expanded, and there were a few signs of reaching out to other minorities. In February 1948, LULAC's supreme council, meeting in Santa Fe, New Mexico, approved a resolution supporting the JACL's campaign for equal naturalization rights for Asian aliens and for evacuation claims legislation to reimburse Issei and Nisei for losses during their wartime removal. In 1949, Edward Roybal, a Mexican American activist, ran for the seat on the Los Angeles City Council representing Boyle Heights, Central Avenue, and Little Tokyo, and assembled an electoral coalition to support his successful candidacy. In particular, he forged a political alliance with African American Assemblyman Augustus Hawkins, and attracted significant support from black voters. The Nisei Progressives, a left-leaning activist group, also mobilized to canvass voters on Roybal's behalf. However, while Roybal won many Nisei votes, he did not really privilege Japanese community concerns. (Elected to Congress a few years later, he became a reliable supporter of immigration reform, and subsequently of redress.) In subsequent decades, under leaders such as Cesar Chavez and Delores Huerta, Chicano movements embraced more-confrontational protest tactics such as boycotts. In the process, Mexican American groups moved toward alliance with

African Americans on different issues, including voting rights legislation and affirmative action.

However, disagreements among Mexican Americans and legal scholars over the nature of their group identity and interests remain explosive. While some writers have argued that the members of "La Raza" are akin to a racial minority in status and should benefit from similar legal protections, many Mexican Americans are still identified, or identify themselves, as "white."[111] Yet if the *Méndez* case did not lead Mexican Americans to identify themselves as a racial minority in common cause with Japanese Americans or African Americans, it did help cement an alliance between the JACL and the NAACP (one which will be discussed further in Chapter 11).

In sum, the relations between Mexican Americans and Japanese Americans in the 1940s remind us that solidarity among racial minorities is possible, but it is neither automatic nor easy to maintain. Minority groups can and do come together at various times, but their interests, attitudes, and priorities are often quite different. Furthermore, in the face of a dominant culture of white supremacy, it is tempting and sometimes profitable for members of a racialized group to identify themselves with the white population and to seek equality by distancing themselves from more identifiably nonwhite minorities. In any case, if the *Méndez* case presents an example of a genuine victory won through the action of an interracial coalition, it also reveals why such victories are rare and difficult to achieve.

7. From *Kuichi* to Comrades

Japanese American Views of Jews in the 1930s and 1940s

Several years ago, as part of my research into the wartime confinement of Japanese Americans, I came across some correspondence by Kiyoshi Okamoto. Okamoto, a Hawaiian-born Nisei, was the founder of the Heart Mountain Fair Play Committee, which campaigned for restoration of civil rights to confined Japanese Americans during World War II and protested conscription of Nisei from the camps. I was surprised to discover that Okamoto's letters seeking outside aid were laced with nasty remarks about Jews and what he considered the baneful Jewish influence over the Roosevelt administration.[1] I mentioned to a Nisei friend the irony of prejudice expressed by a man fighting prejudice, and he responded that "anti-Semitism was endemic within West Coast Japanese communities" during his childhood. This was corroborated by the memoirs of a Japanese student who migrated to the West Coast during the 1930s and recalled, "As a teenager in prewar Japan I had read a little anti Semitic literature based on the Protocols of the Elders of Zion and the alleged Jewish plot to conquer the world. In California, among the Japanese immigrants and their children I had become aware of a strong prejudice against the Jewish people."[2] Another Nisei friend told me that the Issei had even developed a special code word, *kuichi*, to designate their Jewish neighbors: *ku* (the word for the number 9) + *ichi* (the word for 1) = *ju* (the word for 10), a homonym for the English word *Jew*. While the term (like *Jew* itself) was not invariably negative, it had definite pejorative connotations, hence its in-group use.

I was aware of the large-scale literature on black-Jewish connections and tensions, but I had seen almost nothing written on Jews and Japanese Americans. This data went against what little I had seen, such as George Sanchez's study of Los Angeles's multiracial Boyle Heights section (an area also treated more recently in Allison Varzally's book), or Masayo

139

Duus's account of the Nisei soldier unit that liberated Dachau. All these were positive about interracial friendship and alliances.[3] At the same time, there is a small but fascinating literature on Jewish reactions to Japanese Americans, notably to their wartime removal.[4] I resolved to study the question of ethnic Japanese attitudes toward Jews, and to collect every piece of evidence I could to determine the extent of group sentiment. Since the subject of prejudice is a shameful and embarrassing one, many people do not want to talk about it at all, and individual memories are not altogether trustworthy. I have thus eschewed oral history and concentrated largely on documents from the period, especially published sources, plus diaries and other materials, which are less tainted by afterthought or tricks of memory. Unfortunately, such a method also inevitably means relying on the viewpoint of a literate and educated minority. Furthermore, since I do not speak Japanese, I have restricted myself to works written in English by Nisei or by westernized Issei, plus a few translations. The resulting sample is admittedly incomplete, and may not be representative.

Still, with all these limitations in mind, I would say that the available evidence indicates that West Coast Japanese Americans, both aliens and citizens, expressed complex attitudes in regard to Jews in the World War II era. While they expressed a certain abstract awareness, if not sympathy, for the plight of persecuted European Jews, their expressions of opinion regarding Jewish immigration and Jewish Americans were marked by widespread hostility. Their opinions both reflected mainstream prejudice and drew from popular stereotypes.[5]

To begin with, Jewish Americans were largely absent from the West Coast Japanese press in the years before 1938, even as the two communities remained rather aloof. There were occasional positive or neutral features—one 1932 *Nichi Bei Shimbun* article described a Jewish "lochinvar" who had written the newspaper asking for a Japanese girl of light complexion to marry, and offering to take the bride's name and move to Japan with her. A piece the following year reported that the Northern California Board of rabbis had voted a resolution to repeal the 1924 Japanese exclusion law and grant Japan an immigration quota.[6] One columnist cited a friend's argument that all the world's great musical soloists were Jews: "As a race, the Jewish people are endowed richly with highly expressive, almost extravagantly overt, temperament."[7] In Mary Oyama Mittwer's 1936 short story "Coming of Age," a Nisei woman voting for the first time is approached by two "curly-headed" Jewish children to support their candidate. The following year, she took her fellow Nisei to task for parroting popular anti-Jewish attitudes. Mittwer retorted that she had numerous friends who were "young people of Hebrew extraction" whom she considered "more intellectual, cultured, and educated than the average Nisei."[8] Richard Tori spoke at length of the curious friendship he had formed with a Jewish classmate.[9]

More often, though, short stories and news reports portrayed "the Jew" negatively, as a dishonest businessman or pawnbroker. For example, Tooru Kanazawa published a short story in *Kashu Mainichi* in 1933, "The Mandarin Diamond," which centered on a ruse by which Yan Kee, a Chinese merchant, revenged himself on Abie Goldstein, a Jewish shopkeeper who had previously cheated him. Kazumaro "Buddy" Uno's 1936 short story "Resurrection" features a fat and repulsive Jewish pawnbroker.[10] In 1934, the *Japanese American Courier* warned its readers against a confidence scam operated by a "Jew" and a "Russian." The Russian would be asked by the Jew to sell him an allegedly valuable set of sealskin furs, would refuse on the grounds that he hated Jews, and would induce the mark to buy the package (in fact cheap rabbit furs) and resell them at a profit to the Jew. A 1936 news article described a Los Angeles shopkeeper, Sam Cohen, who tried, "with all the ingenuity of a partially deranged Jewish salesman," to fob off a decrepit fishing rod on a Nisei, and then clubbed him with a lead pipe when the man objected. A letter the same year by a Nisei, published under the name "Salemite," contended that money-worship had degraded the Jews, despite their inspiring cultural background. "Some of the richest and most brilliant men have come from the Jewish race, but still to this day we find that the Jews are not recognized as essential inhabitants of this earth."[11]

Even jovial treatments of Jews underlined stereotypical features. Joe Oyama, describing groups of soapbox orators in L.A.'s Pershing Square, noted," You hear the Jews severely criticize the Church only to turn around and praise the Main Street religion.... Jews love to argue. A defense mechanism at work you would call it."[12] John Fujii's discussion of the New York theater referred to "the Jew and the Negro" as "the other underprivileged classes in America" but underlined the Semitic look of audiences, especially "the smartly gowned, lorgnette-wearing Jewess."[13]

The developing international crisis of anti-Semitism at first left only a few echoes in the ethnic Japanese press. At the dawn of the Hitler regime, the *Japanese American Courier* ran an editorial describing the anti-Jewish boycotts as a regrettable example of racial persecution.[14] The next year Larry Tajiri associated Nazi attacks on German Jews with the plight of Nisei, adding a note of competition: "We look askance at Nazi Germany and the persecution of the Jews, but one can look closer to home to find less violent but equally shocking examples of bias and intolerances." In 1935, James Omura warned that a boycott of the Berlin Olympics over Germany's exclusion of Jewish athletes would be unwise.[15] In 1936, Taishi Matsumoto asked rhetorically, "Do we want a Fascist inclined government, nationalistic as in Germany where the Jews are persecuted . . . ?"[16] Meanwhile, in a letter defending the thesis that Japanese Americans should integrate with other groups, an Issei contributor declared that that Jews and Japanese were similar in facing prejudice:

> The main reason the Germans hate the Jews is "isolation and class breeding," and not because they run everything there. Even in this country they hate the Jews because of such traits. I know several Jewish people throughout the state and to me they are the same as any other people but their parents are the ones who are blamed for this ill feeling. . . . There is no reason for such feeling toward the Jews by the white people. Doesn't everybody celebrate the birth of a baby born to a Jewish mother about 1900 years ago?[17]

In early 1938, *New World-Sun* columnist Saburo Kido began including occasional discussions of anti-Semitism in his column "Timely Topics." In February 1938, even as he expressed his respect for Adolf Hitler's dynamic character and leadership, he declared his opposition to the persecution of German Jews: "As a member of a minority race which has faced discriminations and persecutions in this country, we cannot help but feel sorry for those of the Jewish race." In Summer 1938, he exposed the racist character of the German American Bund, and soon after warned of the spread of European anti-Semitism and its potential consequences for America:

> It is possible that even in the United States, such a movement [anti-Semitism] may gain impetus. The general opinion seems to be that the Jews control Wall Street and the financial power of this nation. One of these days a rabid agitation may win the public into believing that the Jews may be the source of this country's economic ills. Any intelligent person will know that such is not the case, but one cannot tell how much a mob psychology may be fanned on false rumors.[18]

Kido's voice remained largely solitary, however, and it was not until the large-scale pogrom of Kristallnacht in November 1938, that the ethnic Japanese newspapers began to comment more frequently on Nazi persecution of European Jews, if at first in rather measured terms. Sei Fujii, Issei editor and a warm partisan of Japan's conquest of China, accepted the absurd claims of the German government that it had been forced to act after the murder of a German embassy secretary in France by a Jewish student. He added, rather naively:

Jews in Germany are receiving sympathy from all over the world, especially from the United States. Among the Jews, there are bad ones but at the same time, there are exceedingly good ones. Germany may have good reasons for taking this unusual measure against the Jewish race, but if there is any case where an innocent Jew is made to suffer for the wrong done by [a] fellow member of his race, I hope eventually the German government will see to it that those innocent and deserving ones are given full protection.

Fujii concluded that England and the United States were blameworthy for Germany's actions because they would not accept Jewish refugees.[19] Similarly, James Tsurutani justified mass repression on the eve of Kristallnacht by repeating as fact an absurd allegation from an American doctor that at the Berlin Hospital over three-fourths of the doctors were Jews and that they routinely offered Jewish patients preference over Germans, who had to wait four or five days for care.[20] (How the German nurses acquiesced in this alleged scheme was left unsaid.) Soon after, with no apparent sense of irony, Tsurutani commented that he was surprised at how passively most Nisei took the German persecution of Jews. "I'm certain that a major portion of our animosity toward this much kicked around racial group is purely personal . . . based upon business relationships and daily contacts in commercial trade."[21] Togo Tanaka deplored the widespread criticism in Japanese communities of President Roosevelt's expressions of "humanitarian . . . helpfulness" to the persecuted Jews of Germany, and claimed that Nisei should not let their negative feelings about Jews sway their support. "Whatever the individual nisei's personal feeling toward the Jews may or may not be, it would be an indefensible and foolish contention for a second generation Japanese to condone or agree with, in principle, the persecution of a racial minority in any country."[22]

In the months that followed, as the Nazis first took over Czechoslovakia and then invaded Poland, triggering World War II in Europe, Japanese American press coverage of European Jews became more frequent. Several newspapers featured photos of ghettos, refugees, or Jews wearing yellow stars.[23] The *Japanese American Courier* recounted the sad story of the refugee ship *St. Louis* (the real-life inspiration for *Voyage of the Damned*), which was refused entry by the United States and Latin American governments and forced to return to Europe. However, such rhetorical sympathy for the Jews was tempered by universal agreement that the American government should not admit Jewish refugees. Columnist Helen Aoki, speaking for *Rafu Shimpo*, expressed sympathy for the persecution of a "cultured race" but insisted that the United States, "a country that spends a large portion of its taxes on relief," could not help the refugees without endangering its own progress: she cited the collective verdict as "Keep the Jews out of here."[24] Similarly, the *Japanese American Courier* editorialized its approval of a 1939 conference in Washington on finding underdeveloped countries to serve as havens for refugees. "It is of interest in this country to recall that for many years the poor, persecuted and oppressed found refuge in the United States. Now this is a thing of the past. We need all our territory and resources."[25]

Meanwhile, the Nikkei press began to draw parallels between German anti-Semitism and American racism: Saburo Kido deplored Germany's "heinous crimes" against the Jews and said that American whites acted similarly to nonwhites.[26] An editorial in *Kashu Mainichi* claimed that even if persecution of German Jews received the greatest attention, Jews in America faced the same troubles as Japanese and Negroes: "Except that the color of their skin bears no physical distinction from those of Caucasian Americans, the Jews in America have had experiences of discrimination: much of whose character would be immediately recognizable by the Japanese—housing restrictions, professional restrictions, and so on. We are, then, not alone in our problems."[27] Columnist Larry Tajiri agreed:

> Racial prejudice isn't something that Hitler invented, though the author of *Mein Kampf* has been a master at exploiting it for political purposes. We have always had racial prejudices, in varying degrees, in this country though the founding fathers or Abe Lincoln never willed it so. . . . On the Atlantic seaboard this prejudice is strongest against the Americans of Jewish extraction, in the southern states it is directed against the Negro race. In many west coast communities there is feeling against the Japanese, Chinese and the Filipino.[28]

A few Nisei held up the Jews (using slightly stereotyped characteristics) as models for Japanese Americans. One Los Angeles columnist deplored rivalries among Nisei, who were insufficiently group-conscious: "We see in the progressive, hustling Jewish folk the opposite tendency. They stick together. In New York every Jewish family is responsible for bringing over at least one Jewish refugee. Refugees who canvass from door to door can expect sales from Jews."[29] Similarly, Roku Sugahara compared Little Tokyo's Issei businessmen with local Jewish merchants. "Just a few miles east of here on Brooklyn Avenue there is a bustling and prosperous Jewish community. They do not have more people than we do, but they have ideas and plans. It is a bee-hive of activity, whereas on East First Street a person can fire a shot-gun down the streets without touching a solitary soul."[30] Tad Uyeno praised Jewish Americans and asked rhetorically, "Where did all this stupid talk emanate that the Jews should be persecuted here in America?"[31]

Yet the attention to Jews was by no means entirely positive. In a widely reprinted report, Thomas Yamate, president of the Southern California Retail Produce Workers' Union, asserted that competition (implicitly unfair) from Jewish merchants was driving Japanese American produce stands out of business, and insisted doubtfully that there were ten Jewish-owned fruit stands for every Japanese one. Tsuyoshi Matsumoto, a Japanese-born Christian minister, reported widespread prejudice and injustice against the Jews: "Some of my most respected American friends shamelessly admit their violent anti-Jewish sentiments." Matsumoto added that many Nisei now expressed dislike for Jews, and reminded his readers that their unjust words made for further difficulties for Jews and other "much abused minority groups."[32] At the same time, a progressive writers group in Los Angeles bemoaned the strong prejudices the Nisei held against blacks, Mexican Americans, and Jews, citing a typically heard complaint about businessmen: "Those damn Jews will gyp you out of your pants. They lie, they cheat... Most of them are radicals, too."[33] Sam Hohri thought that the plight of black Americans deserved more consideration. In one column, he deplored the failure of the mainstream U.S. press to take racial discrimination seriously, then added bitterly, "Yet these same men and papers weep and cry against the European practice of black-listing Jews and part-Jews."[34]

Meanwhile, pro-Japanese propagandists lauded Tokyo's enlightened policy toward Jews, and complained of Jewish attacks on Japan as a fascist nation because of Tokyo's aggression in China.[35] Various Nisei columnists expanded on this line of argument. Howard Imazeki charged that the protest movement for an economic boycott of Japan was being financed, not only by China, but by "American importers of Japanese goods—mostly Jews—whose interest is purely selfish." Imazeki contended, with doubtful logic, that these merchants sponsored the boycott in order to reduce demand for Japanese goods, so that they could then buy them at a cheaper rate.[36] Togo Tanaka insisted that the production of flyers by an antifascist group urging a boycott of Japanese goods was tantamount to saying "no Japanese is fit to exist." He charged that this propaganda was being produced by motion picture people "of Hebrew blood," who were thus inciting anti-Japanese prejudice similar to the anti-Semitism in Europe they loudly deplored.[37] James Hamanaka wrote a letter expressing anger that Jewish picketers and "Jewish influenced, owned or controlled" newspapers protested anti-Jewish meetings by German-Americans, even as "Jewish" meetings advocated "hate and boycott" against Japan.

(Reader Kiyoko Matsuzawa, it must be said, responded by deploring the open Jew-baiting of Hamanaka's letter, and praised the great power for good demonstrated by the Jews and their role in inspiring others to patience and sympathy for the underdog.)[38]

In September 1941, the Nisei press reported on the fallout from a speech by Charles Lindbergh in which the aviator and isolationist leader complained of the "Jewish influence" in the country. The editor of *New World-Sun* in San Francisco contended that Lindbergh's speech cost him a large part of his Nisei following, who rejected any attempt to stir up racial animosity or religious conflict. Conversely, in October *Rafu Shimpo* published a photo of a signboard that proclaimed "Adolf Loves Lindy," alongside a "plague on both your houses" editorial: "We don't like the signboard any more than we liked Lindbergh's reference to Jews in his speech. Both, we feel, were unnecessary, out of place, in bad taste." Yet the editors claimed that the signboard was worse than Lindbergh's efforts, because it was a harbinger of just the kind of "hysteria mongering" that could be turned against Japanese Americans.[39]

The Japanese bombing of Pearl Harbor in December 1941 and the widespread suspicion thrown on West Coast Japanese Americans (plus the confinement of most Issei leaders) over the weeks that followed led the community to turn inward, and self-criticism was drowned out by calls for unity. By authority of Executive Order 9066, the West Coast communities were removed from their homes during spring 1942, and their members were forced to store or dispose of their property at fire sale prices before leaving. As Ellen Eisenberg has shown, West Coast Jewish communities maintained a prudent silence on Executive Order 9066 and commented only in the most muted and indirect fashion on the need to support aliens.[40] Nevertheless, few Japanese Americans seemed aware of the various individual West Coast Jews—broadcaster George Knox Roth, scientist J. Robert Oppenheimer, union official Louis Goldblatt, and lawyers A. L. Wirin, Fred Okrand, and Ernest Besig—who did spring to their defense—admittedly not always specifically *as* Jews. Instead, numerous Japanese Americans scapegoated Jews as scavengers who bought their belongings cheaply at the time of evacuation. A Hawaiian Issei sent to the mainland commented in his diary, "Quite a few Jews took advantage of unlucky Japanese and secretly paid next to nothing for furniture and other goods."[41]

These rumors, it must be said, were not limited to Japanese Americans, but revealed a generalized hostility. Occidental College president Remsen Bird wrote Eleanor Roosevelt, "Sometime I want to explore very precisely the story of the Jewish junk dealers and the disestablishment of the

Japanese-Americans. What a tale is running around our town of their misbehavior at Terminal Island and Little Tokyo in this connection. Maybe it's true—maybe it's propaganda. It isn't enough to just say it is propaganda. It is important to look into just what the facts are." Mrs. Roosevelt responded, "I am disturbed by your story of the junk dealers and your intimation about their actions as concerns the Japanese. I hope when you do run it into the ground, you will let me know what you find."[42] No evidence survives, alas, of any such inquiry.

The fallout from this episode continued to influence ethnic Japanese in their hostile attitudes toward Jews throughout their confinement. One novel drafted during the war reproduced a discussion in camp about Jews:

> "A Jewish salesman told me all those Jews who came to buy things just before evacuation were New York Jews," Gary spoke up. "One of them [the Jews] offered Mochizuki fifty dollars for five hundred dollars worth of cameras in his store and when Mochizuki told him nothing doing, he told Mochizuki, 'The government will confiscate them pretty soon anyway,'" Mike said. "You don't like Jews?" Jim asked. "Right after evacuation I listened to an open radio forum and the only one who stood up on two feet and denounced the whole evacuation was a Jew."[43]

A writer in the *Poston News-Courier*, recounting anti-Nisei letters in the *Los Angeles Times*, noted that one of them was from "a Jew." This led Poston high school principal Miles Cary to object to the "subtle suggestion of race prejudice on your part."[44]

In contrast, the confinement of Japanese Americans, and then the processes of resettlement and return, brought Larry Tajiri and other Nisei liberals to public prominence., They used their platform to denounce anti-Semitism in America, as part of their larger solidarity with minorities generally. In an essay for the magazine *Asia and the Americas*, Tajiri noted, "Before evacuation . . . regional prejudices against Filipinos, Mexicans, Negroes, and Jews were accepted by many Japanese Americans, just as these earlier victims of discrimination sometimes echo the propaganda of the professional 'yellow peril' mongers." Now, he said, Japanese Americans were growing aware of their status as a minority among other minorities.[45] Under Tajiri's editorship the *Pacific Citizen* printed a long extract from a piece by sociologist Tom Shibutani that had appeared in the Rohwer camp's annual, *The Pen*:

> It seems the only salvation for the Nisei or for anyone in a racial minority is to throw off the narrow interest in local and personal problems, and to join in the larger battle for a better world. . . . It

might be well for all of us to begin in our own backyards by getting rid of our own prejudices against people of other races and creeds. By being prejudiced against the Negroes, Jews, Chinese and Filipinos, the Nisei are contributing to their own self-destruction. We cannot take part in a sincere all-out drive for democracy if we ourselves are to foster any part of fascistic ideology.[46]

Tajiri likewise ran occasional stories of Jewish groups supporting the rights of Japanese Americans.[47]

Like Tajiri, Joe Grant Masaoka denounced all forms of the color line, and warned that the racial tensions caused by discrimination against African Americans and other groups might lead to race riots. Masoka reserved his most powerful scorn for discrimination against Jews, reminding his readers that it was a problem in the United states as well as in Germany. "Though war may have touched off race hysteria against the Nisei in colleges, they do have a greater acceptance than Jews. One Jew in seeking to further his medical education confided to his fellow medic Nisei student that he had been refused in 37 other institutions."[48]

The visible empathy that the Nisei felt with Jews victimized by prejudice was expressed most eloquently by Tajiri and by Bill Hosokawa after the liberation of the Nazi death camp at Maidenek in November 1944. These first indications of the atrocities of the Holocaust moved them deeply. Each referred to the genocide as a warning about the evils of racial and religious prejudice against any group. Hosokawa stated, "The Nazis have demonstrated how hatred can spread. We know that the same process can be repeated in this country—minus the gruesome details of course, but still in a manner blighting to democracy—with discrimination against the Negroes, the Jews, the Catholics and others."[49]

In the postwar period, the dynamic between Jewish and Japanese communities was transformed, especially on the West Coast, and members of the two groups drew closer. First, many resettlers who left the camps found housing or employment in Jewish areas—one Seattleite in a synagogue.[50] Second, individual Jews became active within the ethnic Japanese community. A. L. Wirin was named the JACL's official counsel, while the roots and consequences of mass removal were the subject of well-publicized studies by such scholars as Milton R. Konvitz, Morton Grodzins, and Leonard Broom (aka Leonard Bloom). Jewish groups such as B'nai Brith and the American Jewish Congress supported civil rights for Nisei. There were numerous marriages between Nisei and Jews, especially outside the West Coast—one notable case was the union between designer/author Michi Nishiura and Walter Weglyn, a Holocaust survivor.

Still, there was little examination in the Nisei press of the fate of Jewish displaced persons in Europe or refugee policy—even the refugees at Fort Orange who had been cared for by the WRA failed to excite comment—or of anti-Semitism in America, apart from Mary Oyama's crusading *Rafu Shimpo* column "New World a-Coming." *The Pacific Citizen* put occasional information in its "Minorities" column, inaugurated in 1947, which contained information on other racial and ethnic groups. In 1949 it recounted the story of Atsuko Kiyota Szekeres, a Nisei woman from Los Angeles who posed as Jewish to search through DP camps for her Hungarian Jewish husband, who had been sent to a concentration camp.[51] Japanese vernaculars also dutifully reported the aid of Jewish groups. Togo Tanaka, paying homage to the American Jewish Congress for providing the funds to open a monthly Nisei newspaper, noted that the Jews had a healthy suspicion of assimilation and focused on maintenance of ethnic press and institutions.[52] Yet the fledgling ethnic press outside the West Coast was more attentive to anti-Semitism. For instance,, Joe Oyama used his column in the New York–based *Hokubei Shimpo* to denounce the use of the word *kuichi* as reflecting Nazi-like attitudes toward Jews, as well as West Coast racism toward Nisei. "The word is an act of aggression. It leads toward morally wounding and finally killing a fellow human being. The word hits below the belt."[53] While Oyama's piece was picked up by *Chicago Shimpo*, it did not appear in the West Coast or the nationwide ethnic Japanese press.

Perhaps ironically, one forum in which several Nisei writers addressed issues relating to Jews and anti-Semitism was the African American press. In his *Chicago Defender* column, S. I. Hayakawa repeatedly denounced anti-Semitism as equally as loathsome as prejudice against blacks, and discoursed on the absurdity of Christian religious prejudice against Jews. In one mordant 1944 column he related the story of a Nisei woman who was hired to work at a factory job with African Americans. While the woman's new co-workers objected to her presence on ethnic grounds, she soon managed to win their support. According to Hayakawa, when one co-worker afterward apologized to the Nisei woman for her initially prejudiced attitude, the Nisei responded, "I especially like being here because before I came I was working for a bunch of Jews, and I hate Jews."[54] Meanwhile, Larry Tajiri contributed an extended article to *Now*, a black-owned race-relations magazine, on the confluence between Nazi racial ideology in Europe and prejudice against Jews and racial minorities in the United States.[55] Hisaye Yamamoto likewise included a few discussions of Jewish topics in her "Small Talk" column in the *Los Angeles Tribune*. For example, in one piece she described her respect for a Jewish author who refused to change his name in order to avoid anti-Semitism.⁵⁶ Somewhat less positively, in a guest piece for the *Tribune* Yoné Stafford, a biracial Nisei from Massachusetts, argued, "Now having met many Nisei, I realize how they and the Jews make such a god of education and ignore the very necessary and vital function of experience—getting to know people—rubbing their elbows with the rest of the world."⁵⁷

There were further hints of mutual respect and even identification between the two groups in the postwar years. Psychiatrist Joe Yamamoto, who left Heart Mountain to attend the University of Minnesota, later recounted his shock in 1946 at hearing his medical fraternity brothers, who had accepted him, express prejudice against a Jewish candidate.⁵⁸ Mr. and Mrs. Yoshio Terao and their son, Sam, after resettling in Chicago, purchased and operated Ida's Restaurant, a kosher delicatessen with a largely Jewish clientele.⁵⁹ John Okada's 1957 novel *No-No Boy* described the reaction of a Jewish wholesaler to the attack on Pearl Harbor. "Herman Fine listened to the radio and cried without tears for the Japanese, who . . . had taken their place beside the Jew. The Jew was used to suffering. The writing for them was etched in caked and dried blood over countless generations upon countless generations. The Japanese did not know."⁶⁰

Still, hints of bad feeling remained below the surface. In 1947 Henry Mori complained in *Rafu Shimpo* that the Hollywood movie *Crossfire*, which portrayed an anti-Semitic murder, was limited to asking sympathetic tolerance only for the Jewish minority, and made no mention of the wartime removal of the Japanese Americans or the patriotic contributions of Nisei soldiers. (Ironically, the movie was adapted from a novel, *The Brick Foxhole*, that had portrayed homophobia as the inspiration for the hate crime, an aspect that was wholly erased from the movie.) Other Japanese Americans, mainly older ones, continued to express hostile attitudes toward Jews as selfish and power-hungry. An Issei analyst lecturing at Tule Lake in 1945 charged:

> Today the Americans are more concerned about the Jews than the Japanese problem. The Jews who have immigrated from Europe make up 40% of the population in New York, and so they control the economic powers of the city. Formerly the Americans discriminated [against]the Jews. In those days the Jewish youths consisted 40% at Columbia University. And so if the Americans were careless about this situation everything would have been in the hands of the Jews. Recently the power of the Jews became so strong that the public did not discriminate them anymore, and on top of that they have the political and economical control in America today.⁶¹

Similarly, Kumezo Hachimonji (himself, ironically, a graduate of Columbia University) wrote an essay in his private diary in 1952 pondering why Jews were so disliked everywhere: in Japan, where there were no Jews; in California, where people met them sometimes; and in New York, where people met them every day. Hachimonji noted that when he lived in New York in the 1920s he had heard Jews denounced for sharp business practices, yet he admitted that those he had dealt with were honorable. In a poignant passage, he admitted he could not figure out why he disliked Jews (a trait deplored by his son Ike, an army veteran). "Inwardly I still feel the Jews are selfish. They love their own people vehemently but perhaps hate the so-called Gentiles." After justifying himself by deploring the displacement by the Israelis of the Arabs in Palestine, he tacitly confessed his real reason for hating Jews. "Inwardly I dislike them because such disliking was in the atmosphere. And it was planted deep in my feeling, without my knowing of it. I am prejudiced against the Jews without knowing why I may be prejudiced against them." At the same time, acknowledging that hatred of Jews was a "poison," Hachimonji expressed his gratitude that the younger generation was less prejudiced and more tolerant.[62]

There was evidence of public anti-Semitism among Nisei as well. In 1950, Larry Tajiri denounced Kiyoshi Okamoto for stoking prejudice during that year's congressional elections. As head of an organization called Fair Play United, he claimed, Okamoto had circulated a letter to Nisei voters in California to urge their support of Richard Nixon for U.S. senator, claiming that Nixon helped draft the bill "to control the Jew-Communist conspiracy." (Okamoto didn't use the word *Jew*, Tajiri noted caustically, but a derogatory word with the same meaning.)[63] In 1955 another scurrilous anti-Semitic letter was put out, purportedly by an organization called Niseis for Kawakita. Though the letter may have been a forgery by non-Japanese meant to sow ill feeling between Jews and Nisei, and it was rapidly disavowed by the JACL, the text was lent plausibility by its resemblance to actual productions.[64]

It is no doubt risky to try to interpret such impressionistic data as I have collected, and my conclusions are necessary tentative. What seems clear from a review of the sources, especially the Japanese vernacular press, is the distinction between popular attitudes toward Jews in Europe and in America during the prewar and war era. Throughout this period, the Nazi treatment of Jews became a reference point for Japanese Americans in defining their own condition—much as references to the wartime "internment" became common coin among black radicals a generation later. As editor James Omura reminded the Tolan Committee during its 1942 hearings on removal,

"Has the Gestapo come to America? Have we not risen in righteous anger against Hitler's treatment of the Jews?"

Yet in a period of rising domestic anti-Semitism, such references did not automatically translate into solidarity with Jewish Americans. (Indeed, James Omura's brother took him to task for his anti-Semitism in a 1945 letter.)[65] Rather, Japanese Americans publicly expressed casual hostility toward Jews, whereas they generally referred to African Americans or ethnic Chinese (at least publicly) in more respectful terms. This does not mean anti-Semitism was necessarily more vicious or prevalent than prejudice against these other groups. It does indicate that a rhetorical climate existed in which overt stereotyping was accepted. Such feeling surely informed the scapegoating of Jews as chief scavengers during removal—a charge no historian has upheld—and may have impeded intergroup alliances from forming once war broke out. In Canada, which had no such history of Japanese-Jewish hostility, a large fraction of the Nisei who resettled in eastern cities found jobs or housing in Jewish communities.

What explains the anti-Jewish attitudes among Issei and Nisei? As Kumezo Hachimonji suggested, a good deal of it must have been absorbed unconsciously either from Japanese culture (whose anti-Semitic elements, fortified by European racism, have been well described by John Dower and others)[66] or from mainstream white prejudice, the more so as the community bore a strong imprint of Christian missionaries. There was also a certain tension born of economic competition. Furthermore, supporters of Japan—and one should not underestimate their strength in the prewar community—were inflamed by criticism of Tokyo as a fascist regime allied with Hitler, and easily imbibed propaganda linking Jews with communism. The news of the Holocaust did not shake this loathing, at least at first, any more than it did in the case of mainstream Americans.

In addition, given the paucity of regular intergroup contact and lack of visible marks identifying Jews who were not Orthodox, many Japanese Americans were not able to distinguish Jews from other whites unless specifically informed. Thus, renowned Jewish friends of Nisei and Issei such as the sociologists Morris and Marvin Opler, who might have served as counterexamples to hostile stereotypes, probably passed with their ethnicity largely unacknowledged. Indeed, the fact that Japanese Americans saw Jews as white, and therefore not suffering burdens of the same type or importance, is significant. The left-wing activist Karl Yoneda forms an interesting case study. Yoneda worked primarily with Jews inside the Communist Party, and he married a Jewish woman, Elaine Black, who later accompanied her husband to Manzanar. According to the testimony of Yoneda's friend and comrade Koji Ariyoshi, while at Manzanar Elaine assisted and won the admiration of Issei and Nisei "who were prejudiced against Elaine's people because of incessant anti-Semitic propaganda they had been exposed to."[67] Yet while Yoneda's own memoir *Ganbatte* is centered on struggles for racial equality, notably those of blacks and Japanese Americans, he makes no reference to anti-Semitism or to relations between Japanese Americans and Jews (apart from mentioning in passing his loving connection with his wife's parents).[68] Similarly, in an extract from his camp diary, Charles Kikuchi recorded a revealing exchange with Karl Akiya, a fellow activist. Akiya saw anti-Japanese discrimination in race and color terms, as more like that against blacks, and seemed not to accept any kinship with Jews. Kikuchi, conversely, underlined the similarity between the essentially economic discrimination against both Japanese Americans and Jews, and said that the plight of blacks was not comparable.[69]

Whatever the case was, signs of community anti-Semitism did fade in the years that passed. As West Coast Issei and Nisei moved away from the Little Tokyos (and especially to the East), they met and befriended more Jews—schools and universities may well have been a particular point of contact, given the importance of learning to both groups and their outstanding presence in higher education. Meanwhile, as younger generations of Nisei and Sansei grew more engaged in politics, their awareness of discrimination against Jews and their sense of solidarity began to increase.

Top: A section of the Winona Housing Project, Burbank, California, in November 1945, where trailer homes were provided for returned evacuees while they were securing permanent homes in and around Los Angeles. Photographer: Tom Parker. Courtesy Bancroft Library, University of California, Berkeley.

Bottom: Miné Okubo, Nisei, who resettled to New York from the Topaz Center, is showing one of her drawings to Read Lewis, executive director of the Community Council for American Unity, and M. Margaret Anderson, editor of the Council quarterly, *Common Ground*, at the opening of an exhibit of Okubo's drawing and paintings of center life under the Council's auspices, March 6, 1945, at the American Common, New York. Photographer: Toge Fujihira. Courtesy Bancroft Library, University of California, Berkeley.

Above: Unpacking belongings in a temporary trailer home at the Winona Housing Project in Burbank, California, where returned evacuees found temporary living quarters until they were able to secure homes in or around Los Angeles, November 1945. Photographer: Tom Parker. Courtesy Bancroft Library, University of California, Berkeley.

Opposite, Top: Joe Oyama, Asami Kawachi Oyama, and Carol Levy cleaning up the supper dishes in the kitchen of the New York City apartment they shared with several other evacuees, April 25, 1944. Prior to evacuation to Santa Anita the preceding May, Mr. Oyama was assistant editor of the English section of a Japanese American daily in Los Angeles, and Mrs. Oyama was studying journalism at Los Angeles City College. While at Santa Anita, they were both on the staff of the *Pacemaker*, he as city editor and she as women's editor. He kept up with his journalistic interest by serving as editor of the *News Letter of the Japanese-American Committee for Democracy*. Courtesy Bancroft Library, University of California, Berkeley.

Opposite, Bottom: While lunching in one of New York City's famous Automat restaurants just off Fifth Avenue, May Tomio, Granada, and Akira Kashiki, Colorado River, obtained pieces of pie from the food receptacles, August 1944. Photographer: Hikaru Iwasaki. Courtesy Bancroft Library, University of California, Berkeley.

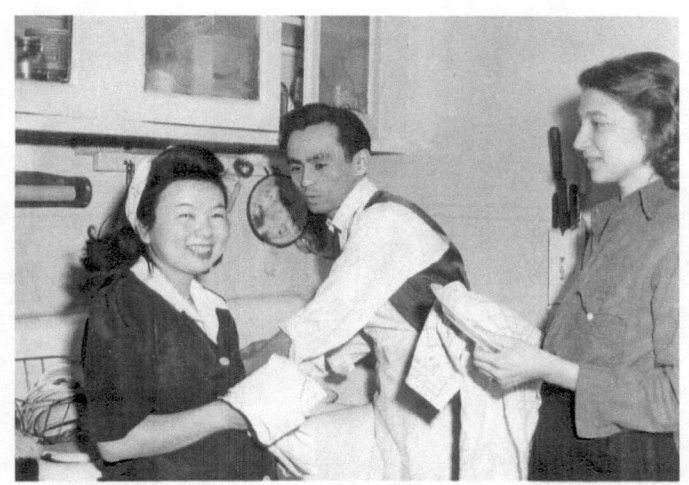

Miné Okubo, frontispiece for Robert O'Brien, *The College Nisei*, 1949. Courtesy Estate of Miné Okubo.

Opposite, Top: Ken Shimizu, extreme left, meets other delegates of various racial backgrounds during the City-Wide Unity Conference held in New York City on March 17, 1945, at the Society for Ethical Culture under the auspices of the Interracial Youth Committee. Others shown with Shimizu are, left to right, Theodora Jaffe, of Jewish descent, a student at the Fieldston School of Ethical Culture; JoAnn McKee, born in Germany, who came to the United States just before the outbreak of World War II, representing Christ Church–Methodist; and Charles Speed, a student at Frederick Douglas Junior High School, representing the Abyssinian Baptist Church. Photographer: Toge Fujihira. Courtesy Bancroft Library, University of California, Berkeley.

Opposite, Bottom: Kiichi Uyeda from Manzanar (right), the first returnee to Little Tokyo, now Bronzeville, Los Angeles, opens the Bronzeville 5-10-25 Cents Store, assisted by his friend Matsuo Yoshida from Colorado River, May 14, 1945. Photographer: Charles E. Mace. Courtesy Bancroft Library, University of California, Berkeley.

Top Left: S. I. Hayakawa, ca. 1946, by Ken Uyehara. Courtesy Hayakawa family.

Top Right: Forrest LaViolette. Courtesy Tulane University.

Bottom Right: Hugh Macbeth Jr., by Toyo Miyatake. Courtesy Hugh Macbeth Jr.

Opposite: Cover, *Crossroads*, 1948. Courtesy Bancroft Library, University of California, Berkeley.

THE LOS ANGELES NISEI WEEKLY
CROSSROADS

TOP--NIGHT SCENE, LI'L TOKYO, 1948--A typical crowd of night idlers gathered in front of a television set avidly watching a grunt an groan wrestling session. BELOW--Nisei voters take time out from their busy office routine to register for the '48 elections at an open-air desk set up on the corner of East First and San Pedro.

EAST FIRST AND SAN PEDRO--Nisei Crossroads of the world, in the heart of Los Angeles' Li'l Tokyo--business and social focal point for more than 30,000 Japanese American returnees. Gradually reconverting from a wartime Bronzeville, the pre-war residents are re-establishing old businesses and busily setting up new ones. ◆ Old Japanese magazines and a rash of new ones from Occupied Japan on sale at a Weller Street bookshop for literature-starved Issei.

From interim stops thru-out the land and overseas, the Nisei have come home again--more hopeful, more aggressive, to re-build and make their life an integral part of the whole community.

Larry Tajiri, in his days as *Denver Post* drama critic. Courtesy Tajiri family.

PART IV

African American Supporters of Japanese Americans, and the Shift in Nisei Views of African Americans

8. African American Responses to the Wartime Confinement of Japanese Americans

Scholars of United States history and literature have devoted increasing attention over the past generation to the study of past encounters between African Americans and Asian Americans. Beyond the importance of the question in academic terms, the rediscovery of the history of black-Asian relations has a particular urgency about it. Even after the end of the twentieth century, in a world of changing global alliances and power relations, people of African and Asian ancestry in the United States remain widely stereotyped in popular thought as "naturally" and fundamentally opposed, an image that results in good part from simplistic mass media accounts of episodic hostility and violent conflict between black and Korean communities in Los Angeles and elsewhere during the early 1990s. As the United States transforms itself into a society that is no longer majority white Anglo, historical discussion of the various complex ways in which members of the different groups have seen each other and formed intergroup coalitions can help correct some serious and ultimately dangerous misconceptions that foster racial tension and stall joint efforts against discrimination.[1]

A central element of the historical narrative of interracial connections is missing: the response of African Americans nationwide to the mass exclusion and incarceration of West Coast Japanese Americans during World War II. Despite the efforts of a handful of scholars who have uncovered various pieces of the question, it remains largely obscure. Not only is it worth looking closely at the reaction of African Americans, the primary racialized group within American society, to the wartime confinement of Japanese Americans, a classic instance of official discrimination informed by race, but the disproportionate support that black communities and individuals offered Japanese Americans proved crucial to the postwar alliance between the two groups in movements for civil rights. In order to address this gap, I will provide a summary history, and then offer some suggestions of areas for further investigation.

In order to put into context the wartime encounters between blacks and Japanese Americans, it should be noted immediately that members of these two groups have come into contact since the dawn of Japanese migration to the United States. For example, Joseph Heco, who was the first Japanese to become an American citizen, saw black slaves during a visit to a plantation near Baltimore in the 1850s, and was fascinated by their strange manners and eccentric dancing.[2] Mazumizu Kuninosuke, who came to California in 1869 as a member of the Wakamatsu colony, the first Japanese settlement in the continental United States, married an African American woman in the 1880s, following the settlement's dissolution.[3] Jenichiro Oyabe, who arrived in the United States in 1888, studied alongside black classmates at the African American colleges Hampton Institute and Howard University. Oyabe was in the vanguard of a number of Japanese students and professors who would affiliate with historically black colleges and universities during the twentieth century.[4]

During the early 1900s there was significant interaction in Pacific coast cities such as Seattle, San Francisco, and Los Angeles between the pockets of Japanese American and African American populations.[5] In these cities, where restrictive covenants effectively kept Japanese Americans confined in nonwhite districts, a number of Issei settled in homes alongside African Americans and Latinos. In neighborhoods such as Los Angeles's Boyle Heights, Japanese-operated groceries and restaurants served a partly black clientele. Nisei children attended school and joined in street life with their African American neighbors. Nisei jazz enthusiasts frequented black nightclubs, while Japanese American musicians and bands on the West Coast played together with black colleagues.[6] The Japanese press also reprinted statistics on lynchings provided by Tuskegee Institute. The English sections of the Japanese American newspapers *Kashu Mainichi* and *Rafu Shimpo* printed reports by Nisei columnists Joe Oyama, Eddie Shimano, Yasuo Sasaki, and Tokumi Hamako, who toured the South and wrote sensitively about Jim Crow conditions (although the coverage was often condescending in its depictions of black southerners). Black lawyers such as Walter Gordon, Loren Miller, and Hugh Macbeth connected with Nisei lawyers in fighting segregation and restrictive covenants.

Outside the West Coast, Japanese expatriate intellectuals formed bonds with African Americans. In New York, artist Eitaro Ishigaki painted a black history mural for a Harlem courthouse, while he, Isamu Noguchi, and Hideo Noda each produced artworks of lynchings. Chicagoan Jun Fujita photographed beatings of African Americans during the 1919 race riot. Some of the connection between the two groups was a by-product of African Americans' respect for and interest in Japan. As the first of the nonwhite world powers, and as a country that had pressed unsuccessfully at the Versailles Peace Conference in 1919 for racial equality to be enshrined in the covenant of the League of Nations, Japan was esteemed by many African Americans. As scholars such as Marc Gallicchio and Reginald Kearney have shown, African American leaders such as W. E. B. Du Bois, as well as black nationalist groups such as Marcus Garvey's United Negro Improvement Association, encouraged African Americans to ally themselves with Japan's international policy. During the 1930s, Japanese propagandists such as Yasuichi Hikide and Satokata Takahashi attracted a significant following in African American ghettos. African Americans also viewed Japanese immigration more sympathetically than their white counterparts, and in some cases protested the exclusionary policy of the United States government.[7]

These various zones of contact notwithstanding, the mass of Japanese Americans and African Americans remained distant from each other in the decades before World War II. Japanese American settlement was concentrated in rural districts of the Pacific coast states and Hawaii, where African Americans made up only a tiny fraction of 1 percent of the inhabitants. Conversely, few Japanese migrated to the black population centers in the South and the industrial North—the Chicago area had barely 400 residents of Japanese ancestry in 1940.[8] Also, while both groups were exposed to racial prejudice and economic discrimination, their principal legal problems and social concerns were different. Throughout the prewar era, the Japanese community was dominated by the immigrant generation. Forbidden by federal statute from becoming American citizens—and ultimately from immigrating at all—the Issei were barred on that basis by state laws from owning agricultural land or taking up various professions.[9] Although their children, who represented two-thirds of the West Coast Japanese population, were American citizens, the majority of the Nisei were under eighteen years old during this period, and while they were excluded by social prejudice from housing and employment opportunities, they did not generally face state-imposed segregation (apart from laws banning racial intermarriage). Thus, the fledgling Nisei organizations such as the JACL focused on Issei problems and issues. In contrast, virtually all blacks were American-born citizens, but the majority living in the South were denied their rights to citizenship and equal education by means of Jim Crow laws, entrenched prejudice, and racial violence, while others throughout the county were subjected to widespread race-based discrimination by custom.

Even such interactions as did exist between the two groups in these years were not always positive. Issei writers anxious to portray themselves as modern and acculturated to American values frequently expressed conventional white stereotypes of African Americans as lazy, boisterous, and inferior. Lawyer Masuji Miyakawa commented that if an individual Negro or Chinese had a "character [that] is so base that it tends to produce degeneration of the community, to lower the standard of living of those around him, or in any way to appear antagonistic to the customs of society, he must suffer the consequences."[10] Many African Americans, in turn, shared widespread white nativist suspicions of "orientals" and felt threatened by competition from Japanese laborers. Although deploring the racism involved, a number of black authors expressed opportunistic support for the exclusion of Japanese immigrants under the 1924 Immigration Act on the grounds that it would aid black economic empowerment.[11] African Americans in West Coast cities complained of discrimination against them by Japanese merchants.[12] As the editor of the short-lived Bronzeville magazine *Spotlight* put it, "In the prewar days a great deal of hatred existed between Negroes and Japs. The whites fawned upon the Japanese and made them feel as though they were whites, despite the fact that they were not accorded all civil liberties. The Japs invaded the domestic field, long the bailiwick of the Negro, in Los Angeles. . . . The domestic working Negro and the Jap piled up hatred against each other."[13] Lester Granger of the National Urban League, with some exaggeration, even ascribed the failure of Japanese propaganda about Tokyo's role as "liberator" of the colored races to attract West Coast African Americans in large part to what he termed the "contemptuous hostility" of the Issei, whose attitude resembled that of southern whites.[14]

African Americans differed in their initial reactions to the removal and confinement of West Coast Japanese Americans. When the army began the roundup of Japanese Americans in the Pacific coast states in early spring 1942, many if not most local blacks were indifferent, especially those who were not longtime residents. Maya Angelou, who moved to San Francisco in early 1942, noted the absence of sympathy or support for the dispossessed Japanese among the masses of black war workers who migrated to the West Coast, many of whom settled in the abandoned Japanese American neighborhoods. Angelou asserted that these blacks, who had never known the people involved, could hardly be expected to champion their cause.

Another reason for [their] indifference to the Japanese removal was more subtle but was more profoundly felt. The Japanese were not whitefolks. Their eyes, language, and customs belied the white skin and proved to their dark successors that since they didn't have to be feared, neither did they have to be considered. All this was decided unconsciously.[15]

Meanwhile, the institutional leadership was silent. The vast majority of black newspapers, like their mainstream white counterparts, failed to speak out on behalf of Japanese Americans in the weeks following the proclamation of Executive Order 9066. As Cheryl Greenberg points out, neither the NAACP nor the National Urban League took any official position against the order. Like many liberal church groups, Jewish groups, and civil rights organizations (including the American Civil Liberties Union), the national NAACP declined to oppose the Roosevelt administration in a time of war. Indeed, when Socialist Party leader Norman Thomas, the only nationwide political figure to oppose mass removal, asked NAACP executive secretary Walter White to sign a petition to President Roosevelt protesting Executive Order 9066, White put him off with the excuse that he would have to be granted permission by the association's board of directors to take such a step. The NAACP's 1942 annual convention considered a resolution calling attention to the racial bias inherent in the evacuation, but did not formally approve it.[16]

In fact, a number of local blacks initially welcomed mass removal. John Robert Badger, West Coast correspondent of the *Chicago Defender* newspaper, approved the imprisonment of "disloyal" Japanese as a chance for native-born citizens to show their loyalty.[17] Other African American supporters of removal were motivated by economic considerations, as was the case in 1924. The directors of the Los Angeles National Negro Business League opportunistically seized on the dispossession of the Issei and Nisei as a chance for blacks to take their place and gain a foothold in California agriculture. Editor Charlotta Bass of the *California Eagle*, the leading black paper in Los Angeles, served as a platform for this view (a stand she later recanted), as did the smaller *Los Angeles Sentinel*. William Greenwell, head of the NAACP's Salinas branch, favored the recruitment of African American farmers to replace confined Nikkei, and he invited Assistant National Secretary Roy Wilkins to visit the West Coast in spring 1942 to facilitate the process. Wilkins soon decided that such a policy would be impracticable as well as undesirable, since it would not increase overall African American economic opportunity.[18]

Notwithstanding the lack of collective action, individual blacks, especially those from cities such as Los Angeles, Seattle, and New York where there was prewar contact between the two groups, began fighting on behalf of Japanese Americans even before Executive Order 9066 was declared. A few individuals, such as longtime resident Samuel Thompson of Los Angeles, spoke out publicly in favor of equal treatment for Japanese Americans The weekly *Los Angeles Tribune*, smallest of the three African American newspapers in the City of Angels, speedily opposed the order.[19] Los Angeles attorney Hugh E. Macbeth, as will be discussed in Chapter 9, became a tireless champion of the rights of Issei and Nisei. Columnist George Schuyler of the *Pittsburgh Courier*, who had warned shortly after Pearl Harbor that concentration camps would be the likely end product of the shameful prejudice against "the Japanese" on the West Coast, denounced the confinement of Japanese Americans as an antidemocratic and racist effort instigated by lazy whites bent on taking over the land the Japanese Americans had worked hard to build up.[20]

One outstanding early supporter of Japanese Americans was the singer/activist Paul Robeson. In February 1942, as widespread pressure built up for the expulsion of all Japanese Americans from the Pacific coast, liberal California congressman John Tolan announced that his Committee on Defense Migration would open hearings on the Japanese situation. Robeson, then in California, was approached by the sculptor Isamu Noguchi, who had founded a progressive group called Nisei Writers and Artists Mobilization for Democracy. Noguchi asked Robeson to appear before the commission as part of a blue-ribbon panel of prominent non-Asians who would testify to the loyalty of Japanese Americans and thereby help avert mass evacuation. Robeson readily agreed.[21] Shortly thereafter, when President Franklin D. Roosevelt signed Executive Order 9066 and mass removal became a fait accompli, the idea of a celebrity panel was dropped. Robeson's promise of action nonetheless impressed many Nisei.

After the issuing of Executive Order 9066, African Americans outside the West Coast began to react. During spring 1942 Norman Thomas (using information that had been sent to him by Hugh E. Macbeth) organized a petition to the president under the auspices of the Post War World Council. The petition's text denounced Executive Order 9066 as undemocratic and called for its rescission. Among the approximately 200 signers were at least 14 African Americans, including a number of distinguished intellectuals and activists such as W. E. B. Du Bois, Charles S. Johnson, Willard Townsend, Channing Tobias, and E. Franklin Frazier.[22] Other African American leaders such as Thurgood Marshall and A. Philip Randolph signed letters asking the government to institute immediate hearings to judge the loyalty of Japanese Americans on an individual basis.[23]

There were other demonstrations of pro–Japanese American sentiment that did not directly challenge the government's policy. For instance, although New York clergyman and city councilman Adam Clayton Powell Jr.'s newspaper the *People's Voice* editorially supported mass removal, Powell joined the board of the Japanese American Committee for Democracy, an antifascist group (as also did subsequently attorney Earl Dickerson). Bayard Rustin, a field secretary for the pacifist and egalitarian group Fellowship of Reconciliation, assisted confined Japanese Americans during his tours of the country during 1942.[24] Fisk University sociologist Charles S. Johnson hired Hawaiian-born Nisei Jitsuichi Masuoka to join his department in 1942, and invited a Nisei observer to attend the first Fisk University Race Relations Institute in 1942—the only nonwhite, nonblack delegate.[25] Johnson's journal *Monthly Summary of Race Relations*, founded in 1943, listed items on Japanese Americans contributed by JACL president Saburo Kido.

As the war continued and Japanese Americans appeared less as economic competitors and more in the guise of victims of persecution, various African Americans expressed support for their rights. Some of the most forceful critics of the government's policy were teachers. One was Layle Lane, a New York–based educator and columnist who had led efforts to unionize southern black teachers during the 1930s (and who later became the first black woman vice president of the United Federation of Teachers). Sensitive to the economics of racial and gender discrimination in Jim Crow states, Lane drew on this understanding in discussing Japanese Americans. During a 1943 meeting of the Civil Rights Defense Committee, a multigroup coalition in New York, she referred to the placing of Japanese Americans in concentration camps as "a disgraceful blot" on the country's record, and analyzed its economic ramifications. Lane pointed out that Japanese American teachers (who, like their African American counterparts, were predominantly women) were exploited. The confined Nisei received a maximum salary of $19 per month, while white teachers performing the same work received $150 per month.[26] In 1944, when the names of Nisei veterans were stripped from a memorial post by the American Legion chapter in Hood River, Oregon, Dr. Charles E. Rochelle, a World War I veteran, mobilized the local branch of the Colored American Legion in Evansville, Indiana, to rally on behalf of the Nisei veterans and demonstrate that the Legion was not all reactionary. (Rochelle, who had been the first African American to graduate from the University of

California, Berkeley, with a doctorate in education, likewise used his influence to arrange for a Nisei former classmate to be hired by the Chicago public school system.) *The Journal of Negro Education* also frequently mentioned Japanese Americans during the war years. In 1943 educator Margaret C. McCulloch denounced in its pages "the will of the white man to supremacy," noting: "In the military forces it has been stronger than the will to victory, sacrificing needed military manpower to a determination to hold down and segregate the Negro, and now the Japanese-American likewise. These are ominous signs."[27]

In tandem with the shift in popular sentiment, the African American press soon grew more vocal, in a fashion that differed from the overall silence of the mainstream white press during the war years. The first noticeable shift came when a few African American columnists deplored mass removal and pointed out that no Italian and German aliens (let alone U.S. citizens) were subjected to similar treatment.[28] In March 1942, the Socialist Workers Party organ the *Militant*, directed by Afro-Caribbean American radical C. L. R. James, criticized the official roundup of Japanese Americans as a Nazi doctrine:

> When Vigilante Terror broke out against persons of Japanese descent on the West Coast, President Roosevelt issued an order empowering the Army arbitrarily to drive all persons of Japanese descent, citizens and noncitizens alike, from their homes and farms. Attorney General Biddle, a self-styled guardian of civil liberties, hastened to approve of it as a measure for the "safety" of the threatened victims of reactionary terrorism. Hitler is a past master in applying this concept of "justice." Every time he undertakes a new invasion, or some other new blow at the masses, he explains that he does it "for their own good," to "protect" them.[29]

In fall 1942 the NAACP magazine, the *Crisis*, published an article by a white activist, Harry Paxton Howard. Using a rhetorical strategy that would soon become frequent among black critics, Howard underlined the centrality of racial bias in inspiring the government's policy and reminded African Americans that if the government could arbitrarily confine American citizens of Japanese ancestry and violate their civil rights on a racial basis, it could do the same to blacks.[30]

Indeed, as C. K. Doreski has shown, sometimes African Americans were stronger in their critiques than Japanese Americans. In 1943, the *Chicago Defender* (which, as noted, had supported mass removal in early 1942) hired African American poet/activist Langston Hughes to write a column. At the same time, in part as an expression of solidarity with Japanese Americans, the *Defender* engaged Canadian-born Nisei academic S. I. Hayakawa to write a daily column. Hayakawa's criticism of official treatment of Japanese Americans was largely muted, to say the least. In contrast, Hughes published a number of sharply critical pieces, calling for unity between racial minorities, including blacks, Latinos, and Japanese Americans, and equated the race-based confinement of Japanese Americans in camps with the race-based confinement of African Americans in ghettos.[31]

Individual blacks also wrote pieces outside of the African American press to express support for the inmates. Richard Tynes and George Schuyler contributed pieces to the JACL organ the *Pacific Citizen* calling for interracial unity. Future journalist William A. Hilliard, then a teenager in Portland, Oregon, sent a note to the *Minidoka Irrigator*, a Japanese American camp newspaper, denouncing racial discrimination and expressing his support for the inmates: "I think you people are doing a swell job despite your handicaps."[32] Lester Granger, director of the National Urban League, argued in *Far East Survey* that the confinement of the Japanese Americans, and especially the U.S. Supreme Court's ruling in the notorious 1944 case *Korematsu v. United States*, represented a dangerous precedent for the rights of blacks in the postwar era, and he called for African Americans to be vigilant:

> The disgraceful record which we established in the evacuation of Japanese Americans from the West Coast has made a lasting impression upon thoughtful Negro leaders. They realize that racial prejudice, almost alone, dictated the unconstitutional dispossession of more than 100,000 persons from their dwellings, and, in many cases, robbed them of their household and personal property.... That decision is grim warning that, when public hysteria is strong enough, not even the American Constitution can protect a minority in its right to "life, liberty, and the pursuit of happiness."[33]

Furthermore, periodicals investigated in depth the question of the Japanese Americans. One of the most open was *The War Worker*, a bimonthly race relations journal founded in 1943 by Bill and Elizabeth Cummings, an interracial black-white couple in Los Angeles.[34] In one of their first issues, Chester Himes, a black writer from Los Angeles who moved into the house of his friend Mary Oyama Mittwer after she was removed, wrote a short story purporting to be the diary of a confined Nisei.[35] Shortly afterward, the journal (renamed *Now*) published a multipart story on the return to the West Coast of the Nittas, a Japanese American family. Beginning in mid-1945, *Now* featured a regular column written by Nisei journalist Larry Tajiri. Other issues also included information on Japanese Americans.

The National Urban League and the NAACP likewise became more visible in opposition once removal began. As early as mid-1942, C. L. Dellums, an organizer with the Oakland NAACP and the Brotherhood of Sleeping Car Porters, sent letters to the national NAACP asking it to intervene. (His nephew, future congressman and Oakland mayor Ronald Dellums, later recalled being upset as a boy when his Japanese American friends left, and shouting at soldiers not to take them away.)[36] In response to Dellums's request, NAACP secretary Walter White contacted Justice Department representatives to inquire into the conditions to which Japanese Americans were subjected. Although he confessed that the condition of Japanese Americans was technically outside his organization's purview, he suggested that the government establish hearing boards to test the inmates' loyalty.[37] Then, when a bill was introduced in Congress in mid-1942 to legalize the imprisonment of all people of Japanese ancestry, with the goal of stripping Japanese Americans of their citizenship, the NAACP's board did formally vote to oppose the bill on the grounds that it encouraged racial discrimination.

Moreover, a number of local NAACP and Urban League chapters took steps to aid inmates. The Seattle NAACP raised funds to support Gordon Hirabayashi's Supreme Court challenge to Executive Order 9066, and branch president Fred Shorter organized aid for his subsequent draft resistance campaign. George Squires of the Seattle Urban League made a speech at the University of Washington in 1943 asserting that "if Japanese American could be evacuated, so could Negroes." Southern California NAACP chairman Thomas L. Griffith, an attorney, volunteered to represent the JACL in legal cases, and he was a signatory of the JACL's brief in *Regan v. King*.[38] The Denver NAACP branch co-sponsored a public meeting in 1944 to oppose a law that would have prevented Japanese aliens from owning land in Colorado. The San Francisco and Los Angeles branches organized welcomes for Japanese Americans and deplored efforts to create friction between the two communities. In mid-1944, the San Francisco NAACP passed a resolution drawn up by branch president Joseph James calling for "fair treatment of loyal Japanese-Americans and condemning efforts of reactionary interests to incite suspicion among Americans of African ancestry for Americans of Japanese ancestry."[39] The following year, James joined a delegation that met with state attorney general Robert Kenny to discuss ways to end violence against returning Issei and Nisei.[40]

The national NAACP likewise became more active in the latter part of the war, in part as the result of the efforts of Milton R. Konvitz, a white scholar and civil rights lawyer who also worked with the ACLU.[41] In May

1944, under prodding from Konvitz, NAACP leader Roy Wilkins issued a public telegram in the name of the association scoring New York mayor Fiorello La Guardia for opposing the resettlement of Japanese Americans in New York. Wilkins then helped organize a well-attended public rally to support the admission of resettlers into New York, and delivered a speech praising the loyalty of Japanese Americans.[42]

Shortly thereafter, in May 1944, NAACP secretary Walter White sprang into action. Upon learning that President Franklin Roosevelt intended to delay the closing of the camps until after the November 1944 election, White and American Friends Service Committee field secretary Clarence Pickett put together a proposal for a series of protests by blacks on behalf of the inmates. White and Pickett asked Eleanor Roosevelt to convey their plan to the president in hopes that it would sway him. FDR relayed back through his wife that protests by one racial minority group on behalf of another would provoke a racist backlash, and advised them to avoid any specifically black protest. White was promised an off-the-record meeting with the president over the Japanese Americans, but he was unsuccessful in his attempts to arrange it.[43]

The NAACP also promoted Japanese Americans in the press. In June 1945, NAACP publicity director Consuelo Young-Megahy sent out a press release on Japanese Americans to the *New York Times*, the *Chicago Sun*, and other newspapers. In her letter, Young-Megahy pointed to an editorial in the army newspaper *Stars and Stripes* extolling the remarkable contributions of Nisei soldiers, and she contrasted their patriotism with "the impunity from legal punishment with which [the] outrages against Americans of Japanese ancestry have been committed, plus the continued segregation and discrimination practiced against Negroes."[44] Meanwhile, the *Crisis* (which, as noted, had published Harry Paxton Howard's article in fall 1942) opened its pages to Nisei journalists. In January 1945, the *Crisis* published Ina Sugihara's "Our Stake in a Permanent FEPC." In the years that followed, a selection of articles by Sugihara, Sachiye Mizuki, and George Yamada appeared in its pages.

The narrative of African Americans and wartime Japanese confinement needs to be further fleshed out in a number of ways, in order to deal with some central intellectual issues. The first is the distinctive role of black women dissenters. Although Cheryl Greenberg has noted the failure of the National Council of Negro Women to protest Executive Order 9066, the nature and development of black women's attitudes toward the Japanese Americans, and the importance of gender in shaping black responses, remain substantially unexplored.

There are numerous examples of African American women who spoke out in support of Japanese Americans. One outstanding dissident was columnist Erna P. Harris of the *Los Angeles Tribune*. Although less renowned a figure than Schuyler or Hughes, she proved the most forthright and fearless critic among African American columnists of the treatment of Japanese Americans. In late November 1943, reports of rioting among "disloyal Japanese" at the government's "segregation center" at Tule Lake brought anti–Japanese American sentiment in Southern California to a climax. Politicians and organizations called for a military takeover of the camps and for the end of resettlement. *The Los Angeles Times* published a reader poll on December 7, the second anniversary of the Pearl Harbor attack, in which a large majority supported confinement and postwar deportation of all Japanese Americans. In a column, Harris decried the hysteria over "disloyalty," laying into the bigots and expressing sympathy for the rioters and other Japanese Americans who had been "set on" as part of the inflammatory campaigns of the Hearst press:

> Eighteen months ago the evacuation of the Issei and Nisei was being called a matter of military necessity on threat of imminent invasion. In a few months it was called protective custody for their own safety— such cannibals are we, their erstwhile neighbors, alleged to be. But now, as the interests which have long wanted them eliminated from California in the hysteria of war-bred hatred dare to come out into the open, there comes the call for their permanent exclusion from California, for treating them as war prisoners, for depriving them of citizenship, and from a man pledged to enforce the law, [Los Angeles County] Sheriff [Eugene] Biscailuz, comes a plea for sending many of them to Japan in exchange for prisoners of war. Such a move would involve some American citizens. If citizenship is to become a matter of racial or national predeterminism or of periodic authoritarian changes, who will be safe from the whims of the powerful?[45]

Exactly how gender factors determined the response of black women to Japanese wartime confinement likewise remains to be settled. In this context, *California Eagle* editor Charlotta Bass's comment that she "shed no tears" for the Japanese Americans at the time of the roundup is perhaps revealing.[46] Similarly, it is fascinating to ruminate on the gender politics of Margaret C. McCullough's and Consuelo Young-Megahy's protests over discrimination against Nisei and African Americans in the military. In her June 1945 press release on Japanese American soldiers, Young-Megahy commented that "the editorial cited in *Stars and Stripes* [about Nisei soldiers] gives us reason to hope that the men in the army will have learned from their fight for democracy more about what democracy means than any noncombattant." This ready equation of maleness and military service with citizenship left Japanese American women, like African American women, implicitly subordinate.⁴⁷

Perhaps the most complex case of the role of gender in black women's responses to Japanese Americans was the evolution of the views of Pauli Murray, whose activism for racial and gender equality was heavily informed by her friendships with other women. During spring 1942 Murray, then a law student at Howard University, became active in the defense of Odell Waller, a North Carolina sharecropper sentenced to death by an all-white jury on flimsy evidence. After being misinformed about the nature of removal by a friend in Oregon, who told her that Japanese Americans were being evacuated for their own protection, Murray wrote an angry letter to President Roosevelt calling attention to racial violence. If the Japanese Americans, she commented ironically, could be transported away from danger, why could the government not move southern blacks to protect them from lynching? Her letter, which she herself later termed "ill-conceived," received a blistering reply from First Lady Eleanor Roosevelt (who had previously struggled to dissuade her husband from approving Executive Order 9066). In a rare display of anger (mixed with some odd ethnic categorization) Mrs. Roosevelt wrote Murray:

> I wonder how many of our colored people in the South would like to be evacuated and treated as though they were not as rightfully here as other people? I am deeply concerned that we have had to do that to the Japanese who are American citizens, but we are at war with Japan and they have only been citizens for a very short time. We would feel a resentment if we had to do this for citizens who have been here as long as most of the white people.⁴⁸

Not only did Mrs. Roosevelt's reply cause Murray to realize she had been taken in by propaganda about the plight of Japanese Americans, but it also sparked a lifelong friendship between the two women based on their common interest in human rights.

Although Murray did not involve herself further in direct challenges to the removal of Issei and Nisei, she credited a Japanese American friend, Miyeko Takita, whom she met while studying at University of California, Berkeley, in the latter months of the war, with expanding her perspective on the race problem and helping begin her broader education on the place of civil rights within human rights. As an inmate at Topaz, Takita had, in Murray's words, "suffered the terrible paradox of World War II in ways I could only imagine."⁴⁹ Murray became a prominent advocate of Japanese

American rights in the postwar years, when as attorney for the American Jewish Congress she drafted eloquent briefs in support of civil rights for Nisei, and later she was a co-founder of the feminist group National Organization for Women.[50]

Another area that requires further exploration is the factor of religion in shaping African American responses to the government's policy toward Japanese Americans. This is a fundamental question both because of the dominant role of the church in African American life and also because of the participation of diverse religious groups such as the Quakers, the Mennonites, and the Baptist Home Mission Society in protesting the official policy and aiding the inmates. The existing record, while sparse, gives some indication of the presence of religious leaders among the supporters of Japanese Americans. George Haynes of the Federal Council of Churches wrote a bimonthly newsletter in which he repeatedly attacked the treatment of Japanese Americans in the camps. In June 1945, Rev. Benjamin Mays, president of Morehouse College, made a commencement address at Howard University calling for the students to fight injustice at any price. "We are tied together with an inescapable destiny. What affects one, affects all. . . . The injustice against loyal Japanese Americans is injustice against America."[51] A number of black churchmen leading interracial congregations, such as Dr. Howard Thurman in San Francisco and Dr. John Yancey in Chicago, supported Japanese American resettlers and denounced discrimination, while Rev. Charles Kingsley opened the doors of Pilgrim House in Los Angeles to Japanese Americans on an equal basis. However, with the possible exception of Adam Clayton Powell, little has been uncovered in regard to the attitudes of prominent black religious leaders and groups. Did the National Baptist Convention, Inc. or the African Methodist Episcopal Church, for example, address the subject or aid Japanese Americans?

In sum, while much remains to be done to flesh out the nature and range of African American reactions to Japanese American removal, even the incomplete narrative that has already been uncovered demonstrates great variety of responses, and challenges simplistic descriptions. Still, what remains most clear is the disproportionate support offered by blacks to confined Japanese Americans, and the extent to which they were able to draw connections between their own condition and the plight of the inmates. This identity of interest, and the bonds between the groups that resulted, would have powerful consequences for postwar events.

9. The Los Angeles Defender
Hugh E. Macbeth and Japanese Americans

The long history of relations between Asian Americans and African Americans has been marked by a complex succession of interactions, in which individuals have at different times expressed curiosity, disdain, admiration, hostility, envy, affection, rivalry, xenophobia, and sympathy for the other. Probably the most common sentiment has been indifference—members of these two population groups have simply not been in a position either to make trouble for the other group or to do them much good. Historians have only begun to document some of the striking, if less common, incidences of mutual support and friendship between blacks and Asians.

One of the most notable cases of such collaboration was occasioned by the wartime removal and incarceration of West Coast Japanese Americans. The arbitrariness and race-based nature of the government's actions toward a group of nonwhite American citizens and residents struck a responsive chord among many African Americans. Conversely, the disproportionate presence of blacks among critics and opponents of the government's policy helped to inspire a lasting bond with many Nisei, and to draw representatives of the two groups together in postwar legal struggles for civil rights.

Perhaps the most outstanding black supporter of the rights of Japanese Americans during World War II was Hugh E. Macbeth,[1] an attorney in Los Angeles who was executive secretary of the California Race Relations Commission. An early and fervent advocate for equal justice, Macbeth dedicated himself to fighting Executive Order 9066 through fact-finding, lobbying, and public speeches. The legal challenges he helped bring, though unsuccessful in reversing the policy, ultimately resulted in an important postwar victory for Japanese Americans.

Hugh Ellwood Macbeth had a colorful and slightly checkered prewar career. He was born in Charleston, South Carolina, in 1884, the oldest of eight children. His father, Arthur Macbeth, the son of a Scottish immigrant father and a free black mother, was a pioneering black portrait photographer. (A Macbeth family legend claims that Arthur Macbeth's mother had been sired by the Bullochs, the family of Theodore Roosevelt's mother, and certainly Arthur Macbeth strongly suggests TR in his photos, which show him with mustache and pince-nez.) In 1905, after attending Avery Normal School and Fisk University, the young Hugh decided to become a lawyer. As he later told the tale, he decided to attend Harvard University. Ignorant of the admissions process, he traveled to Cambridge and managed to see the law dean, James Baer Ames. Ames initially refused to admit him, explaining that Macbeth would do better at Tuskegee—Harvard, he explained, trained lawyers for "leadership in railroads, banks, and big business." Macbeth then explained that he wished to study at Harvard in order to find out why colored people had lived in the United States for 300 years without sharing in the leadership of big business. Dean Ames then relented and admitted him, stating, "Young man, you have won your first law case."

After graduating from Harvard in 1908, Hugh Macbeth married, had a child, and settled in Baltimore, where his father had moved the family and established his photography business. Unable to support himself through the law, he first worked for a shoe company, and subsequently assumed editorship of a new African American newspaper, the *Baltimore Advocate* (later known as the *Baltimore Times*). During his tenure on the newspaper, Macbeth stirred up controversy through his attacks on local ministers and political figures. He also sparked opposition among the black community's solidly Republican leadership by supporting Theodore Roosevelt's Bull Moose Party candidacy and attending the party's convention (at least until Roosevelt excluded black delegates from the convention). These were the first demonstrations of the maverick style and shifting political stance that were to characterize his entire career.

In 1913, Macbeth gave up management of the paper and headed west to Los Angeles, then still a growing city of some 400,000, including perhaps 10,000 blacks. He praised the city enthusiastically to his wife as "God's Country."[2] The couple's happiness was shadowed in 1914 when their young daughter was killed in an automobile accident; a second child, Hugh Macbeth Jr., was born in 1919. In the decades following his move to Los Angeles, Macbeth became an important player in local law and politics, although lack of available sources make knowing the extent of his involvement difficult. His activity was bifurcated. On one hand, he remained an active proponent of the rights of African Americans. In a 1914 letter to Booker T. Washington, Macbeth spoke of his efforts to persuade local newspapers to run a greater number of positive stories on black communities. In the first years after World War I, Macbeth became a leading local supporter of Marcus Garvey's black nationalist movement, the United Negro Improvement Association. Meanwhile, hoping to combine freedom from discrimination with profit, Macbeth formed a syndicate with local businessmen to purchase land in Baja California, Mexico, and encourage black colonization in "Little Liberia." While the project ultimately fizzled due to diplomatic obstacles and poor management, he retained a close interest in Mexico and would later serve as an advisor to the Mexican government at the 1945 Latin American conference that resulted in the Act of Chapultepec.

During the 1920s and 1930s, Macbeth worked actively within the Los Angeles African American community. The law firm he formed with his brother, Gobert, regularly represented black litigants and criminal defendants, including such notable names as jazz great Jelly Roll Morton. In 1928, the Macbeth brothers brought a successful civil rights suit on behalf of Elizabeth Slaughter, a black UCLA student who had been removed from a public beach and imprisoned under a municipal racial segregation ordinance. Macbeth also undertook various cases challenging racially restrictive covenants in housing. In 1940, he joined forces with the celebrated white attorney Jerry Geisler in a suit against the American Legion over its policy of excluding black boxers from fight cards at Hollywood Legion Stadium, and he proved that blacks had been systematically refused access based on their race. The overturning of the policy won Macbeth plaudits in black communities nationwide. In 1941, he testified before the federal Fair Employment Practices Committee on behalf of blacks excluded from shipbuilding industries.

At the same time, Macbeth refused to associate himself solely with African American interests. His law firm had mostly white clients, and he sought to contribute to the larger society. After serving briefly as assistant district attorney in 1916–17, Macbeth allied himself with local good-government movements. During the 1920s, he joined campaigns against police protection of gambling and vice activities in the largely black Central Avenue District, and later claimed that the evidence he collected resulted in the indictment of municipal officials for corruption. (Ironically, in 1930 Macbeth would himself be implicated in the defense of Curtis

Mosby and George Brown, Central Avenue businessmen accused of violating Prohibition-era liquor laws.) His most important political intervention came in 1934, which he was named general counsel for the Utopian Society of America, a largely white fraternity and economic reform group that claimed some 600,000 members. The Utopians lobbied for relief funds and old-age pensions for destitute victims of the Great Depression and urged bringing together unemployed workers and farmers with surpluses to sell. The Utopians were early backers and idea men for Upton Sinclair's unsuccessful social democratic "End Poverty in California" gubernatorial campaign. Although Macbeth's reaching beyond the black community made him subject to criticism by local blacks, in 1936 he was named resident consul in Los Angeles for the Republic of Liberia, a tribute to his broad interests and political connections. He remained in the largely symbolic post for almost a decade.

In keeping with his larger focus, Macbeth maintained significant contacts with Japanese Americans during the prewar years. He settled in the Jefferson Park district of Los Angeles, then largely a Japanese area. Hugh Macbeth Jr. later recalled that as a child he attended Japanese school with his Nisei friends after the regular school day finished, since otherwise he would have no children in the neighborhood to play with. There he studied Japanese language and judo—and also absorbed endemic community prejudices against Chinese and Filipinos. Meanwhile, the Macbeth family took in an orphaned Japanese American boy, Kenji Horita, who celebrated all his birthdays with his adoptive family and established a lasting bond with Mrs. Macbeth.[3]

Macbeth's social contacts ultimately evolved into political ties. In 1937, Macbeth founded the United Races of America, a multiracial group dedicated to fighting all forms of racial prejudice, which he termed "a peculiar form of lunacy," and he invited Asian Americans to collaborate in its activities. The following year, Republican California governor Frank Merriam, who was facing a tough reelection campaign, created the California Race Relations Commission in a move to foster racial amity and secure liberal support. Macbeth, who had drawn up the legislation establishing the commission, was named executive secretary, and the commission's bureaus were housed in his downtown Los Angeles law office. Presumably with his collaboration, thirteen other commissioners, representing a selection of racial minority groups, were chosen for the board, including Issei newspaperman Sei Fujii and Chinese American minister Kei T. Wong. At the invitation of his fellow commissioners, Macbeth scheduled community forums in Little Tokyo and other areas, and solicited evidence of discrimination.

Despite these connections, it was the aftermath of the Japanese attack on Pearl Harbor that dramatically shifted Macbeth's political orientation toward a focus on Japanese Americans. In the first week of January 1942, Macbeth traveled to Guadalupe and Santa Barbara, California, with an unidentified Nisei friend (presumably Tooru Takahashi) to investigate the cases of Issei who had been rounded up by the Justice Department during December and sent to an internment camp in Missoula, Montana. Following interviews with the internees' families, he discovered that all those taken were prosperous truck farmers with large families and that none was suspected of sabotage. He swiftly came to the conclusion that the charges were trumped up by white agricultural interests anxious to grab the Issei farmers' land, an impression confirmed when a friendly FBI agent informed him that the agency had arrested suspects whose names figured on a secret list that had been maintained for several years.[4] Macbeth prepared to defend the interned farmers but was stymied by the government's refusal to allow counsel at hearings.

Outraged by the arrests, Macbeth turned to organizing support for Japanese Americans among liberal and church groups on the West Coast, and to speaking in favor of the rights of Japanese Americans in public forums such as George Knox Roth's radio show. In Macbeth's words, "You never know in this world when you are going to get your block knocked off, and you might as well be certain it's something you stand for."[5] As a result of his influence, the California Race Relations Commission and the Santa Barbara Ministers Alliance would eventually become the only two Southern California organizations to officially oppose evacuation. Macbeth's efforts also attracted some less favorable attention from Los Angeles police commissioner Al Cohn. In January 1942, Cohn sent city mayor Fletcher Bowron a secret report featuring wild charges that Japanese spies had infiltrated the Central Avenue district by buying up pool halls and restaurants, and were using marijuana to spread antiwhite propaganda among Negroes and Mexicans. Cohn identified Macbeth as their agent:

> A colored attorney, Hugh E. Macbeth . . . has seen fit to champion a Japanese private detective who has endeavoured to secure a permit to carry concealed weapons. Macbeth has written the Attorney General in Washington, D.C. complaining about "discrimination" and the rights of minority groups, etc. This is all tied in with the very dangerous condition being fostered and pressed by the Japanese in colored town.[6]

In addition to his local efforts, Macbeth moved to organizing on a nationwide scale, in hopes of averting federal action against Japanese Americans. Using the Race Relations Committee's assistant, Ann Ray, a Socialist Party member, as a conduit, he undertook an extensive correspondence with Socialist leader Norman Thomas. Macbeth was largely responsible for Thomas becoming the only national political figure to oppose mass evacuation, as Thomas made extensive use of information provided by Macbeth on the treatment of Japanese Americans when he wrote a series of articles in the Socialist newspaper, the *Weekly Call*, and in radio speeches. Macbeth continued to collaborate with Thomas during the months that followed Executive Order 9066. Most notably, Macbeth was featured as a co-signer and sponsor of Thomas's widely distributed pamphlet, *Democracy and the Japanese Americans*, which denounced the government's policy as "totalitarian justice" and called for the end of confinement and for reparations.[7]

The announcement of Executive Order 9066 on February 19, 1942, was a major blow to Macbeth. Deciding that military control over Japanese Americans could no longer be averted, given the frenzied state of West Coast public opinion, he altered his strategy. On February 22 he sent President Roosevelt a telegram, hoping to shape the government's policy to defend the community:

> Now that your recent Executive Order, transferring jurisdiction of Japanese aliens and citizens to the United States military officials, has allayed fears of those who felt in danger of Japanese sabotage on the Pacific Coast, will you consider a plan of productive work for the liberty-loving Japanese by permitting them voluntarily, under military surveillance and with government assistance, to resume their normal activities as cooperative producers of agricultural products, and thus contribute to our nation's defense? . . . Such a plan will go far to remove the sufferings of efficient loyal American citizens who are victims of the racial complexities incident to our defense efforts.

Macbeth privately admitted that by his strategy of organizing guards for farmers he was trying to make the best of a bad situation.

> Our Commission is very doubtful as to how well the Agricultural production work will go under [military surveillance]. However, the hysteria is so universal and pronounced that I feel it would be endangering the lives of Japanese farmers to have them work in the present state of public minds without the benefit of bayonets and rifles to keep them from being murdered in their fields or in the huts in which they live on the agricultural lands.[8]

He was nevertheless revolted by the "heart-rending scenes" that were provoked by the government's orders.

> Families are being torn up by the roots from their homes which they have spent twenty, thirty, forty and forty-five years in building. They are being shifted out—they know not where. Japanese citizens who have been loyal and self-sacrificing are being embittered. From a military standpoint I seriously doubt that good has been accomplished by the order. I am afraid that the net result will be an invitation to serious bombings of our Western Coastal region.[9]

Given these feelings of outrage and pessimism, Macbeth's attempts to bring about cooperation with the military were halfhearted. In early March, he wrote General John DeWitt to pass along a proposal that loyal Japanese American farmers be permitted to collaborate with the government by forming an Inter-Mountain Cooperative Farmers' Association and moving voluntarily to Utah to form colonies. (Ironically, the apparent designer of this proposal was San Francisco–area nurseryman Hi Korematsu, whose brother Fred would soon challenge mass removal in court.) Even in making this offer, however, Macbeth could not restrain himself from lecturing the general that his creation of "martial law zones" had left Japanese Americans "deeply hurt" and bitter over their sense that "the real cause of their inability to enjoy the same status as other loyal American citizens is due to general and deep seated American racial prejudice against orientals and particularly against Japanese."[10] Perhaps not surprisingly, the general seems not to have responded to Macbeth's overtures.

Even as he resigned himself to preliminary removal, Macbeth remained interested in bringing a constitutional challenge to the government's orders. With Norman Thomas's assistance, Macbeth had first contacted the American Civil Liberties Union in early February 1942 to press for action (he planned a trip to Washington to brief ACLU director Roger Baldwin, although it is not clear whether that trip took place).[11] Soon after Executive Order 9066 was issued, he told Norman Thomas, "I think it is very necessary that several suits be started by American citizens who have no suspicion or enemy-alien blood in them to test the extent and validity of General DeWitt's order and its supporting Presidential decree."[12] He offered to use the Race Relations Commission's investigatory powers to facilitate such suits. "Once the worst has come to pass in the announcement of the military zones, our commission can then proceed with its factual survey and protest for its end purpose of the reduction of these military zones and the eventual return of the great majority of the interned Japanese to their former places of residence."[13] Thomas agreed to work on pushing the ACLU to act. However, to his and Macbeth's dismay, a pro-administration faction on the board quickly called a board member referendum, in the wake of which the national ACLU formally voted not to challenge the constitutionality of Executive Order 9066. Although local branches were permitted to contest its arbitrary application to Japanese Americans, the narrow grounds on which they had to argue left opponents of Executive Order 9066 in a weakened position.

In May 1942, Macbeth visited the Santa Anita Assembly Center with his wife and brother to see friends and collect information on living conditions. Shortly afterward, with encouragement from liberal California congressman Jerry Voorhis, Macbeth traveled to Washington to meet with federal officials regarding race relations, including the treatment of Japanese Americans. The primary goal of his trip was to lobby for the creation of a new cabinet post in interracial affairs—and, ironically in view of his attempts to undo the arbitrary government power and racial bias of Executive Order 9066, for an executive order making all racial discrimination a treasonable military offense.[14] While in Washington, he attempted to secure a meeting with President Roosevelt in order to plead for justice. According to his son, he even used a White House cook as a back channel. (African American White House butler Alonzo Fields, who enjoyed a privileged relationship of trust with FDR, may have been consulted.) Macbeth was unable to persuade the president to see him. He did, however, meet with Justice Department officials, and on his return, he wrote to Norman Thomas that they had a green light to proceed with a legal challenge:

> I want you to know in confidence that the Department of Justice *would not be antagonized* by a *real effort* to test the validity of the Japanese evacuee procedure in our Supreme Court. However, they would like it to be a very serious effort with able outstanding Counsel from the East as well as from the West. I understand that an effort is being started in California by the local branch of the A.C.L.U. Please advise me as to what if any help I can render in the premises.[15]

Macbeth soon found a pair of cases challenging the constitutionality of General DeWitt's evacuation orders: the combined habeas corpus suits of Ernest Kinzo Wakayama and his wife, Toki Wakayama. Ernest Wakayama, born in Hawaii in 1897, was a veteran of World War I and an officer of the American Legion. A onetime postman, he worked as secretary/treasurer of the Western Fishermen's Union.[16] Toki Wakayama had been born in California in 1914. While at the Santa Anita Assembly Center, the Wakayamas decided to have ACLU lawyers Fred Okrand and Edgar Camp file a petition on Mrs. Wakayama's behalf for a writ of habeas corpus (by the time it was filed on August 20, 1942, they had been moved to Manzanar). The principal argument of the petition was that the military necessity claimed by the army for evacuation did not exist, and also that General DeWitt's exclusion order was arbitrary and encroached on the rights of civilian authorities.[17] The attorney who assumed chief direction of the case on behalf of the ACLU was A. L. Wirin, a progressive Jewish lawyer. (Warned by partners in his law firm that the labor union clients who provided most of their business would be unhappy about his defending "Japs," Wirin courageously left the firm and set up his own practice in order to defend the Wakayamas.)[18] Presumably at the behest of Wirin, Macbeth chose to join the Wakayamas' defense team (another black lawyer, NAACP counsel Loren Miller, also signed the Wakayamas' petition as counsel, but did not actively participate in the case).

In October 1942, the Wakayamas' petition was heard by a panel of three federal judges, Campbell E. Beaumont, J. E. T. O'Connor, and Harry Hollzer, sitting en banc. A. L. Wirin argued that the authority to remove American citizens from a military area did not include the authority to confine them. In his supporting brief, Macbeth charged that a race-based confinement constituted unconstitutional discrimination. In his oral argument, which Wirin praised as "magnificent," he urged the judges to overturn evacuation as an unwarranted discrimination against a people because of race.[19] U.S. attorney Leo Silverstein, with California attorney general Earl Warren joining him, submitted amicus briefs supporting continued confinement. Sensing victory, Macbeth wrote the national ACLU to request that $50,000 be set aside to pursue the case. The judges, however, delayed consideration. On February 4, 1943, Judge Hollzer granted the Wakayamas a writ of habeas corpus and set the case down for a full hearing. However, by this time the Wakayamas no longer wished to proceed. Worn down by large-scale official harassment at Manzanar, including beatings and ostracism, the Wakayamas withdrew their suit and filed requests for "repatriation" to Japan.

Although his chief constitutional case had collapsed, during 1943 Macbeth continued to press in different avenues for the release of Japanese Americans from camp. He wrote President Roosevelt in March 1943 urging him to release Japanese Americans to California so they could do their patriotic duty in improving farm production. He bombarded War Relocation Authority director Dillon S. Myer with letters. While the WRA director repeatedly acknowledged his letters with thanks, Macbeth was unable to make any headway with him. Macbeth received even less encouragement in his dealings with the head of the Office of War Information. Following a message from Macbeth in early 1944, OWI director Elmer Davis became so alarmed about the lawyer's ideas that he wrote to FBI director J. Edgar Hoover, to check up on Macbeth's organization and associations.[20] Meanwhile, in the face of widespread anti-Japanese sentiment in Los Angeles, Macbeth spoke out in favor of the return of confined Japanese Americans to their homes on the West Coast. During a public forum in April 1943, he remarked: "The question of racial identity of the Japanese is out of the question. It does not matter to me if they are Japanese, Jews, Negroes, or Germans. I claim that the moment the so-called power of government steps in and takes any people out of their homes, the very essence of democracy has been ruined."[21] In mid-1945, after exclusion of Japanese Americans from the West Coast was lifted, Macbeth applied for a park permit to host a ceremony welcoming returning Japanese Americans to California, although it is not recorded whether any event took place. He also contributed to helping Japanese Americans on a personal level. When Chiyoko Sakamoto, the first Nisei woman to be admitted to the California bar, returned from camp, she was unable to find a job in her field. Macbeth hired her as an associate, thus helping launch her career. (Following Gobert Macbeth's death in 1943, Hugh Macbeth Jr., a Boalt Hall graduate, also began practice with his father.)

During this period, Macbeth began working with the Japanese American Citizens League. In late 1942, the case of *Regan v. King*, in which the Native Sons of the Golden West brought suit to overturn Nisei voting rights and birthright citizenship, was brought on appeal before the United States Court of Appeals for the Ninth Circuit. The JACL resolved to submit an amicus brief in favor of suffrage rights. Both because their own lawyers were confined in camps and to broaden their representation, JACL leaders obtained the aid of A. L. Wirin. Doubtless at Wirin's suggestion, they then reached out to Hugh Macbeth, who not only agreed to join on the brief but who in turn recruited the NAACP's Southern California branch president, Thomas L. Griffith.

The JACL's amicus, which listed Macbeth and Griffith among the counsel, was filed on February 17, 1943, two days before oral argument in the case. The brief included a section termed "Interests of Negroes and this case." In this section, whose prose and contents bear the mark of Macbeth, the brief drew larger connections between opponents of equality for Japanese Americans and blacks, and added that if the Native Sons lawsuit was successful, the next step of such "Hitlerism" would be the introduction of a constitutional amendment to deprive Negroes of citizenship.[22]

In early 1944, Macbeth signed the JACL's amicus curiae brief for the appellant in *Korematsu v. United States*, the Supreme Court case that upheld the constitutionality of race-based "evacuation." Shortly after, in April 1944, he volunteered to travel to the Amache camp in eastern Colorado to counsel families of inmate draft resisters.[23] Meanwhile, he undertook what would become his most important contribution to the rights of Japanese Americans.

In 1943–44, the California state legislature, hoping to forestall the return of West Coast Japanese Americans from camp, provided funds for the state attorney general's office to bring escheat suits to enforce the state's Alien Land Act against Japanese Americans. Macbeth responded by joining forces with A. L. Wirin, by then JACL counsel, in a group of lawsuits challenging the constitutionality of California's Alien Land Act. In February 1945, the case of *People v. Oyama*, together with a companion case, *People v. Hirose*, was argued in San Diego County Superior Court. In their memorandum of law, Wirin and Macbeth argued that even if the Alien Land Act had been upheld by the U.S. Supreme Court in the 1920s, "many living waters have [since] run under the bridges of the Constitution"; the times and circumstances had changed sufficiently that the decisions were no longer controlling.[24] Moreover, they claimed, the Alien Land Act was conceived in race prejudice and penalized the defendants solely because of race, and was thereby unconstitutional. In an overt (and audacious) reference to the *Korematsu* case, then less than two months old, Wirin and Macbeth asserted that "discrimination because of race is constitutionally justified only when required by pressing public necessity, under circumstances of direct emergency and peril."[25]

The Superior Court judge refused the demurrer, arguing that the constitutional questions were not appropriate for a trial court to examine. At this point, for reasons that are not clear, Macbeth officially withdrew from the case. However, he remained interested in the case, which on appeal became *Oyama v. California*, as it was taken up to the U.S. Supreme Court. It was Hugh Macbeth Jr. (following the ideas of University of California law professor Dudley McGovney) who proposed to Wirin what became the winning appellate strategy, namely, that the case be argued on the basis of the law's discriminatory impact on American citizens of Japanese ancestry. In January 1948 the Supreme Court, in a 6–3 vote, struck down all enforcement of the Alien Land Act. The ruling not only reversed historical discrimination against Japanese aliens but enshrined as Supreme Court doctrine the principle of "strict scrutiny" of racial classifications. By making use of this principle, African Americans were able to challenge Jim Crow legislation in further civil rights victories in the years that followed, with the campaign culminating in the legendary 1954–55 Supreme Court decisions known as *Brown v. Board of Education*.[26]

Hugh E. Macbeth did not survive to see most of the changes he set in motion—he died in mid-1956, not long after the *Brown* decisions were issued. His career has been little studied, in part because he did not preserve his own records or correspondence. Yet, as a historian, I have found it gratifying to chase down Macbeth's story. His attachment to democratic principle and passion for building bridges remain potent lessons for our times.

10. Crusaders in Gotham
The JACD and Interracial Activism

The most unique element of 1940s New York Japanese community life, and one in which resettlers would also play a prominent role, was the development of a mass Nikkei political action group, the Japanese American Committee for Democracy. The JACD has been effectively ignored in the history of Japanese Americans, no doubt as a result of its close relationship to the Communist Party. The number of actual Party members in the JACD seems to have been small, though this is a matter of dispute, and the group's militants were by no means simple party-liners. Nevertheless, the JACD's platform and activities were shaped in significant ways by the Communist Party and by its wartime strategy of total victory over fascism, most notably in the JACD's emphasis on encouraging the Nisei to look beyond their own group interests in support of a larger war for democracy. On one hand, this principle led the group not only to demonstrate its support for the war effort through numerous activities but also to reach out in important ways to other groups such as African Americans, championing equal rights for all. On the other hand, the JACD's support for the anti-Axis struggle led it to approve uncritically the confinement of West Coast Japanese Americans and to downplay the injustice done to Japanese Americans afterward.

The JACD was first founded in New York in 1940 as the Committee for Democratic Treatment for Japanese Residents in Eastern States. Although it was a mixed Issei-Nisei group from the beginning, its first leader was Rev. Alfred Akamatsu, the young Issei pastor of New York's Japanese Methodist Church, and its leadership boasted many radical Issei sympathizers. Its goals, which resembled those of the JACL and of the fledgling Fair Play Committees on the West Coast, was to inculcate pro-American and pro-democratic sentiment within the Japanese community while mobilizing public opinion in favor of loyal Japanese Americans. Its initial board was composed of white liberals such as ACLU director Roger Baldwin, writer Pearl S. Buck, and progressive Protestant clergyman John Haynes Holmes. In part because of resistance by the largely pro-Japanese Issei leadership of New York's prewar ethnic Japanese community, the group remained largely dormant through the U.S. entry into war in December 1941, when the committee was rechristened the Japanese American Committee for Democracy. At a mass meeting of 150 Nikkei shortly after Pearl Harbor, the new organization elected a chairman, Thomas Komuro, established a structure of six subcommittees, and began a regular newsletter (Nisei journalist Larry Tajiri, who had relocated to New York in 1940–41, contributed to the first issue of the newsletter before returning to the West Coast). Yoshitaka Takagi, a radical Issei, became the secretary and chief mover of the group.

In early January 1942, the JACD drafted and approved a constitution and by-laws, with its official goals being to "mobilize all loyal Americans of Japanese ancestry and Japanese residents of our community loyal to the United States for the defense of American democracy; establish better understanding between the Japanese community and the greater American public and thus facilitate our participation in the full scheme of American life; promote the economic, social, and cultural status of our community." The committee's newsletter urged Japanese Americans to show their patriotism despite the discrimination they faced. The JACD organized public demonstrations of Japanese American loyalty such as war bond rallies, blood drives, and art exhibitions. A number of its members volunteered for work in the Foreign Language Division of the Office of War Information, the government information service, as translators or writers. Although the JACD board sent letters to Filipino, Chinese, and Korean organizations suggesting cooperative action, there were no immediate responses.[1]

During the early part of 1942, the JACD devoted itself primarily to the organization of social service work within the Japanese community. Under the leadership of Akamatsu, the JACD organized a social study of the New York Japanese community, to determine where aid was most needed.[2] Meanwhile, the Vocations and Welfare Committee provided information about collecting unemployment insurance to Japanese Americans left unemployed by the closure of Japanese businesses and laying off of municipal civil service workers, and JACD members organized an employment service to find work for the displaced residents.

The issuing of Executive Order 9066 on February 19, 1942, cast the JACD into a conflict (one even starker than the JACL faced on the West Coast) between its twin goals of support for the war effort and advocacy of Nikkei civil rights. Immediately after the order was issued, the JACD wrote a letter to the government supporting mass removal. As the group's newsletter reported:

> In effect, our letter stated that while we realized that the majority of Japanese Americans are innocent, at the same time we recognized the possibility of fifth columnists working in their midst. As our committee is pledged to the full support of national defense, we offered to back whatever action the government deemed necessary to protect the strategic coastal zones and vital industrial areas. This would entail terrific sacrifices, such sacrifices as others are making. But this is war time [sic] and sacrifices are necessary on the part of all.[3]

The policy of support for the government effectively tied the group's hands as far as protesting the violation of the constitutional rights of Japanese Americans. In mid-March 1942, the JACD sent a letter to Attorney General Biddle asking him to establish a federal agency to create jobs for Japanese Americans unable to find work because of suspicion by potential employers. The following month, when members of the Tolan Committee, which was investigating the effect of the wartime "evacuation," came to New York, JACD representatives repeated the request for federal intervention in favor of equal opportunity, stating that "discrimination against the loyal elements of any racial group would necessarily injure the essential strength of our unity ... [and] contribute directly to the enemy's policy of 'divide and conquer' " as well as wasting skills and lowering war production." In May 1942, JACD members attending a conference of the Communist-allied American Committee for the Protection of the Foreign Born approved a resolution calling for the setting up of loyalty boards for "Germans, Italians, and Japanese" to determine individual guilt. In summer 1942 the JACD issued a resolution opposing a bill introduced by Tennessee senator Tom Stewart to intern all people of Japanese ancestry. However, rather than criticizing the bill for its racism and violation of the citizenship rights of Japanese Americans, the JACD protested the bill on the ground that it misrepresented them as Japanese citizens owing primary allegiance to Japan.[4]

The fundamental contradiction between the JACD's policies of opposing discrimination and offering absolute support to the government was laid bare in June 1942 when Socialist Party leader Norman Thomas, a longtime adversary of the Communist Party, organized a public meeting through the Post War World Council to protest Executive Order 9066. At the meeting, Mike Masaoka of the Japanese American Citizens League (which had been bitterly denounced in Japanese American communities for urging the Nisei to show their patriotism by collaborating with the government) argued that the treatment of Japanese Americans was "a test of democracy" and warned, "If they can do that to one group they can do it to other groups." With Masaoka's support, Thomas introduced a resolution calling for the immediate establishment of hearing boards to determine the loyalty of the "evacuees" and warning against the "military internment of unaccused persons in concentration camps."[5]

Although this resolution resembled in practical terms the one the JACD had approved in May, the group objected to Thomas's criticism of official policy. JACD leader Teru Matsumoto immediately offered a counterresolution supporting all measures to help ensure victory, and endorsing the government's claim that "military considerations made necessary the evacuation of all Americans of Japanese ancestry from certain areas on the West Coast." The JACD resolution was handily defeated, but Thomas's passed only narrowly, and its effectiveness was neutralized.[6] In a letter to the government, JACD secretary Yoshitaka Takagi defended the group's spoiler role:

> We disagree utterly with any tendencies to take the type of attitude . . . that the fact of evacuation should be protested now, as a peacetime measure might, in the light of personal discomfort or some such similar basis. We feel that such an attitude has nothing realistic or constructive about it, and indeed, tends to work toward disunity among the minority groups by distorting their just problems into separate interests . . . and when this general attitude is coupled with criticism of our government in the carrying out of its serious duties, we are even more concerned.[7]

Even as it sought to quell criticism of government discrimination against Japanese Americans, the JACD turned its attention to a large victory rally designed to promote "the end of all racial discrimination and the establishment of a mighty People's Front against fascism." None of the speakers, apart from Pearl S. Buck, discussed the discrimination facing Japanese Americans, let alone denounced the injustice of the government's actions toward them. Rather, the keynote speakers, African American leader Adam Clayton Powell Jr. and Chinese musician Liu Liang Mo, focused on forging equality for their respective minority groups and on friendship for the Soviet Union. Powell stated "that in all the allied nations except the United States men of all races fought side by side, but in the United States the Negro was relegated to mess halls and toilet duties."[8] "A democratic conduct of the war, he concluded, "was the pattern for victory, the pattern set by the Russian Army, a People's Army, a democratic army of all Russia." Liu called for friendship between China and Japan. Urging tolerance and study rather than hatred of Russia, "the eastern bulwark of the United Nations," Liu called for the immediate opening of a second front in Europe to relieve the Soviet Union (the chief goal of Communist Party propaganda during that period).[9] The same policy of self-abnegation that the JACD had showed at its victory rally was manifested in June 1942, when an invitation the group had received to join in New York City's official victory parade was abruptly rescinded by Mayor Fiorello LaGuardia, who justified his ban on the clearly spurious ground that the presence of Japanese Americans among the marchers would lead to violence. Although the JACD publicly termed the mayor's act "ill-advised," its leaders urged acceptance of the decision in a spirit of unity.

The JACD's intransigent attitude cost it in popularity among many liberals. Roger Baldwin and several other board members, all of them white, resigned their posts over the group's support for mass removal. Nisei sociologist T. Scott Miyakawa, disgusted by the JACD's policy, formed a short-lived rival group, the Townshend Harris Society, in order to support the war effort while simultaneously protesting the official actions. Ironically, the JACD's policy failed to bring the group the kind of government sponsorship and influence gained by the JACL. Although government agencies, notably the Office of War Information and the War Relocation Authority, did remain in correspondence with the JACD and coordinated with its members on projects such as propaganda broadcasts to Japan, no official patronage was forthcoming, and the FBI continued to keep the group's meetings and newsletter under close surveillance.

By late fall 1942, the removal and confinement of Japanese Americans was complete. The JACD was thus freed of its burden of defending the policy. While it did not call directly for the closing of the camps, which would constitute criticism of the government, it turned to pushing resettlement, especially once it became official policy. In February 1943, the JACD invited WRA director Dillon Myer to a forum on "Japanese Americans in the victory program" designed to determine, among other things, "what is being done to permanently resettle [the inmates] and can they be integrated into the American community." A positive program on Japanese Americans, the JACD claimed, was essential, as "only then will discrimination and suspicion based on prejudice be ended, and reactionary legislation and deliberate divisionism fostered around the Japanese Americans problem be exposed as an aid to our enemies."[10] In the following months, JACD members volunteered their services to the government as liaisons for resettlement, and worked to find sponsors and housing so that inmates could leave the camps. In coalition with the National Maritime Union, JACD leaders lobbied the War Department and the WRA to speed up the release of Japanese American merchant seamen from the camps to reduce shortages in shipping.[11]

By mid-1943, the JACD's encouragement to resettlers began to bring results for the group itself. As the camps began opening, the Nisei artists and intellectuals who were liberated were recruited to come to New York. Many of these people joined the JACD or attended its meetings. (Others were attracted to the Arts Council of the JACD, founded in 1943 under the direction of the famed painter Yasuo Kuniyoshi. The Arts Council was a semi-independent group that took advantage of the community's artistic resources to hold exhibitions, raise money for war relief, and issue its own statements denouncing a negotiated peace with Japan.)

The new arrivals transformed the JACD. Relying on dues and small gifts from outside sympathizers, the group established a permanent office and hired its first paid staffer, Nori Ikeda Lafferty, a former journalist for the San Francisco–based CP newspaper *People's World*. From being an organization with a mixed Issei-Nisei membership and New York–based focus, the JACD became a mass Nisei-based organization urging political action on a nationwide scale (by the end of 1944, all of the Issei board members had been asked to resign to make way for Nisei leadership). In the process, its mandate expanded from pro-Allied activism and community service to social activities and antiracist lobbying. In addition to continuing its blood drives and political meetings, during mid-1943 the JACD sponsored a Japanese translation of former ambassador Joseph Grew's *Ten Years in Japan*, and established a sizable lending library in its office. At the same time, many of the new arrivals were young, and to serve them the organization became a center of social life—there were dances and picnics to permit Nisei to meet for dating purposes. The JACD also sponsored (presumably with the assistance of folk musician Pete Seeger, husband of sometime JACD activist Toshi Aline Ohta) concerts by folk singers Leadbelly and Woody Guthrie.

Even as it moved to embrace resettlement, the JACD pledged itself to a national and interracial struggle for equality. In December 1942, the committee held a 1st Remember Pearl Harbor meeting, at which Charles Collins of the Negro Labor Committee offered a stirring speech connecting the war between democracy and fascism with the struggle of minority peoples against colonialism. At this meeting the JACD also approved a resolution stating that one of its primary goals was "to fight against discrimination on the basis of race, color, creed, national origin, or noncitizenship, in the interest of national unity."[12] In the months that followed, the JACD threw itself into reaching out to other groups. In tandem with the Chinese Hand Laundry Alliance, its members lobbied on behalf of the Immigration Bill sponsored by left-wing congressman Vito Marcantonio that would repeal restrictions on all "orientals," and also endorsed the congressional repeal of the Chinese Exclusion Act, which was signed into law in October 1943. The JACD also praised the efforts of the federal Fair Employment Practices Committee to end discrimination in war industries, and welcomed its extension to Nisei. (Impressed by the group's stand, in midyear Earl Dickerson, who had been the sole African American member of the FEPC before being dismissed for excessive militancy, joined the JACD advisory board.) In November 1943 the JACD newsletter contained an editorial encapsulating its official platform:

> The fight against fascism is not the fight alone of "majorities" nor of "minorities." Neither is it the fight of Negroes alone against Jim Crow, nor of the Jews alone against anti-Semitism, nor of Ibero-Americans alone against a "zoot suit" identification, nor of Japanese Americans as psychological enemies [sic]. The role of Japanese Americans this sphere is clear cut. We must be in the forefront of the struggle against any act of racism, There can be no compromise on this score.... It is singularly absurd, and totally fascistic, for Japanese Americans to practice Jim Crow and Anti-Semitism at the same time they profess Americanism—or democracy.[13]

The JACD accorded particular emphasis to equality for African Americans as the most notable victims of racial discrimination. In addition to calling for a permanent FEPC "to liberate the economically restricted Negro," the JACD focused its lobbying efforts on fighting the poll tax, which was (especially after the Supreme Court overturned the white primary in 1944) the most common method of disenfranchisement of African Americans in the South. In April 1944, the JACD ran a special legislative bulletin analyzing the failure of the Senate to approve cloture on an anti-poll-tax bill and listing the votes. "Abolition of the poll tax," wrote the author, Ernest Iiyama, "is not a Negro issue although Negroes are intensely concerned, nor a southern issue although the poll tax law is associated mostly with southern states. It is a question of vast importance to all of democratic America," in which he explicitly included the Nisei.[14] That same month, the JACD held a discussion called "National Minority Groups—Their Status," in which speakers discussed the status of the Filipino and of Japanese minorities, as well as African Americans. Presiding officer Joe Tamura pointed out that African Americans were just as intelligent as whites, and called for an end to prejudice. Making the ritual nod to the Soviet Union and its alleged elimination of racism, he added, "In Russia racial persecution and discrimination is illegal. They have welcomed racial programs."[15] The JACD invited speakers from the Communist-sponsored National Negro Congress to address their meetings, and joined with NNC members in a rally in fall 1944 supporting the reelection of President Franklin Roosevelt.[16]

Even after the West Coast was reopened in January 1945 and Japanese Americans began to leave the camps in large numbers and to return to their Pacific Coast homes, the JACD remained fixed on the dual mission of welcoming Japanese Americans to New York and improving the condition of African Americans, whose equality they connected with their own as a minority group in white America. The JACD collaborated with other groups in forming resettlement committees to replace the WRA after the agency's liquidation in 1946, and some of its members began a short-lived community newspaper, *The Nisei Weekender*. The JACD also marched in May Day parades, calling for the democratization of Japan. In mid-1945 the JACD's legislative subcommittee sent protest letters condemning the refusal of major-league baseball teams to hire black players.[17]

In September 1945, following the end of the war, the FEPC was disbanded. Chizu Iiyama lamented in the JACD *Newsletter*:

> We should remember that to retain their stranglehold on the feudal economy of the South, the Southern landowners (who send their representatives to Congress via the Poll Tax) must keep the races divided—to pit white against black. It also is part of a pattern of reactionary industrialists in the north, to keep the people from uniting their forces.[18]

In March 1946, the JACD organized a meeting protesting the shooting of an African American veteran in suburban New York after he complained about being refused service in a restaurant. The group's newsletter noted acidly, "The fact that this incident took place in New York, and not in the deep South was noted, and the membership condemned the dangerous trend of violence and terror against the Negroes and other minority groups."[19] The JACD called for a thorough government investigation of the case, and collected funds for a contribution to the slain man's widow.

In January 1948, the JACD held a dance to raise money for further lobbying against the poll tax. It was one of the committee's last events.[20] Soon after, the organization morphed into the Nisei for Wallace, formed to support Henry Wallace's third-party candidacy. After the election the new formation once again changed its name, this time to Nisei Progressives. Its membership sponsored a newsletter, the *Bandwagon*, and organized trips and get-togethers. However, between the dispersal of Japanese Americans from New York in the postwar years and the rise of McCarthyism, which frightened many progressive Americans away from further political action, by late 1950 the group had faded away.

The JACD, especially as reformulated after 1943 by resettled Japanese Americans from the camps, was a rare example of an outspoken Nisei activist group, and it also contributed strongly to bringing Japanese American New Yorkers into a cohesive and politically engaged community. However, its success was ephemeral. A few JACD members, such as Ernest and Chizu Iiyama and Karl Akiya, continued their activism after leaving the group, often working alongside African Americans. Others, such as Minn Matsuda and Kazu Iijima, profited from the JACD experience in the late 1960s when they became involved in Asian American political organizing, notably through a new group, Asian Americans for Action. However, the short history of the JACD suggests that their efforts to build interracial coalitions did not succeed in establishing either a durable political consciousness among Nisei or genuine links with other groups. In 1945 the FBI reported, "Sources advise that there is no program planned for cooperation with the Negroes as a minority group and only contact has been occasional Negro speaker at JACD panel groups." Another informant stated that "to his knowledge the JACD is not interested in Negro groups. He pointed out that in the past the JACD had invited Negro speakers on occasion but that the Negro groups never so much as invited representatives from the JACD."[21] Even if we discount this as evidence from a hostile source, there was effectively no mention of the JACD in the African American press during the time, which suggests the narrow base of its appeal as a coalition partner.

The history of the JACD stands in ironic counterpoint to African American writer Harold Cruse's famous denunciation of the Communist Party in his classic polemic *The Crisis of the Negro Intellectual* for manipulating Harlem blacks into concentrating on issues marginal to their (nationalist) group struggle.[22] Under the influence of the party line, the JACD refused to criticize mass removal during 1942, and even blocked the efforts of non-Japanese to do so. Even after the group moved toward advocacy of resettlement and welcomed former camp inmates who violently opposed mass incarceration, the JACD's membership chose to focus on the goal of racial equality for African Americans. The breadth of vision of the JACD's activists, and their clear desire to support other groups, shows remarkable perception and foresight. Still, the rewards they received for this commitment were meager. Now, durable coalitions between minority groups are something of a rarity in American history, for a number of reasons. Still, it is difficult to escape the conclusion that the JACD's activism was stunted by the refusal of its members to concentrate the same energy on protesting undemocratic and biased treatment of Japanese Americans as it devoted to other minority groups, and perhaps other groups sensed this and kept their distance.

PART V

The Rise and Fall of Postwar Coalitions for Civil Rights

11. From *Korematsu* to *Brown*

Nisei and the Postwar Struggle for Civil Rights

The story of the United States Supreme Court's epochal 1954 ruling in *Brown v. Board of Education* and the legal struggle for civil rights led by the NAACP during the decade following World War II occupies a central place in many Americans' understanding both of the history of democracy in the United States and of the African American experience.[1] Under the direction of chief counsel Thurgood Marshall, the NAACP's Legal Defense and Education Fund and allied attorneys brought a series of civil rights cases before the U.S. Supreme Court. Its campaign culminated triumphantly in *Brown* and its companion case *Bolling v. Sharpe*, in which the Court struck down school segregation.[2]

In was in the *Bolling* case that the Court clearly and definitively established its doctrine of "strict scrutiny." According to this doctrine, race was a "suspect classification" under the Constitution, meaning that the Court would subject to a searching examination any government action that involved a racial classification, rather than assume its constitutionality, and that it would hold the action to be unconstitutional unless it served a compelling state interest and was narrowly tailored to meet that interest. The Court's doctrine of strict scrutiny removed the constitutional underpinnings of Jim Crow and thus paved the way for its subsequent civil rights decisions during the 1960s.

One crucial element of the story of *Brown v. Board of Education* and the battle for black equality has been obscured in the popular narrative: the role of the Nisei in the legal struggle leading up to *Brown*. The Nisei contribution took different forms: For example, lawyers for the Japanese American Citizens League consulted on different occasions with NAACP counsel on the preparation of civil rights cases before the Supreme Court and lower courts, and the JACL participated in these cases as amicus curiae. Beyond the force of their arguments, the presence of the Nisei alongside African Americans served a powerful symbolic function, particularly in the decade following the mass wartime removal and incarceration of Japanese Americans. It operated to remind both judges and the nation that racial prejudice was not simply a "black problem" but a complex phenomenon of global dimensions, and it highlighted the dangerous consequences of race-based legislation.

However, the most decisive contribution of the Japanese Americans to the legal struggle for civil rights was in laying the foundation for the doctrine of strict scrutiny on which *Brown* and the other cases were based. The doctrine was developed in significant part from principles first enunciated in the cases involving Japanese American challenges to their wartime incarceration. These principles were then elaborated and reinforced immediately after World War II in a set of cases brought by the JACL concerning the rights of Japanese Americans to live and work free of discriminatory restrictions. In the years that followed, the NAACP built upon these cases in its fight against segregation, and the Court finally absorbed and explicitly enshrined the principles first enunciated in those cases.

The story of Japanese Americans and strict scrutiny begins with *Hirabayashi v. United States* and *Korematsu v. United States*.[3] In these cases, the Court justified its upholding of race-based restrictions on American citizens of Japanese ancestry on the grounds of the exceptional demands of wartime military necessity. In the case of *Hirabayashi*, the Court sanctioned a special curfew and registration requirements for Japanese Americans. Engaging in some judicial hairsplitting, the Court considered these questions separately from the mass removal and confinement that followed, which it refused to address. Chief Justice Harlan Stone, in order to underline the exceptional nature of the action, wrote that as a general rule, "distinctions between citizens solely because of their ancestry are by their very nature odious to a free people whose institutions are founded upon the doctrine of equality. For that reason, legislative classification or discrimination based on race alone has often been held to be a denial of equal protection."[4] However, Stone was writing for a unanimous Court, and kept his discussion of the issues involved in the case to a minimum to avoid dissents. As it was, Justice Frank Murphy strongly objected to the race-based curfew and circulated a dissent, which he was persuaded only under great pressure to transform into a concurrence and preserve unanimity.[5]

The *Korematsu* case, in contrast, involved the right of the army to undertake the mass removal of American citizens of Japanese ancestry from the West Coast. Once again, the majority of the Court chose to frame the issue simply as "evacuation," isolated from the consequent confinement of Japanese Americans. Nevertheless, the Court split on the decision. In a ringing dissent, Justice Murphy charged that the Court's action amounted to "a legalization of racism."[6] This clearly stung the author of the majority opinion, Justice Hugo Black, a southerner sensitive to the question of racial discrimination.[7] Black vigorously rejected any suggestion that racism had guided either the Court or the officials responsible for evacuation: "To cast this case," he insisted, "into outlines of racial prejudice, without reference to the real military dangers which were presented, merely confuses the issue."[8] Still, to buttress his conclusion, Black felt compelled to add to his original draft opinion some preliminary language distinguishing the case and justifying the extraordinary military urgency that led the Court to its ruling:

> It should be noted, to begin with, that all legal restrictions which curtail the civil rights of a single racial group are immediately suspect. That is not to say that all such restrictions are unconstitutional. It is to say that courts must subject them to the most rigid scrutiny. Pressing public necessity may sometimes justify the existence of such restrictions; racial antagonism never can.[9]

This belatedly inserted and somewhat defensive passage may well have been considered dicta by the justices.[10] In that sense it resembled the first appearances in the opinions of the Court of the idea of a privileged level of scrutiny for legislation in the area of minority rights. In footnote 4 of his opinion in the 1938 case *United States v. Carolene Products Co.* Justice Stone had noted that legislation involving racial minority groups or other "discrete and insular minorities" might well be subjected to "more exacting judicial scrutiny."[11] Later, in the 1942 case *Skinner v. Oklahoma*, the Court had stated that "strict scrutiny" of legislative classifications was necessary in the case of basic civil rights, although this did not involve a racial classification but one of different classes of felons.[12] Nevertheless, the Court did not further mention such a doctrine or cite these passages in civil rights cases such as *Morgan v. Virginia* during the immediate postwar years.[13] This would change as Japanese Americans became engaged in the issue of equal rights to residence, both through their efforts to fight the California Alien Land Act and through their participation in the larger multigroup struggle against restrictive covenants.

California's Alien Land Act, originally enacted in 1913, barred all "aliens ineligible to citizenship" from owning, acquiring, leasing, occupying, or transferring agricultural land. The law, which soon inspired similar statutes in other West Coast states, was designed to preserve white farmers from competition by Issei farmers—who, as Asians, were barred from naturalization by federal law—and to stigmatize the Issei as undesirables.[14] Challenges to the constitutionality of the Alien Land Acts by Japanese Americans were defeated in the United States Supreme Court during the 1920s. In *Ozawa v. United States, Terrace v. Thompson,* and *Porterfield v. Webb,* the Court ruled that Congress could constitutionally make rational distinctions in the classification of aliens such that some were eligible for citizenship and others not, and that the states did not violate the equal protection clause of the Fourteenth Amendment in limiting agricultural land ownership to citizens and aliens eligible for citizenship.[15] As a result of the law, Issei farmers were forced either to depend on white friends to buy and hold their land for them or to place the title to their land in the names of their American-born children, who were citizens. This was a gray area at the very least, legally speaking, as the law provided that any property acquired or transferred "with intent to prevent, evade, or avoid" the statute's provisions would "escheat" to the state as of the date of acquisition. Section 9(a) of the law (the product of a 1920 amendment) made explicit the legal presumption of such intent whenever an ineligible alien paid for land that was transferred to a citizen or eligible alien.[16]

The Alien Land Acts remained largely unenforced throughout the 1920s and 1930s. In the words of a contemporary commentator, "Legal loopholes, administrative inactivity and public indifference enabled Japanese aliens to circumvent many of the prohibitions."[17] However, during World War II, white Californians lobbied for strict enforcement of the statute to discourage return to the state by incarcerated Japanese Americans. In 1944 and 1945, as Japanese Americans began preparing to leave the camps, the California legislature appropriated money for the state's attorney general to initiate escheat proceedings to take land purchased with the funds of Japanese American aliens away from its owners. Even though by 1946 there were barely 10,000 "aliens ineligible to citizenship" farming in California, most of whom were elderly, these escheat proceedings were enormously damaging to all Japanese Americans. Title companies refused to insure Japanese American farmland except at exorbitant rates, and numerous families lost their land or were forced to pay large sums to the state government (usually half the assessed value of the land) in order to be left alone.[18] In all, fifty-nine escheat actions were brought by the state of California against Japanese aliens in the five years after 1942, compared with fourteen in the previous thirty years.[19]

In early 1945, Fred and Kajiro Oyama brought a legal challenge to the Alien Land Act. Fred was a Nisei from the San Clemente area who had been given two small parcels of land bought by Kajiro, his Issei father, during the 1930s. The Oyamas were forced to leave their land in spring 1942, when West Coast Japanese Americans were excluded. While the Oyamas were away, state attorney general Robert Kenny commenced an escheat proceeding, claiming that the land had been transferred to Fred in order to evade the Alien Land Act.[20] With the aid of neighbors Kazaburo Koda and Shichinosuke Asano, the Oyamas organized the Society for the Promotion of Japanese-American Civil Rights to fund a test case.[21] The Oyamas' case was taken up by JACL counsel A. L. Wirin, a white Jewish lawyer who was also head of the Southern California branch of the American Civil Liberties Union, and by Hugh Macbeth, an African American lawyer from Los Angeles who had worked with the JACL's legal committee on several cases, most recently the organization's amicus brief in *Korematsu*. In February 1945, the case of *People v. Oyama*, together with a companion case, *People v. Hirose*, was argued in San Diego County Superior Court. In their memorandum of law, Wirin and Macbeth argued that even if the Alien Land Act had been upheld by the U.S. Supreme Court in the 1920s, "many living waters have [since] run under the bridges of the Constitution"; the times and circumstances had changed sufficiently that the decisions were no longer controlling.[22] Moreover, the Alien Land Act was conceived in race prejudice and penalized the defendants solely because of race, and was thereby unconstitutional. In an overt reference to the *Korematsu* case, then less than two months old, Wirin and Macbeth asserted that "discrimination because of race is constitutionally justified only when required by pressing public necessity, under circumstances of direct emergency and peril."[23]

In March 1945 Superior Court judge Charles G. Haines ruled against the Oyamas, on the ground that he was bound by the earlier decisions of the courts. Haines's opinion implicitly rejected the imposition of a higher standard of scrutiny for racial classifications: "Whether in view of changed views on the subject of race, classifications stressing that consideration have ceased to be reasonable in such as sense as to render them obnoxious to limitations expressed in the Federal Constitution, is a question not very appropriate for consideration by a trial court."[24]

Shortly thereafter, Wirin appealed *People v. Oyama* to the California Supreme Court.[25] The *People v. Hirose* case was not appealed, and perhaps as a result, Macbeth withdrew from the case at this point.[26] Instead, San Francisco attorney James Purcell (who had previously represented Mitsuye

Endo before the Supreme Court in her habeas corpus case challenging her confinement), working on behalf of the Civil Liberties Defense League of California, agreed to support Wirin's efforts.[27] The *Oyama* case was heard in California Supreme Court in March 1946. By this time, prewar and wartime public hostility to Japanese Americans on the West Coast had eased. In November 1946 a voter initiative in California to extend the Alien Land Act was resoundingly defeated at the polls. A federal judge in Orange County, citing the legal principle proclaimed by Stone in the *Hirabayashi* case as authority, had struck down segregated schools for Mexican Americans in *Méndez v. Westminster*.[28] Nevertheless, a few days before the election the California Supreme Court issued a decision that upheld the attorney general's action. Although the right of an American citizen minor to receive and hold property from an alien ineligible to citizenship had been established in the 1922 California Supreme Court case *Estate of Tetsubumi Yano*, the California court largely ignored in its ruling the impact of the law on Fred Oyama.[29] Rather, the California high court judges, once again citing the United States Supreme Court's 1923 decisions on the Alien Land Act as precedent, held that the state's action in classifying aliens according to eligibility to citizenship had a rational basis.[30]

Following the California court ruling, Wirin, with the aid of both the JACL and the ACLU, decided to petition the United States Supreme Court to hear the case. Purcell and the Civil Liberties Defense League withdrew from the case, fearing that the Supreme Court would merely reaffirm the holding.[31] Instead, Wirin joined forces on the appeal with his new law partners, Fred Okrand and former JACL president Saburo Kido (who together submitted an amicus brief in the name of the JACL). Meanwhile, in hopes of showcasing the case's importance, he sought an appellate lawyer with a national reputation to argue the case before the Supreme Court. With the aid of Charles Horsky, a Washington attorney who had put together the ACLU's amicus brief in the *Korematsu* case, the JACL contacted Dean Acheson, a distinguished Washington lawyer and former U.S. undersecretary of state (who was shortly to become President Truman's secretary of state). Acheson agreed to serve without fee as chief counsel in oral argument on the case, now called *Oyama v. California*.[32]

Wirin and his colleagues retooled their strategy in their appeal to the Supreme Court. Rather than emphasizing the rights of aliens in the appellant's brief, dated September 1947, the JACL lawyers led off their case by arguing that the Alien Land Act violated the Fourteenth Amendment rights of citizens of Japanese ancestry by imposing solely on them, and not on citizens of any other ancestry, the burden of proof that any land they received from a parent ineligible to citizenship was intended as a gift and was not made in order to avoid escheat under the Alien Land Act.[33] The JACL attorneys then bolstered their case by means of a "strict scrutiny" argument. Because the Alien Land Act was expressly race-based and anti-Japanese, it was not subject to the presumption of constitutionality that the Court usually granted to state legislative classifications. On the contrary, cases involving civil liberties, whether they concerned citizens or aliens, faced a more rigorous constitutional test than cases involving ordinary commercial transactions. "Indeed," Wirin asserted, "the presumption—and it is a strong presumption—is against any 'race' legislation."[34] The Court should examine rigorously the intent and effect of the law. As authority for this proposition, Wirin audaciously cited Justice Black's language in *Korematsu v. United States*: "[T]o begin with, . . . all legal restrictions which curtail the civil rights of a single racial group are immediately suspect. . . . Pressing public necessity may sometimes justify the existence of such restrictions; racial antagonism never can."[35]

While the citation of *Korematsu* in support of civil rights was seemingly unprecedented in arguments before the Supreme Court, Wirin's position on "strict scrutiny" echoed arguments that had appeared in several law journal articles on alien land legislation over the previous months. For example, Edwin Ferguson, onetime solicitor for the WRA, had written in early 1947 that a higher standard was necessary in judging alien land law cases:

> It should not be enough to indulge in speculative justifications of the law . . . or to plead ignorance of local conditions and the possibility of a "rational basis" for the legislative judgment. Restrictive legislation stemming from race prejudice, particularly against a minority that is unable to participate in the political process, calls for more searching inquiry. Such an inquiry would reveal, it is submitted, that the alien land law is unjust and unjustifiable legislation, and that it clearly violates the rights protected by the Fourteenth Amendment.[36]

On January 19, 1948, the Supreme Court handed victory to the plaintiffs by a 6–3 margin. Chief Justice Fred Vinson, in the majority opinion, agreed that the act violated the Fourteenth Amendment rights of citizens of Japanese ancestry. He thus found it unnecessary to examine the issue of whether Japanese aliens were also entitled to the protection of the Fourteenth Amendment. As a result, the Supreme Court's decision did not explicitly overturn the Alien Land Act, though in practice it suspended all enforcement of it in California. Nevertheless, the chief justice left no doubt that only a truly "compelling justification" could sustain any racially discriminatory statute.[37] "There remains the question of whether discrimination between citizens on the basis of their racial descent, as revealed in this case, is justifiable. Here we start with the proposition that only the most exceptional circumstances can excuse discrimination on that basis in the face of the equal protection clause."[38] Furthermore, Vinson declared, the Court had the duty to examine whether a law, even if fair on its face, had a discriminatory intent or effect. Contrary to the normal practice of appellate courts, the Court could take account not only of the legal issues involved but also of "those factual matters with which they are commingled." Thus, the majority of the Court tacitly accepted the JACL's argument that laws involving race or color faced a more rigorous test than the Court usually applied to state laws, and would now require a showing of exceptional circumstances to justify them. The novelty of this position was recognized in several law journal articles in the period that followed.[39]

Several of the justices went even further in their analysis than Vinson's majority opinion. In a concurrence, Justice Hugo Black stated that the Court should have overturned the Alien Land Act because its basic provisions violated the equal protection clause of the Fourteenth Amendment in discriminating against Japanese aliens. "If there is one purpose of the Fourteenth Amendment that is wholly outside the realm of doubt," the author of the *Korematsu* opinion pointedly commented, "it is that the Amendment was designed to bar states from denying to some groups, on account of their race or color, any rights, privileges, and opportunities accorded to other groups."[40] In a second concurrence, Justice Frank Murphy presented a detailed account of the history of California's Alien Land Act, which he denounced as a blatant expression of racism and of an "anti-Oriental virus."[41] Murphy cast particular scorn on the claims of the act's defenders regarding "the alleged disloyalty, clannishness, inability to assimilate, racial inferiority and racial undesirability of the Japanese."[42] The uncompromising language of Murphy's opinion led Justice William O. Douglas to send him a curious letter asking him to tone down or withdraw the concurrence:

> In *Oyama* you are 100 per cent right in your position and I would like to join you. The difficulty is that I fear your opinion as written will be translated by the Russians into Korean, Chinese and Japanese and widely circulated in the Orient. The racial prejudice represented by the legislation is unmistakable. But it does not represent the viewpoint of the people of our nation. In fact, it does not represent the views of a majority of Californians. A few vested interests have put the thing

through. But the Russians will utilize it against all of our people. That is most unjust. I wanted to submit this angle to you for your consideration.[43]

Although the majority opinion did not cite *Korematsu*, the specter of the wartime confinement of the Japanese Americans hung over the Supreme Court and clearly helped shape the decision. The Court that decided *Oyama* was, with only two exceptions, the same Court whose members had upheld the constitutionality of the army curfew and evacuation of people of Japanese ancestry a few years before.[44] The government's claims of military necessity and Japanese American disloyalty, which the justices had then accepted as sufficient to justify removal, were swiftly discredited after the end of the war by commentators such as Eugene Rostow.[45] In the months before the Court rendered its decision, the United States President's Committee on Civil Rights, in its historic report *To Secure These Rights*, had advocated an investigation of the wartime injustice to Japanese Americans and had called for legislation compensating them for their losses.[46] The Court was only too conscious of the connection between the discriminatory provisions of the Alien Land Act and the pressures that had led to the internment, although Chief Justice Vinson's majority opinion took pains to distinguish the Court's ruling in *Oyama* from that in *Hirabayashi*. Vinson referred to *Hirabayashi* as a war measure that had presented "exceptional circumstances," contrary to the "general rule" against racial distinctions mentioned in that case.[47] Still, Justice Murphy, citing his dissenting opinion in *Korematsu*, explicitly connected the bigoted attitudes that underlay the Alien Land Act with the "misrepresentations, halftruths and distortions" that made up the government's case for exclusion. Paraphrasing the language of that dissent and thereby emphasizing the link, he then called on the Court to overturn its previous decisions that gave sanction to legalized racism.[48]

In addition to defending the rights of Japanese American farmers, both the opinion in *Oyama* and the JACL attorneys who brought the test case would provide strong support for the NAACP's contemporaneous fight against restrictive covenants. Restrictive covenants—reciprocal promises by groups of homeowners, usually included in the deeds to their homes—expressed the promise not to sell or rent those homes to members of minority or "colored" groups such as blacks, Native Americans, Latinos, Asian Americans, and Jews, and to make future buyers' signing of the covenants an express condition of sale. The covenants were effective means of perpetuating housing segregation in urban areas. The U.S. Supreme Court had previously rejected an attack on the constitutionality of restrictive covenants in *Corrigan v. Buckley*. Because the covenants were private agreements, the Court held, they did not violate the equal protection clause of the Fourteenth Amendment, which prohibited racial discrimination only by state governments.[49]

During the postwar years when there where chronic housing shortages, however, restrictive covenants cut sharply into the total housing available for minority groups and fostered extreme overcrowding in ghetto areas. This made them a crucial public policy issue. In 1946, the NAACP and its allies again sought to disarm restrictive covenants by bringing lawsuits on behalf of the African American buyers and renters of houses covered by restrictive covenants and the white sellers, all of whom had been enjoined in state court by the owners of other houses subject to the covenants who sought to enforce the covenants, vacate the sales, and evict the buyers and renters. When a St. Louis case, *Shelley v. Kraemer*, and a Detroit case, *McGhee v. Sipes*, ended in defeat in the respective state supreme courts, NAACP lawyers successfully petitioned for certiorari to the U.S. Supreme Court, which consolidated the two cases under the title *Shelley v. Kraemer*.[50] NAACP lawyers hoped to persuade the Court that even if restrictive covenants were private agreements, judicial enforcement of them by state courts constituted discriminatory state action, which violated the equal protection clause of the Fourteenth Amendment. The Supreme Court also agreed to hear *Hurd v. Hodge*, a case that involved a restrictive covenant in the District of Columbia, where the Fourteenth Amendment did not apply.[51]

In its preparation for the briefs in the restrictive covenant cases, the NAACP turned to Los Angeles lawyer Loren Miler, a recognized expert on the subject of housing discrimination, who in turn sought assistance from his longtime ally A. L. Wirin.[52] In December 1945, Miller had won the first victory over restrictive covenants, successfully defending Ethel Waters and a number of other black entertainers who had bought houses in Los Angeles's West Adams Heights district from eviction under a restrictive covenant. Superior Court judge Thurmond Clarke had ruled in that case that the restrictive covenants in and of themselves violated the Fourteenth Amendment.[53] Following the decision, Wirin, who had long been involved in fighting restrictive covenants on behalf of the ACLU, persuaded the JACL to support a multiethnic struggle against restrictive covenants in the Los Angeles area. In 1946 Miller and Wirin began a widely publicized and ultimately triumphant campaign against restrictive covenants on publicly owned land in South Pasadena.[54] However, Wirin's experience was generally less successful. In 1946, with legal advice from Miller, the JACL sponsored a suit in *Kim v. Superior Court* and *Amer v. Superior Court*, representing, respectively, a Chinese American and a Korean American ex-GI, each of whom had purchased a home subject to restrictive covenants excluding "Mongolians." In August 1947, the California high court upheld enforcement of both the restrictive covenants in question.[55]

After securing Miller's assistance, the NAACP scheduled a conference in Chicago over Labor Day weekend 1947. The purpose of the conference, which was attended by civil rights lawyers and representatives of liberal organizations from all over the country, was to formulate strategies for fighting *Shelley v. Kraemer* and *Hurd v. Hodge*, the restrictive covenant cases then pending before the Supreme Court. In the end, the consensus of the conferees was that the NAACP should prepare a "Brandeis brief," that is, a brief that concentrated less on legal precedent than on presenting sociological and statistical data (in this case, on the negative effects of restrictive covenants). In pursuit of this plan, the NAACP distributed supporting materials to the representatives of the other groups for them to use in writing amicus curiae briefs that would contain data on the harmful and degrading effects of restrictive covenants.[56]

During the afternoon of September 6, Charles H. Houston, lead counsel in the District of Columbia *Hurd v. Hodge* case, brought up the question of the optimum timing of the hearing in the two restrictive covenant cases. A. L. Wirin, who was attending the conference, announced, "The Supreme Court has granted certiorari in the Japanese Alien [sic] and Land Law case. Would it be advisable to have the restrictive covenant cases come up at the same time?" Attorney Frank Donner, of the CIO's Washington, D.C., office, replied, "It would be helpful to have them together. The Supreme Court will probably do so anyway."[57]

No doubt hoping to emphasize the connection between the restrictive covenant cases and *Oyama*, the JACL decided following the conference to submit to the Court an amicus brief that would provide information on restrictive covenants against Japanese Americans. On September 16, 1947, Ina Sugihara, a Nisei active in the New York branch of the JACL who had attended the conference as a representative of the Protestant Council of New York City (and reported on it for *the Pacific Citizen*), wrote Marian Wynn Perry of the NAACP that the national JACL wished to file an amicus brief supporting the NAACP in the restrictive covenant cases, but that it needed information on how to file such a brief since it had never done one before.[58] Perry sent the requested materials to JACL attorney Masao Satow and enclosed a note saying, "We are very happy you are going to join us in these cases."⁵⁹ The firm of Wirin, Kido, and Okrand then began work on the brief. Frank Chuman, a Nisei former camp inmate who was the firm's new associate, did much of the initial drafting.

Meanwhile, Miller and Wirin together petitioned the Supreme Court to grant certiorari in the *Kim* and *Amer* cases, and they filed a separate amicus brief in the name of the JACL urging the Court to hear the two cases because they illustrated how restrictive covenants affected racial groups other than African Americans.⁶⁰ On October 31, 1947, Wirin wrote Thurgood Marshall, asking that the NAACP also file an amicus brief in support of granting certiorari in *Kim* and *Amer*.⁶¹ Although Marshall privately expressed his gratitude for Wirin's efforts to bring the cases as support for the NAACP, he seems not to have drafted the requested amicus brief—no doubt he had too much work on his plate already.⁶² In the end, the Court did not move to grant certiorari in either *Kim* or *Amer*, and the decisions in *Shelley v. Kraemer* and *Hurd v. Hodge* eventually mooted the two cases.⁶³

The JACL's own brief in the restrictive covenant cases (which, for reasons that are not clear, was nominally addressed only to *Hurd v. Hodge*) was filed on December 1, 1947. In it, Wirin, Kido, Okrand, and Chuman described how restrictive covenants were used to discriminate against Japanese Americans, making it impossible for Nisei veterans to find housing for their families and forcing citizens of Japanese ancestry to live in overcrowded and unhealthy "Little Tokyo" areas.⁶⁴ Charles Houston apparently believed that the information presented by the JACL about restrictive covenants in South Pasadena and the attempts to turn the South San Francisco peninsula into an all-white area was of sufficient importance that he cited the JACL brief in the petitioner's reply brief in *Hurd*. No other amicus brief received a similar compliment.⁶⁵

During fall 1947, twenty-eight organizations filed amicus briefs supporting the NAACP's position in *Shelley v. Kraemer* and *Hurd v. Hodge*. Many of these, such as the ACLU and the American Jewish Congress, were groups that had filed amicus briefs in *Oyama*. One crucial supporter, the United States Justice Department, had not.⁶⁶ In November 1947, U.S. Attorney General Tom Clark agreed to have the federal government file an amicus brief against the enforcement of restrictive covenants. Clark's decision was heavily publicized, since it marked the first time the Justice Department had ever intervened as amicus curiae in a civil rights case. The decision to file a brief was the product of a complex set of pressures and causes, including political calculation regarding the upcoming presidential election, internal lobbying by officials in the Justice Department and the Indian Bureau (which opposed restrictive covenants against Native Americans), and the report of the President's Committee on Civil Rights, which called for the banning of restrictive covenants.[67] The treatment of the Japanese Americans also may have played a role in Clark's decision. Clark had been a central participant in formulating the West Coast evacuation policy during spring 1942, and he later publicly expressed his remorse over his actions.[68]

In any event, the government's amicus brief, which declared that judicial enforcement of restrictive covenants was contrary to the public policy of the United States, referred prominently to the wartime Japanese American cases in its argument. It not only cited the language from *Hirabayashi* about race-based distinctions in law being "odious to a free people" but also quoted, as the JACL had done shortly before in its *Oyama* brief, from the passage in the *Korematsu* opinion to describe the "attitude" the Supreme Court should adopt in dealing with state action based on racial distinctions: "All legal restrictions which curtail the civil rights of a single racial group are immediately suspect. That is not to say that all such restrictions are unconstitutional. It is to say that courts must subject them to the most rigid scrutiny. Pressing public necessity may sometimes justify the existence of such restrictions; racial antagonism never can."[69]

The government's brief concluded that since distinctions based on race or color were constitutionally invidious and could be justified, if at all, only by "the weightiest countervailing interests," the Court should make the most searching inquiry into the sufficiency of any grounds asserted to justify racially discriminatory legislation. The government asked the Court to apply this doctrine, and thereby strike down judicial enforcement of restrictive covenants.[70]

On May 3, 1948, the Court issued its decisions in *Shelley v. Kraemer* and *Hurd v. Hodge*. By a 6–0 margin (Justices Reed, Jackson, and Rutledge recused themselves from both cases), the Court determined that restrictive covenants based on race or ancestry violated the equal protection clause of the Fourteenth Amendment and were thereby unenforceable in the courts.[71] Chief Justice Vinson's unanimous opinion in *Shelley* relied heavily on *Oyama* (which it cited in two places), particularly in its central conclusion, namely, that any government action "which denied equal enjoyment of property rights to a designated class of citizens based on race or color was not a legitimate exercise of the state's police power but violated the guarantee of the equal protection of the laws."[72] While the petitioners in *Shelley* and *Hurd* were African Americans—although Hurd himself insisted he was a Mohawk Indian—the Court acknowledged in a footnote its understanding that restrictive covenants were used to discriminate against various groups, including "Japanese" among others. Indeed, the covenant at issue in *Shelley* explicitly banned use by "people of the Negro or Mongolian race."[73]

The companion opinion in *Hurd* reached the same result as *Shelley*. However, since *Hurd* involved the District of Columbia, whose residents were not protected by the Fourteenth Amendment, the Court reached its decision on other grounds. The plaintiffs had sought to persuade the Court that the due process clause of the Fifth Amendment encompassed a guarantee of equal protection similar to that of the equal protection clause of the Fourteenth Amendment. For this purpose, the *Hurd* plaintiffs cited both *Hirabayashi* and *Korematsu*, which had been decided on the basis of the Fifth Amendment. However, the justices were not ready to explore this issue, which they stated was unnecessary in order to decide the case. Instead, the Court premised its conclusion on the existence of a federal statute, the Civil Rights Act of 1866, which had expressly provided that all citizens had equal rights to "real and personal property."[74]

A third case, *Takahashi v. California Fish and Game Commission*, further extended the evolution of strict scrutiny.[75] Torao Takahashi was one of approximately 700 licensed Issei commercial fishermen who worked in California in the years before World War II. In 1943, while Takahashi and the rest of the West Coast Japanese Americans were incarcerated in camps, the California legislature amended its Fish and Game Law to bar all "Japanese aliens" from being granted fishing licenses. The clear purpose of the new law, which was part of the wave of anti-Japanese legislation introduced in the legislature during that year, was to express hostility toward the Japanese Americans and to discourage them from returning to California following their release from the camps by making it impossible for them to practice their trade. In 1945, amid concerns that the statute unconstitutionally singled out Japanese aliens, the legislature amended its wording to deny fishing licenses to "aliens ineligible to citizenship," among whom Japanese were effectively the only representatives. In 1945, after Takahashi returned to California and was denied a fishing license, the JACL and the Southern California Japanese Fishermen's Association together agreed to sponsor a test case, and A. L. Wirin, assisted by his partners John Maeno and Saburo Kido, served as counsel.[76]

Unlike the Oyamas, Takahashi was initially victorious. In 1946, the Los Angeles County Superior Court ruled that Takahashi had a constitutional right to fish outside the three-mile belt representing the state's territorial waters. The Superior Court bitingly characterized the law as an example of anti-Japanese discrimination, "the thin veil used to conceal a purpose being too transparent."[77] The state appealed to the California Supreme Court, which in October 1947 overturned the Superior Court's decision. By a narrow 4–3 vote, the high court ruled that the state had a proprietary interest in the fish in its ocean waters and could constitutionally restrict fishing licenses to citizens and aliens eligible for citizenship in order to preserve its natural resources.[78] This decision attracted widespread negative comment in the national press. The President's Committee on Civil Rights called for the statute's repeal.[79]

Wirin waited to decide whether to appeal *Takahashi* until the Court had ruled on the *Oyama* case.[80] Once the Court issued the *Oyama* decision, the appeal was a foregone conclusion. Although the main opinion in *Oyama* had deliberately avoided deciding whether race-based discrimination against aliens violated the Fourteenth Amendment, four of the justices in *Oyama* had already joined in concurring opinions stating that discrimination against Japanese aliens on the basis of race or ancestry violated the equal protection clause of the Fourteenth Amendment. Indeed, in his concurring opinion, Justice Black had pointed to the statute in *Takahashi* as an example of such discrimination against Japanese aliens.[81] Thus, even before the Supreme Court acted on a petition for certiorari, there appeared to be four justices ready to rule in the JACL's favor.

Nevertheless, Wirin was taking no chances. In October 1947, at the same time he wrote Marshall about the *Kim* and *Amer* cases, he also informed Marshall that *Takahashi* had been decided in California and was now being appealed to the Supreme Court. He asked that the NAACP prepare an amicus brief in support of granting certiorari. On December 31, 1947, Samuel Ishikawa of the JACL's Anti-Discrimination Committee met with Marian Wynn Perry of the NAACP and repeated Wirin's request. Ishikawa then also proposed that the NAACP contact the U.S. attorney general to urge the government to submit an amicus brief, as it had in *Shelley*.[82] Solicitor General Philip Perlman, cheered by the positive reception of the government's *Shelley* brief, was inspired to intervene on behalf of Japanese Americans.[83] In February 1948, Perlman wrote to the JACL lawyers that the government had decided to file a brief in support of their case. The Takahashi case, Pearlman said, "raises civil liberties issues of such national importance and affecting such a large number of persons as to warrant intervention by the Government."[84] Thus, barely three years after the *Korematsu* decision, the same Justice Department that had defended mass violation of the civil liberties of Japanese Americans now was officially committed to their defense. Ishikawa wrote Perry to express his gratitude to the NAACP for its lobbying of the attorney general.[85]

In March 1948, the Supreme Court granted certiorari in *Takahashi*. The NAACP then agreed to submit an amicus brief in support of the JACL. Both the appellant's brief and the NAACP's amicus brief, in which the National Lawyers Guild joined, argued that the California fishing law denied legal residents of the United States the opportunity to earn a living in a common occupation because of their Japanese ancestry. Both briefs asserted that the law was racist in purpose and effect (the NAACP brief pointed out that the fishing law had the same purpose and effect as the Alien Land Act that the Court had recently addressed in *Oyama*) and thus violated the appellant's rights to equal protection and due process under the Fourteenth Amendment as well as the United Nations Charter. In addition, both briefs charged that the California law improperly interfered with the supreme right of the federal government to make immigration and foreign policy, since its primary effect was to exclude aliens legally admitted to the United States from residing in the state.[86]

Oddly, neither the JACL nor the NAACP lawyers attempted to build upon the JACL's contention in its *Oyama* brief that "pressing public necessity" was required to constitutionally justify a racially discriminatory statue, even though the Court had tacitly accepted this doctrine in its *Oyama* opinion. Rather, both the JACL and the NAACP lawyers held to the less rigorous legal standard of whether the law's racial distinctions bore a "rational relationship" to its purpose. Both briefs devoted much of their argument to demonstrating that there was no rational relationship between preventing Japanese aliens from commercial fishing and the state's ostensible interest in conservation.[87]

In contrast, the argument for a higher standard and heightened scrutiny was put forward in a short amicus brief by the Justice Department. As in its amicus brief in *Shelley*, written two months before, the department took the position in its *Takahashi* brief that any racial classifications were prima facie invalid and that the state had an obligation to justify any race-based legislation under the Fourteenth Amendment. Courts, meanwhile, should subject any purported justification to the "most searching inquiry." The Justice Department called upon the Court to exercise heightened scrutiny of the California fishing law because it involved a race-based classification, and to thereafter overturn it because California could not show, as *Korematsu* required, that the law was required by "pressing public necessity."[88]

On April 22 and 23, 1948, the Court heard oral argument in *Takahashi*. As in *Oyama*, Dean Acheson served as chief counsel for the JACL. Six weeks later, on June 7, 1948, the Court announced its decision. The same justices who had previously voted with the majorities in *Oyama* and in

Shelley (plus Burton, who had dissented in *Oyama*, and Rutledge, who had recused himself in the restrictive covenant cases) struck down the California fishing law. Justice Black, writing for the majority, held that the protection of the Fourteenth Amendment extended to aliens as well as citizens.[89] Black based his opinion on the rights of aliens under the Fourteenth Amendment. In addition, he agreed with the petitioner's claims that a state law infringed on the federal government's exclusive authority over immigration when it prevented an alien lawfully admitted to the United States from earning a living in the same manner as other residents of the state. Finally, Black stated, he was unable to find any "special public interest" in support of California's discriminatory fishing law that would serve as a legitimate basis for upholding it.[90] Although he refused to address the question of whether the law was prompted by racial hostility against the Japanese, he "vigorously denied" that it was simply a conservation measure.[91] Although Black played down the racial aspects of the case, Justice Murphy issued a concurring opinion, as in *Oyama*, that provided an extended exposition of the anti-Japanese history of the California law and the racist intent of the lawmakers.

The *Takahashi* victory halted California's historic legal discrimination against Japanese aliens, although the Issei did not attain full equality until 1952, when Congress passed the McCarran-Walter Immigration Act. That act removed all racial and national restrictions on the naturalization of immigrants, thus eliminating in a stroke the category of "aliens ineligible to citizenship." A far more lasting product of the case was its contribution to the development of the "strict scrutiny" doctrine as a weapon in eliminating Jim Crow, as Thurgood Marshall recognized in an article published shortly afterward.[92]

By the time the *Takahashi* case was argued, NAACP lawyers were reaching the end stages of a long-term legal assault on racial segregation. According to the Supreme Court's then-prevailing "separate but equal" doctrine, first enunciated in the 1896 case *Plessy v. Ferguson*, racial segregation was not unconstitutional as long as the separate facilities provided were "substantially equal."[93] Beginning in the 1930s, NAACP lawyers, following a plan developed by Nathan Margold, decided that public education would be a promising field for litigation, because public schools involved a heavy investment by states and because the inequalities in segregated education were so apparent. In the mid-1930s, then NAACP chief counsel Charles H. Houston decided as a first step to fight educational inequality without directly addressing *Plessy* by challenging the exclusion of African Americans from higher education. Successful court suits would establish a record and a momentum in favor of nonsegregated equality by forcing southern states to either admit blacks to white institutions or maintain a prohibitively expensive dual educational system. In 1938, the NAACP won its first Supreme Court victory in the educational field in *Missouri ex rel. Gaines v. Canada*. The Court ordered the University of Missouri's Law School to admit Lloyd Gaines, an African American, since it maintained no law school for blacks.[94]

After the end of World War II, the NAACP expanded its efforts to secure the admission of African Americans to graduate and law schools. In 1948, the Court issued a per curiam opinion in the case of *Sipuel v. Board of Regents of University of Oklahoma* reaffirming its ruling in *Gaines* that a state must provide to all persons equal facilities to those it provided for whites, and ordering that it must provide those facilities as soon as it did for whites.[95] Following this victory, the NAACP brought two further cases, *McLaurin v. Oklahoma* and *Sweatt v. Painter*, which grew out of the Court's rulings in *Gaines* and *Sipuel*. *McLaurin* involved an African American who had been admitted to the University of Oklahoma's School of Education, but once inside was made to sit in a separate area of his classroom (originally in an alcove, later in a cordoned-off row of seats) and restricted to his own special assigned table in the school's cafeteria and library.[96] *Sweatt* concerned the deeper question of "equality." Heman Marion Sweatt had applied for admission to the University of Texas Law School. In order to avoid being forced to admit him, Texas state authorities had established a separate law school for blacks in a "temporary" location in the basement of the state's capitol in Austin.[97]

On January 7, 1949, the NAACP held a conference of civil rights lawyers and supporting organizations on the upcoming *McLaurin* and *Sweatt* cases. A number of liberal, labor, and Jewish groups were invited, with the JACL being the only racial minority organization included.[98] As in the restrictive covenant cases, the NAACP sought to coordinate strategies and encourage the writing of amicus briefs. The JACL complied with a short brief (which was formally addressed only to *McLaurin*) signed by Edward Ennis, the former Justice Department lawyer who had been named JACL counsel, as well as by a group of fifteen Nisei lawyers listed as "of counsel" (including Minoru Yasui, whose conviction for disobeying wartime evacuation orders had been upheld by the Supreme Court simultaneously with the *Hirabayashi* decision).[99] The JACL brief stated that separate facilities for blacks and other racial minorities were never equal in practice, and asked the Court to overturn the *Plessy* "separate but equal" doctrine on that basis. Subtly connecting Jim Crow with the wartime internment cases, the brief further argued that "during the recent war hostilities an unfortunate and mistaken exercise of the war power involving racial discrimination was allowed as a temporary emergency matter" but that "since the end of hostilities racial discrimination by governmental action has been consistently condemned as unconstitutional." As evidence of this trend, the brief cited *Oyama, Shelley,* and *Takahashi.*[100]

Meanwhile, in its appellant's brief in *McLaurin*, the NAACP lawyers adopted for the first time a version of the "strict scrutiny" argument that the JACL had first put forward and the Justice Department had subsequently expanded. The NAACP brief argued that laws involving racial or religious classifications were subject to a special test. "In the absence of an overriding public necessity, this Court has never allowed governmental regulation of this constitutionally preferred area and has nullified all such unreasonable and irrational classifications."[101] The NAACP contended that in the matter at hand the state had not and could not show the clear and "overwhelming public necessity" required to legitimize racial classifications. As the JACL had done in *Oyama* and the Justice Department had done in *Shelley* and *Takahashi*, the NAACP held that governmental action based on race or color bore a presumption of unconstitutionality. In support of this assertion, it cited large sections from the "recent decisions" of *Hirabayashi, Korematsu, Oyama,* and *Takahashi* and their concurrences to show that "racial distinctions have incurred such constitutional odium" as to be "presumptively void."

On June 5, 1950, the Supreme Court unanimously ruled in favor of the African American petitioners in both *McLaurin* and *Sweatt*, finding in both cases that the education being offered to the petitioners was not equal to that of whites and thus violated the Fourteenth Amendment's equal protection clause. Since the Court found that the facilities were unequal, it did not explicitly address whether the *Plessy* doctrine was wrong or irrelevant. However, in a move that was significant for the NAACP position, the Court concluded in *Sweatt* that equality of schooling rested in part on "intangible" factors such as a school's reputation and the opportunity to exchange ideas with other students, and in *McLaurin* that no matter how nominal the differences were in the facilities afforded McLaurin and those offered to his fellow students, they signified that the state set him apart on a racial basis and thus handicapped him in his pursuit of effective graduate education.[102]

The way was now prepared for a direct assault on "separate but equal" in the central area of primary education. This had always been the NAACP's ultimate goal. The previous graduate school cases had affected only a very few people. The school cases the NAACP prepared to bring would affect thousands of children. In fall 1950, Thurgood Marshall and the NAACP lawyers directed or assisted in the bringing of five separate lawsuits that challenged segregation in school districts in Kansas, South Carolina, Virginia, Delaware, and the District of Columbia. The NAACP provided massive expert witness testimony from educators and psychologists on the harmful effects of segregation on African American children (notably the famous "doll" experiments of Drs. Mamie and Kenneth B. Clark). In four of the cases, the lower courts ruled that "separate but equal" education did not violate the constitutional rights of African Americans, even though the Kansas judge found that segregated schools were harmful to African American children. Only in the Delaware case did the local judicial authorities order the district schools desegregated. In 1952, the U.S. Supreme Court granted certiorari in all five cases, which were consolidated under the title of the Kansas case, *Brown v. Board of Education of Topeka, Kansas*.[103]

The galaxy of appellate briefs submitted by Marshall and his colleagues on these cases included an impressive mass of sociological and psychological data. Their legal arguments against segregation resembled those in *McLaurin* and *Sweatt*. As in those briefs, the NAACP lawyers argued that the Court should exercise "strict scrutiny" in judging laws involving race or color. Since classifications based on race served no "legitimate state purpose," they were not defensible.[104]

On December 9, 1952, the five cases that collectively comprised *Brown v. Board of Education* were argued in the U.S. Supreme Court. The Court immediately found itself deadlocked over whether there was any basis in the Fourteenth Amendment on which to overrule *Plessy v. Ferguson*. In order to clarify the issues and to gain further time to resolve its own inner conflict, the Court asked the parties to return the following fall for reargument on the question of whether the framers of the Fourteenth Amendment had intended to forbid segregated schools. In September 1953, as the two sides were preparing their briefs, Chief Justice Fred Vinson suddenly died. His replacement as Chief Justice was California governor Earl Warren.[105] Ironically, during spring 1942 Warren, then California's attorney general, had been among the principal instigators of the removal of the Japanese Americans. Although Warren never publicly discussed his wartime actions in regard to Japanese Americans in the years that followed, in his posthumously published autobiography he expressed his profound regret over them.[106]

In December 1953, the *Brown* reargument took place. In their conference afterward, the justices found a majority in support of overturning

Plessy. In the months that followed, Chief Justice Warren prepared the opinion of the Court and successfully exerted pressure on potential dissenters to join the majority (the two most reluctant justices were Jackson and Reed, the dissenters in *Oyama* and *Takahashi*).[107] On May 17, 1954, the U.S. Supreme Court unanimously declared that segregated schools violated the equal protection clause of the Fourteenth Amendment. The decision was based primarily not on legal precedent but on evolving standards of fair treatment and the demonstrated psychological harm imposed on African American children by segregation. As the Court declared in ringing tones: "We conclude that in the field of public education the doctrine of 'separate but equal' has no place. Separate educational facilities are inherently unequal."[108]

Somewhat lost in the glare of attention over the *Brown* decision was Chief Justice Warren's opinion in the companion case, *Bolling v. Sharpe.* In *Bolling,* as previously in *Hurd v. Hodge,* the Court had to deal with racial discrimination in the District of Columbia, where the Fourteenth Amendment did not apply. Unlike in *Hurd,* however, there was no specific statute that the Court could say prohibited racial segregation in the District's schools. The brief submitted by NAACP lawyer James Nabrit, counsel for the petitioners in *Bolling,* had taken up and built upon the argument previously made by the petitioners in *Hurd,* namely, that the due process clause of the Fifth Amendment barred racial distinctions in federal law the same way that the equal protection clause of the Fourteenth Amendment did with regard to state law.[109] Warren's opinion relied on this argument. Due process and equal protection were not mutually exclusive, Warren stated. Although the first was not as explicit a guarantee as the second, both stem from "our American ideal of fairness," and discrimination may be so unjustifiable as to violate due process. "Liberty," he continued, is not confined to "mere freedom from bodily restraint." Rather, it extends to the "full range of conduct which the individual is free to pursue, and it cannot be restricted except for a proper governmental objective." Since segregation in public schools was not reasonably related to any "proper governmental objective," it imposed an arbitrary deprivation of the liberty of African American children that violated the Fifth Amendment's due process clause. In any case, Warren concluded, it would be "unthinkable" that the Constitution should impose a lesser duty on the federal government than on the states.[110]

In support of his assertion that segregation was not related to any legitimate governmental purpose, Warren expressly adopted the "strict scrutiny" doctrine that first the JACL, then the Justice Department, and finally the NAACP had urged on the Court. Citing *Korematsu* and *Hirabayashi* in a footnote, the opinion stated: "Classifications based solely upon race must be scrutinized with particular case, since they are contrary to our traditions and hence constitutionally suspect." Almost ten years after World War II, the man who had done so much to deprive West Coast Japanese Americans of their liberty used the cases that endorsed those shameful actions as support for ending a shameful era of segregation in the nation's schools.[111]

Both the Supreme Court's rejection of the "separate but equal" rule in *Brown* and its adoption of the "strict scrutiny" doctrine in *Bolling* are landmarks in American history. Since 1954, the "strict scrutiny" doctrine has become central to the Court's approach to racial issues During the 1950s and 1960s, the Court relied on "strict scrutiny" to strike down state and local segregation laws, as well as to remove restrictions on the rights of African Americans to vote. Beginning in the 1990s, the Court has used "strict scrutiny" as a basis for curtailing affirmative action laws and "racial gerrymandering" of electoral districts.[112]

The role of the *Korematsu* case, both as precedent and as warning, in the evolution of equal protection deserves further attention. (It is a historical irony that *Korematsu*, whose practical impact compared to the *Endo* case was effectively nil, should have had such a full and contentious afterlife.)[113] Furthermore, the postwar Japanese American cases and the role of Japanese Americans in the restrictive covenant cases have been unjustly ignored in the history of civil rights in the United States. A. L. Wirin, in later years, stated that the *Oyama* and *Takahashi* cases were the most important he had ever handled, "because they were able to establish principles which were the forerunners of the United States Supreme Court cases involving Negroes and affording them the rights to equal treatment and equal protection of the law under the [Fourteenth] Amendment."[114] The critical place of these cases in the development of the "strict scrutiny" doctrine reminds us once again how richly the struggles of Japanese Americans have contributed to building the edifice of American freedom.

12. An Uneasy Alliance

Blacks and Japanese Americans, 1954–1965

The interaction between Nisei and African Americans in the period from the 1940s to the 1960s offers a revealing window into the complexities of American society and race relations. Although members of both groups suffered continuing race-based discrimination in differing forms and degrees, their experience did not necessarily bring them together. Encounters between individuals involved a variety of reciprocal reactions: friendship, fear, hostility, sympathy, competition, disdain, solidarity, envy, suspicion, desire for emulation, and (perhaps most often) indifference. During the early postwar years, members of the two communities formed numerous ties, and on a group level the two minorities achieved a fragile alliance. Newspaper editors and civil rights organizations from both groups formally endorsed equal rights for all, and the two joined in legal struggles against racial segregation and exclusion, as we have seen. Yet as time went on they increasingly diverged in their collective interests and attitudes. By the 1960s, a few Japanese Americans actively supported the protests of Rev. Dr. Martin Luther King Jr. and his colleagues. Nevertheless, many Nisei expressed negative attitudes toward the black freedom movement, which they considered at best as irrelevant to their interests and at worst as a threat to social stability. African Americans, conversely, found little to share with their erstwhile allies.

As previously noted, until World War II Japanese American and African Americans were largely distant. The removal and confinement of Japanese Americans brought them into large-scale contact with African Americans. First, a substantial number of Issei and Nisei were transported to the South, near black areas. Two government camps, Rohwer and Jerome, were established in Arkansas, and housed at their height a combined population of 20,000 Japanese American inmates. In mid-1943, after the famous all-Nisei 442nd "Go for Broke" combat team was formed, volunteers were sent to Fort Shelby, Mississippi, for training. Many Nisei, exposed for the first time to a Jim Crow society, were horrified by the treatment of blacks. Furthermore, tens of thousands of Nisei who left the camps during and after the war became acquainted with African Americans. Beginning in late 1942, Nisei college students and other inmates whom the government adjudged to be "loyal" and who found job sponsors were resettled by the government outside the West Coast. By the end of the war, almost one-half of the mainland Japanese American population lived outside the West Coast.

Nisei resettlers in cities such as New York, Cleveland, Washington, and Chicago, barred by poverty or racial discrimination from more affluent areas, moved into or alongside majority black areas and gained African American friends and neighbors. Many resettlers experienced a warm welcome from African Americans, and intellectuals such as Charles Kikuchi felt a powerful sense of identification and kinship.[1] There remained, however, identifiable undercurrents of strain. John Howard has shown that Japanese American inmates in Arkansas confronted by a Jim Crow system tended to ally themselves with whites.[2] Many Japanese Americans who resettled in the "black belt" of northern and midwestern cities shunned their black neighbors and reacted in bigoted fashion.[3] In January 1944, a white Chicago woman, Marie Harlowe Pulley, complained in *the Pacific Citizen* that Nisei resettlers on Chicago's South Side were refusing to associate with African Americans, even though blacks had courageously welcomed them and had provided the majority of the housing occupied by Nisei resettlers.[4]

At the same time, as previously mentioned, during the war years the African Americans who migrated in waves to the West Coast could find housing only in the "evacuated" Japanese American neighborhoods of the West Coast. When the Japanese Americans who returned to the West Coast at the end of the war, African Americans organized to welcome them. The returnees settled in the prewar Little Tokyos alongside the newer black arrivals, even as others found housing in predominantly Latino and African American neighborhoods such as the Watts district of Los Angeles.

The coming together of African Americans and Japanese Americans was spiritual as well as geographical. During the war years, as noted, many blacks expressed public sympathy for Japanese Americans and criticized the government's removal policy. Black supporters of "fair play" such as Langston Hughes, Hugh E. Macbeth, and George Schuyler took outstanding roles in defense of the rights of American citizens of Japanese ancestry, including sponsoring civil rights groups, bringing lawsuits, writing newspaper articles, signing petitions, visiting government camps, and lobbying officials. Many Nisei, especially those involved in community leadership, were grateful for the efforts of black supporters of "fair play" during the war years, and they reminded their friends that the discrimination against blacks was even worse. The experience of being excluded and confined on a racial basis gave these young Nisei a genuine feeling of kinship with African Americans, who faced prejudice and exclusion on the basis of their race.[5] As the Nisei emerged from the camps and attempted to establish independent lives in their new homes, they sought to build group identity that did not carry the stigmas of association with Japan or double allegiance. The example of blacks showed that it was possible to be entirely American without surrendering an ethnic group culture and identity, and many Nisei looked to blacks as models of struggle and pride.

This identification was neither universal nor absolute. Many Nisei unquestioningly absorbed dominant white social attitudes of black inferiority and inherent criminality. Even among those who questioned or opposed the racial status quo, the Nisei were often reluctant to involve themselves in protesting racial injustice against African Americans. Nisei civil rights advocates frequently complained of friends who told them that the Nisei had enough troubles without becoming involved with extraneous causes, and that it was not in their group interest to support the rights of a despised minority, especially when it would only accentuate their own racial difference.

Despite these limitations, a black-Nisei alliance emerged during the postwar years. The very real problem of racial discrimination, intermixed with sense of gratitude to their previous supporters, catalyzed a significant group of Nisei intellectuals to argue that it was in the self-interest of Japanese Americans to support the rights of African Americans. In 1946, writer Mary Oyama Mittwer (who had rented her Los Angeles home to African American writer Chester Himes and his family after being removed) argued that the Nisei had a duty as a minority group to support equal rights for all, especially since so many groups had "stuck their necks out" to support the citizenship rights of Japanese Americans. "We must be courageous and be willing to stick up for those even worse off than we are.... If we are such Casper Milquetoasts that we would not be willing to suffer a bit for the sake of other fellow Americans—the Jews, the Negroes, the Filipinos, the Mexican Americans—we certainly deserve to be stepped on and pushed around."[6] Shortly afterward, Togo Tanaka excoriated a Japanese American businessmen's association in Los Angeles for hiring Nisei ex-GIs as guards to prevent robberies by what they referred to as black "hoodlums." Tanaka pointed out that they were giving in to a destructive strategy of blaming the victims of prejudice for systemic ghetto problems:

> The truth [is] that color is only incidental to the fact that crime is always high in run-down, overcrowded, near-slum areas of segregation such as Little Tokyo-Bronzeville. There is [however] little evidence that [the business] leaders are concerned about the real reason why their business district suffers a high crime rate, causing them to dish out of their own pockets for a police protection they pay for in taxes but obviously do not get. There also seems little awareness on their part that they have been unwittingly maneuvered by members of the majority group to take issue with a minority group with which they have much more in common and with whose welfare their own is more immediately linked.[7]

Tanaka's advocacy of Japanese Americans aligning themselves with blacks to overcome the divide-and-conquer strategy of the white establishment was echoed in the writings of African American intellectuals. George Schuyler noted in the *Pittsburgh Courier:*

> Japanese can learn more than they ever dreamed of from colored Americans. And the reverse is equally true . . . We are indeed peculiar brothers, who face discrimination, ostracism, and exploitation in common but are so enamoured with ourselves that we cannot band together and face the common enemy. Colored Americans, Japanese, Chinese, Mexicans, and Filipinos would do well to know each other better.[8]

The postwar black-Nisei alliance expressed itself in diverse forms. Activists such as Bayard Rustin, Canada Lee, Sam Hohri, Ina Sugihara, and Pauli Murray contributed to each other's newspapers, addressed social and political group meetings, and joined in multigroup activities. To serve as a bridge between the communities, Nisei writer Hisaye Yamamoto was hired as a columnist by the African American *Los Angeles Tribune,* while S. I. Hayakawa wrote a column for the *Chicago Defender.* Community members formed interracial churches, housing developments, and schools. Antifascist and left-wing organizations in the two communities, notably the Japanese American Committee for Democracy and the Civil Rights Congress in New York, forged partnerships. Sociologists Horace Cayton and Setsuko Matsunaga Nishi published joint research, as did Charles S. Johnson and Jitsuichi Masuoka. Black and Nisei artists and musicians worked together.

A small number of Nisei even joined black colleagues in nonviolent pacifist and civil rights actions through the Fellowship of Reconciliation and the Congress of Racial Equality (CORE).. Indeed, in April 1942, when James Farmer first came up with the idea for a Gandhian protest movement against discrimination, he brought together a half-dozen activists to form a group. Farmer later stated that one of the group was Robert Chino, and that it was Chino who came up with the idea of calling the group CORE, as representing the center of things and the place of action. Chino then was present in the interracial group of twenty-eight activists who participated in CORE'S very first civil rights sit-in, a protest held in May 1942 at Jack Spratt's in Chicago, a restaurant that did not serve blacks.[9] Nisei in Los Angeles, New York, Toronto, and elsewhere were active in other protest actions in the years that followed.

One notable activist who worked to join blacks and Nisei was the celebrated performer Paul Robeson. Robeson, who had been among the first African Americans to oppose Executive Order 9066, continued to keep himself informed of the conditions of the Nisei in the years that followed the end of the war, and to advocate interracialism. In 1946, he publicly opposed the Canadian government's movement to deport thousands of citizens and residents of Japanese ancestry to Japan. As a symbol of his solidarity, Robeson signed on as an honorary life member of the Japanese Canadian Committee for Democracy.[10] Meanwhile, he sang and spoke before Japanese American audiences on several occasions. In April 1946, he gave a concert in Salt Lake City, then home of the Japanese American Citizens League, to an audience composed in significant part of Japanese Americans. Although he did not refer directly to the Nisei in his remarks, his talk was widely reported in the Nisei press. Community reaction was so favorable that a coalition of Japanese American groups in Chicago invited Robeson to be a guest speaker at a testimonial banquet honoring Nisei veterans on Memorial Day, 1946. At the banquet, which was heavily publicized in the Nisei press, Robeson strongly denounced racial discrimination in America as a fascist doctrine and reminded the veterans that the victorious struggle against fascism had to be extended to the home territory. "Your fight is my fight," he told the veterans.[11] The following year, Robeson returned to Salt Lake City to give another concert. After the concert, he told an interviewer that he was

> sharply aware of the evacuation and of wartime prejudice against the Nisei. He said he would like to include a Japanese song in his program, a song of the common people to help fight discrimination against Americans of Japanese origin. It is all part of one problem, he noted,

this matter of discrimination and it may be the foremost question facing us today in the atomic age.[12]

Perhaps the most dedicated champions of alliance between Nisei and blacks were the leaders of the Japanese American Citizens League, the largest Nisei political group. The JACL creed of "Better Americans in a Greater America" and its citizens-only membership gave it a reputation as a conservative, ultrapatriotic organization, and it was reviled among many Nisei for its policy of collaboration with Japanese American removal during World War II. Nevertheless, the JACL was by no means monolithic. Larry Tajiri, as editor of the JACL organ the *Pacific Citizen*, ran numerous pro-black articles and editorials. As he put it starkly in a 1944 editorial for the *Pacific Citizen*:

> It has often been said the four freedoms must be made free to all Japanese Americans or all Americans are harmed; the four freedoms must be made free to all Americans or the Nisei will be harmed. We know how horrible, how vicious and unthinking race prejudice can be. We must not be guilty of it ourselves.[13]

During the first postwar years Tajiri drastically increased the journal's coverage of civil rights issues. The editorial page campaigned vigorously for a permanent Fair Employment Practices Committee and for legislation to repeal poll taxes. In August 1947 Tajiri inaugurated a weekly roundup of news of other minorities, which he placed in a prominent space on the editorial page. The *Pacific Citizen* published a series of reports on speeches to Nisei groups by African Americans such as Pauli Murray and Bayard Rustin urging the Nisei to involve themselves fully in the larger struggle of minorities. Tajiri also called for interracial engagement in his own column for the paper. For example, in 1947, in discussing images of minorities in Hollywood films, he stressed the primacy of African Americans struggles.

> The ... extension of democracy to all Americans will be measured in its approach to the Negro whose present and past predicament is the domestic question of our time. The patterns of anti-Orientalism on the Pacific coast and anti-Mexican prejudice in the Southwest are by-products of the second-class citizenship of the American Negro.[14]

Even as Tajiri lobbied the Nisei in the *Pacific Citizen*, Mike Masaoka brokered political ties. In 1942, hoping to advise federal officials and influence official policy on Japanese Americans, he persuaded the JACL to open a Washington office under his direction. He actively sought help from the National Association for the Advancement of Colored People and other

African American groups. Masaoka renewed these ties after the war, when he became an influential lobbyist. In 1947, he served as advisor to the President's Committee on Civil Rights, and called for federal action in support of African Americans. In 1950, he became the JACL's representative on the Leadership Conference on Civil Rights (LCCR), a joint civil rights lobbying group and clearinghouse organized by the NAACP. The JACL was the only nonblack minority association among the LCCR's founding members.

As has been noted, the JACL's collaboration with the NAACP's Legal Defense Fund in the series of civil rights cases decided by the United States Supreme Court during the postwar years was its primary contribution to the black-Japanese alliance. The two groups initially worked together to expand the compass of the Fourteenth Amendment in cases involving land ownership and housing, and their partnership lasted through the Supreme Court rulings in *Brown v. Board of Education* and *Bolling v. Sharpe*, which set the stage for the civil rights revolution. Yet by the time the cases were decided, the JACL and the NAACP had largely ceased their collaboration, although they retained their respective memberships in the Leadership Conference on Civil Rights, and the JACL continued to print legislative reports endorsing civil rights legislation. When in 1953 Walter White suggested that the JACL help fund an emergency civil rights mobilization, Mike Masaoka replied that the JACL had barely enough funds for its own budget.[15]

On a larger level, the separation between the two groups reflected the growing distance between African Americans and Japanese Americans. The reasons for this are not entirely clear, but a few general trends stand out. One is the exceptional circumstances of their postwar alliance. The collaboration between blacks and Nisei was forged at a time when both groups were victimized by legal and economic discrimination, which they sought to counter through lawsuits, public information campaigns, and government lobbying. Once the principles of legal equality and color-blindness were established, either by legislation or by court order, such a strategy became less compelling. Their partnership also suffered from the decline of the surrounding intergroup movement for equality—CORE was largely inactive for the balance of the 1950s—as well as the eclipse of the large interlocking network of associations that supported civil rights for all Americans, including the American Council on Race Relations, the Common Council for American Unity, the American Veterans Committee, and various Jewish organizations.

Meanwhile, postwar idealism declined among Japanese Americans and radical and oppositional voices became less prominent in the 1950s—a casualty of McCarthyism, Cold War nationalism, and postwar affluence. The Nisei, a small and (outside Hawaii) politically weak minority, felt obliged to adopt an accommodationist political stance toward integration and established institutions, emphasizing their good citizenship and seeking favors from conservative whites. This policy, in turn, paid them important dividends. For example, Congress passed the Evacuation Claims Act in 1948 to reimburse actual losses by Japanese Americans during removal, although the sums ultimately awarded were generally paltry. Similarly, the McCarran-Walter Immigration Act of 1952, otherwise a monument of xenophobia, reopened Japanese immigration and granted naturalization rights to the Issei, thus excising the final basis for legal discrimination against them.[16] Nisei were thus less inclined to support African Americans, who still faced substantial institutional restrictions on their rights, ones they could not overcome through quiet struggle and conservative alliances. As mentioned, even those Nisei who questioned or opposed racial injustice against African Americans were often reluctant to involve themselves in protesting. They also felt pressure, both discreet and not so discreet, from white supporters to remain silent. In one notable example, in March 1954 Col. Sidney Mashbir, who had commanded 4,000 Nisei in the Military Intelligence Service during World War II and extolled their contributions afterward, warned Japanese Americans to distance themselves from other minority groups and not let themselves be used as "a cudgel" by those seeking "social" equality, especially since "confusing" races was a Communist idea. "I do not see why you should stick with other minority groups. It is following the Communist line."[17]

Whatever the cause, Nisei (like most white Americans, especially outside the southern states) remained largely aloof from the black freedom struggle as it developed in the years after *Brown v. Board of Education*.[18] The Montgomery bus boycott of 1955–56, in which black residents refused to ride segregated city buses in the "cradle of the Confederacy," was the first major victory of the movement. Montgomery showed the power of nonviolent struggle by minorities and brought the young leader of the boycott forces, Martin Luther King Jr., to national prominence. Although King and the organization he formed, the Southern Christian Leadership Conference, organized a series of actions in the following years, there was little effective change. However, in February 1960 four black college students in Greensboro, North Carolina, sat in protest at a lunch counter after being denied service. The Greensboro sit-in ignited a movement of similar actions by African American southerners and their white allies that succeeded in opening up public accommodations throughout the South. By mid-1960, an umbrella group, the Student Nonviolent Coordinating Committee (SNCC), was formed with the goal of promoting racial integration through nonviolent struggle. SNCC activists moved into Mississippi to engage in civil rights education and voter registration. Their actions were matched by those of the renascent CORE, which among other activities organized the interracial Freedom Rides, mass long-distance bus rides by demonstrators designed to test laws desegregating interstate buses.

In early 1963, SNCC and CORE pooled their efforts with those of King's organization to sponsor a mass campaign in Birmingham, Alabama, which proved to be the climactic event of the civil rights struggle. Media images and accounts of attacks on nonviolent demonstrators (including children and young adolescents) by police armed with attack dogs and water cannons sparked international protest and brought the problem of racial equality into widespread debate. In June 1963, after Birmingham city officials reluctantly agreed to a desegregation plan, President John F. Kennedy put the moral authority of the White House behind racial equality in a nationally televised address in which he proposed landmark civil rights legislation to ban discrimination in employment and public accommodations. King and his colleagues, in hopes of building support and dramatizing the need for such legislation, joined in a March on Washington organized by veteran militants A. Philip Randolph and Bayard Rustin. The march and rally, which took place on August 28, 1963, attracted a reported 250,000 participants. King electrified both the participants and the large television audience with his "I Have a Dream" speech, which became an instant classic. A year later, the Civil Rights Act of 1964 opened public accommodations to blacks and outlawed job discrimination. [19]

The nationwide debate over civil rights during the early 1960s revealed grave divisions among Japanese Americans. On one hand, there were throughout the period scattered community voices advocating greater involvement by the Nisei against racial injustice. Harlem-based activists Bill and Mary (Yuri) Kochiyama organized support for Freedom Riders and formed the Harlem Parents Committee to fight for racial integration of public schools. In the process, Yuri Kochiyama became notable for her warm friendship with Malcolm X.[20] In 1961 journalist Tooru Kanazawa deplored segregation and noted that the movement of black Americans for their rights was part of a larger international struggle by Asian and African people against colonialism. "We are identified with that struggle, preferred status or not, will we or nill we."[21] In early 1963, John Yoshino, a staffer for President Kennedy's Committee for Equal Employment, negotiated the desegregation of restaurants on the highway route between

New York and Washington. Meanwhile, Issei minister Rev. Daisuke Kitagawa, addressing a world council of churchmen, claimed that blacks and other people of color, "who are far less tolerant of white people than their leaders are," had "cast the vote of non-confidence in the Christian leadership among white people." He called on the Church "to do everything in her power" to regain such confidence or imperil her soul and her survival.[22] When a coalition of activists in San Francisco organized a Human Rights March in spring 1963 in the wake of the Birmingham demonstrations, a trio of Nisei ministers in San Francisco, Nick Iyoya, James Nakamura, and Lloyd Wake, produced a powerful statement urging Japanese Americans to join in support: "What has happened and is happening in Birmingham lies heavily upon the consciences of all concerned Americans. Furthermore, the de facto segregation in relation to housing and employment in San Francisco is a moral blight upon our city." Playing on the JACL slogan, the trio contended that by marching, "we can also indicate that we are sincere about being 'Better Americans in a Greater America,' when any person is denied his God-given human rights on account of his color or national origin; neither can we be 'better Americans' by being concerned about only our rights and freedoms while others are denied theirs."[23] In early August 1963, the distinguished Canadian-born Nisei semanticist S. I. Hayakawa delivered a widely publicized lecture in which asserted that the way the nation handled the civil rights question would determine its place in the world. Anticipating the later advent of affirmative action and "magnet schools," Hayakawa called for a number of special public-private measures to ensure equality, including initiatives in the recruiting of minorities by labor unions and businesses, the end of segregation in public accommodations, and efforts to increase educational opportunity, such as through incentive bonuses to attract talented teachers to schools for the underprivileged.[24] Hayakawa's speech was also foresightful in underlining the role of television, which showed young blacks images of consumerist fantasy that could not be realized, in sparking discontent.[25]

However, these positive statements were largely overshadowed by a number of more hostile remarks. As early as 1961, Clifford Uyeda, president of the San Francisco JACL, proclaimed that Japanese Americans had overcome far greater discrimination than present-day Negroes without aping their "excessive crime rate," and added that "the re-education of the minority groups themselves toward better citizenship" was more important than legislation in fostering equality.[26] Interviews on the mass protest movement uncovered more bitter disdain among Nisei. First, an anonymous gardener in Gardena, California, was quoted in an article in the *Saturday Evening Post* as saying that Negroes should work their own way up the social ladder. According to playwright/critic Samuel A. Boyea, a black man from British Guyana and himself a JACL member, the comment drew a bitter reaction among "many California Negroes." Boyea remarked that "such statements do a disservice to the Nisei who, by their fine example of family loyalty and kindness to children of all races, usually save an integrated neighborhood from going to pot."[27]

Moreover, on June 29, 1963, Howard Imazeki, editor of the San Francisco newspaper *Hokubei Mainichi*, published an editorial calling on Negroes to do some "soul searching." He admitted that it was difficult for Nisei to "really appreciate the suffering and agony of our Negro Americans." Yet despite their history of victimization, of "discrimination, exploitation and even violence comparable to that of the Negroes," he insisted that Japanese and Chinese Americans had crime rates far lower even than that of whites, and many had grown wealthy.[28] Conversely, while he had met outstanding Negro leaders, Imazeki continued, his primary contact was with "lesser Negroes who make a great number of our people afraid to come out to Nihonmachi [Japantown] at night." He thus counseled African Americans to be patient—"Do not say, impatiently, there is no time. Life is long, and America will be here for centuries and centuries after we are gone"—and challenged the black community to make a more concerted effort to better itself in tandem with any movement to break down social and economic barriers.

> They blame society for their womenfolk giving birth to illegitimate children and for living on welfare checks. They blame society for petty thefts and rapes being perpetrated by their manfolks in Nihonmachi. In short, they blame all of their antisocial habits and cultural maladjustment on the "unjust" community in which they live. We have yet to hear any Negro voice "blaming" themselves for their social maladjustment. We once told a prominent San Francisco Negro leader at an NAACP gathering that one doesn't have to have a penny in his pocket to check himself from stealing or raping a woman, for that was what he had implied in his chip on the shoulderish defense of Negro misbehavior.
>
> What we are trying to say most sincerely here is that the Negro community leaders should do a little soul searching of their own today and see if their back yards couldn't be tidied up a bit, find if their children couldn't be given a little community push and more encouragement for education, and examine if there is not one rock too many on their shoulders needlessly.[29]

Excerpts from Imazeki's editorial were rapidly distributed via the Associated Press to newspapers throughout the country, and it was widely reprinted and reported on in the following months (sometimes in tandem with reports of calls for community self-improvement by African Americans).[30] In July, segregationist Louisiana representative Joe D. Waggoner Jr. cited the piece on the floor of Congress and inserted its text into the *Congressional Record* as evidence against the civil rights bill.[31]

As the editorial (often in condensed form) appeared in journals throughout the country, it drew strong reactions, both positive and negative. Imazeki claimed that he received no fewer than 160 letters, with most readers contacting him privately to express their agreement. In any case, he printed in the *Hokubei* a broad selection from named individuals of various racial backgrounds. The thirty-odd published letters written by those identifying themselves as white, coming from around the country, were without exception positive—many of Imazeki's readers praised his courage and said that he had expressed their own thoughts. In contrast, the newspaper published a dozen letters by those identifying themselves as African Americans. Apart from one anonymous missive, all were hostile, though they ranged in tone from dignified rebuttal to abusive remarks about alleged Japanese American support for Japan during World War II. In contrast, *Hokubei* printed only a small number of letters from Japanese Americans. Most were from scholars or ministers who objected to Imazeki's ideas. Conversely, one Nisei reader insisted that Imazeki had "hit the nail on the head, dead center," and affirmed that the Negro must concentrate on improving himself instead of asking for equal rights: "No law of any kind will make a person a first-class citizen. All the demonstrations they are having only cause more hatred toward the Negro people."[32]

Meanwhile, a set of largely hostile letters inspired by Imazeki's column appeared in the mainstream press. A black Chicago writer summed up the opposing case: "The Negro is discriminated against more than the Japanese. They are not faced with the everyday suffering of the American Negro."[33] Black activist George Butler asked that Nisei refrain from "sniping" at another minority group when they were locked in a "life and death struggle for basic rights" by questioning whether their teeth were brushed or their pants pressed.[34] Civil rights lawyer Loren Miller, a longtime JACL collaborator, complained that Imazeki had been "brainwashed" and reminded his readers of the past assistance that blacks had rendered to Nisei:

> We remarked a few lines ago that a few Negroes supported the evacuation of Japanese in World War II. Most did not. They protested

and they said that race and race alone was the root of the policy. And in the meanwhile Negroes broke down the restrictive covenants that barred Japanese from good housing along with us. . . . And our lawyers broke down the anti-intermarriage laws that cast a reflection on us all—Japanese, Negroes, and other darker races alike. Negroes urged Congress to end laws barring Japanese from citizenship.[35]

Some of the most heated objections to Imazeki's words came from Nisei. The JACL formally disassociated itself from Imazeki's words. Hollywood minister George Aki said that he felt "hurt and embarrassed" by the editorial because it "gave the assumption that the Nisei were superior or felt superior to the Negroes."[36] *New York Nichibei* editor Taxi Kusonoki, who lobbied Congress to enact "civil [human] rights legislation with teeth in it," took Imazeki to task, though without mentioning his name.[37] It was immoral, she maintained, for outsiders to call on blacks who were demanding the same basic rights as all others to "slow down" or "straighten yourself out first," and to justify their arguments by proceeding "to cite 'reasons' that are not reasons at all but rationalizations of the worst sort." The Nisei, who had themselves been victims of an "immoral action" that had put them behind barbed-wire enclosures in the name of national security, should know better.[38] Bill and Mary Kochiyama produced a full-scale broadside against what they called Imazeki's "asinine" argument: "To say we were shocked, embarrassed, anguished and enraged could hardly suffice. At the same time we acknowledge his right to express himself as he believes, and also recognize that [his article] may be representative of the thinking of many Nisei in California and across the country." The Kochiyamas retorted that there was no possible comparison between the condition of the Nisei, even their wartime removal, and "the agonizing and brutal inflictions of three hundred years of enslavement and one hundred years of humiliation and insults." They reminded Imazeki of continuing barriers to black advancement:

> We wonder if the writer has ever closely been associated with the Negro people on a personal basis, to hear first-hand from the Negro parents and children themselves? Does he know how many times they have been turned away while looking for a job, an apartment, or home advertised as available; how often they have been ignored while waiting to be served; and often being waited on and served with disdain; also the many places they cannot yet dare dream of being served? Did he ever stop to think of the superficial acceptance, outright ostracism, and social segregation the Negro undergoes, all of which discourages human and individual betterment.[39]

The Kochiyamas closed by citing the inspiring example of the African Americans who maintained their "irrepressible fervor for total freedom despite indignities and affronts," and who sought growth and education in the face of degrading conditions.[40]

The controversy inspired by Howard Imazeki's column mirrored a rancorous debate that developed within the JACL over the attitude to take toward black struggles. In mid-1963, the organization was invited by King and the organizers of the March on Washington to send representatives to the rally. National president K. Patrick Okura and executive secretary Mike Masaoka announced their intention to accept. Numerous local chapter presidents quickly objected that the JACL should not identify itself too closely with the controversial movement, since it was not their fight and would alienate useful white allies. As Okura later recalled, "There were a number of older Nisei who were fairly well established in business and who were proud that we had pulled ourselves up by our bootstraps following the Evacuation. . . . It was the feeling of the great majority of our chapter leaders that what the blacks did was their business, their problem, and that they should improve their lot the same as we had, and we shouldn't get involved in the civil rights movement."[41] Furthermore, many Nisei disapproved of direct action. As former JACL president Saburo Kido stated, "What can be gained by the Negroes in demonstrating when everything is being done to improve conditions? Marches will not change things overnight." Kido warned that marches in cities such as Los Angeles risked poisoning a friendly atmosphere and bringing about a negative reaction.[42] The JACL newspaper *Pacific Citizen* invited prominent Nisei to comment on whether the organization should march. All responded that the JACL should, of course, fully support equality, and that the decision to march was an individual matter, but most added that the organization should not do so as an official matter. A pair of Chicago Nisei argued that "emotional street demonstrations" that "disrupt the civil rights of others, disrupt traffic and the free and normal flow of community life" were not justifiable.[43]

The conflict became further heated in mid-July after the *Pacific Citizen* reprinted Imazeki's column. Dozens of readers wrote in to express their opinions. Many objected to Imazeki's stance and insisted that he did not speak for the entire community. However, Clifford Uyeda (himself a future JACL president) praised Imazeki for his insight and denounced black demonstrators as a menace to civil rights legislation. "Violence and threats are their current method. . . . Congress cannot be intimidated into voting for equality. It must be persuaded." Blacks, he concluded, must show good citizenship and loyalty to their country, as the Issei and Nisei had done.[44] Uyeda added another letter the following week condemning black leaders for minimizing "the sordid record of violence and crime" in black communities. Given the excessive crime rate in African American areas, Uyeda commented, how could blacks be trusted to be good neighbors if permitted to move elsewhere?[45]

Throughout this debate, the national JACL, hoping not to further divide the community, avoided setting an official policy. However, in late July, San Francisco television host John Hart invited JACL Pacific Southwest regional leader Isaac Matsushige to his program to discuss Imazeki's comments. After Dr. Christopher Taylor of the Los Angeles NAACP asserted that Imazeki did not speak for all Japanese Americans, Matsushige was asked how much help blacks could expect from the Nisei. Although Matsushige had written numerous columns favorable to civil rights, he responded that the Japanese did not demonstrate publicly because they believed that violence and emotional demands were not methods to gain their rights.[46] Although he spoke as an individual, his position and comments seemed to connote JACL approval of the Imazeki column. It became obvious that the national JACL needed to speak authoritatively on the subject of civil rights.

Therefore, in late July 1963 JACL president Pat Okura convened an emergency national board meeting to set policy. In hopes of overriding opposition to civil rights protest from local chapters, Okura set the meeting for his home town of Omaha, Nebraska. That way, the delegates could be at a remove from constituents in West Coast communities, which the national leaders considered particularly insular. Meanwhile, Okura appointed a committee of national JACL leaders to draft a somewhat amorphous "Memorandum on Policy Regarding Civil Rights." Masaoka, national director Masao Satow, and Denver attorney Minoru Yasui (who had previously challenged Japanese American removal before the Supreme Court) were named to the committee, but anecdotal evidence suggests that the text was largely created by a pair of officers: third vice president William M. Marutani and past president Frank F. Chuman. Both had experience in civil rights matters.[47] Marutani had publicly championed the rights of black Americans and made various speeches on "civil rights and the Nisei."[48] Chuman, a former member of the JACL legal team that had worked together with the NAACP in challenging racial exclusion, served as president of the Los Angeles Human Relations Commission. A few weeks before arriving in Omaha, Chuman had presided over a public meeting in which black leaders announced a timetable for "total integration" of city housing and schools. Pronouncing the demands "justified," Chuman warned of violence if the problems were not resolved in a cooperative way.[49]

In any case, the document the committee produced called upon JACL chapters and members to "participate actively and significantly in all responsible and constructive activities which focus public attention upon legitimate civil rights issues."[50] It formally endorsed President Kennedy's civil rights program as the minimum acceptable to the JACL, promised lobbying efforts to strengthen it, announced that the JACL would make a $2,000 contribution to the Leadership Conference on Civil Rights for lobbying expenses, and provided that JACL representatives could attend the March on Washington on an individual basis. In an attempt to make the action more palatable to conservatives, the statement characterized the JACL's presence in the march in distinctly nonmilitant terms, as designed to "petition for redress of grievances" and "to be welcomed by the President of the United States." Following a strong campaign by Okura, the document was adopted by the conference as official policy and sent to the chapters.

The issuing of the statement was carried on various television news programs throughout the nation and was carried in its entirety by the *Los Angeles Herald-Express*, an African American weekly newspaper. The statement was hailed by the national Conference of Christians and Jews and the National Urban League. It did not stop the disagreements. Two Los Angeles Nisei newspapers, *Kashu Mainichi* and *Crossroads*, complained that the policy was overly "meek" and defensive. Conversely, various chapters objected to the donation to the LCCR, noting that the JACL's constitution barred national headquarters from making donations to outside groups without formally consulting the membership. There was also resistance to the organizational mandate. At a public "discussion" on civil rights sponsored by the Orange County JACL, chapter board members expressed opposition to any participation by the JACL in the March on Washington, stating that Nisei presence in demonstrations would "not enhance" their status in the county. Board members stated that they would even refuse to sit on any human rights council if one were formed.[51]

In any case, Japanese Americans were not prominent in the great march of August 1963. Official mandates notwithstanding, only some thirty-five JACL representatives attended the event grouped under the organization's banner, and while seats were set aside on the main platform for Masaoka and Okura, they were unable to make their way through the crowd to their places.[52] The JACL group's presence was complemented by that of a few hundred other Nisei, mainly from New York, Philadelphia, and Washington. The following week, Rev. Alfred Akamatsu of New York, who had brought a busload of Nisei parishioners to the March, published a lengthy eyewitness account. Akamatsu, who (like many marchers of all colors) had originally feared violence by extreme racists, was impressed by the order and optimism that pervaded the march. "As we entered the city, we went through the slums of Washington, and the most heart-warming experience for us was to see the Negro people waving us welcome. There was hope in their eyes. For this was their day."[53] Akamatsu told his Nisei readers that they had the duty of translating the uplift that they, too, must feel into militant action. "More of us must join the Negroes in various demonstrations. We need courage, and our faith must equal this demand. But more important than all these is the re-examination of our own attitude toward the Negroes and other minorities." Citing Dr. King's speech, he asked, "Can we accept them as individuals, 'not judged by the color of their skin but by the content of their character?'"[54]

Despite Akamatsu's appeal, the issue of black-Nisei brotherhood was far from settled. The controversy sparked by Imazeki's comments was renewed by the appearance of the full text of his June 29 column in the *Christian Science Monitor* and other newspapers. Meanwhile, a letter appeared in the *Chicago Tribune* under the name of Austin Herschel. It suggested that Asian Americans were "another race that has been subjected to even greater prejudice and discrimination," and noted that Asians could provide a model for other groups (by implication, blacks) because they handled discrimination with "quiet dignity" and had worked through achievement and greater citizenship to secure acceptance. "[Asian] children do not contribute unduly to the school dropout problem; few are sired by unknown fathers; few become criminals. The Asian does not create slums."[55]

The Herschel letter drew a retort from Malcolm Christian, whose letter offers a rare window on African American attitudes toward the Nisei during the period.[56] Significantly, although by 1963 virtually all Japanese Americans were native-born and spoke English as their native language, Christian focused on their status as immigrants and outsiders: "So long as Asian immigrants remain in such negligible numbers, and self-segregated conditions as not to pose problems for those areas desired exclusively for white people," they would be tolerated and privileged.[57] Negroes, in contrast, being more numerous, were more threatening to and disliked by white people because of the specter of economic competition and intermarriage, and could not segregate themselves. "Asians and many other foreign-born Americans, having their own distinctive forms of religious worship, language, customs and self-segregation tendencies, more easily ignore unkind or unlawful indignities by withdrawing to their own sympathetic group nucleus."[58] William Marutani followed Christian's letter with a stinging column in the *Pacific Citizen* attacking Nisei who expressed pride at overcoming discrimination and who said of blacks, "We did it; why can't they?" Marutani denounced such an attitude as "pharisaic" and concluded rhetorically, "Can anyone set himself up as the Supreme judge and declare that before a Negro can breathe freely and fully the air of freedom he must first show himself worthy by running society's race abreast[?]"[59] Dr. Hisaji Quintus Sakai added a letter deploring the fact that too many Nisei, who believed the fatuous statement that "if the Negro would improve himself, prejudice would disappear," were guilty of ignorance and unconscious racism.[60]

In November 1963, President John F. Kennedy was assassinated. His successor, Lyndon Johnson, pushed Kennedy's civil rights bill as a priority. During the first months of 1964, attention was focused on Congress as the bill slowly passed through the various stages. There was little public discussion of the larger question of civil rights among Nisei.[61] Still, Mike Masaoka traveled around to JACL chapters in different cities, urging Japanese Americans to join other minorities in support of the president's program.[62] Senator Daniel Inouye of Hawaii, a strong supporter of the civil rights bill (though criticized by liberals for voting against the elimination of the filibuster, the device traditionally used by white southerners to block civil rights legislation), masqueraded as a newspaper reporter in Maryland and quizzed local residents on their feelings about the bill. Inouye found that, because of his Japanese ancestry, white suburbanites told him honestly their fears, believing that because of his Japanese ancestry he was indifferent. To his great surprise, Inouye found that an enormous amount of misinformation existed as to the bill's provisions. "They thought it would take away their jobs, integrate their neighborhoods, ruin their businesses, and all sorts of things. Almost all thought of it as a 'Negro Bill.' . . . The civil rights bill won't cure the situation by itself but I think maybe we're on the way."[63]

On July 2, 1964, more than a year after the bill was introduced, President Johnson signed it into law. In the wake of the law's passage, the emotions stirred by the civil rights question once again cast a shadow over the Japanese community. In July 1964, the JACL held its biennial convention in Detroit. The convention publicity emphasized the connection to the civil rights struggle. At the conference, past non-Japanese supporters of equality for Japanese Americans were honored, and JACL officials presented awards to the winners of a student essay contest the organization had sponsored on the issue of civil rights. JACL president Pat Okura invited NAACP director Roy Wilkins to present the keynote address. Wilkins praised the recently signed civil rights bill as granting full citizenship at last to the Negro. "It is a matter for the heart—none is so poor that he does not have a heart; none is so rich that he can do without a heart." Wilkins then asked the JACL's help in carrying out the "monumental task" of ensuring that the civil rights measures were promptly and fully implemented.[64] The official JACL releases praised Wilkins and his speech. According to an eyewitness, however, Wilkins's speech produced only polite applause, and when he asked for financial help for the NAACP and other black groups to continue the struggle, he was met with an embarrassed and dismissive silence by the delegates.[65] Meanwhile, Pat Okura, who ran for an unprecedented second term as JACL president, was defeated in the balloting—at least in part as a punishment for his advocacy of civil rights.

In the wake of the convention, Japanese Americans in California, home of the majority of Japanese Americans on the mainland, became embroiled in debates over Proposition 14. The proposition (actually an initiative), placed on the ballot by the California Real Estate Association in response to the 1963 Rumford Fair Housing Act passed by the state legislature, gave property owners a constitutional right to discriminate against racial and religious minorities in housing sales and rental. The issue gained significant national attention, apart from its intrinsic importance, since it served as a harbinger of a feared white "backlash" against civil rights following the federal law. The campaign for the proposed constitutional amendment was run parallel to the presidential campaign of conservative Republican senator Barry Goldwater, who had voted against the civil rights bill in the Senate. (Although Goldwater, like many Republican leaders, remained officially neutral on the measure, his vice presidential candidate, Rep. William Miller of New York, officially endorsed Proposition 14.)

Proposition 14 offered tangible proof of the division among Japanese Americans and of the gap between the JACL and ordinary Nisei. During the July 1964 convention, the national JACL went on record against Proposition 14, appropriated $5,000 to oppose it, and offered organizational support to the "no" campaign.[66] Jerry Enomoto, first national JACL vice president and chair of its State Committee Against Proposition 14, asserted that, if passed, the law and its provisions could be used just as easily against Japanese Americans as against others. "It favors no minority. Taking away all the tricky words of the California Real Estate Association and their ilk, it simply gives legal license to refuse us housing on the basis of our Japanese ancestry, our Negro birth or our Jewish faith."[67] In August 1964, an umbrella group, the Japanese Americans Against Proposition 14, was formed at a meeting in Oakland. Frank Chuman, who organized a leafleting campaign in conjunction with Chinese American and Korean American groups, compiled a roster of affiliated Japanese community organizations that included a diverse assortment of newspapers, religious congregations, chambers of commerce—even the San Fernando Valley Landscape Gardeners Association.[68] Nisei activists toured Christian and Buddhist churches and spoke with community groups. Readers' letters in Nisei newspapers decried Nisei real estate agents and other supporters of Proposition 14 as hypocrites who sought equality with whites while denying it to blacks. Mary Ikuta, sounding the alarm over the proposition in the pages of *Kashu Mainichi*, reminded her readers that the barbed-wire fences of the war were not far gone, and bigotry could all too easily rise again.[69]

By the beginning of September, JACL officers resolved to "go for broke" (borrowing the slogan of the World War II all-Nisei 442nd Regimental Combat Team) to defeat Proposition 14. JACL national leaders called for volunteers to serve in the campaign. Some two dozen local chapters of the JACL officially voted resolutions opposing the initiative, and chapters in such places as San Mateo and Orange County participated in newspaper campaigns or held debates or informational meetings. Chapter presidents solicited donations to the "no" campaign, registered Nikkei voters and provided them with anti–Proposition 14 literature, and distributed "No on 14" campaign buttons featuring the Japanese character for "house." JACL delegates planned a joint fund-raiser, "Oriental Americans Against Proposition 14," and invited other Asian American organizations to coordinate efforts. The event, a combination dinner and rally, took place on October 14. Some 450 Asian Americans, the majority of whom were Nisei, listened to California governor Pat Brown present in depth the case for fair housing.

Meanwhile, the JACL spread its message through the *Pacific Citizen*. During fall 1964, the newspaper provided updates on the progress of the "no" campaign. Editors and columnists repeatedly reminded readers that the proposition was directed by the same forces that had denied Japanese Americans fair housing in previous decades. The *Pacific Citizen* campaign climaxed with the appearance of an unprecedented special issue, dated October 16, 1964, that was devoted entirely to the "no" campaign. Edited by Mas Satow and Tad Masaoka and entitled "Why Californians Are Voting No on Proposition 14," it mixed reports of Japanese American efforts for the "no" campaign with descriptions of continuing housing discrimination against Japanese Americans.

As Election Day neared and the polls favored Proposition 14, the "no" side heightened its rhetoric. San Francisco JACL president Eddie Moriguchi testified before a committee of the California State Senate that Japanese Americans in the Bay Area were not exempt from discrimination in housing and would be significantly harmed by such a law as Proposition 14. Despite the success of the Japanese Americans in overcoming the effects of wartime evacuation, he remarked, "being welcomed as a neighbor is a true test of acceptance, and these instances of housing discrimination are enough to remind us that we still do not have the full acceptance of our fellow Americans." In a clear reference to opponents of black equality, Moriguchi added, "There are those who contend that members of minority groups must prove themselves before they are accepted, but do not give these minorities the chance to prove themselves. How can one prove himself a good neighbor unless given the opportunity to do so?"[70]

At the same time, there was significant, if quiet, community support for Proposition 14. Even opponents of the measure admitted that many Nisei said privately that they did not wish to be "forced to rent apartments to Negroes."[71] After buttonholing friends and neighbors, Mary Ikuta found many Nisei who intended to vote yes or were not sure. "The main reason given was their desire to escape or protect themselves from the Negro influx."[72] Dr. Richard Iwata of Los Angeles appeared in television advertisements in favor of the measure, claiming, "I am against discrimination . . . but want to reserve the basic human right to dispose of property as I see fit."[73] When pressed by community activists to state the reasons for his support, he remarked that American society was built on racial distinctions. Negroes might have greater physical strength and musical talent, he proclaimed, but "as a race, they have greater delinquency and crime. " Conversely, he stated that compared with other races, the Japanese race "can be said to be more industrious, loyal to its parents, scholarly in education, trustworthy in its financial credits, and skillful with its hand."[74] Conservative columnist George "Horse" Yoshinaga proudly avowed his support for the measure.[75] A poll of UCLA students conducted by a political science professor found 49 percent of Asian students in favor of Proposition 14, and 37 percent against (figures for black students, conversely, were 12 percent for and 77 percent against, with Jewish students 22 percent for and 64 percent against and Mexican Americans 35 percent in favor and 41 percent opposed). Considering the likelihood of undercounting in such responses by those who did not wish to appear to favor discrimination, the real total no doubt represented a solid majority.[76] While a separate poll taken in October 1964 revealed that Asian American respondents intended to vote against the proposition by a significant majority, in fact the authors of the poll interviewed only a small contingent of urban voters, notably those in San Francisco's Chinatown, who presumably were mostly ethnic Chinese, and did not take tallies from the more conservative suburban middle-class electorate.[77]

To sway voters in support of Proposition 14, the Nisei for Goldwater group, led by Dr. Tetsuro Tanabe of Montebello, circulated a leaflet written by former war hero Ben Kuroki (who had been honored by the JACL shortly before) extolling the conservative position. The Goldwaterites did not all explicitly endorse Proposition 14, but they were known to be in sympathy.[78] (At the same time, Yoshiro Kikuchi, a member of the Japanese Diet, aroused rancor among local Nisei on the West Coast and Hawaii by endorsing Barry Goldwater and making speeches on his behalf.)[79]

On Election Day 1964, President Lyndon Johnson won a large majority against Republican candidate Barry Goldwater, in California as in other states. (In the same election, Patsy Takemoto Mink of Hawaii, a Nisei, became the first woman of color ever elected to the U.S. Congress.) However, Proposition 14 passed by a margin of almost two-thirds. The *Pacific Citizen* predictably denounced the passage of the initiative. In marked contrast, *Rafu Shimpo*, which had refused to take an open editorial position on the question during the entire campaign, telegraphed its own editorial view by reprinting an Associated Press article that presented the position that Proposition 14 was a justified defense of the "basic human right" to control of property.[80]

Although Proposition 14 was immediately blocked by court challenges and ultimately struck down as unconstitutional, first by the California Supreme Court and then by the United States Supreme Court, the damage had been done. In particular, many historians have attributed to Proposition 14 a share of responsibility for the large-scale riot that erupted in Watts in August 1965.[81] Resentment against Nisei may have been part of the package. While many local blacks watched over longtime Japanese neighbors or employers to guard them from attacks during the riot, Nisei-owned businesses in the Watts area lost an estimated $1 million in lost sales, stolen goods, and damage. In a tragic instance of interracial solidarity, a Japanese American teenager and an African American friend who went to investigate a shop were killed by police who mistook them for looters.[82]

The Watts riot reflected an ever more complex and ambivalent pattern of black-Nisei relations during the years after 1964. On one hand, a fraction of Japanese Americans, particularly college students, continued to sympathize with blacks suffering racial injustice and to support protest efforts. Various West Coast Sansei, including Marilyn Kashiwagi and Howard Iriyama, had joined voter registration efforts in Mississippi. In late 1964, Martin Luther King Jr. and his allies organized a protest movement in Selma, Alabama, on behalf of voting rights for African Americans. Numerous younger Japanese Americans, including Steve Kiyoshi Kuromiya and Todd Endo, traveled to Alabama to participate. The protesters organized a march from Selma to Montgomery for March 7, 1965, but their attempts to march were greeted with violent repression by local law officials. (Kuromiya was badly beaten by sheriffs during a nonviolent protest at the Alabama Capitol in Montgomery the following week). Following the violence, numerous Japanese Americans traveled to Selma to express support for the protesters and their cause—Tomi Kanazawa Knaefler organized a multiracial delegation whose members flew in from Hawaii for the rescheduled march.[83]

At the end of March 1965, President Lyndon Johnson, inspired by the protests and the national mood of support, introduced a historic voting rights bill in Congress. The JACL lobbied through the Leadership Conference on Civil Rights for rapid passage of the law, as well for as a ban on any amendments that might weaken it. After the Voting Rights Act was signed into law in August 1965, JACL counsel William Marutani traveled to Bogalusa, Louisiana, for several weeks as a volunteer lawyer to ensure enforcement of the law. (He would return the following year at JACL expense.) JACL officers continued to lobby for equal rights, while Nisei representatives in Congress and state legislatures supported civil rights laws.

On the other hand, by that time many Japanese community members had abandoned even their rhetorical support for African Americans. As critics such as Harry Kitano and Daniel Okimoto noted, during this period an increasing number of Nisei tended to take the attitude "We overcame the barriers of racial prejudice without help from anyone. Why can't they?" As Okimoto put it crisply, "The Nisei community is in little danger of winning medals for social crusading on behalf of those outside its circle."[84] When Martin Luther King Jr. was assassinated in April 1968, the event was hardly noted in the Japanese American press, apart from the ensuing urban riots, nor was there much visible mourning.

In 1966–67, the NAACP and JACL joined together once more as allies in a Supreme Court struggle. The case was *Loving v. Virginia*, which challenged antimiscegenation laws. The JACL had been interested for many years in overturning laws preventing Asians from marrying whites, as such laws not only represented a mark of inferiority but also became troublesome as the Nisei became a largely exogamous group.[85] Since "miscegenation" was traditionally the greatest bugaboo of white racists, the ban on intermarriage represented the final legal barrier to equal rights for minorities. Although neither the NAACP nor its Legal Defense Fund brought the case, both organizations supported the petitioners with amicus briefs. JACL counsel William Marutani received special permission to present arguments on behalf of Japanese Americans, since as "orientals" they were also subject to these laws.[86] On June 12, 1967, the Court unanimously declared that all laws that imposed racial bars on marriage were unconstitutional. However, just as the *Loving* decision stood in many ways as the final legal hurdle to equality for the civil rights movement, the case also represented a last hurrah, a throwback to a past era of alliance between blacks and Nisei that had already largely faded.

Epilogue

In 1969, Bill Hosokawa, an esteemed Nisei journalist and associate editor of the *Denver Post*, produced a popular historical study of Japanese Americans. His principal goal, as he described it, was to tell the inspiring tale of the Japanese community's social ascension, despite the exceptional level of exclusion and discrimination its members had faced relative to other immigrants. As former U.S. Ambassador to Japan Edwin O. Reischauer stated in the book's preface, the history of Japanese Americans was "the great American success story writ large—a Horatio Alger tale on an ethnic scale," and a source of inspiration for other minorities seeking equality.[1] Notably, to explain how Nisei had attained such success, in contrast to what he termed "the often unproductive struggles of other minorities to win social respect and economic security," Hosokawa approvingly cited a 1966 *New York Times Magazine* article by University of California, Berkeley sociologist William Petersen, who found that Nisei, uniquely among nonwhite groups, absorbed cultural values of hard work and diligence from their immigrant parents, and this heritage of group pride allowed them to overcome obstacles.[2]

Even before its official publication, Hosokawa's book was the subject of a series of bulletins in the Japanese American press.[3] The anticipation among community members was understandable. The work promised to be a landmark, as it was not only a rare full-length history of Japanese Americans but also the first one ever produced by a Nisei. In addition to the air of legitimacy conferred on the work by the author's ethnic identity, the study bore a certain weight of official community patronage. The book had been formally commissioned by the Japanese American Research Project, and Hosokawa drew substantial material from the project's files at the library of the University of California, Los Angeles. While Hosokawa insisted that he was entirely a free agent and not responsible to any organization for his views, he had long been a stalwart member of the Japanese American Citizens League, which had raised the funds to establish the Japanese American Research Project several years earlier, and was a regular columnist for the *Pacific Citizen*, the JACL newspaper. His status led many Nisei to assume that the book would reflect a typical JACL version of the group's history.

No doubt for this reason, when Hosokawa announced that the work's original working title, *Americans with Japanese Faces*, had been changed to *Nisei: The Quiet Americans* (a play on the title of Graham Greene's celebrated novel), the news ignited a firestorm of controversy in the Japanese vernacular press, one that persisted through publication of the book and crystallized the dissatisfaction with Hosokawa's approach. Various individuals (implicitly belying the book's title by their actions) wrote in community media to complain that Hosokawa sought to reproduce invidious ingrained stereotypes of Japanese Americans as conformist and passive. Among the first to protest was Rev. Roy Sano. The preceding year, in a set of public critiques of Petersen, Sano had strenuously rejected the notion that cultural values were responsible for promoting Nisei over other minorities. Far from forming a model of adaptation for other minorities, he maintained, Nisei success was chiefly a product of the actions of these other minorities, who had "opened the door" for inclusion of nonwhites through organized protest. Now Sano added that Hosokawa's use of the phrase "quiet Americans" was both misleading and ideologically biased: "An accurate reading of our history will demonstrate how assertive we have been in our own way. . . . Have we forgotten all the vigils, protests, strikes, demonstrations, and even a few acts of violence in camp?"[4] Amplifying Sano's critique, activist Raymond Okamura accused Hosokawa of furnishing a "propaganda device" for the Nisei and denigrating other nonwhite groups, who had challenged discrimination more openly. "It may be historically accurate to describe the Nisei as quiet and docile, but to glorify this, as a matter of pride, in 1969 is absurd. Far too often, the nice little orientals have been used as an example for other minorities to follow."[5] Sano and Okamura's writings reflected (and anticipated) the evolving critique of the "model minority" thesis by Asian American militants in the decades that followed.

In a review article some months after the book's publication, Yoshio Kishi attempted the audacious feat of synthesizing Hosokawa's "quiet Americans" image of the Nisei, the assumptions that underlay it, and the arguments of his critics by grounding them all in the specific historical experience of Japanese Americans, in particular their wartime confinement, which had violated their fundamental rights:

> The consequence of this shocking violation was twofold: The first was a re-examination by the Nisei of the American dream and a re-assessment of the means whereby they could adjust to the stern reality of the American scene. This led briefly to such activist groups as the Japanese American Committee for Democracy after World War II, an expression of militancy that withered away during the McCarthy era in the Fifties.
> The second was a withdrawal by the Nisei from any deep involvement, social or political, with a society that had already stigmatized them as outsiders. This led to the appearance of the stereotype, the neuter who has been characterized as patient, quiet industrious, passive, untroublesome and unmilitant. It is this image that is perpetuated by Hosokawa's Nisei (the Quiet Americans) and is at the same time a product of that mentality. This is the shameful legacy of the concentration camps.[6]

What the chapters in this collection suggest, I think, is that Kishi may have been on to something. To a large degree, during the 1940s and 1950s and into the 1960s, the Nisei concentrated on blending into the larger American society and overcoming racial and ethnic prejudice primarily through educational and occupational achievement, rather than by political or social protest. Wherever they resettled, whether on the West Coast or outside, during this period the Nisei faced enormous pressure, both from official sources and their own communities, to assimilate and avoid being perceived as different or threatening. Many Nisei removed the most conspicuous signs of their racial and cultural differences—anglicizing their first names, refusing to speak Japanese or eat Japanese food, and immersing themselves in mainstream American popular and consumer culture.

Still, as I have tried to document, the varieties of "assimilation" took a great many different forms. What is more, the evidence suggests that the experience of individuals was both more complex and less cohesive than the "quiet American" stereotype would indicate. For one thing, the assimilationist drive of the Nisei, while obviously shaped by the camp experience and fears of a future recurrence if they did not "Americanize," resembles in many respects contemporary developments among other marginalized groups who did not experience any such race-based incarceration. (It would be useful for a sociologist to compare the experience of the Nisei with that of Armenian or Italian Americans, or especially Jews: during the generation that followed World War II many Jewish Americans, especially the children of immigrants, anglicized their names, abandoned Yiddish language and culture, and adopted dominant white cultural patterns.)

Moreover, in the case of the Nisei, as to some degree with that of other minorities, the drive to assimilate was tied up with a sense of being powerless to alter American society. Yet in the same fashion, the consciousness of being members of a small and exposed group of outsiders pushed many Nisei toward a feeling of sympathetic identification with other minorities. This feeling was especially potent in the first years after the end of World War II, as Issei and Nisei were being released from the camps and beginning the process of rebuilding their lives in a largely unfamiliar and often hostile environment. Nisei reached out to groups such as Mexican Americans and Jews, and in the process were forced to reconsider some of the negative images they had previously held of these groups

With no other minority was the Nisei's feeling of identification stronger than with African Americans. Both groups felt called upon to justify their group identity and to build separate institutions that would not be judged as inferior. What is more, the two were victimized by various forms of legal and economic discrimination, which they sought to counter through lawsuits, public information campaigns, and government lobbying. As a result, representatives of both minorities found it useful to join in alliance with the other. The cement of this alliance was a small leadership group of writers, lawyers, and activists. They were intellectually linked by a common sense of democratic idealism and faith in legal change, as well as common membership in the larger interlocking network of committees and organizations that sprang up in the postwar years to support civil rights for all Americans.

Nevertheless, the connection between the larger communities was always tenuous, given their lack of common history and mutual understanding, and relations became increasingly distant by the 1950s. . Even during the heyday of interminority relations in the early postwar years, many Nisei had unquestioningly absorbed dominant white social attitudes of black inferiority and inherent criminality. Such attitudes became more common with greater distance. Once the principles of legal equality and racial integration were established, there was less room for collaboration between the groups. Direct action and mass protest replaced the slow and costly process of litigation as the weapon of choice in the black freedom struggle. Conversely, once legal bars had fallen, Nisei had the means to rise in the American social hierarchy. As prewar and wartime anti-Japanese prejudice waned and the Nisei experienced greater social and economic opportunity, they moved out of inner-city areas to largely white suburbs in search of greater social and economic opportunity. They literally left behind their black friends and neighbors, who continued to face housing and school discrimination. Similarly, as Japanese Americans increasingly associated (and intermarried) with whites, they felt less of a kinship with blacks.

The Nisei community's political orientation also shifted over the course of the postwar generation. Although Japanese Americans continued to speak in favor of equal rights for African Americans, and their representatives in Congress and state legislatures were active supporters of civil rights laws, radical voices became less prominent (in part a casualty of McCarthyism) and—as in the case of other groups, such as Jews and labor unions—the community adopted a more accommodationist stance toward established institutions. As the black freedom movement developed, and gave rise to black power, numerous white commentators disseminated conservative images of Asian Americans as a "model minority" who had apparently achieved social and economic parity through the established system without political action or government aid. It was tempting for Nisei to buy into such images of themselves, and many preferred to celebrate the remarkable success of their own community and to question why blacks could not follow their example. As Mike Masaoka described the conflict, not without sympathy, "Oddly, the Japanese American community was split on the issue of civil rights advocacy. Some of the older Nisei . . . were seeking peace and tranquility. Largely by their own efforts they had gained status and social acceptance, which they guarded jealously."[7] Even when these Nisei acknowledged the harsh psychological effects of wartime removal of their continuing racial marginalization in a white-dominated society, they saw African Americans less as fellow minorities than as a threat to their new privileged position.

As a result, expressions of solidarity between the two groups grew increasingly rare and hedged as the 1960s went on. During the black power era, many African American militants referred to the wartime injustice of the camps as an illustration of American racism and repression of people of color. Yet they did not consider Japanese Americans as authentic allies. Educated blacks, following somewhat in the vein of Malcolm Christian, continued to refer to insular community social structures as the main reason for lack of civil rights protest by Nisei. When J. Alfred Cannon, a Los Angeles doctor, addressed an interracial community meeting in Los Angeles shortly after the Watts riot and was asked about the lack of visible movements among other minorities, he pointed out that silence among

Mexican Americans and Japanese Americans did not necessarily mean those groups were content. "At the same time, they may be better able to relate to society than Negroes because they contribute 'subcultures' with their own language and particular heritage."[8] When James Farmer of CORE was asked shortly afterward about the lack of Nisei involvement in civil rights protest, he pointed to a sprinkling of Asian American workers in Mississippi, then commented that "Oriental Americans" had "more tightly-knit structures" that encouraged self-help and deterred outside involvement.[9]

Conversely, angry expressions of discontent became more frequent. On August 28, 1963—the same day as the March on Washington—a group of black demonstrators in Fresno, California, picketed two Nisei-owned grocery stores that they alleged had refused them service.[10] In 1965, a Los Angeles funeral home operated by African Americans sought a zoning change to move into the multiracial Cranshaw district, and drew opposition from associations of local businessmen. A group of black ministers complained that while blacks had been the only ones to befriend the Nisei in the years after the war, the Japanese Americans were now fighting the funeral home because "they are now white and don't want Negroes around." Although a local black-owned weekly accused the ministers of making such statements in exchange for a payoff, they clearly were playing to an existing current of resentment.[11] Similarly, in early 1967 an anonymous black who referred to himself as an "ex-GI" scornfully dismissed anti–Vietnam War activism and racial solidarity among nonwhites:

> [Blacks] are citizens here and should work towards improving the race
> situation right here in the U.S. rather than espousing the cause of
> some Asians who couldn't care less about us, even though they are not
> white. To show the total disregard they have for U.S. Negroes,
> Orientals who live in this country are quick to discriminate against us.
> On several occasions, we have had to fight the civil rights battle in
> Chinese and Japanese restaurants. Funny how it happens that they
> don't want Negro soldiers fighting against them when there is a war
> on, but at any other time, they[,] like the whites, feel superior to us.[12]

Despite these tensions, relations between the two groups took a more positive turn by the end of the 1960s, as a new generation of younger Nisei and Sansei (third-generation Japanese Americans) came of age. Less shaped than their elders by the traumas of the wartime experience, they were more critical of accommodationist policies against racial discrimination. Ironically, even as the NAACP was rejected as old-fashioned and elitist by the young militants of the Student Nonviolent Coordinating Committee and other more radical groups during the black freedom movement, the JACL was challenged by a new generation of Japanese American activists who emerged at the end of the 1960s. Inspired by the civil rights and black power movements, the younger Nisei and Sansei called on Japanese Americans to take pride in their group culture and history. They readily defined themselves in racial terms as "Asian American," forging close relations on a durable level with members of other ethnic Asian communities. On a more short-term basis, they sought to revive the legacy of struggle by joining often-ephemeral "Third World Peoples Alliances" and calling for solidarity with African Americans against white domination.[13] Meanwhile, groups of Asian American activists organized a national movement to seek reparations from the government for the wartime removal and confinement of Issei and Nisei, a campaign that ultimately triumphed in 1988 with the enactment of federal redress legislation.[14]

Yet the issue of Japanese American redress did not mark a watershed in black-Nisei relations. Clearly, the redress campaign benefited from the legacy of the black freedom movement, which reshaped national consciousness regarding the rights of minorities, and redress activists described their efforts within a larger multiracial framework. Their cause received substantial support from an older generation of African American legislators who saw the question as a matter of civil rights. Still, black support for redress outside the halls of Congress was lukewarm at best, especially as the movement became more narrowly political, and grew focused largely on Japanese American patriotism. If the success of redress may have led Japanese Americans to look more favorably in retrospect on the movement for black equality than many did in 1963–64, it played a rather limited role at best in inspiring them to support further measures for black advancement.

Notes

INTRODUCTION

1. Japanese Americans are conventionally divided up by generation. The first-generation immigrants are referred to as "Issei," while the second generation, American citizens by birth, are referred to as "Nisei."
2. There is no single volume on postwar Japanese communities: it is perhaps symptomatic that the best-known group history, Bill Hosokawa's *Nisei: The Quiet Americans* (New York: Morrow, 1969), devotes barely forty pages of its five hundred to the years after 1945. There is, though, a small assortment of related works. Lon Kurashige, *Japanese American Celebration and Conflict* (Berkeley: University of California Press, 2002) contains a section on postwar community in Los Angeles. Kevin Leonard, *The Battle for Los Angeles* (Albuquerque: University of New Mexico Press, 2006), Allison Varzally, *Making a Nonwhite California* (Berkeley: University of California Press, 2006), and Mark Brilliant, *The Color of America Has Changed: How Racial Diversity Shaped Civil Rights Reform in California, 1941–1978* (New York: Oxford University Press, 2010) cover postwar interracial politics, as does a portion of Scott Kurashige's *The Shifting Grounds of Race: Black and Japanese Americans in the Making of Multiethnic Los Angeles* (Princeton, NJ: Princeton University Press, 2008). There have also appeared down through the years a selection of sociological and psychological portraits of Japanese communities, including, for example, Harry H. L. Kitano, *Japanese Americans: The Evolution of a Subculture* (Englewood Cliffs, NJ: Prentice-Hall, 1969); Jere Takahashi, *Nisei/Sansei: Shifting Japanese American Identities and Politics* (Philadelphia: Temple University Press, 1998); and Dorothy Swaine Thomas with Charles Kikuchi and James Sakoda, *The Salvage* (Berkeley: University of California Press, 1952). One might add William Petersen's informative but tendentious work, *Japanese Americans: Oppression and Success* (New York: Random House, 1971).
3. I am a bit abashed at being obliged to limit my discussion to the mainland, as I have often complained of books on Japanese Americans that ignore

Hawaii. However, the compelling story of the 150,000 "local Japanese" and their postwar struggle for political and economic influence is sufficiently discrete and well-documented that it really lies outside the framework of this study. See, for example, Tom Coffman, *The Island Edge of America* (Honolulu: University of Hawaii Press, 2003) and Franklin Odo, *No Sword to Bury* (Philadelphia: Temple University Press, 2004). Also largely (though not entirely) beyond the scope of this volume is the postwar experience of Japanese Canadians, following their own wartime confinement. See Roy Miki, *Redress: Inside the Japanese Canadian Call for Justice* (Vancouver: Rainforest Books, 2004).

4. Primary material on Japanese Americans in the generation after the war ranges from memoirs of individuals and collected oral histories to the published output of the Japanese vernacular newspapers of the period. Among the most striking and insightful works, in my view, are the final chapters of Jeanne Wakatsuki Houston and James D. Houston, *Farewell to Manzanar* (Boston: Houghton Mifflin, 2002 [1972]); Daniel I. Okimoto, *American in Disguise* (New York: Walker/Weatherhill, 1971); Gene Oishi, *In Search of Hiroshi* (Rutland, VT: Charles E. Tuttle, 1988); and the collections "Nanka Nikkei Voices: Resettlement Years, 1945–1955," Los Angeles, Japanese American Historical Society of Southern California, 1998, and Brian Komei Dempster, ed., *Making Home from War: Stories of Japanese American Exile and Resettlement* (Berkeley, CA: Heyday Books, 2011).

5. Winthrop D. Jordan, *White over Black: American Attitudes Toward the Negro, 1550–1812* (New York: Penguin Books, 1971 [1968]), vii.

6. John Modell, *The Economics and Politics of Racial Accommodation: The Japanese of Los Angeles, 1900–1942* (Urbana: University of Illinois Press, 1977).

7. On the history of the Japanese Evacuation Claims Act and its place as a "pyrrhic victory" for Japanese Americans on the road to redress, see Greg Robinson, *A Tragedy of Democracy: Japanese Confinement in North America* (New York: Columbia University Press, 2009), ch. 6.

8. Naoko Shibusawa, *America's Geisha Ally* (Cambridge, MA: Harvard University Press, 2006) is a fascinating study of how "Japaneseness" was revalued and reabsorbed into Cold War U.S. culture, though it does not delve into the place of Japanese Americans in the transformation. Caroline Chung Simpson's *An Absent Presence: Japanese Americans in Postwar Culture* (Seattle: University of Washington Press, 2002) describes the erasure of the wartime confinement as an element in U.S. political life after the war.

1. POLITICAL SCIENCE?

1. For the use of social scientists in both Japanese American camps and the M Project, see generally David Price, *Anthropological Intelligence: The Deployment and Neglect of American Anthropology in the Second World War* (Durham, NC: Duke University Press, 2008).

2. Franklin Roosevelt, column in the *Macon Telegraph*, April 21, 1925, reprinted in *F.D.R. Columnist*, ed. Donald Scott Carmichael (Chicago: Pellegrini and Cudahy, 1947), 38. During the early years of the Depression, Roosevelt put forth various schemes to resettle the urban unemployed, largely immigrants, on agricultural land. However, his plans ignored economic and cultural realities. Resettlement under the New Deal was implemented only in piecemeal fashion and not directed primarily toward urban immigrants. Frank Freidel, *Franklin D. Roosevelt: The Triumph* (Boston: Little, Brown, 1956), 225–26.

3. Franklin Roosevelt, column in the *Macon Telegraph*, April 30, 1925, in *F.D.R. Columnist*, 41. For Roosevelt's 1920s racial views, see Greg Robinson, *By Order of the President: FDR and the Internment of Japanese Americans* (Cambridge, MA: Harvard University Press, 2001), 36–43.

4. On FDR and Bowman, see Neil Smith, *American Empire: Roosevelt's Geographer and the Prelude to Globalization* (Berkeley: University of California Press, 2004).

5. Blanche Wiesen Cook, *Eleanor Roosevelt*, vol. 2: *1933–1938* (New York: Vintage, 1999), 560–61.

6. Robert Strausz-Hupé, *In My Time*, 188.

7. Ladislas Farago, "Refugees: The Solution as F.D.R. Saw It," *United Nations World*, June-July 1947.

8. On the M Project, see Price, *Anthropological Intelligence*, 125–37.

9. Ales Hrdlicka, "The Full-Blooded American Negro," *American Journal of Physical Anthropology* XII, 1 (July-September 1928): 155.

10. Letter, Franklin D. Roosevelt to W. L. Mackenzie King, 1942, reprinted in Normand Lester, *Le livre noir du Canada anglais* (Montreal: Les Intouchables, 2001).

11. Letter, Ales Hrdlicka to Franklin D. Roosevelt, May 27, 1942, Jack Carter file, President's Secretary's File, Office Files, Franklin D. Roosevelt Presidential Library, Hyde Park, NY (hereafter "Carter file").

12. Ibid.

13. Memo, FDR to Cordell Hull, June 5, 1942, Office File 5325, Franklin D. Roosevelt Presidential Library (henceforth "FDRL").

14. Memo, Henry Wallace to FDR, June 5, 1942, Office File 5325, FDRL.

15. Memo, John Franklin Carter to Ales Hrdlicka, July 30, 1942, Carter file.

16. For Carter and his team, see Robinson, *By Order of the President*, 65–70, 78–83.

17. Ibid.

18. Ibid.

19. Memo, John Franklin Carter to Roosevelt, July 30, 1942, Carter file.

20. Memo, FDR to John Franklin Carter, July 30, 1942, Carter file.

21. Memo, John Franklin Carter to Grace Tully, August 3, 1942, Carter file.

22. John Franklin Carter Oral History, June 1966, FDRL, 22.

23. Letter, John Franklin Carter to Harry S. Truman, November 6, 1945, John Franklin Carter file, Rose Conway file, Harry S. Truman Library, Independence, MO.

24. John Franklin Carter, memo to President Harry Truman, May 7, 1945, John Franklin Carter File, Harry S. Truman Library.

25. Henry Field, *M Project for FDR* (privately printed, 1963), 327–28. "This time we must not prop up Europe with billions of dollars for if we do, we shall eventually become the most despised and finally hated nation on Earth. Everyone wants to be helped in adversity. But later, it is only human to become envious of the wealth of a great benefactor, then jealousy, and finally hatred, overcomes all other sentiments." Ibid.

26. Henry Wallace Diary, May 22, 1943, Henry Wallace Papers, University of Iowa, microfilm copy in Library of Congress.

27. Jay Franklin (John Franklin Carter), *The Catoctin Conversation* (New York: Charles Scribner's Sons, 1947), 175.

28. Letter, Secretary of War to the President, July 7, 1942, Official File 197-A (Japan), FDRL.

29. "Mrs. F. D. Roosevelt Visits," *Gila River News-Courier*, April 25, 1943, 1.

30. Hung Wai Ching, "Visit to White House for Conference with President F.D. Roosevelt, May 9, 1943," Hung Wai Ching File, Morale Committee Files, Box 1, RASRL Papers, Special Collections, University of Hawaii–Manoa, Honolulu, HI. I am indebted to Tom Coffman for calling my attention to this document.

31. Robinson, *By Order of the President*, 196–97.

32. Henry L. Stimson Diary, May 26, 1944, 3–4, Henry L. Stimson Papers, Yale University Library. On the May cabinet meeting, see Robinson, *By Order of the President*, 218.

33. Letter, Harold Ickes to FDR, June 2, 1944, Official File 4849, FDRL.

34. Memorandum, FDR to E. R. Stettinius Jr. and Harold Ickes, June 12, 1944, Official File 4849, FDRL.

35. Letter, Gen. C. H. Bonesteel to John J. McCloy, July 31, 1944, RG 107, ASW014.311, National Archives, Washington, DC. Bonesteel noted that those who were scattered would face racial hostility and be vulnerable to economic retaliation.

36. Franklin D. Roosevelt, press conference no. 982, November 21, 1944, in *Complete Presidential Press Conferences of Franklin D. Roosevelt* (New York: Da Capo Press, 1973), 24:247–48.

37. Robert Strausz-Hupé, *In My Time* (New York: W. W. Norton, 1965), 193.

38. The situation of Japanese Canadians forms a striking contrast with that of their counterparts south of the 49th parallel. In Canada, where the cabinet acted independently of Parliament under the War Measures Act, the government formally confiscated and sold the properties of Japanese Canadians, and pressured those it confined to move east and scatter themselves, under pain of postwar deportation to Japan. Thus, Japanese Canadians settled in small colonies in the eastern part of the country, and even after the Pacific coast was belatedly reopened in spring 1949 they did not return in large numbers. See Greg Robinson, *A Tragedy of Democracy: Japanese Confinement in North America* (New York: Columbia University Press, 2009), ch. 6.

2. FORREST LAVIOLETTE

1. Forrest LaViolette, "Une Esquisse de l'Histoire de la Famille de John Emmanuel LaViolette," private document. For information on the LaViolette family and a document tracing their history, I am indebted to Ms. Peggy LaViolette Powell.
2. Author interview with S. Frank Miyamoto, Seattle, January 2005. Miyamoto also attributes LaViolette's interest in Japan to missionaries he met in his early youth, to the point where the young LaViolette for a time dreamed of becoming a missionary himself.
3. Forrest LaViolette academic vita, Peggy LaViolette Powell collection.
4. LaViolette file, Reed College Library, Portland, Oregon. I am indebted to special collections librarian Gay Walker for her assistance in locating this information.
5. Ibid.
6. Shotaro Frank Miyamoto, "Social Solidarity Among the Japanese in Seattle," *University of Washington Publications in the Social Sciences* 11, no. 2 (December 1939): 57–130. In his preface, Miyamoto thanks LaViolette, "with whom I had the good fortune to work on related problems," for offering "some of the basic insights into Japanese community life."
7. Author telephone interview with Michi De Sola, June 2005.
8. Ibid. Yasumura's own links with the *Courier* were familial as well as communal, as her brother-in-law, John McGilvrey (Maki), had been a longtime writer and editor for the newspaper. Upon his return to Seattle from Japan in 1939, Maki was named a lecturer in Oriental studies at the University of Washington, and also became a friend and advisor to LaViolette. For Maki's career, see John M. Maki, *Voyage Through the Twentieth Century* (Amherst, MA: Modern Memoirs Publishing, 2004).
9. Yuji Ichioka, "A Study in Dualism: James Yoshinori Sakamoto and the *Japanese American Courier*, 1928–1942," *Amerasia Journal* 13, no. 2 (1986): 49–81.
10. Forrest LaViolette, "Citizenship of Japanese," Part I, *Japanese-American Courier*, July 2, 1938, 1.
11. Forrest LaViolette, "Citizenship of Japanese," Part II, *Japanese-American Courier*, July 9, 1938, 1. In an oddly futuristic reference, he stated, "It is a commonly known that the family in oriental civilizations is far more important as a social unit than in Post-Colonial America."
12. Forrest LaViolette, "Citizenship of Japanese," Part IV, *Japanese-American Courier*, July 30, 1938, 1.
13. Forrest LaViolette, *Americans of Japanese Ancestry: A Study of Assimilation in the American Community* (Toronto: Canadian Institute of International Affairs, 1945).
14. "Japanese Sons and Daughters Found Help Building America," *Christian Science Monitor*, February 18, 1939, 1.
15. Letter, Gay Walker to author, September 6, 2005.

16. "Expert on Japanese Problem Joins Staff at McGill," *Montreal Star*, September 27, 1940.

17. Forrest E. LaViolette, "The American-Born Japanese and the World Crisis," *Canadian Journal of Economics and Political Science* 7, no. 4 (1941): 517–52.

18. Ibid.

19. There is evidence that LaViolette may have attempted (vainly) to secure admission to McGill for one of his friends. See correspondence, Forrest LaViolette papers, Special Collections, Tulane University. For dissenters, see Robert Shaffer, "Cracks in the Consensus: Defending the Rights of Japanese Americans During World War II," *Radical History Review* 72 (1998): 104–5.

20. Forrest LaViolette, "The Problem of Community Disorganization," Heart Mountain Community Analysis Section report, May 16, 1943, Reel 16, Community Analysis Reports and Community Analysis Trend Reports of the War Relocation Authority, 1942–1946, War Relocation Authority papers, RG 210, National Archives (henceforth WRA papers).

21. Ibid. The role of community analysts and the tension between their roles as objective information gatherers and informants for camp administration have been highlighted by a number of studies in recent times, most notably Yuji Ichioka, ed., *Views from Within: The Japanese Evacuation and Resettlement Study* (Los Angeles: UCLA Asian American Studies Center, 1987), and Lane Ryo Hirabayashi, *The Politics of Fieldwork: Research in a Japanese American Concentration Camp* (Tucson: University of Arizona Press, 1999). A more positive assessment of the role of community analysts is found in Edward H. Spicer et al., *Impounded People: Japanese-Americans in the Relocation Centers* (Tucson: University of Arizona Press, 1969 [1946]).

22. Forrest LaViolette, "Discrimination in Education," Heart Mountain Community Analysis Section report, July 1943, WRA papers.

23. Forrest LaViolette, "An Analysis of Family Composition of Those Individuals Who Intend to or Have Applied for Repatriation and Who Answered Question Twenty-Eight Unsatisfactorily," undated [June 1943], WRA papers. For the history of the Fair Play Committee, see, for example, Eric Muller, *Free to Die for Their Country* (Chicago: University of Chicago Press, 2001).

24. "Japs in West Well Treated," *Globe and Mail*, December 20, 1943, 21.

25. Forrest E. LaViolette, "Pride or Prejudice?" *Far Eastern Survey* 12, no. 24 (December 29, 1944): 233–34.

26. Forrest E. LaViolette, review of Allan Bosworth, *America's Concentration Camps*, *Pacific Affairs* 41, no. 1 (Spring 1968): 148–49.

27. Forrest E. LaViolette, review of Alexander Leighton, *The Governing of Men*, *International Affairs (Royal Institute of International Affairs)* 22, no. 2 (March 1946): 283.

28. Forrest E. LaViolette, review of Roger Daniels, *The Decision to Relocate the Japanese Americans*, *Pacific Affairs* 48, no. 4 (Winter 1975–76): 658–59; Forrest LaViolette, review of Jacobus tenBroek et al., *Prejudice, War and the Constitution*, *American Sociological Review* 20, no. 4 (August 1955): 489–90.

29. Forrest E. LaViolette, review of Edward Spicer et al., *Impounded People, Pacific Affairs* 44, no. 1 (Spring 1971): 158–59.

30. See Forrest E. LaViolette, "Japanese Evacuation in Canada," *Far Eastern Survey* 11, no. 15 (July 27, 1942), 163–67; Forrest E. LaViolette, "Two Years of Japanese Evacuation in Canada," *Far Eastern Survey*, 13, no. 11 (May 31, 1944): 93–100.

31. LaViolette, "Japanese Evacuation in Canada,", 167.

32. LaViolette, "Two Years of Japanese Evacuation in Canada," 97.

33. "LaViolette tells of Canadian Evacuee Problem During Visit," *Heart Mountain Sentinel*, September 23, 1944, 2.

34. Forrest E. LaViolette, *The Japanese Canadians*, pamphlet, Toronto: Canadian Institute of International Affairs, 1945; see also "The Japanese Canadians, "*Nisei Affairs* 1, no. 4 (January 1946).

35. Forrest E. LaViolette, *The Canadian Japanese and World War II: A Sociological and Psychological Account* (Toronto: University of Toronto Press, 1948).

36. Tamotsu Shibutani, review of Forrest LaViolette, *The Canadian Japanese and World War II, American Journal of Sociology* 54, no. 4 (January 1949): 387–88. Other reviewers included Carey McWilliams (*Far Eastern Survey*, November 3, 1948), Marvin K. Opler (*American Anthropologist*, July-September 1949), and Robert O'Brien (*Social Forces*, December 1950).

37. Kimiaki Nakashima, "Introduction," in "The Economic Aspects of Japanese Evacuation from the Canadian Pacific Coast: A Contribution to the Study of Economic Consequences of the Relocation of Social Groups and Displaced Persons," M.A. thesis, Department of Sociology, McGill University, 1946.

38. "Jap Problem Here Outlined at Club," *Montreal Gazette*, February 12, 1945.

39. "Canada's Jap Problem Cited," *Montreal Star*, February 13, 1945.

40. "Picked up in Passing," *Lethbridge Herald*, February 26, 1935, 2.

41. F. E. LaViolette, "Social Psychological Characteristics of Evacuated Japanese," *Canadian Journal of Economics and Political Science* II, no. 3 (August 1945): 420–31, cited in "Our Own Japanese," *Winnipeg Free Press*, September 7, 1945, 6.

42. For Montreal Committee on Canadian Citizenship, see Greg Robinson, "Two Other Solitudes? Historical Encounters Between Japanese Canadians and French Canadians," in Greg Donaghy and Patricia Roy, eds., *Contradictory Impulses: Canada and Japan in the 20th Century* (Vancouver: University of British Columbia Press, 2008), 140–57.

43. In a notable article, one that was confirmed in 2005 by Hurricane Katrina and its aftermath, he analyzed the dangers resulting from overcrowding in the French Quarter and the expense of living Uptown, which relegated many poor blacks to the "swampland" downriver and low-lying areas. Forrest E. LaViolette and Joseph T. Taylor, "Negro Housing in New Orleans," Special Research Report to the Commission on Race and Housing, September 1957,

LC-TU, 17, reprinted in Nathan Glazer and Davis McEntire, eds., *Studies in Housing and Minority Groups* (Berkeley: University of California Press, 1960), 155–78.

44. Ann Gomer Sunahara, *The Politics of Racism: The Uprooting of Canadian Japanese During World War II* (Toronto: Lorimer, 1981), 210.

45. Rolf Knight, *A Voyage Through Mid-Century*, http://www.rolfknight.ca/VoyageT.pdf, p. 59.

3. JAPANTOWN BORN AND REBORN

1. Widespread government surveillance of Japanese communities and plans for wartime confinement of leaders had begun long before the war, and helped create a climate of anti-Japanese opinion. See Greg Robinson, *A Tragedy of Democracy* (New York, Columbia University Press, 2009), ch. 1.

2. For the government's decision, see, for example, Allen R. Bosworth, *America's Concentration Camps* (New York: Norton, 1967); Roger Daniels, *Prisoners Without Trial: Japanese Americans in World War II* (New York: Hill and Wang, 1993); Audrie Girdner and Anne Loftis, *The Great Betrayal* (New York: Macmillan, 1969); Peter Irons, *Justice at War* (New York: Oxford University Press, 1983); United States Commission on Wartime Relocation and Internment of Civilians, *Personal Justice Denied* (Seattle: University of Washington Press, 1996 [1982]).

3. See, for example, Michi Nishiura Weglyn, *Years of Infamy* (Seattle: University of Washington Press, 1996 [1976]).

4. U.S. Department of the Interior, War Relocation Authority, *The Evacuated People: A Quantitative Description* (New York: AMS Press, 1975 [1946]). Slightly more men than women left camp during the war, but since thousands of males either volunteered for the army or were conscripted after January 1944, when Nisei were again made draft-eligible, eventually the majority of the resettler population was female.

5. For WRA efforts to aid returnees, see Kevin Allen Leonard, "Years of Hope, Days of Fear," Ph.D. dissertation, Department of History, University of California, Davis, 1992, 232 and passim. This aspect is downplayed somewhat in Leonard's book *The Battle for Los Angeles: Racial Ideology and World War II* (Albuquerque: University of New Mexico Press, 2006).

6. The overview in the following four paragraphs appears in somewhat different form in my introduction to Brian Komei Dempster, ed., *Making Home From War: Stories of Japanese American Exile and Resettlement* (Berkeley: Heyday Books, 2011), viii–xiii.

7. U.S. Department of the Interior, War Relocation Authority, *The Relocation Program* (New York: AMS Press, 1975 [1946]).

8. For resettlement generally, see U.S. Department of the Interior, War Agency Liquidation Unit, *People in Motion: The Postwar Adjustment of the Evacuated Japanese Americans* (Washington, DC: U.S. Government Printing Office, 1947); Dorothy Swaine Thomas, assisted by Charles Kikuchi and James

Sakoda, *The Salvage: Japanese American Evacuation and Resettlement* (Berkeley: University of California Press, 1952).

9. "Editorial Denounces Gov. Wallgren's Stand," *Pacific Citizen*, January 27, 1945, 3.

10. War Relocation Authority, *The Evacuated People*, 43.

11. U.S. Department of the Interior, War Agency Liquidation Unit, *People in Motion*, 159–62.

12. "JACL Opens Chapter in Detroit," *Utah Nippo*, June 12, 1946.

13. Report of Detroit Resettlement Committee, July 1945. Papers of Detroit District Relocation Office, War Relocation Authority, Japanese Evacuation and Resettlement Survey Records, Reel 10, Bancroft Library.

14. Dale Oka, "Just Incidentally," *Pacific Citizen*, April 15, 1944.

15. Cited in Dale Oka, "Just Incidentally," *Pacific Citizen*, April 22, 1944.

16. Arthur Juntunen, "2,000 Jap-Americans 'Adopt' Detroit, More Are Expected to Come," *Detroit Free Press*, clipping in War Relocation Authority Papers, RG 210, National Archives, Washington, DC.

17. Author interview with Marian Yoshiki-Kovanick, San Marino, CA, January 2004.

18. Letter, T. Scott Miyakawa to Roger Baldwin, October 31, 1944, ACLU papers, Princeton University (microfilm copy in Library of Congress).

19. "CIO, FEPC Action Ends Walkout over Nisei Worker," *Pacific Citizen*, May 6, 1944, 3.

20. For New York's early Japanese American communities, see T. Scott Miyakawa, "Early New York Issei Founders of Japanese American Trade," in Hilary Conroy and T. Scott Miyakawa, *East Across the Pacific: Historical and Sociological Studies of Japanese Immigration and Assimilation* (New York: ABC-CLIO, 1972), 156–86; Mitziko Sawada, *Tokyo Life, New York Dreams: Urban Japanese Visions of America, 1890–1924* (Berkeley: University of California Press, 1996); Akiko S. Hosler, *Japanese Immigrant Entrepreneurs in New York City: A New Wave of Ethnic Business* (New York: Garland, 1998), ch. 1; Eiichiro Azuma, "Issei in New York, 1876–1941," *Japanese American National Museum Quarterly*, Summer 1998, 5–8.

21. See, for example, Masayo Duus, *The Life of Isamu Noguchi: Journey Without Borders* (Princeton, NJ: Princeton University Press, 2004); Bunji Omura, *The Last Genro* (Philadelphia: Lippincott, 1938); K. K. Kawakami, *Joikichi Takamine: A Record of His American Achievements* (New York: M. E. Rudge, 1928); Helen Caldwell, *Michio Ito: The Dancer and His Dances* (Berkeley: University of California Press, 1977); Toru Asano, *Amerika ni Mananda Nihon no Gakatachi: Kuniyoshi, Shimizu, Ishigaki, Noda to Amerikan Shiin kaiga [Japanese Painters Who Studied in USA and the American Scene]* (Tokyo, 1982). One study estimates that the city was home to no fewer than 100 artists of Japanese ancestry in the interwar period. Mitsutoshi Oda, "Japanese Artists in New York Between the World wars: A New Chapter in American Art," http://www.brickhaus.com/amoore/magazine/oba.html, searched August 31, 2011.

22. Toru Matsumoto and Marion O. Lerrigo, *A Brother Is a Stranger* (New York: John Day, 1946); Taro Yashima, *The New Sun* (New York: Henry Holt, 1943); Ayako Ishigaki, *Restless Wave: My Life in Two Worlds* (New York: Feminist Press at the City University of New York, 2004 [1940]).

23. M. Ishikawa, "Study of the Intermarried Japanese Families in U.S.A.," *Cultural Nippon*, October 1935, 457–87, cited in Forrest L. LaViolette, *Americans of Japanese Ancestry: A Study of Assimilation in the American Community* (Toronto: Canadian Institute of International Affairs, 1945), 121.

24. Kathleen Tamagawa, *Holy Prayers in a Horse's Ear* (New York: R. Long and R. R. Smith, 1932); Karl S. Nakagawa, *The Rendezvous of Mysteries* (Philadelphia: Dorrance, 1928); Kay Karl Endow, *Transpacific Wings* (Los Angeles: Wetzel, 1935); Kimi Gengo, *To One who Mourns at the Death of the Emperor* (New York: Pilgrim House, 1934); Kikuko Miyakawa, *Starpoint* (New York: House of Field, 1940).

25. Phil Tajitsu Nash, "A Giant of Journalism," *Asiaweek*, November 22–28, 2002, 3.

26. Yi-Chun Tricia Lin and Greg Robinson, "Afterword," in Ishigaki, *Restless Wave*, 257–58.

27. War Relocation Authority, *The Evacuated People*, 44. WRA statistics list 874 people as relocating directly to New York City from camp during 1943–44, and 1,162 in the fifteen months after January 1945. As with Detroit, these statistics ignore the sizable population that first resettled elsewhere. This figure also does not include the 1,500 resettlers employed at the Seabrook Farms plant in nearby New Jersey.

28. U.S. Department of the Interior, War Agency Liquidation Unit, *People in Motion*, 159–62.

29. Alfred Saburo Akamatsu, "The Function and Type of Program of a Japanese Minority Church in New York City: A Proposal for the Establishment of the Japanese American Church of Christ in New York," Ph.D. dissertation, Teacher's College, Columbia University, 1948. In addition to their community center and social welfare role, they were places for Nisei boys and girls to meet for dating—the only acceptable pairings in the largely endogamous community. Sid Yamasaki, "New York New York My Home Town," in *Nanka Nikkei Voices: Resettlement Years, 1945–1955* (Los Angeles: Japanese American Historical Society of Southern California, 1998), 19.

30. Author interview with Sanae Kawaguchi Moorehead, New York, June 2001.

31. Major Sherman A. Amsden to War Relocation Authority, December 30, 1944. Employment Division file, Mid-Atlantic (New York) Resettlement Office, RG 210, War Relocation Authority Papers, National Archives (hereafter WRA papers).

32. U.S. Commission on Wartime Relocation and Internment of Civilians, *Personal Justice Denied* (Seattle: University of Washington Press, 1996), 203; Greg Robinson, *By Order of the President* (Cambridge, MA: Harvard University Press, 2001), 213.

33. Letter, T Stover, A&P, to War Relocation Authority, August 16, 1943. Employment Division file, Mid-Atlantic (New York) Resettlement Office, WRA papers.

34. Employment Division file, Mid-Atlantic (New York) Resettlement Office, WRA papers.

35. "Coastal Japanese Number 60 Percent Pre-War Count," *Rafu Shimpo*, August 26, 1947, 1.

36. "Initiative Eases U.S. Racial Problems in West," *Christian Science Monitor*, January 26, 1945, 1.

37. While various public opinion polls conducted by the West Coast press, notably the notorious *Los Angeles Times* poll times for the anniversary of the Pearl Harbor attack, showed wide support for deporting all Japanese Americans, a more scientific poll carried out at the University of Southern California in early 1944 showed a majority in favor of welcoming loyal Issei and Nisei back to the region. "S.C. Poll Favors Return of Japs," *Los Angeles Times*, March 9, 1944, A1.

38. "Pasadena School Board Rules Nisei Girl Must Be Accepted," *Los Angeles Times*, September 21, 1944, 1; "Tolerance Plea Made for Japs," *Los Angeles Times*, January 2, 1945, A8. See also Girdner and Loftis, *The Great Betrayal*, 380–81.

39. "Sheriffs Warned to Protect Nisei," *New York Times*, March 18, 1945, 18.

40. *New Canadian*, January 27, 1945, 2.

41. "Bowron Lauds Good Conduct of Japanese Americans," *Los Angeles Daily News*, September 24, 1946. Masaoka nonetheless added that Japanese Americans faced an acute housing shortage, and still had trouble finding suitable employment.

42. Lawrence E. Davies, "Pacific States," *New York Times*, February 10, 1946; Larry Tajiri, "Evacuees and Relief," *Pacific Citizen*, January 19, 1946, 3.

43. Scott Kurashige, *The Shifting Grounds of Race: Blacks and Japanese Americans in the Making of Multiethnic Los Angeles* (Princeton: Princeton University Press, 2008); Samuel Ishikawa, "Common Ground," September 10, 1945; Japanese minority files, John Anson Ford Papers, Huntington Library, San Marino, CA.

44. "Church Fights Ouster by Nisei," *Pittsburgh Courier*, February 24, 1945, 15.

45. *ACLU Bulletin*, Summer 1947, 224.

46. George J. Sanchez, "What's Good for Boyle Heights Is Good for the Jews: Creating Multiculturalism on the Eastside During the 1950s," *American Quarterly* 56, no. 3 (2004): 663–61; "War Altered Los Angeles's International Colonies," *Los Angeles Times*, December 14, 1947, A1.

47. "Trailer Homes for Returning Evacuees," *Pacific Citizen*, December 1, 1945, 1. "Irated Residents of Lomita Send Protest to WRA," *Rafu Shimpo*, April 26, 1946, 1.

48. "1300 Evacuees Get Temporary Housing in Los Angeles Area," *Pacific Citizen* November 17, 1945, 1; "87 Winona Families Ready to Move into New

Locale," "Final Exodus of Winonans Begins Monday as Two Nisei Get Lease on Site," *Rafu Shimpo*, July 17, 1947, November 7, 1947, 1. See also generally Charlotte Brooks, *Alien Neighbors, Foreign Friends: Asian Americans, Housing, and the Transformation of Urban California* (Chicago: University of Chicago Press, 2009), 166.

49. "Return to County Service Discouraged," *Los Angeles Times*, January 11, 1945, 2.

50. "Nisei Physician Denied Old Post," *Los Angeles Times*, April 12, 1945, 11.

51. Press release, Church Federation of Los Angeles, June 1945; "Memo of Discrimination," September 25, 1945, Japanese American file, John Anson Ford Papers, Huntington Library, San Marino, CA.

52. "Terror Keeps U.S. Japs from Returning Home," *Chicago Tribune*, March 23, 1945, 12; "Nisei Girls Take Family Reins in Return to Still Hostile West," *New York Herald Tribune*, September 23, 1945, 12.

53. In January 1942, there were only forty-three Los Angeles municipal employees of Japanese ancestry. All were all ordered to go on "voluntary" leaves of absence; the four who refused were summarily suspended. "Eviction of Jap Aliens Sought," *Los Angeles Times*, January 28, 1942, 1. An indication of the nature of prewar discrimination is that public schools in the Los Angeles area refused to employ a single Nisei teacher. In contrast, there was a large set of Nisei public school teachers (and even a Nisei school principal, Shigeo Yoshida) in Hawaii, and even a pair of Nisei schoolteachers, the Hinata sisters, among the tiny Japanese population of New Orleans.

54. "Terror Keeps U.S. Japs from Returning Home."

55. Kurashige, *The Shifting Grounds of Race*, 197.

56. "Pilgrim House Story," *Los Angeles Tribune*, October 25, 1947, 7. See also Naoko Masuda, "Race Relations in Little Tokyo During the Postwar Period: The Resettlement of Japanese Americans and the Activities of 'Pilgrim House,'" *Journal of American and Canadian Studies* 22 (2004): 56–74. For a critical view, see Kariann Yakota, "From Little Tokyo to Bronzeville and Back," M.A. thesis, Department of History, UCLA, 1994, which underlines the lack of solidarity and friendship between the African American and Japanese American groups.

57. Minnie Lomax, "Japanese-Negro Relations Do Stink; Leaders Plan on Action," *Loa Angeles Tribune*, March 8, 1947, 2; "Getting Down to Cases," *Los Angeles Tribune*, March 15, 1947, 2.

58. Charles E. Gibson, "Little Tokyo Hums with Activity, but It's Bad," *Pittsburgh Courier*, March 15, 1947, 3; "Nisei, Negro Groups Learning to Live and Work Together," *Pacific Citizen*, March 8, 1947, 3.

59. "Little Tokyo's Discord Aired at Conference," *Los Angeles Times*, March 4, 1947, A1; "Du Bois Warns Minorities to Reason, to Get Acquainted," *Los Angeles Tribune*, March 22, 1947, 1; "Los Angeles Groups Join Hands to Make Brotherhood a Reality," *Chicago Defender*, March 15, 1947, 2.

4. BIRTH OF A CITIZEN

1. The debate over the production of protest fiction and its stifling effect on creativity was memorably dissected in James Baldwin's essay "Everyone's Protest Novel," in his *Notes of a Native Son* (New York: Harper & Row, 1956), 13–23, and Ralph Ellison's polemical dialogue with Irving Howe, "The World and the Jug," in Ellison's *Shadow and Act* (New York: Random House, 1964), 107–44.

2. Pamela Stennes Wright, " 'Hitting a Straight Lick with a Crooked Stick': Strategies of Negotiation in Women's Autobiographies from the U.S. 1940s: Zora Neale Hurston, Mine Okubo, and Amelia Grothe," Ph.D. diss., University of California, San Diego, 1993, cited in Elena Tajima Creef, *Imaging Japanese America: The Visual Construction of Citizenship, Nation, and the Body* (New York: New York University Press, 2004), 78. See also the essays by Stella Oh, Vivian Fumiko Chin, and Heather Fryer in Greg Robinson and Elena Tajima Creef, eds., *Miné Okubo: Following Her Own Road* (Seattle: University of Washington Press, 2008), in which an earlier version of the current essay also appeared.

3. Creef, *Imaging Japanese America*, 78.

4. The theme of locating resistance has been a common element in accounts of Japanese American incarceration. In the introduction to his selection of sociologist Richard Nishimoto's reports from Poston, Lane Hirabayashi offers a classic statement of this trend: "My selections and interpretations are highly motivated by my conclusion that popular resistance by Japanese Americans in WRA camps during World War II has been highly underreported and misinterpreted." Richard Nishimoto, *Inside an American Concentration Camp: Japanese American Resistance at Poston, Arizona*, ed. Lane Ryo Hirabayashi (Tucson: University of Arizona Press, 1995), cited in *Journal of American History* 82, no. 4. (Mar. 1996): 1629.

5. See, for example, introductory biographical paragraph, "Issei, Nisei, Kibei," *Fortune*, April, 1944, 21.

6. Miné Okubo, "Preface to the 1983 Edition," in *Citizen 13660* (Seattle: University of Washington Press, 1983), ix.

7. Ibid.

8. "Excerpts from Comments on 'Citizen 13660' by Miné Okubo," press release, Columbia University Press, September 20, 1946, 6, private collection on file with author. Deutsch may have been exaggerating Okubo's fixed goals and comic purpose, although Okubo did not differ enough to forbid the letter from being used in her publicity.

9. In 1939–40, Okubo exhibited her paintings at the Fine Arts palace built on Treasure Island for the San Francisco World's Fair. In November 1940 she contributed four paintings to the San Francisco Society of Women Artists' fifteenth annual show. *San Francisco News* critic Emile Hodel praised Okubo as "an accomplished artist whose Japanese tradition fuses beautifully with

American forthrightness." "Art Work of Mine Okubo, Berkeley Nisei Artist, Given High Praise at Show," *Nichi Bei*, November 11, 1940, 1. In the 1941 painting show Okubo won the $200 Anne Bremer Memorial Prize for her painting "Miyo and Cat." Okubo would continue to contribute to the museum shows as her principal means of showing her work. In 1944 she won the Art Association Purchase Prize and in 1948 the Museum Annual Prize. In spring 1946 she won praise for her entries in a show of watercolors. "Nisei Artist Has Watercolors on Exhibit," *Utah Nippo*, April 26, 1946, 1; "Artists Take Part in S.F. Exhibition," *Rafu Shimpo*, September 28, 1948, 1.

10. Dorothy Fuccinelli, "Review of the Art Association's Annual Exhibition of Drawings and Prints," *California Art and Architecture* 60, no. 3 (April 1943): 12. Several current-day viewers have singled out "On Guard," with its sensitive depiction of freezing MPs on a lonely outpost building a fire to keep warm, as testimony to Okubo's remarkable humanity in humanizing her captors.

11. Ruth Hunt Gefvert, "American Refugees: Outline of a Unit of Study About Japanese Americans," pamphlet, Philadelphia, Committee on Educational Materials for Children of the American Friends Service Committee, 1943, 47–48.

12. Miné Okubo, "An Evacuee's Hopes and Memories," *This World*, August 29, 1943, 12–13, reprinted in Robinson and Creef, eds., *Miné Okubo: Following Her Own Road*, 40–45. See also "Miné Okubo's Art, Article, Published in Coast Magazine," *Pacific Citizen*, September 11, 1943, 4.

13. U.S. Senate, 78th Congress, First Session, Document Number 96, "Message from the President of the United States Transmitting Report on Senate Resolution No. 166 Relating to Segregation of Loyal and Disloyal Japanese in Relocation Centers and Plans for Future Operations of Such Centers," September 14, 1943, 2.

14. The WRA's strong efforts in these fields led historian Kevin Leonard to compare the agency's role to that of the Freedmen's Bureau in supporting African Americans during Reconstruction. Kevin Allen Leonard, "Years of Hope, Days of Fear: The Impact of World War II on Race Relations in Los Angeles," Ph.D. diss., University of California, Davis, 1992, ch. 5.

15. On the "providential" nature of Japanese American resettlement as defined in government circles, see Greg Robinson, *By Order of the President* (Cambridge, MA: Harvard University Press), 236–39.

16. For a recent restatement of this thesis, see Bill Hosokawa, "Afterword 2002," in *Nisei: The Quiet Americans*, rev. ed. (Boulder: University Press of Colorado, 2002), 529.

17. WRA teams also compiled press clippings and added sociological data on Japanese Americans collected in the camps by government social scientists and members of the University of California's Japanese Evacuation and Resettlement Study. The methodological and ethical faults of these studies have nevertheless been analyzed and justly critiqued. See, for example, Yuji Ichioka, ed., *Views from Within: The Japanese American Evacuation and*

Resettlement Study (Los Angeles: Asian American Studies Center, University of California at Los Angeles, 1989).

18. A notable example of these efforts is the WRA's protest over a series in the newspaper comic strip *Superman* that was set in a Japanese American camp. See Gordon H. Chang, "'Superman Is About to Visit the Relocation Centers' and the Limits of Wartime Liberalism," *Amerasia Journal* 19, no.1 (1993): 37–59. For official influence on film images, see also Clayton R. Koppes and Gregory D. Black, *Hollywood Goes to War: How Politics, Profits, and Propaganda Shaped World War II Movies* (Berkeley: University of California Press, 1990).

19. Paul La Rosa, "An Artist Remembers," *New York Daily News*, October 3, 1983, M3. A contemporary issue of the *Topaz Times* lists her as having departed for New York in the last two weeks of January 1944. "Keep Posted," *Topaz Times*, February 1, 1944, 3. Certainly, planning for the April 1944 issue and the preparation by Okubo's preparation of the numerous new illustrations for the articles on Japan would have made a short deadline impracticable.

20. Miné Okubo, quoted in Deborah Genensman and Mindy Roseman, *Beyond Words: Images from America's Concentration Camps* (Ithaca, NY: Cornell University Press, 1987), 74. The story of how *Fortune* became interested in Okubo's work shifted somewhat over time. In a later interview, Okubo recalled being told that by a lucky chance a *Fortune* staff member had seen some of her paintings in a Los Angeles art gallery, and was thereafter able to track her down and arrange for her release to New York. Dennis Dugan, "Artist Gets a Second Look," *Newsday*, September 21, 1983, 35. Her *New York Times* obituary stated, with greater plausibility, that the prize awarded Okubo's drawing "On Guard" in the 1943 San Francisco Museum of Art show catalyzed *Fortune*'s interest. "Miné Okubo, 88, Dies; Art Chronicled Internment Camps," *New York Times*, February 25, 2001, 29.

21. Robinson, *By Order of the President*, 187.

22. Miné Okubo, "Testimony Before the Commission on Wartime Relocation and Internment of Civilians."

23. In the same month that *Fortune*'s article appeared, the weekly photomagazine *Life*, published by Time, Inc., ran a story on harassment of Japanese American resettlers in New Jersey. See Robert Shaffer, "Mr. Yamamoto and Japanese Americans in New Jersey," *Journal of American History* 84, no. 1 (Spring 1998): 454–56. While it may be coincidence, the timing of the two articles could reflect an overall push by Time Inc. to run stories on Japanese American resettlement.

24. "New Yorkers Honor Miné Okubo," *Colorado Times*, March 24, 1945, 1.

25. Ibid. Her illustrations appeared in such diverse publications as the *Saturday Review of Literature*, the *New York Times*, *Survey Graphic*, and *Lamp* (the last of these being the house organ of the Standard Oil Company).

26. *New York Times Book Review*, October 15, 1944, 7.

27. Okubo later claimed, with some exaggeration, that Anderson was the only person who had ever really worked to advance her career without selfish motive. Okubo also recalled with gratitude how Anderson had often had her as a guest at her summer home in upstate New York, where Okubo was able to relax and beat the New York City heat. Miné Okubo, comment to author, September 1998.

28. For more on M. Margaret Anderson and *Common Ground*, see Deborah Ann Overmyer, "Common Ground and America's Minorities, 1940–1949," Ph.D. diss., University of Cincinnati, 1984.

29. M. Margaret Anderson, "Get the Evacuees Out!" *Common Ground* 3, no. 2 (Summer 1943): 65–66.

30. Letter, M. Margaret Anderson to Norman Thomas, December 27, 1943, correspondence file, microfilm reel 15, Norman Thomas Papers, New York Public Library.

31. Letter, M. Margaret Anderson to Eleanor Roosevelt, February 28, 1945, series 100 correspondence, Eleanor Roosevelt Papers, Franklin D. Roosevelt Library.

32. Monthly report, Reports Division, New York Office, War Relocation Authority, April 1945, War Relocation Authority Papers, RG 210, National Archives.

33. "Nisei's Drawings of Life in a War Relocation Center," *New York Herald Tribune*, March 14, 1945, 32. Two of Okubo's sketches accompanied the interview. One sketch portrayed the arrival at Topaz, and the other a Japanese American woman teaching school at the camp. Interestingly, Okubo's description of the school image changed drastically in the eighteen-month period between its appearance in the *New York Herald Tribune* and its final publication in *Citizen 13660*. In the earlier version, Okubo's caption reads simply "Discipline was lax at Topaz, Utah, when schools were first opened." Conversely, in her book Okubo accompanied the same image with a more positive but pointed commentary: "School organization was an improvement over Tanforan. The curriculum followed the requirements of the state of Utah and the school was staffed by Caucasian teachers and by teachers selected from among the evacuees; the latter received only the standard camp wages." Okubo, *Citizen 13660*, 166.

34. "Artist Tells of Her Internment in Horse Stall," *New York Herald Tribune*, March 14, 1945, 32.

35. "Display Art Work Done by Nisei," *Utah Nippo*, September 18, 1946.

36. "Nisei Art Exhibit Opens in San Francisco," *Utah Nippo*, July 12, 1946.

37. Review, cited in "Life of the Nisei," *Utah Nippo*, April 26, 1946, 1.

38. "Display Art Work Done by Nisei," *Utah Nippo*, September 18, 1946, 1.

39. "Stories in Area Newspapers," monthly report, Reports Division, New York Office, War Relocation Authority, June 1945, 11, War Relocation Authority Papers, RG 210, National Archives.

40. "Biographies of Nisei Women in 'Glamour' Magazine," *Colorado Times*, January 23, 1946, 1.

41. Shirley Sun, *Mine Okubo: An American Experience* [exhibition catalog] (San Francisco: East Wind Printers, 1972), 29.

42. Letter, M. Margaret Anderson to Larry Tajiri, January 14, 1946, "T" Correspondence File, Common Council for American Unity Files, American Council for Nationalities Service Papers, Immigration History Research Center, University of Minnesota (hereafter Anderson papers).

43. Okubo, *Citizen 13660*, viii.

44. Naoko Shibusawa, " 'The Artist Belongs to the People': The Odyssey of Taro Yashima," *Journal of Asian American Studies* 8, no. 3 (October 2005): 257–75. Okubo later recalled having met Yashima at the time she resettled in New York, although she was unable to say whether his work had influenced the style of her book. Miné Okubo, conversation with author, New York, 1999.

45. Miné Okubo, "Miné Okubo Says," in bulletin, *People Through Books* 2, no. 2 (September-October 1946), published for the Library Service, East and West Association, 5.

46. Okubo, *Citizen 13660*, 68, 172.

47. Ibid., 177.

48. Ibid., 209.

49. Okubo, "Miné Okubo Says."

50. "Excerpts from Comments on 'Citizen 13660' by Miné Okubo," 4, 5.

51. M. Margaret Anderson, "Concentration Camp Boarders, Strictly American Plan," *New York Times Book Review*, September 22, 1946, 7.

52. Cited in "Miné Okubo to Exhibit at Basement Shop," *New York Nichibei*, September 29, 1983, 2.

53. Alfred McClung Lee, "Concentration Camp, U.S. Model," *Saturday Review*, September 28, 1946.

54. Harold L. Ickes, "Mass Hysteria Hits Harmless Jap Residents," *Austin American*, September 23, 1946, 1. *New York Herald Tribune* columnist Gerald W. Johnson also used the term "concentration camp" to describe the government's camps.

55. Letter, M. Margaret Anderson to Larry Tajiri, December 12, 1946, Anderson papers.

56. MOT (Marion O. Tajiri), "Citizen 13660," *Pacific Citizen*, cited in "Bookshelf," *Pacific Citizen*, November 4, 1983, 5. (Also reprinted in *New Canadian*, December 22, 1946, 3.)

57. "North American Journal," *Hokubei Shimpo*, September 12, 1946, 1. I am indebted to Mr. Junichiro Koji for his translation of this article.

58. Mary Ikeda, "Citizen 13660 ... Reviewed," *JACD Newsletter*, September 1946, 5.

59. Alice M. Togo, "Citizen 13660," *Pacific Affairs* 20, no. 1 (Mar. 1947): 122.

60. Setsuko Matsunaga Nishi, "Book Review of *Citizen 13660*," *American Journal of Sociology* 52, no. 5 (March 1947): 463–64.

61. La Rosa, "An Artist Remembers."

62. Roger Daniels, "Words Do Matter," in Louis Fiset and Gail M. Nomura, eds., *Nikkei in the Pacific Northwest* (Seattle: University of Washington Press, 2005), 202–3.

63. Miné Okubo, "Introduction to the 1983 Edition," in *Citizen 13660*, vii.

64. See Okubo, "Testimony Before the Commission on Wartime Relocation and Internment of Civilians," in Robinson and Creef, eds., *Miné Okubo: Following Her Own Road*, 46–49.

65. "Miné Okubo to Exhibit at Basement Shop," *New York Nichibei*, September 29, 1983, 2:1.

66. La Rosa, "An Artist Remembers."

67. "Miné Okubo, 88, Dies."

5. THE "NEW NISEI" AND IDENTITY POLITICS

1. Eddie Shimano, "Blueprint for a Slum," *Common Ground*, Fall 1943, 78.

2. Mary Oyama, editorial, *Pacific Citizen*, July 3, 1943, 2.

3. Ina Sugihara, "I Don't Want to Go Back," *Commonweal*, July 20, 1945, 330–32.

4. Sam Hohri, "I Don't Want to Go Back," *Commonweal*, September 21, 1945, 552–53.

5. Sam Hohri, "The Nisei Situation as Part of America's Race Problem," *Pacific Citizen*, June 25, 1945.

6. For Larry Tajiri's career and thought see Greg Robinson, ed., *Pacific Citizens: Larry and Guyo Tajiri and Japanese American Journalism in the World War II Era* (Urbana: University of Illinois Press, 2012); David K. Yoo, *Growing Up Nisei: Race, Generation, and Culture Among Japanese Americans of California, 1924–1949* (Urbana, IL: University of Illinois Press, 2000), 124–48.

7. Larry Tajiri, "Democracy Corrects Its Own Mistakes," *Asia and the Americas*, April 1943, 213–16.

8. Larry Tajiri, "Farewell to Little Tokyo," *Common Ground* 4, no. 2 (Winter 1944): 90–95.

9. Ibid.

10. Biographical information on Ina Sugihara comes mainly from author's telephone interview, Ina Sugihara Jones, June 2001; Ina Sugihara Jones, conversation with author, November 2001, New York City; and James Sugihara, letter to author, December 28, 2007.

11. James Farmer, *Lay Bare the Heart: An Autobiography of the Civil Rights Movement* (New York, Plume, 1985), 152, 162.

12. Ina Sugihara, "Our Stake in a Permanent FEPC," *The Crisis*, January, 1945, 15.

13. Ibid.

14. No biography exists of S. I. Hayakawa, though various sources list one by Gerald Haslam in preparation. The most probing extant discussion of his ideas is in Daryl J. Maeda, *Chains of Babylon: The Rise of Asian America* (Minneapolis: University of Minnesota Press, 2009), ch. 2.

15. For Hayakawa's early career, see, for example, R. F. Fox, "A Conversation with the Hayakawas," *English Journal* 80, no. 2 (February 1991): 36–40; "Interview with S. I. Hayakawa," in Amy Takichi et al., eds., *Roots: An Asian American Reader* (Los Angeles: UCLA Asian American Studies Center, 1971), 19–23.

16. Author interview with Robert W. Frase, Washington, DC, October 22, 2002.

17. The thesis led to Hayakawa's first book, an anthology of selections from Holmes's writings for which he produced an introduction. Oliver Wendell Holmes, *Representative Selections* (New York: American Book Company, 1939).

18. Ken Adachi, *The Enemy That Never Was* (Toronto: McLelland & Stewart, 1976), 162–63. The delegates were challenged by anti-Asian British Columbia MPs as to whether their very polish and superb assimilation indicated that they were exceptions or representative of the larger group.

19. Samuel I. Hayakawa, "A Japanese American Goes to Japan," *Asia*, March 1937, 269–73.

20. Samuel I. Hayakawa, "My Japanese Father and I," *Asia*, April 1937, 331–33.

21. S. I. Hayakawa, *Language in Action* (New York: Harcourt Brace, 1939).

22. Author interview with Robert W. Frase, October 22, 2002.

23. C. K. Doreski, " 'Kin in Some Way': The *Chicago Defender* Reads the Japanese Internment, 1942–1945," in Todd Vogel, ed., *The Black Press: New Literary and Historical Essays* (New Brunswick, NJ: Rutgers University Press, 2001), 161–86.

24. On postwar Japanese Americans in Chicago, see Charlotte Brooks, "In the Twilight Zone Between Black and White." There is also Jacalyn Harden's compelling but unreliable book *Double Cross: Japanese Americans in Black and White Chicago* (Minneapolis: University of Minnesota Press, 2003).

25. Author interview with Setsuko Matsunaga Nishi, New York, December 27, 2007.

26. "S. I. Hayakawa, Semanticist, Criticizes Support of Walter-McCarran Act," *Chicago Shimpo*, September 13, 1952; Richard Akagi, "An Open Letter," *Chicago Shimpo*, October 11, 1952.

27. See, for example, Ryochi Fujii, "Commends Truman on Courageous Veto Stand," *Chicago Shimpo*, September 16, 1950.

28. S. I. Hayakawa, letter to California Intercollegiate Nisei Organization, cited in "Are Social Organizations Necessary?" *New Canadian*, January 14, 1956, 2.

29. "What Dr. Hayakawa Said," *New Canadian*, January 21, 1956, 2.

30. "Three Letters to the Editor," *New Canadian*, January 21, 1946, 2; Kangu Kunitsugu, "Reply to Dr. Hayakawa," *Crossroads*, November 1956, reprinted in *New Canadian*, November 24, 1956, 2.

31. "Americans Talk Back," *New Canadian*, February 4, 1956, 2.

32. "Hayakawa Calls Nisei 'Intermediary,'" *New York Nichibei*, March 6, 1969; "Pickets, Dissenter Counter Hayakawa," *New York Nichibei*, May 8, 1969.

33. See "Testimony on S. 2116 Before the Subcommittee of the Committee on Appropriations, Senator Ted Stevens, Chairman, Los Angeles, August 16, 1984, presented by S. I. Hayakawa of Mill Valley, CA," Commission on Wartime Relocation and Internment of Civilians Collection, DENSHO archive, http://archive.densho.org/main.aspx, searched September 1, 2011.

34. "More Rights Action Urged by Hayakawa," *New York Times*, August 14, 1963, 26; "Revolt of Negro Credited to TV," *Washington Post*, September 2, 1963, A2.

35. Harlan Trott, "World's Eye View of Racial Conflict," *Christian Science Monitor*, October 11, 1963, 6. The controversy over JACL participation in the march is discussed later in this volume.

36. S. I. Hayakawa, "The Woman Who Was Not Tokyo Rose," *Redlands Daily Facts*, March 20, 1976, April 3, 1976, B-1.

37. Gaylord Shaw, "Ford Achieves His Final Day's Goal—An Empty Desk," *Los Angeles Times*, January 20, 1977, 1.

38. "Hayakawa's 'Internment' Remark Draws Criticism," *New Canadian*, April 11, 1980; Gene Maeroff, "Should Professed Homosexuals Be Allowed to Teach?" *New York Times*, June 24, 1977, 26. Two years later, he publicly asserted that there was a link between marijuana and homosexuality, and thus opposed decriminalization. "Hayakawa Hint Link Between Pot and Homosexuality," *New Canadian*, January 9, 1979, 1.

6. JAPANESE AMERICANS AND MEXICAN AMERICANS

1. *Méndez v. Westminster School District of Orange County*, 64 F.Supp. 544, 161 F2d 774 (1947).

2. For the equation of *Brown* and *Méndez*, see, for example, Christopher Hilger, "A Local Desegregation Case—Eight Years Before *Brown v. Board of Education*," *Orange County Lawyer* 43 (2001), 30–31; Vicki L. Ruiz, "We Always Tell Our Children That They Are Americans: *Méndez v. Westminster* and the California Road to *Brown v. Board of Education*," *College Board Review* no. 200 (Fall 2003); Jim Newton, "Ahead of the Curve on Integration," *Los Angeles Times*, May 16, 2004, M3.

3. Ronald Takaki, *Double Victory: A Multicultural History of American in World War II* (Boston: Little, Brown, 2000), 223. For other sources that highlight the interracial aspect of the case, see Christopher Arriola, "Knocking on the Schoolhouse Door: *Mendez v. Westminster*, Equal Protection,

Public Education, and Mexican Americans in the 1940s," *La Raza Law Journal* 8, no. 2 (1995): 203–4; Sandra Robbie, "*Méndez v. Westminster*: For All the Children, Para Todos los Niños," documentary film, Real Orange Films, 2002. Since the original version of this essay came out, there have been more nuanced and balanced views of the relations between the different groups in the case. See, for example, the excellent study by Mark Brilliant, *The Color of America Has Changed: How Racial Diversity Shaped Civil Rights Reform in California, 1941–1978* (Berkeley: University of California Press, 2010).

4. California Education Code §§8003 and 8004 permitted individual school districts the option of providing separate schools for "Indian children or children of Chinese, Japanese, or Mongolian parentage," and forbade the children of these groups from attending other schools once such separate schools were established. The law originally provided for the educational segregation of African Americans as well, but following civil rights protest by black Californians the law was amended in 1880 to remove black children from the list of groups that could be segregated. Although the law included "Mongolian" children starting in 1885, "Japanese" children were not explicitly listed until 1921. Charles Wollenberg, *All Deliberate Speed: Segregation and Exclusion in California Schools, 1853–1973* (Berkeley: University of California Press, 1976), 24ff. In 1940, under pressure from the Florin JACL, the local school board ended segregation. "Sansei Voted as President of Students," *Rafu Shimpo*, December 6, 1940, 1:2. The Walnut Grove "Oriental" school remained open until mass removal in 1942.

5. See, for example, Matt Garcia, *A World of Their Own: Race, Labor, and Citrus in the Making of Greater Los Angeles, 1900–1970* (Chapel Hill: University of North Carolina Press, 2001); Albert Camarillo, *Chicanos in a Changing Society: From Mexican Pueblos to American Barrios in Santa Barbara and Southern California* (Cambridge, MA: Harvard University Press, 1979).

6. Gilbert Gonzalez, *Labor and Community: Mexican Citrus Worker Villages in a Southern California County, 1900–1950* (Urbana: University of Illinois Press, 1974), 7.

7. Ibid. See also George Sanchez, *Becoming Mexican American: Ethnicity, Culture and Identity in Chicano Los Angeles, 1900–1945* (New York: Oxford University Press, 1993).

8. Charles Wollenberg, "*Mendez v. Westminster*: Race, Nationality and Segregation in California Schools," *California Historical Quarterly* 53 (Winter 1974): 317–20.

9. Superior Court of the State of California, San Diego County, Petition for a Writ of Mandate, February 13, 1931. See Robert R. Alvarez, "National Politics and Local Responses: The Nation's First Successful School Desegregation Court Case," in Henry T. Trueba and Concha Delgado-Gaitan, eds., *School and Society: Learning Content Through Culture* (New York: Praeger, 1988), 37–52. The authors are indebted to Anne Knupfer for this reference. Alvarez refers to the case only as the Lemon Grove case.

10. Alvarez, "National Politics and Local Responses." See also Gary A. Greenfield and Don B. Kates Jr., "Mexican Americans, Racial Discrimination, and the Civil Rights Act of 1866," *California Law Review* 63 (1975): 682.

11. United States. Bureau of the Census, "Japanese Population of the State of California, by County, 1890–1940," in U.S. Congress, House of Representatives, *National Defense Migration* (Washington, DC: Government Printing Office, 1942), 97; Wollenberg, *All Deliberate Speed*, 73; Arriola, "Knocking on the Schoolhouse Door," 176–77.

12. Guadalupe San Miguel Jr., "The Struggle Against Separate and Unequal Schools: Middle Class Mexican Americans and the Desegregation Campaign in Texas, 1929–1957," *History of Education Quarterly* 23 (Fall 1983): 343–59.

13. Petition for a Writ of Mandate, 6.

14. J. Russell Smith, *North America* (New York: Harcourt Brace, 1925), 504. For an intriguing discussion of the life and economics of borderland Asian communities, see Irwin A. Tang, ed., *Asian Texans: Our Histories and Our Lives* (College Station, TX: It Works, 2008). On the history of Japanese Mexicans see generally Daniel M. Masterson with Sayaka Funada-Classen, *The Japanese in Latin America* (Urbana, IL: University of Illinois Press, 2004).

15. Gilbert Gonzalez, "The Los Angeles County Strike of 1933," Paper WP7, Center for Research on Latinos in a Global Society, University of California, Irvine, 1996; Tomas Almaguer, *Racial Fault Lines: The Historical Origins of White Supremacy in California* (Berkeley: University of California Press, 1994).

16. For a poignant account of a friendship between two girls, see Ines Macaulay, "We Are Many People Living Together," *Christian Science Monitor*, August 15, 1945, 18.

17. "Nisei Plays Mexican Jazz," *Nichi Bei*, January 25, 1938, E-4; for Nisei in music, see George Yoshida, *Reminiscing in Swingtime: Japanese Americans in American Popular Music, 1925–1960* (San Francisco: National Japanese American Historical Society, 1997).

18. Tad Uyeno, "Lancer's Column," *Rafu Shimpo*, November 16, 1941, 4:4.

19. Mario Garcia, "Americans All: The Mexican American Generation and the Politics of Wartime Los Angeles, 1941–45," *Social Science Quarterly* 65, no. 2 (June 1984): 278–89.

20. Kevin Allen Leonard, " 'Brothers Under the Skin'? African Americans, Mexican Americans, and World War II in California," in Roger W. Lotchin, ed., *The Way We Really Were: The Golden State in the Second Great War* (Urbana: University of Illinois Press, 2000), 192, 195–96.

21. On Lazo, see "Stand Up for Justice: The Ralph Lazo Story," documentary, NCRR, John Esaki, 2004. On Gabaldon, see, for example, Gregg Kakeseko, "Pied Piper Returning to Saipan," *Honolulu Star-Bulletin*, June 6, 2004. See Gilbert Sanchez's testimony at Los Angeles CWRIC hearings, CWRIC papers, RG 220, National Archives.

22. Gladys Shimasaki, "A Visit with a Congressman," *Washington JACL Newsletter*, May 1964, reprinted in *Pacific Citizen*, February 19, 1965. The article's author states that she met Roybal through Robert Y. Kodama, a former classmate and personal friend of the congressman.
23. "Un japones reune fondos para comprar un canon para Estados Unidos," *La Prensa*, January 11, 1942, 1.
24. "Extranjeros que expresan su lealtad sé han dirigido a Roosevelt gran número de organizaciones," *La Prensa*, February 8, 1942, 2.
25. "Plazo a los extranjeros en California para el dia 15 deben abandonar sus casas," *La Prensa*, February 14, 1942, 3. Cecil's figures were not founded in fact, as there had not been any detectable mass violence or killings in those areas.
26. Talbot Lake, "150,000 japoneses son leales a los Estados Unidos," *La Prensa*, February 21,1942, 8.
27. Ibid.
28. "Americanos de origen japonés que instruyen al ejército de Ee.Uu.," *La Prensa*, March 8, 1942, 8.
29. Stanton Delaplane, "Japoneses en el territorio americano," *La Prensa*, March 31, 1942, 8.
30. Joseph Kalmer, "La quinta colmna los nipones han cometido flagrantes transgresiones al derecho internacional en México y demás países," *La Prensa*, April 26, 1942, 8.
31. The series of photos showed, in order, "the roomy houses of a Japanese evacuee camp in California; medical care; carrying wood for heating Japanese evacuated from the strategic zones to be sent to isolation centers, [where] the United States observe some of the ideals for which they are fighting." "Singulares obras de explotacion agricola reciben trato humanitario los japoneses internados en los Estados Unidos," *La Prensa*, October 20, 1942, 3.
32. "Concentrationes contra el sabotaje," *La Opinión*, January 30, 1942, 1.
33. Ibid. The rather doubtful nature of such an assertion by a Nisei is reinforced by the fact that a search of California birth records and government records of confined Japanese Americans by the author has failed to uncover any such name. While there were associations of Japanese American fishermen, moreover, it is unclear if there ever was one such as described here.
34. "Redada ayer en la Isla Terminal," *La Opinión*, February 3, 1942, 1.
35. "Solo dicen Shikatagani," *La Opinión*, February 4, 1942, 8. The Spanish phrase means roughly "what will happen, will happen."
36. "Nueva oficina de la Dra. Ichioka," *La Opinión*, February 3, 1942, 1:1.
37. "Propaganda pro-Japon confiscada," *La Opinión*, February 13, 1942, 8.
38. "Los Angeles centro de espionaje," *La Opinión*, February 7, 1942, 1; "Nueva redada de japoneses en la region del puerto," *La Opinión*, February 8, 1942; "Gran exodo de japoneses evacuaron ya varias zonas/viene una comision del Congres," *La Opinión*, February 18, 1942, 8.
39. "Cien extranjeros mas detenidos," *La Opinión*, February 21, 1942, 8.

40. "Se predice una invasion del Canada," *La Opinión*, February 13, 1942, 1.

41. For the removal in Mexico, see Greg Robinson, *A Tragedy of Democracy* (New York: Columbia University Press, 2009), 145–48; Daniel M. Masterson with Sayaka Funada-Classen, *The Japanese in Latin America*, 125–28. It should be mentioned that *La Prensa*, which cited former president Cardenas dismissing any Japanese threat to Mexico, presented only a single article on the progress of mass exclusion in Mexico. "No será otra Pearl Harbor Baja California el Gral. Lázaro Cárdenas fortifica lodos los puntos," *La Prensa*, February 10, 1942, 8; "El traslado de nipones continua," *La Prensa*, February 26, 1942, 1.

42. "El Japon prepara un ataque contra Mexico," *La Opinión*, February 14, 1942, 1.

43. "Frente al peligro," *La Opinión*, February 26, 1942, 2.

44. "Evacuacion," *La Opinión*, March 19, 1942, 8. In fact, Alice Tatsuni, the person shown, was not an alien, but a U.S. citizen of Japanese ancestry.

45. "Llegan mil japoneses a Manzanar," *La Opinión*, March 25, 1942.

46. Stanton Delaplane, "Japoneses en el territorio americano," *La Opinión*, March 31, 1942.

47. "Comenzar ayer el exodo de los nipones," *La Opinión*, March 25, 1942.

48. "1500 nipones van rumbo a Manzanar ya," *La Opinión*, May 2, 1942, 1.

49. "Mas nipones evacuados" and "1000 salieron de Pasadena," *La Opinión*, May 8, 1942, 8. Emphasis added.

50. "Un ejemplo de democracia es la concentration de nipones en el Campo de Owens Valley," *La Opinión*, April 13, 1942, 3.

51. "Como a su casa," *La Opinión*, July 2, 1942, 2.

52. "Mexicanos en lugar de japoneses," *La Opinión*, February 28, 1942, 1.

53. "Terminaran la evacuation de japoneses," *La Opinión*, April 27, 1942, 1–3.

54. "La gran oportunidad," *La Opinión*, April 27, 1942, 5. A few days later, the newspaper reported that 4,000 farms had been transferred. It also reported, however, that "the LA City Council unanimously approved a resolution opposing the importing of Mexican braceros. "4200 ranchos son trasposadas," *La Opinión*, April 29, 1942; "Opocision al proyecto de traer pizcadores de Mexico a California," *La Opinión*, May 1, 1942, 8.

55. José Ruiz Velis, "El 'Piqueno Tokyo' ha muerto," *La Opinión*, April 19, 1942, 7.

56. Geoffrey Perrett, *Days of Sadness, Years of Triumph* (Baltimore: Penguin Books, 1974), 314–16; Carey McWilliams, *North from Mexico: The Spanish-Speaking People of the United States* (Westport, CT: Greenwood Press, 1968 [1948]), 228–51. The verdict was subsequently overturned on appeal.

57. Ibid. See also Mauricio Mazon, *The Zoot Suit Riots: The Psychology of Symbolic Annihilation* (Austin: University of Texas Press, 1984).

58. Garcia, "Americans All." The Sleepy Lagoon verdict prompted African Americans to defend publicly the rights of their Mexican American "neighbors" (in the words of the African American newspaper *California Eagle*). For African American reactions to the Sleepy Lagoon case, see, for example,

Kevin Allen Leonard, " 'In the Interest of All Races': African Americans and Interracial Cooperation in Los Angeles During and After World War II," in Lawrence B. De Graaf, Kevin Mulroy, and Quintard Taylor, eds., *Seeking El Dorado: African Americans in California* (Los Angeles: Autry Museum of Western Heritage, 2001), 333–34.

59. *Japanese American Committee for Democracy Newsletter*, March 1944, 5; *Manzanar Free Press*, January 30, 1943, 2. See also "Zoot Suit Gangsters," *Manzanar Free Press*, October 15, 1942, 2.

60. See, for example, Harry H. L. Kitano, *Japanese Americans: The Evolution of a Subculture* (Englewood Cliffs, NJ: Prentice-Hall, 1969); Bill Hosokawa, *JACL in Search of Justice* (New York: Morrow, 1982).

61. Frank Chuman, *The Bamboo People: The Law and Japanese Americans* (Del Mar, CA: Publishers, Inc., 1976).

62. "Form Antidiscrimination Body to Seek Fair Play," *Rafu Shimpo*, July 23, 1946; "JACL Establishes Defense Fund for Civil Rights Cases," *Pacific Citizen*, December 7, 1946.

63. "Stress JACL Must Work for All Minorities," *Pacific Citizen*, February 8, 1947.

64. Garcia, "Americans All." In 1945, the assembly voted to repeal §§8003 and 8004, but the legislation subsequently died in the state senate.

65. Lawrence E. Davies, "Segregation of Mexican American Students Stirs Court Fight," *New York Times*, December 22, 1946, IV, 6:4.

66. Judgment of Dismissal, *A. T. Collison and R. L. Wood v. Nellie Garcia et al.*, Superior Court of the County of Los Angeles, Civil Case Series I, No. 498206, February 9, 1945. See also "Judge Rules in Covenant Suit," *Los Angeles Times*, February 17, 1945.

67. Garcia, "Americans All," 285, 287. See also generally Mario T. Garcia, *Mexican Americans: Leadership, Ideology and Identity, 1930–1960* (New Haven: Yale University Press, 1989).

68. Garcia, "Americans All," 285, 287.

69. Neil Foley, "Partly Colored or Other White: Mexican Americans and Their Problem with the Color Line," lecture delivered at the Labor and Working Class Historians luncheon at the Organization of American Historians Meeting, April 1, 2000, www.lawcha.org/resources/talks/beyondbw.html. See generally Neil Foley, "Becoming Hispanic: Mexican Americans and the Faustian Pact with Whiteness," in Neil Foley, ed., *Reflexiones 1997: New Directions in Mexican American Studies* (Austin, TX: CMAS Books, 1998), 53–70.

70. Robbie, "*Méndez v. Westminster*: For the Sake of the Children"; César Arredondo, "Court Case Changed O.C. Schools," *Orange County Register*, September 24, 2002, S3:1–5.

71. Petition, *Westminster School District et al. v. Gonzalo Méndez*; Christopher Arriola, "Knocking on the Schoolhouse Door." Arriola describes Marcus as "an African American civil rights lawyer," but this is doubtful. More plausibly, especially given his family name, members of the Marcus family described David Marcus as Jewish.

72. *Méndez v. Westminster*, record of trial, 116, 121, and passim. Cited in *Westminster School District of Orange County, et al. v. Gonzalo Méndez, et al. Motion and Brief of the United Jewish Congress as Amicus Curiae*, 17; *Westminster School District of Orange County, et al. v. Gonzalo Méndez, et al. Brief for the American Civil Liberties Union, and the National Lawyers Guild, Los Angeles Chapter as Amicus Curiae*, 16.

73. Ogle's decision not to assert that Mexicans were "Indians" and thus subject to the California school segregation law may have constituted lawyer's error. The question of the Mexicans' racial classification had never been clearly judicially determined, and certainly not in California. In 1929 state attorney general Ulysses S. Webb issued an advisory opinion that segregation of schoolchildren of Mexican ancestry was not supported by law because they were members of the white race, but the opinion was nonbinding. In 1931, Assemblyman George Bliss, who had established a segregated Mexican school in his hometown of Carpinteria on the grounds that it was an "Indian school," introduced an amendment to §§8003 and 8004 to provide for segregation of "Indian" children "whether born in the United States or not," presumably as a means to provide legal support for the segregation of Mexican Americans. The assembly, anxious to avoid alienating Mexico through such a provision, killed the bill. Alvarez, "National Politics and Local Responses," 44.

74. For more on "whiteness," see, for example, Ian F. Haney López, *White by Law: The Legal Construction of Race* (New York: New York University Press, 1998); George Lipsitz, *The Possessive Investment in Whiteness: How White People Benefit from Identity Politics* (Philadelphia: Temple University Press, 1998).

75. *Méndez v. Westminster School District of Orange County*, 64 F. Supp. 543, 549 (1946).

76. See, for example, Warren's comment that "to separate [children in grade and high schools] from others of similar age and qualifications solely because of their race generates a feeling of inferiority as to their status in the community that may affect their hearts and minds in a way unlikely ever to be undone." *Brown v. Board of Education*, 347 U.S. 483, 494 (1954).

77. *Méndez v. Westminster School District of Orange County*, at 549.

78. Ibid., at 550.

79. Ibid., at 549.

80. Ibid., at 548. Ironically, the language quoted by McCormick came from *Hirabayashi v. United States*, 320 U.S. 81 (1943), one of the "internment" cases that upheld the constitutionality of wartime restrictions imposed on Japanese Americans on the basis of their ancestry.

81. *Westminster School District of Orange County, et al. v. Gonzalo Méndez, et al., Brief of Appellants; Westminster School District of Orange County, et al. v. Gonzalo Méndez, et al., Appellees' Reply Brief.*

82. Ibid.

83. James A. Ferg-Cadima, "Black, White, and Brown: Latino School Desegregation Efforts in the Pre- and Post–*Brown v. Board of Education* Era,"

pamphlet, Mexican American Legal Defense and Educational Fund, May 2004, 20; see www.maldef.org/pdf/LatinoSegregation.pdf (November 2004).

84. Lawrence Davies, "Segregation of Mexican American Students Stirs Court Fight," *New York Times*, December 22, 1946, IV, 6:4.; "School Segregation Case Is Before U.S. Court Here," *San Francisco Chronicle*, December 10, 1946.

85. Carey McWilliams, "Is Your Name Gonzales?" *Nation*, March 15, 1947, 302.

86. Ibid., 303.

87. *Westminster School District of Orange County, et al. v. Gonzalo Méndez, et al., Motion and Brief of the United Jewish Congress as Amicus Curiae.*

88. *Westminster School District of Orange County, et al. v. Gonzalo Méndez, et al., Motion and Brief of the Attorney General of the State of California as Amicus Curiae.*

89. "Legality of Segregating Grade School Children Challenged," *Utah Nippo*, December 23, 1946, 1:3; "Class Segregation Suit Dismissed," *Utah Nippo*, January 10, 1947, 1:3. See also "Lawsuit Challenges Racial Bias in California Schools," *Chicago Defender*, January 18, 1947, 2; "Kenny Raps Organizations on School Segregation Suit," *Rafu Shimpo*, January 10, 1947, 1:4–5.

90. *Westminster School District of Orange County, et al. v. Gonzalo Méndez, et al., Brief for the American Civil Liberties Union, and the National Lawyers Guild, Los Angeles Chapter, as Amici Curiae, A. L. Wirin, Saburo Kido, of Counsel for Japanese-American Citizens League*, 6. During the lower court case, Wirin had been listed as "of counsel" on the amicus brief submitted by the national ACLU, while African American attorney Loren Miller had submitted a separate brief on behalf of the National Lawyers Guild.

91. *Westminster School District of Orange County, et al. v. Gonzalo Méndez, et al., Brief for the American Civil Liberties Union, and the National Lawyers Guild, Los Angeles Chapter, as Amici Curiae, A. L. Wirin, Saburo Kido, of Counsel for Japanese-American Citizens League*, 6.

92. Ibid., 9. In view of the fact that the Supreme Court had actually ruled in *Korematsu* that the mass removal of Japanese Americans from the West Coast was constitutional, Wirin and Kido's argument here is especially strained.

93. Ibid., 21.

94. Ibid., 17.

95. Lawrence E. Davies, "Pupil Segregation on Coast Is Fought," *New York Times*, December 10, 1946, 28:1. Another sign of the JACL's interest in the *Méndez* case was the significant coverage it received during 1946 and 1947 in the organization's newspaper, the *Pacific Citizen*, and in other ethnic Japanese media. See, for example, "Legality of California School Segregation Argued in Court" and "Segregated Schools," *Pacific Citizen*, December 14, 1946; "School Segregation," *Pacific Citizen*, April 19, 1947.

96. "School Segregation Case Is Before U.S. Court Here," *San Francisco Chronicle*, December 10, 1946.

97. Letter, Thurgood Marshall to Carl Murphy, December 20, 1946, Mendez case, legal files, Series B, 1940–1960, NAACP papers, Library of Congress, Washington, DC.

98. Richard Kluger, *Simple Justice: Brown v. Board of Education and Black America's Struggle for Equality* (New York, Vintage, 1975), 399.

99. *Westminster School District of Orange County, et al. v. Gonzalo Méndez, et al., Motion and Brief for the National Association for the Advancement of Colored People as Amicus Curiae*, 4.

100. Ibid., 25.

101. Ibid., 31.

102. See letter, Robert L. Carter to David C. Marcus, September 13, 1946, informing Marcus of the NAACP's intervention, Mendez case, legal files, Series B, 1940–1960, NAACP papers, Library of Congress, Washington, DC.

103. *Westminster School Dist. of Orange County et al. v. Mendez et. al*, 161 F.2d 774, 780.

104. Ibid.

105. Ibid.

106. Ibid., at 780, n. 7. On the shifting and ambiguous bases of racial distinctions in U.S. law, see Haney López, *White by Law*.

107. *Westminster School Dist. of Orange County et al. v. Mendez et. al*, 161 F.2d 774, at 783.

108. Steven H. Wilson, "*Brown* over 'Other White': Mexican Americans' Legal Arguments and Litigation Strategy in School Desegregation Lawsuits," *Law and History Review* 21, no. 1 (Spring 2003): 145–94.

109. On *Hernández*, see, for example, Kevin R. Johnson, "*Hernández v. Texas*: Legacies of Justice and Injustice," *UCLA Chicano-Latino Law Review* 25 (2005): 153–78.

110. News release, Alianza Hispano-Americano, October 10, 1955; *Joe R. Romero, et al. v. Guy Weakley et al., Motion and Brief for the Japanese American Citizens League et al. as Amicus Curiae*, 2, School Segregation file, Box 32, papers of the ACLU, Southern California Branch, UCLA Library.

111. See, for example, Richard Delgado and Vicky Palacios, "Mexican Americans as a Legally Cognizable Class Under Rule 23 and the Equal Protection Clause," *Notre Dame Law Review* 50 (1975): 323; Greenfield and Kates, "Mexican Americans, Racial Discrimination, and the Civil Rights Act of 1866." See also generally David G. Gutiérrez, *Walls and Mirrors: Mexican Americans, Mexican Immigrants, and the Politics of Ethnicity* (Berkeley: University of California Press, 1995).

7. FROM *KUICHI* TO COMRADES

1. See, for example, Kiyoshi Okamato to M. Margaret Anderson, March 7, 1942, attachment in letter Margaret Anderson to Norman Thomas, March 15, 1943, correspondence file, Norman Thomas Papers, Princeton University.

2. Kiyoaki Mutata, *An Enemy Among Friends* (Tokyo: Kodansha International, 1991), 86.

3. George J. Sanchez, "'What's Good for Boyle Heights Is Good for the Jews': Creating Multiculturalism on the Eastside During the 1950s," *American Quarterly* 56, no. 3 (Fall 2004); Masayo Umezawa Duus, *Unlikely Liberators: The Men of the 100th and the 442nd* (Honolulu: University of Hawaii Press, 2006); Alison Varzally, *Making a Non-White America: Californians Coloring Outside Ethnic Lines, 1925–1955* (Berkeley: University of California Press, 2008). Scott Kurashige mentions an Issei boycott of Jewish shops on First Street, the area that was not yet Little Tokyo, during 1907, but refers to it as a classic merchant-buyer dispute. Scott Kurashige, *The Shifting Grounds of Race* (Princeton, NJ: Princeton University Press, 2007), 41.

4. For Jewish attitudes, see Ellen Eisenberg, *The First to Cry Down Prejudice? Western Jews and Japanese Removal During World War II* (Lanham, MD: Lexington Books, 2008); Cheryl Lynn Greenberg, "Black and Jewish Responses to Japanese Internment," *Journal of American Ethnic History*, Winter 1995, 1–35. One incident that remains unexplored is the reaction of Jews to the San Francisco school crisis during fall 1906, in which the local school board attempted to segregate Japanese school children to stigmatize them, thereby catalyzing nationwide debate. Local rabbi M. S. Levy, an outspoken advocate of Asian immigration restriction, endorsed the city's policy in "Why Japs Are Kept Separate," *Boston Globe*, December 6, 1906, 10.

5. On popular anti-Semitism in the World War II era, see, for example, Henry Feingold, *A Time for Searching: Entering the Mainstream, 1920–1945* (Baltimore: Johns Hopkins University Press, 1995); David Wyman, *The Abandonment of the Jews* (New York: Pantheon Books, 1979), ch. 1; Carey McWilliams, *A Mask for Privilege: Anti-Semitism in America Today* (Boston: Little, Brown, 1948).

6. "Jewish Lochinvar Seeks Japanese Girl of Good Financial Standing for Mate," *Nichi Bei Shimbun*, July 14, 1932; "Quota for Nippon Urged by North Calif. Rabbis," *Nichi Bei Shimbun*, August 7, 1933.

7. Ujinobo Konomi, "Gleanings: Jews and Expression," *Kashu Mainichi*, November 16, 1933.

8. Molly Oyama [Mary Oyama Mittwer], "Coming of Age," *Gyo-Sho* (1936), 9; "Deirdre," "Nisei, Stop Imitating Race Prejudice," *New World-Sun*, July 16, 1937.

9. Richard Tori, "Jap and Jew," *New World-Sun*, February 8, 1937.

10. Buddy Uno, "Resurrection . . . A Nisei Melodrama," *Rafu Shimpo*, April 12, 1936.

11. "Never Try to Haggle Jewish Salesman," *Rafu Shimpo*, May 22, 1936; "A Reel Fight," *Nichi Bei*, May 24, 1936; "Culture of Jews and Greeks Compared," *New World Sun*, April 8, 1936..

12. Joe Oyama, "The Pershing Square," *Rafu Shimpo*, March 29, 1936.

13. T. John Fujii, "A Nisei in Manhattan," *Rafu Shimpo*, March 28, 1937.

14. James Y. Sakamoto, "A Regrettable Move," *Japanese American Courier*, April 1, 1933.

15. Larry Tajiri, "Discriminatory Bugaboos," *Kashu Mainichi*, May 13, 1934; Jimmie Omura, "Drifts," *New World-Sun*, October 5, 1935.

16. Taishi Matsumoto, "Why I Back Roosevelt," *Kashu Mainichi*, October 4, 1936.

17. Cary [], "There Are No Racial Bars in U.S.," letter, *Nichi Bei Shimbun*, August 5, 1935, 4.

18. Saburo Kido, "Herr Hitler," *New World-Sun*, February 22, 1938; "The Bund," *New World-Sun*, February 22, 1938; "Jews," *New World-Sun*, July 19, 1938.

19. "Uncle Fujii Speaks," *Kashu Mainichi*, November 16, November 17, 1938.

20. James Tsurutani, "On the Nose," *Rafu Shimpo*, November 6, 1938.

21. James Tsurutani, "On the Nose," *Rafu Shimpo*, December 4, 1938.

22. Togo Tanaka, "Post Script," *Rafu Shimpo*, November 19, 1938.

23. See, for example, *Nichi Bei*, September 12, 1938; *New World-Sun*, December 21, 1938; *Kashu Mainichi*, November 27, 1941; *Rafu Shimpo*, February 9, 1941. See also G. Abe, "A. Hitler's Ghetto," *Rafu Shimpo*, December 1, 1940.

24. Helen Aoki, "Tid-bits," *Rafu Shimpo*, December 11, 1938.

25. "Greatest Humanitarian Project," *Japanese American Courier*, October 21, 1939.

26. Saburo Kido, *New World Sun*, April 1939, cited in "Pressing Points," *Rafu Shimpo*, April 30, 1939.

27. Sei Fujii, "Vantage Points: Men of Goodwill and Tolerance," *Kashu Mainichi*, October 5, 1941.

28. Larry Tajiri, "Race Prejudice," *Nichi Bei*, August 30, 1940.

29. "Nisei in Manhattan," *Japanese American Mirror*, May 5, 1939, 3.

30. Roku Sugahara, "As I See It," *Japanese American Mirror*, April 28, 1939, 2.

31. Tad Uyeno, "Lancer's Column," *Rafu Shimpo*, October 20, 1940. Ironically, Uyeno had previously rejoiced at Hitler's invasion of Czechoslovakia and Nazi diplomatic victories because Germany was an ally of Japan and had provided aid for Japan's occupation of China. Tad Uyeno, "East Window," *New World-Sun*, September 26, 1938.

32. "Japanese Being Pushed Out," *New World-Sun*, July 17, 1939 (reprint from *Rafu Shimpo*); Tsuyoshi Matsumoto, "Out of Our Lives," *Rafu Shimpo*, October 9, 1941.

33. "The Story of Taro Suzuki, Part II," *Rafu Shimpo*, September 22, 1941, 2.

34. Sam Hohri, "Rambler's Nemesis," *Sangyo Nippo*, March 20, 1940. It is not clear from this brief comment whether Hohri meant to make an issue of Jewish ownership of American newspapers.

35. One notable example among several is Kazumaro "Buddy" Uno, "Japan and the Jews," *Rafu Shimpo*, April 16, 1939. See also "Nippon Has not abandoned Her Principle of Race Equality," *New World-Sun*, December 19, 1938;

"Japan Champion of Racial Equality, Jews in Asia Assured," *Japanese American Review*, December 31, 1938; "Ban on Anti-Semitism Protects Rights of Jewish People in Japan," *Japanese American Review*, June 3, 1939.

36. H.M.I. [Howard M. Imazeki], "Smoking Room," *New World-Sun*, November 14, 1937.

37. Togo Tanaka, "Post Script," *Rafu Shimpo*, December 9, 1938.

38. James Hamanaka, "Jews Are Funny People," *Rafu Shimpo*, Mach 19, 1939; Kiyoko Matsuzawa, "Not for the Nisei," *Rafu Shimpo*, April 2, 1939.

39. "Lindbergh Draws Fire of Americans in attempt to Introduce Racial Hatred," *New Word-Sun*, September 16, 1941. "Story of the Day," *Rafu Shimpo*, October 5, 1941. Earlier that year, *Rafu* deplored the tactics of a merchant "beaten in business by a Jew" who sent out an anti-Semitic mailing. Henry Mori, "Making the Deadline," *Rafu Shimpo*, February 5, 1941.

40. Eisenberg, *The First to Cry Down Injustice?*

41. Yasutaro (Keiho) Soga, *Life Behind Barbed Wire: The World War II Internment Memoirs of a Hawaiian Issei* (Honolulu: University of Hawaii Press, 2008), 81–83.

42. Letter, Remsen Bird to Eleanor Roosevelt, July 11, 1942; letter, Eleanor Roosevelt to Remsen Bird, July 28, 1942, *The Papers of Eleanor Roosevelt, 1933–1945*, microfilm (Lanham, MD: University Press of America, 1986), reel 2.

43. Hiroshi Nakamura, *Treadmill: A Documentary Novel* (Oakville, ON: Treadmill Press, 1996). The reference is presumably to George Knox Roth, a Los Angeles radio broadcaster who devoted himself so dearly to defending the constitutional rights of Japanese Americans that he was removed from his program. On Roth, see Shizue Seigel, *In Good Conscience: Supporting Japanese Americans During the Internment* (San Mateo: AACP, 2006), 57–59.

44. "Poston Lampoon," *Poston Chronicle*, May 6, 1943, 2; Miles E. Cary, "Letter to the Editor," *Poston Chronicle*, May 8, 1943

45. Larry Tajiri, "Farewell to Little Tokyo," *Common Ground*, Spring 1944.

46. Tom Shibutani, "The Copy Desk," *Pacific Citizen*, November 13, 1943.

47. "Jewish Group Urges Justice for Evacuees," *Pacific Citizen*, August 5, 1944. Another piece told of an Indianapolis rabbi who drafted a prayer for parents mourning their child. *Pacific Citizen*, August 15, 1944.

48. Ibid. North of the border, the *New Canadian* was even more supportive of Nisei-Jewish ties. In September 1943 it reported on anti-Semitism and explicitly associated the condition of Jews and of Nisei. In an interview shortly after, Yoshio Arthur Oda noted that Jews experienced far greater prejudice in eastern Canada than Japanese did, but if the Nisei could show some of the fortitude of the Jews, they could succeed as well. "Anti-Semitism a Personal Problem," *New Canadian*, September 14, 1943; "Nisei Need Courage of Jews to Beat Rap," *New Canadian*, November 15, 1943. This did not mean, of course, that Canadian Nisei were immune from prejudice. Eiko Henmi bitterly criticized Nisei who picked up ignorant attitudes from non-Japanese friends. Cinderella [Aiko Henmi] , "Femme Fare," *New Canadian*, March 26, 1952, 8.

49. Bill Hosokawa, "From the Frying Pan," November 15, 1944.
50. "Seattle Jewish Synagogue Hires Returnee from Hunt," *Minidoka Irrigator*, May 12, 1945, 3.
51. "The Strange Journey of Atsuko Kiyota," *Pacific Citizen*, February 5, 1949.
52. Togo Tanaka, "Editorial of the Times," *Colorado Times*, February 19, 1946.
53. Joe Oyama, *Hokubei Shimpo*, cited in *Chicago Shimpo*, May 4, 1948.
54. S. I. Hayakawa, "Second Thoughts," *Chicago Defender*, April 3, 1943, 15; August 12, 1944, 13.
55. Larry Tajiri, "Nazis and the 'Yellow Peril,'" *Now*, first half February 1946.
56. Hisaye Yamamoto, "Small Talk," *Los Angeles Tribune*, May 4, 1946. See also, for example, Hisaye Yamamoto, "Small Talk," *Los Angeles Tribune*, October 5, 1946, which includes the only Nisei discussion of the Palestine question to appear. I am indebted to Hisaye Yamamoto De Soto for sharing these columns.
57. Yoné U. Stafford, "Advice Which Is Cheap," *Los Angeles Tribune*, September [15?]1947.
58. Joe Yamamoto, "Japanese American Identity Crisis," in Eugene B. Brody, ed., *Minority Group Adolescents in the United States* (Baltimore: Williams and Wilkins, 1968), 137.
59. "Terao Cooking: Kosher Style," *Chicago Shimpo*, August 14, 1947.
60. John Okada, *No-No Boy* (Seattle: University of Washington Press, 1979 [1957]), viii.
61. "Prejudice, by an Issei," in "Tule Lake, Resident Reports and Comments, Spring/Summer 1945," Community Analysis report, available at California Digital Library, http://content.cdlib.org/view?docId=kt938nb3b6&, accessed November 15, 2009.
62. Kumezo Hachimonji, "The Jews," diary entry, ca. 1952, Kumezo Hachimonji papers, YRL Special Collections, UCLA.
63. Larry Tajiri, "A Sour Note in California," *Pacific Citizen*, October 21, 1950.
64. "Anti-Semitic Letters Signed by 'Nisei for Kawakita Society' Rapped by JACL; Misunderstanding Among Nisei and Jews Feared," *Pacific Citizen*, May 18, 1956.
65. "You don't especially like Jews, do you? In a parasite economy, if they perchance are the best parasite, can you blame them? In financial dealings I have gotten rooked more often from Japanese than any other people because I had more dealings with them. Cheap tactics are not exclusively the characteristics of the Jews. Others have it, too. You should not look at other minorities from a personal viewpoint only. You should study the history of the Jews in the last 1900 years in this world.... Do you recognize the similarity in the treatment of the Jews and that of the Japanese? You should! The Japanese have the advantage of having come from a nation of power. The Jews on the other hand are not a nationality group. They have no national home. They are a

religious group. Jew is religion, not nation." Letter, Kazushi Matsumoto to James Omura, January 16, 1945, James Omura Papers, Green Library, Stanford University. I am indebted to Arthur Hansen for this reference.

66. See John W. Dower, *War Without Mercy: Race and Power in the Pacific War* (New York: Pantheon, 1987).

67. Koji Ariyoshi, *From Kona to Yenan: The Political Memoirs of Koji Ariyoshi*, ed. Alice M. Beechert and Edward D. Beechert (Honolulu: University of Hawaii Press, 2000), 55.

68. Karl G. Yoneda, *Ganbatte: Sixty Year Struggle of a Kibei Worker* (Los Angeles: UCLA Asian American Studies Center Press, 1983).

69. Charles Kikuchi, *The Kikuchi Diaries: Chronicle from an American Concentration Camp*, ed. John Modell (Urbana: University of Illinois Press, 1973), 75–76. Kikuchi likewise recounted arguments he had had with his embittered (and estranged) father, who claimed that any Jew was a "cheating kike" (198).

8. AFRICAN AMERICAN RESPONSES TO THE WARTIME CONFINEMENT OF JAPANESE AMERICANS

1. A few outstanding examples are Shannon Steen and Heike Raphael-Hernandez, eds., *Afro-Asian Encounters: History, Culture, Politics* (New York: New York University Press, 2006); Diane Fujino, *Heartbeat of Struggle: The Revolutionary Life of Yuri Kochiyama* (Minneapolis: University of Minnesota Press, 2005); Najia Aarim-Heriot, *Chinese Immigrants, African Americans, and Racial Anxiety in the United States, 1848–1882* (Urbana: University of Illinois Press, 2003); Vijay Prashad, *Everybody Was Kung Fu Fighting: Afro-Asian Connections and the Myth of Cultural Purity* (Boston: Beacon Press, 2001); Mark S. Gallicchio, *The African American Encounter with China and Japan: Black Internationalism in Asia, 1895–1945* (Chapel Hill: University of North Carolina Press, 2000); Grace Lee Boggs, *Living for Change: An Autobiography* (Minneapolis: University of Minnesota Press, 1998); Edward T. Chang and Russell C. Leong, eds., *Los Angeles—Struggles Towards Multiethnic Community: Asian American, African American and Latino Perspectives* (Seattle: University of Washington Press, 1994).

2. Joseph Heco, *The Narrative of a Japanese: What He Has Seen and the People He Has Met in the Course of the Last Forty Years*, ed. James Murdoch (Yokohama: Yokohama Printing & Publishing, 1894), 145.

3. Bill Hosokawa, *Nisei: The Quiet Americans* (New York: William Morrow, 1969), 32–33.

4. Jenichiro Oyabe, *A Japanese Robinson Crusoe*, ed. Greg Robinson and Yujin Taguchi (Honolulu: University of Hawaii Press, 2009 [1898]).

5. On prewar Seattle, see Quintard Taylor, *The Forging of a Black Community: Seattle's Central District From 1870 Through the Civil Rights Era* (Seattle: University of Washington Press, 1994), 126–27.

6. See George Yoshida, *Reminiscing in Swingtime: Japanese Americans in American Popular Music, 1925–1960* (San Francisco: National Japanese American Historical Society, 1997); Daniel Widener, " 'Perhaps the Japanese Are to Be Thanked?': Asia, Asian Americans and the Construction of Black California," *Positions: East Asia Cultures Critique* 11, no. 1 (Spring 2003): 141–65; Mark Wild, *Street Meeting: Multiethnic Neighborhoods in Early Twentieth Century Los Angeles* (Berkeley: University of California Press, 2005); George Sanchez, "Working at the Crossroads: American Studies for the Twenty-First Century," Presidential Address to the American Studies Association, *American Quarterly* 54 (2002): 1–23. So familiar was the connection of Japanese Americans with jazz that George Schuyler referred in a novel to a mythical Japanese American jazz composer, Forkrise Sake. See George S. Schuyler, *Black No More* (Boston: Northeastern University Press, 1989 [1931]), 147.

7. See David Hellwig, "Afro-American Reactions to the Japanese and to the Anti-Japanese Movement, 1906–1924," *Phylon* 38 (March 1977): 93–104; Ernest Allen, "When Japan Was 'Champion of the Darker Races': Satokata Takahashi and the Flowering of Black Messianic Nationalism," *Black Scholar* 24 (1994): 23–46.

8. The city of Chicago had 390 residents of Japanese ancestry, while there were 413 in Cook County as a whole. U.S. Census, 1940. See also Bureau of the Census, "Japanese Population in the State of Illinois by Sex and Nativity or Citizenship, for Counties and Cities of 10,000 or More," 1941, Henry Field Papers, Franklin D. Roosevelt Library.

9. Milton R. Konvitz, *The Alien and Asiatic in American Law* (Ithaca, NY: Cornell University Press, 1946).

10. Masuji Miyakawa, *Powers of the American People* (New York: Baker & Taylor, 1908), 34.

11. David J. Hellwig, "Black Leaders and United States Immigration Policy, 1917–1929," *Journal of Negro History* 66, no. 2 (Summer 1984): 117–18.

12. Arnold Shankman, " 'Asiatic Ogre' or 'Desirable Citizen'? The Image of Japanese Americans in the Afro-American Press, 1867–1933," *Pacific Historical Review* XLVI (November 1977): 575–81.

13. Bishop Hilton, "Editorial," *Spotlight*, October 6, 1944, 2.

14. Lester B. Granger, "The Negro Views Peace," *Far Eastern Survey* 14, no. 17 (August 29, 1945): 238.

15. Maya Angelou, "From *I Know Why the Caged Bird Sings*," reprinted in Lawson Fusao Inada, *Only What We Could Carry: The Japanese American Internment Experience* (Berkeley, CA: Heyday Books, 2000), 53–56.

16. NAACP Board Minutes, July 26, 1942; letter, Walter White to Wendell Berge, July 27, 1942, Japanese (Nisei) 1942–1945 file, Series II, NAACP Papers, Library of Congress (hereinafter NAACP Papers).

17. C. K. Doreski, " 'Kin in Some Way': The *Chicago Defender* Reads the Japanese Internment, 1942–1945," in Todd Vogel, ed., *The Black Press: Liter-*

ary and Historical Essays (New Brunswick, NJ: Rutgers University Press, 2001), 162–63.

18. Reginald Kearney, *African American Views of the Japanese: Solidarity or Sedition?* (Albany: State University of New York Press, 1998), 109–10.

19. Ibid., 109–16, esp. 111. The nature of the *Tribune*'s editorial position is difficult to reconstruct, as its 1942 issues have not been preserved in archives.

20. George S. Schuyler, *Pittsburgh Courier*, April 25, April 26, 1942, cited in Robert Shaffer, "Cracks in the Consensus: Defending the Rights of Japanese Americans During World War II," *Radical History Review* 72 (Fall 1998): 84–120. 126 n. 81; George S. Schuyler, *Black and Conservative* (New Rochelle, NY: Arlington House, 1966), 256.

21. Letter, Isamu Noguchi to Carey McWilliams, February 18, 1942, Box 1, Carey McWilliams Papers, Hoover Institution, Stanford University, Stanford, CA. On Robeson's connections with Asia and Asian Americans, see Greg Robinson, "Internationalism and Justice: Paul Robeson, Asia, and Asian Americans," in Shannon Steen and Heike Raphael-Hernandez, eds., *AfroAsian Encounters: Culture, History, Politics* (New York: New York University Press, 2006), 358–81.

22. For petition signers, see letter, Mary W. Hillyer et al. to Franklin D. Roosevelt, April 30, 1942, press release, May 1942, Postwar World Council, Postwar World Council Papers, Norman Thomas Papers, New York Public Library. For Du Bois, see also David Levering Lewis, *W. E. B. Du Bois: The Fight for Equality and the American Century, 1919–1963* (New York: Owl Books, 2001).

23. Greg Robinson, *By Order of the President* (Cambridge, MA: Harvard University Press, 2001), 160.

24. Jervis Anderson, *Bayard Rustin: Troubles I've Seen* (New York: HarperCollins, 1997), 82.

25. For a description of Charles Johnson and the Race Relations Institute, see Robert G. Spinney, *World War II in Nashville: Transformation of the Homefront* (Knoxville: University of Tennessee Press, 1998), 137.

26. Albert Parker, "Layle Lane's Speech," *Militant*, April 3, 1943.

27. Margaret C. McCulloch, "What Should the American Negro Reasonably Expect as the Outcome of a *Real* Peace?" *Journal of Negro Education* 12, No. 4 (Fall 1943): 566.

28. Kearney, *African American Views of the Japanese.*

29. "Protection," *Militant*, March 7, 1942, cited in C. L. R. James et al., *Fighting Racism in World War II* (New York: Pathfinder Books, 1980), 153.

30. Harry Paxton Howard, "Americans in Concentration Camps," *Crisis* 49 (September 1942): 281–84, 301–2.

31. Doreski, "Kin in Some Way."

32. William A. Hilliard, "War Is Dreadful," *Minidoka Irrigator*, April 3, 1943.

33. Granger, "The Negro Views Peace," 239.

34. On *The War Worker*, see Kevin Allen Leonard, *The Battle for Los Angeles*, 187.

35. Edward Margolies and Michel Fabre, *The Several Lives of Chester Himes* (Jackson: University Press of Mississippi, 1997), 49. Himes also briefly addressed the injustice of Japanese removal in his novel *If He Hollers, Let Him Go*. Kevin Allen Leonard, " 'In the Interest of All Races': African Americans and Interracial Cooperation in Los Angeles During and After World War II," in Lawrence B. De Graaf, Kevin Mulroy, and Quintard Taylor, eds., *Seeking El Dorado: African Americans in California* (Los Angeles: Autry Museum of Western Heritage, 2001), 317–18.

36. Shaffer, "Cracks in the Consensus," 104–5; letter, C. L. Dellums to Walter White, July 7, 1942, NAACP Papers; Ronald Dellums, "The Total Community," in Inada, ed., *Only What We Could Carry*, 33–34.

37. Kearney, *African American Views of the Japanese*; Cheryl Lynn Greenberg, "Black and Jewish Responses to Japanese Internment," *Journal of American Ethnic History*, Winter 1995, 15–16.

38. Kaz Oka, "In the Interest of the Nisei," *Poston Chronicle*, March 6, 1943, 3. For the NAACP and *Regan v. King*, see Greg Robinson, "When Birthright Citizenship Was Last 'Reconsidered': *Regan v. King* and Asian Americans," The Faculty Lounge, August 2010, http://www.thefacultylounge.org/2010/08/when-birthright-citizenship-was-last-reconsidered-regan-v-king-and-asian-americans-1.html.

39. Annual Report, San Francisco NAACP, December 4, 1944, correspondence, San Francisco Branch, branches file, Series II, NAACP papers.

40. *San Francisco Chronicle*, June 13, 1945.

41. Konvitz continued his activism on behalf of Japanese Americans throughout the 1940s. In July 1944, he advised JACL leaders on drafting a civil rights bill to protect Japanese Americans in Utah from discrimination. Letter, Milton R. Konvitz to Saburo Kido, July 14, 1944. Civil Rights, Utah, Civil Rights files, Volume 47, American Civil Liberties Union Papers, Library of Congress. He subsequently wrote a major treatise on Japanese American civil rights, *The Alien and Asiatic in American Law* (Ithaca, NY: Cornell University Press, 1946).

42. Letter, Milton Konvitz to Roy Wilkins, April 23, 1944; telegram, Roy Wilkins to Fiorello LaGuardia, April 27, 1944; Nisei 1942–1945 file, NAACP Papers; "New York Meeting Protests Racial Attitude of Mayor," *Pacific Citizen*, May 27, 1944.

43. Letter, Clarence Pickett to Eleanor Roosevelt, June 19, 1944; letter, Eleanor Roosevelt to Clarence Pickett, June 18, 1944, Clarence Pickett Correspondence, Section 70 (Correspondence with Government Departments), Eleanor Roosevelt Papers, 1884–1945, Franklin D. Roosevelt Library; Memo from Miss Randolph to Mr. White, June 21, 1944, Eleanor Roosevelt Correspondence, NAACP Papers.

44. Letter, Consuelo Young to *New York Times* et al., June 13, 1945, Consuelo Young Files, NAACP papers.

45. Erna P. Harris, "Reflections," *Los Angeles Tribune*, November 22, 1943, cited in *Pacific Citizen*, December 4, 1943, 5.
46. Leonard, "'In the Interest of All Races,'" 323.
47. Consuelo Young, letter to *New York Times* et al.
48. Letter, Pauli Murray to Franklin D. Roosevelt, July 30, 1942; letter, Eleanor Roosevelt to Pauli Murray, August 3, 1942, Personal Correspondence, Group 100, Eleanor Roosevelt Papers, Franklin D. Roosevelt Library; Pauli Murray, *Song in a Weary Throat: An American Pilgrimage* (New York: Harper & Row, 1987), 188–89.
49. Murray, *Song in a Weary Throat*, 259–60.
50. See, for example, Everett James Starr, "Young Negro Woman Attorney Speaks to NY JACL," *Pacific Citizen*, February 22, 1947.
51. Benjamin E. Mays, "Democratizing and Christianizing America in This Generation," *Journal of Negro Education* 14, no. 4 (Autumn 1945): 533.

9. THE LOS ANGELES DEFENDER

1. The family name is alternately rendered as "MacBeth" and "Macbeth" in both newspaper articles and public documents. While in the past I have most often used the first of these spellings, after consultation with Hugh Macbeth Jr. I have adopted the version with lowercase "b" as more authentic.
2. Douglas Flamming, *Bound for Freedom: Black Los Angeles in Jim Crow America* (Berkeley: University of California Press, 2005), 23.
3. Author interview, Hugh E. Macbeth Jr., January 19, 2005, San Francisco.
4. Ann Ray to Norman Thomas, January 14, 1942, Chronological Correspondence file, Reel 6, Norman Thomas Papers, New York Public Library (henceforth Norman Thomas papers).
5. Ibid.
6. Al Cohn, report to Mayor Fletcher Bowron, January 21, 1942, 6, Japanese file, Fletcher Bowron Papers, Huntington Library, San Marino, CA.
7. Norman Thomas, *Democracy and the Japanese Americans* (New York: Postwar World Council, 1942), vi.
8. Hugh Macbeth to Norman Thomas, March 2, 1942, Norman Thomas papers.
9. Hugh Macbeth to Norman Thomas, March 9, 1942, Norman Thomas papers.
10. Hugh Macbeth to General John DeWitt, March 4, 1942, Norman Thomas papers.
11. Ann Ray to Norman Thomas, January 23, 1942; Norman Thomas to Hugh Macbeth, February 2, 1942, Norman Thomas papers.
12. Hugh Macbeth to Norman Thomas, March 9, 1942.
13. Hugh Macbeth to Norman Thomas, March 2, 1942.
14. Macbeth publicly repeated these ideas in an address given in Chicago, "Colored American Leadership Comes into Action on Behalf of the Entire

Human Race," June 14, 1942, which he reprinted in *Justice for All Humanity: Colored America Answers the Challenge of Pearl S. Buck*, pamphlet, United Races of America, 1942. Bancroft Library, University of California, Berkeley. Referring to Macbeth's visit to Washington, Ann Ray reported to Thomas, "He said, with a chuckle, that he might need you and [ACLU director] Roger Baldwin to help him get out of jail. He has his address drawn up and is going to first go over it with [attorney general Francis] Biddle and possibly the President. . . . The President may feel it necessary to use his charm upon Macbeth." Ann Ray to Norman Thomas, May 18, 1942, Norman Thomas papers

15. Hugh Macbeth to Norman Thomas, June 26, 1942, Norman Thomas papers (underlined in original).

16. Author correspondence with Edgar Wakayama, March 2006.

17. "Test of Jap Internment Decrees Files in U.S. Court," *Los Angeles Times*, August 20, 1942, A3. Meanwhile, Ernest Wakayama and three other Nisei were charged with felonies for violating a rule of the Wartime Civil Control Administration, the military entity that ran the "assembly centers," by speaking in Japanese at a public meeting and publicly discussing "international affairs" and "the present war with Japan," but Attorney General Biddle quickly ordered those indictments dismissed. Peter Irons, *Justice at War* (New York: Oxford University Press, 1983), 115.

18. Frank Chuman, "Notes on Interview with A. L. Wirin," transcript, December 1971, Box 534, Frank Chuman Papers, Special Collections, University of California, Los Angeles.

19. Letter, A. L. Wirin to Oswald Garrison Villard, October 29, 1942, Reel 243, Vol. 43, ACLU papers, Princeton University.

20. Memo, Elmer Davis to J. Edgar Hoover, January 10, 1944, OWI files, Philleo Nash Papers, Harry S. Truman Library, Independence, MO. The government harassment of Macbeth did not stop with investigation. A few months later, at the request of the U.S. State Department, Macbeth was relieved of his Liberian consulship. See "Liberia Makes Consul Change," *Chicago Defender*, April 8, 1944.

21. "Negro Attorney Upholds Rights of Nisei at West L.A. Forum," *Pacific Citizen*, April 1, 1943, 5.

22. Brief on Behalf of the Japanese American Citizens League, amicus curiae, *John T. Regan v. Cameron King*; February 17, 1943; reel 68, Japanese American Evacuation and Resettlement Records, Bancroft Library, University of California, Berkeley.

23. Deborah K. Lim, "The Lim Report," privately printed, 1990.

24. A. L. Wirin, article for the *Open Forum*, February 24, 1945, attached draft to letter, A. L. Wirin to Clifford Forster, February 19, 1945, Alien Land Law, Japanese Americans file, microfilm papers of the American Civil Liberties Union, Library of Congress.

25. Ibid.

26. For *Oyama v. California* see Chapter 12 in this volume.

10. CRUSADERS IN GOTHAM

1. *JACD Newsletter*, January 15, 1942, 1.
2. Survey Committee, New York, "A Social Study of the Japanese Population in the Greater New York Area, April 24, 1942–June 26, 1942," pamphlet, 1942, Starr East Asian Library, Columbia University.
3. *JACD Newsletter*, February 23, 1942, 1.
4. *JACD Newsletter*, August 1942, 2.
5. Greg Robinson, "Norman Thomas and the Struggle Against Japanese Internment," *Prospects* 29 (2004): 423–24.
6. Ibid.
7. Letter, Yoshitaka Takagi to Bradford Smith, June 24, 1942, Bradford Smith correspondence, Foreign Nationality Groups, Japanese Section, OWI papers, RG 208, National Archives.
8. FBI report internal security, joint report of H. O. Bly and Special Agent D. W. Fults: Japanese American Committee for Democracy, May 8, 1942, Japanese Espionage file, Justice Department, War Division, RG 60, 143-10, National Archives.
9. JACD newsletter, May 5, 1942. Following the meeting Powell accepted a position on the advisory board of the JACD, replacing the liberals who had departed.
10. *JACD Newsletter*, February 1943.
11. Letter, Yoshitaka Takagi to Henry Stimson, March 13, 1943; Takagi to Dillon Myer, March 13, 1943, Associated Groups, RG 210, Subgroup 16, subject correspondence files, WRA papers, National Archives and Records Administration.
12. Letter, Yoshitaki Takagi to Bradford Smith, December 2, 1942, reprinted in *JACD Newsletter*, February 1943. The last clause was not in the resolution presented at the mass meeting, and was only belatedly added.
13. *JACD Newsletter*, November 1943, 3.
14. Ernest Iiyama, "Poll Tax Bulletin," *JACD Newsletter*, April 1944.
15. *JACD Newsletter*, May 1944.
16. "New York Nisei Committee Backs Roosevelt for a 4th 4 Year Term," *Rocky Shimpo*, November 3, 1944; Dyke Miyagawa, "New York Japanese Americans Sponsor Rally for Roosevelt," *Pacific Citizen*, November 4, 1944, 3.
17. *JACD Newsletter*, November 1945.
18. *JACD Newsletter*, September 1945, 3.
19. *JACD Newsletter*, March 1946, 2.
20. Flyer for Barn Dance, March 20, 1948, in Nisei folder II, NAACP Papers, Series II, 1935–1954, Library of Congress.
21. Report of Special Agent Clarence L. Johnson, "Japanese American Committee for Democracy," February 17, 1945, Justice Department, Special War Problems Committee, RG 60, 143-10, National Archives and Records Administration.

22. Harold Cruse, *The Crisis of the Negro Intellectual* (New York: Morrow, 1967).

11. FROM *KOREMATSU* TO *BROWN*

1. *Brown v. Board of Education*, 347 U.S. 483 (1954).
2. *Bolling v. Sharpe*, 347 U.S. 497 (1954).
3. *Kiyoshi Hirabayashi v. United States*, 320 U.S. 81 (1943); *Toyosaburo Korematsu v. United States*, 323 U.S. 214 (1944). See Daniel Sabbagh, "Généologie du principe de color-blindness," in *L'Égalité par le droit: Les paradoxes de la discrimination positive aux Etats-Unis* (Paris: Economica, 2003), 165. For a discussion of *Korematsu* and the origins of strict scrutiny, see Michael Klarman, "An Interpretive History of Modern Equal Protection," *Michigan Law Review* 90 (1991): 213–62; Reggie Oh and Frank Wu, "The Evolution of Race in the Law: The Supreme Court Moves From Approving Internment of Japanese Americans to Disapproving Affirmative Action for African Americans," *Michigan Journal of Race and Law* 1 (1996): 165–93; Neil Gotanda, "The Story of *Korematsu*: The Japanese-American Cases," in Michael C. Darf, ed., *Constitutional Law Stories* (New York: Foundation Press, 2004), 270–73.
4. 380 U.S. 81 (1943) at 100.
5. Peter Irons, *Justice at War: The Story of the Japanese-American Internment Cases* (New York: Oxford University Press, 1983), 242–45. Stone himself seems to have been unhappy about the government's treatment of Japanese Americans and even wrote privately that it was difficult to reconcile with any concept of civil liberties. Greg Robinson, *By Order of the President: FDR and the Internment of Japanese Americans* (Cambridge, MA: Harvard University Press, 2001), 190.
6. 323 U.S. 215, at 242. For Murphy's impact on shaping Fifth Amendment protections, see Matthew J. Perry, "Justice Murphy and the Fifth Amendment Equal Protection Doctrine: A Contribution Unrecognized," *Hastings Constitutional Law Quarterly* 27 (2000): 266–79.
7. For Black's opinion in *Korematsu* and his views on racial matters, see Roger K. Newman, *Hugo Black* (New York: Pantheon, 1994), 313–17.
8. Ibid., 223.
9. Ibid., 216.
10. Michael Jones-Correa has argued cogently that the rule expounded in *Korematsu* came about in a sense by accident, in that the majority wished to "attenuate the shocking nature" of its holding in the case by marking off its decision in that particular case as exceptional, and that otherwise the justices would never have agreed to such an explicit formulation. Michael Jones-Correa, "The Origins and Diffusion of Racial Restrictive Covenants," *Political Science Quarterly* 115 (2001): 115.
11. *United States v. Carolene Products Co.*, 304 U.S. 144, 153 n.4 (1938).
12. *Skinner v. Oklahoma*, 316 U.S. 535 (1942).

13. *Morgan v. Virginia*, 328 U.S. 373 (1946). On the non-use of *Carolene Products*, see Felix Gilman, "The Famous Footnote Four: A History of the Carolene Products Footnote," *South Texas Law Review* 46 (2004): 186–91.

14. Roger Daniels, *The Politics of Prejudice* (Berkeley: University of California Press, 1962).

15. *Ozawa v. United States*, 260 U.S. 178 (1922); *Terrace v. Thompson*, 263 U.S. 197 (1923); *Porterfield v. Webb*, 263 U.S. 225 (1923). On development and constitutional aspects of Alien Land Laws, see, for example, Moritoshi Fukuda, *Legal Problems of Japanese Americans* (Tokyo: Keio Tsushin, 1980), 123–91.

16. Ibid.

17. "The Alien Land Laws—a Reappraisal," *Yale Law Journal* 56 (June 1947): 1018.

18. Bill Hosokawa, *Nisei: The Quiet Americans* (New York: Morrow, 1967), 447–48.

19. *Oyama v. California*, 332 U.S. 633 (1948) at 661.

20. Unlike the overwhelming majority of West Coast Japanese Americans, the Oyamas were not confined in a camp. They were able to migrate to Utah during the short period during spring 1942 when such "voluntary evacuation" was permissible. It was during their stay in Utah that the Oyama family learned of the escheat proceeding. Telephone interview with Fred Oyama, September 2004.

21. Yukio Morita, "The Japanese Americans in the United States Between 1945 and 1965," M.A. thesis, Department of History, Ohio State University, 1967, 47–55.

22. A. L. Wirin, article for *Open Forum*, February 24, 1945, attached draft to letter, A. L. Wirin to Clifford Forster, February 19, 1945, Alien Land Law, Japanese Americans file, microfilm papers of the American Civil Liberties Union, Library of Congress (hereinafter ACLU papers).

23. Ibid.

24. *American Civil Liberties Union Bulletin* no. 1170 (March 19, 1945), ACLU papers.

25. See article, *Open Forum*, March 7, 1945, Housing, Civil Rights Cases, Box 28, Papers of the Southern California American Civil Liberties Union, Special Collections, University of California, Los Angeles.

26. In what was almost certainly a spin-off of the *Hirose* case, Mather Masako Hirose brought an unsuccessful action in San Diego County to quiet title, but trial judge Arthur L Mundo ruled that because of the escheat, Hirose had no claim to the land. Instead, he awarded it to Thomas Gonzalez, who had been engaged as Hirose's manager during the war, and who had taken advantage of the escheat proceeding to take over the property upon paying the balance of the mortgage. Hirose, with A. L. Wirin representing him, then appealed, and in December 1948 the California Supreme Court reversed both the escheat and the "unconscionable" award of the land to Gonzalez. *Thomas Gonzalez et al. v. Mather Masako Hirose et al.*, 33 Cal. 2d 213 (1948).

27. "Retainer Agreement Signed with Attorneys Purcell and Ferriter," *Utah Nippo*, February 13, 1946.

28. *Mendez v. Westminster School District of Orange County*, 64 F. Supp. 543, 546 (S.D. Cal. 1946).

29. *Estate of Tetsubumi Yano*, 206 995 (1922).

30. *People v. Oyama*, 29 Cal. 2d 164, 173 P.2d 794 (1946), and see also "Statement of Attorney A. L. Wirin on California Supreme Court Ruling in the Oyama Test Case," ACLU papers; Frank F. Chuman, *The Bamboo People: The Law and Japanese Americans* (Del Ray, CA: Publisher's Inc., 1976), 80–81.

31. "Oyama Test Case," *Pacific Citizen*, March 5, 1947, 3:2; "CRDU Sudden Act to Drop Oyama Case Stirs JACL," *Rafu Shimpo*, February 13, 1947, 1:5–6.

32. According to A. L. Wirin, Horsky suggested Acheson because he had lost his first two cases before the Supreme Court and wished to burnish his reputation. Frank Chuman, "Notes on Interview with A. L. Wirin," transcript, December 1971, Box 534, Frank Chuman Papers, Special Collections, University of California, Los Angeles. JACL secretary Mike Masaoka gave a more colorful version of Acheson's recruitment. According to Masaoka's account, he went to see Acheson, who asked how much money the JACL could pay. Masaoka responded, "Five hundred dollars." Acheson commented that that would scarcely be enough to pay for the record, and he would have to serve without pay, whereupon Masaoka quickly responded, "We accept—you have a client!" Mike Masaoka and Bill Hosokawa, *They Call Me Moses Masaoka* (New York: Morrow, 1987), 213–14. Acheson's presentation was confined to the argument that the Alien Land Act discriminated against American citizens of Japanese ancestry. "Oyama Test Case," *Pacific Citizen*, November 8, 1947.

33. Brief for Petitioners, *Fred Y. Oyama and Kajiro Oyama v. State of California*, United States Supreme Court, 1947.

34. Ibid., 35.

35. Ibid. One interesting means of tracing the development of Wirin's position on "strict scrutiny" is by comparing the petitioners' brief with Wirin's original petition for certiorari to the Supreme Court. In that document, written in late 1946, Wirin had argued on the basis of *Thomas v. Collins*, 323 U.S. 516, and other precedents that cases involving civil liberties imposed a more rigid test on state action than normal commercial transactions, and that only cases involving a "grave and impending public danger" could justify such action. He proceeded to cite the operative passage in *Korematsu* as support for his claim that the impact of the Alien Land Act on aliens of Japanese origin was similar. However, Wirin then immediately retreated from that position and insisted that the Alien Land Law did not even meet the usual "reasonable classification" test for constitutionality. Petition for certiorari, *Fred Y. Oyama and Kajiro Oyama v. State of California*, 20–21, Mike Masaoka Papers, Marriott Library, University of Utah.

36. Edwin E. Ferguson, "The California Alien Land Law and the Fourteenth Amendment," *California Law Review* 35 (March 1947): 61–90; cited in "Land Law Analysis," *Pacific Citizen*, June 21, 1947. See also "The Alien Land

Laws—a Reappraisal"; D. O. McGovney, "Anti-Japanese Land Laws of California and Ten Other States," *California Law Review* 35 (March 1947): 7–60. Evidence of the importance of the Yale article is the presence of a marked-up reprint in the file with correspondence with A. L. Wirin and director Roger Baldwin, ACLU papers. Hugh E. Macbeth Jr., son of Hugh E. Macbeth Sr. and himself a former student of McGovney's, discussed McGovney's work with A. L. Wirin shortly after the California Supreme Court decision, and recalled that Wirin was particularly impressed with the idea of basing the Supreme Court appeal primarily on the rights of American citizens to receive property. Interview with Hugh E. Macbeth Jr., January 2005.

37. *Oyama v. California*, 332 U.S. 633 (1948) at 640.

38. Ibid. at 646.

39. Ibid. at 637. Examples of law journal articles include R. A. Goater, "Civil Rights and Anti-Japanese Discrimination," *University of Cincinnati Law Review* 18 (January 1949): 81–89; "Conflict Between Local and National Interests in Alien Landholding Restrictions," *University of Chicago Law Review* 16 (Winter 1949): 315–23; "1947–48 Term of the Supreme Court—the Alien's Right to Work," *Columbia Law Review* 49 (February 1949): 257–64. See also Joseph Tussman and Jacobus tenBroek, "The Equal Protection of the Laws," *California Law Review* 37 (June 1949): 341.

40. *Oyama v. California*, at 649.

41. Ibid. at 651 (Murphy, J., concurring).

42. Ibid. at 651, 671.

43. Letter from William O. Douglas to Frank Murphy, January 14, 1948, William O. Douglass Papers, Library of Congress.

44. One contemporary scholar asserted that the *Oyama* decision represented the Supreme Court's atonement for its mistake in *Korematsu*. C. Herman Pritchett, *The Roosevelt Court: A Study in Judicial Politics and Values, 1937–1947* (New York: Macmillan, 1948), 283. See also C. Herman Pritchett, *Civil Liberties and the Vinson Court* (Chicago: University of Chicago Press, 1954).

45. Eugene V. Rostow, "The Japanese American Cases—A Disaster," *Yale Law Journal* 485 (Summer 1945); see also Carey McWilliams, *Prejudice: Japanese-Americans, Symbol of Racial Intolerance* (Boston: Little, Brown, 1944); Miné Okubo, *Citizen 13660* (New York: Columbia University Press, 1946). The War Relocation Authority, the government agency responsible for operating the camps, had cast doubt on the necessity for "evacuation" in its official history. U.S. Department of the Interior, War Relocation Authority, *Wartime Exile: The Exclusion of the Japanese Americans from the West Coast* (Washington, DC: Government Printing Office, 1946).

46. United States President's Committee on Civil Rights, *To Secure These Rights* (Washington, DC: Government Printing Office, 1947), 31, 34.

47. *Oyama v. California*, at 646.

48. Ibid. at 671, 672.

49. *Corrigan v. Buckley*, 271 US 323 (1926). The classic study of restrictive covenants, although it does not mention the role of Japanese Americans, is

Clement Vose, *Caucasians Only: The Supreme Court, the NAACP, and the Restrictive Covenant Cases* (Berkeley: University of California Press, 1959). See also Michael Jones-Correa, "The Origins and Diffusion of Racial Restrictive Covenants," *Political Science Quarterly* 115, no. 4 (Winter 2000–2001).

50. *Shelley v. Kraemer*, 334 U.S. 1 (1948).

51. *Hurd v. Hodge* 334 U.S. 24 (1948); Loren Miller, *The Petitioners: The Story of the Supreme Court of the United States and the Negro* (New York: Pantheon, 1967), 321–26; Mark V. Tushnet, *Making Civil Rights Law: Thurgood Marshall and the Supreme Court, 1936–1961* (New York: Oxford University Press, 1994), 85–90.

52. For Miller's expertise, see Loren Miller, "Restrictive Covenants v. Democracy," in Loren Miller and Bernard J. Sheil, *Racial Restrictive Covenants*, pamphlet, Chicago Council Against Racial and Religious Discrimination, 1946; Loren Miller, "Covenants in the Bear Flag State," *Crisis* 35 (May 1946): 138–40, 153. For Miller and Wirin, see letter, Thurgood Marshall to Loren Miller, February 13, 1947, Loren Miller File, Restrictive Covenant Files, Legal File, NAACP Papers.

53. "Month in Building News," *Architectural Forum*, January 1946.

54. "Housing Segregation Suit Lost by Pasadena FPHA," *Rafu Shimpo*, July 26, 1947, 1:5–6.

55. "Chinese Vet Fights Against Restrictive Covenants," *Rafu Shimpo*, May 15, 1956, 1:3–4; "California Supreme Court Upholds Housing Covenants," *Rafu Shimpo*, August 22, 1947, 1:5–6; "High Court Ruling Hurts Minorities," *Los Angeles Tribune*, August 20, 1947, 1:6. For *Kim* and *Amer*, see also Charlotte Brooks, *Alien Neighbors, Foreign Friends*, 179–83.

56. Richard Kluger, *Simple Justice* (New York: Vintage, 1975), 254–55.

57. "Participation in Restrictive Covenant Cases Considered by JACL-ADC," *Utah Nippo*, September 29, 1947, 1:3–4; "Minutes of Discussion, Sunday Afternoon, *Shelley v. Kraemer* Lawyer Conference," Restrictive Covenant Files, Legal File, B133, NAACP Papers.

58. Letter, Ina Sugihara to Marian Wynn Perry, September 16, 1947, Japanese (Nisei) file, NAACP Papers. The reasons for the JACL's ignorance regarding amicus curiae briefs are not clear. The organization already had submitted such a brief to the Supreme Court in the *Korematsu* case and had intervened in the *Méndez v. Westminster* case and others, including a restrictive covenant case involving African Americans in New York. "Deplore Racial Ban in Housing," *Rafu Shimpo*, January 11, 1947.

59. Letter, Marian Wynn Perry to Masao Satow, September 18, 1947, Japanese (Nisei) file, NAACP Papers.

60. "Add New 'Color' to Supreme Court Case," *Open Forum* 24, no. 21 (October 18, 1947): 1:2.

61. Letter, A. L. Wirin to Thurgood Marshall, October 31, 1947; letter, A. L. Wirin to Thurgood Marshall, December 16, 1947, Japanese (Nisei) file, NAACP Papers.

62. Letter, Thurgood Marshall to Roger Baldwin, December 30, 1947, Japanese (Nisei) file, NAACP papers.
63. Ibid. See also "Supreme Court Declares Restrictive Covenant Out," *Rafu Shimpo*, May 3, 1948, 1:5–6.
64. Brief of the Japanese American Citizens League as amicus curiae, *Hurd v. Hodge*.
65. Ibid., 8, cited in *Hurd* reply brief, 6. Houston also referred during oral argument to the *Kim* and *Amer* cases.
66. There is some evidence that the Justice Department considered and rejected the filing of such a brief in the *Oyama* case. See remarks by Phineas Indritz in "Minutes of Discussion, Sunday Morning, *Shelley v. Kraemer* Lawyer Conference," Restrictive Covenant Files, NAACP Papers. See also letter, Philleo Nash to David K. Niles, April 8, 1947, Correspondence file, Philleo Nash papers, Harry S. Truman Library, Independence, MO.
67. On Clark's role in the government's decision to file an amicus brief, see Kluger, *Simple Justice* (New York: Vintage, 1975), 252–53. Philip Elman (interviewed by Norman Silber), "The Solicitor General's Office, Justice Frankfurter, and Civil Rights Litigation, 1946–1960: An Oral History," *Harvard Law Review* 100 (1987): 818–20.
68. See, for example, Tom C. Clark, "Preface," in Chuman, *The Bamboo People*, vii.
69. Brief of the United States as amicus curiae, *Shelley v. Kraemer et al.*, 48, 53.
70. Ibid., 54. Solicitor general Philip Perlman reaffirmed this position when he stated during oral argument before the Supreme Court that restrictive covenants affected "the lives, health and well-being of not only millions of Negroes but of Jews, Chinese and Japanese." There was no detectable irony in the Justice Department's use of the *Korematsu* case, which it had defended barely two years earlier, to press the Court to defend equal rights for minorities, including Japanese Americans.
71. *Shelley v. Kraemer*, 334 U.S. 1 (1948).
72. Ibid. at 21.
73. Ibid., n. 26 at 21, 4; *Hurd v. Hodge*, 334 U.S. 24 (1948), n. 2.
74. *Hurd v. Hodge* at 30.
75. *Takahashi v. California Fish and Game Commission*, 334 U.S. 410 (1948).
76. Chuman, *The Bamboo People*, 230–31. See also Lillian Takahashi Hoffecker, "A Village Disappeared," *American Heritage*, November-December 2001, 64–71.
77. Los Angeles County Superior Court, *Torao Takahashi v. Fish and Game Commission et al.*, cited in Brief of the Japanese American Citizens League amicus curiae, *Torao Takahashi v. Fish and Game Commission et al.*, 42. See also Robert Kirsch, "Judge Orders Issuance of Fishing License to Issei: Rules Ban Is Unconstitutional," *Rafu Shimpo*, June 14, 1946, 1:5–6.

78. *Torao Takahashi v. Fish and Game Commission et al.,* 30 Cal 2d 719, 185 P.2d 805 (1947).

79. United States President's Committee on Civil Rights, *To Secure These Rights,* 162.

80. "Ask Supreme Court Hearing on Takahashi Case Testing California Fish, Game Code," *Pacific Citizen,* January 17, 1948, 1:1–2.

81. *Oyama v. California,* at 648.

82. Memorandum to Mr. Marshall from Marian Wynn Perry, December 31, 1947, Japanese (Nisei) file, NAACP Papers.

83. Elman, "The Solicitor General's Office, Justice Frankfurter, and Civil Rights Litigation, 1946–1960," 819–20.

84. Letter cited in *Open Forum* 25, no. 4 (1947), 1:1. Presumably the "large number of persons" to whom Perlman [misidentified in the article as "Pearlman"] referred were not the Issei fishermen, of whom there were barely 200, but Japanese Americans and minorities generally.

85. Letter, Samuel Ishikawa to Marian Wynn Perry, February 6, 1948, Japanese (Nisei) file, NAACP papers.

86. Motion and Brief for the National Association for the Advancement of Colored People as amicus curiae, *Toro Takahashi v. California Fish and Game Commission;* Brief for Petitioner, *Toro Takahashi v. California Fish and Game Commission.*

87. Motion and Brief for the National Association for the Advancement of Colored People as amicus curiae, *Toro Takahashi v. California Fish and Game Commission;* Brief for Petitioner, *Toro Takahashi v. California Fish and Game Commission.*

88. Brief for the United States as amicus curiae, *Toro Takahashi v. California Fish and Game Commission,* 5, 6.

89. *Takahashi v. California Fish and Game Commission,* 334 U.S. 410. Although Black had expressed this conclusion in his concurring opinion in *Oyama,* his *Takahashi* opinion cited not *Oyama* on this point but the Court's barely month-old decision in *Hurd v. Hodge.*

90. Ibid.

91. Ibid.

92. Thurgood Marshall, "The Supreme Court as Protector of Civil Rights," *Annals of the American Academy of Political and Social Sciences* 275 (May 1951), reprinted in *Writings of Thurgood Marshall,* ed. Mark V. Tushnet (New York: Laurel Hill Books, 2001), 119–21.

93. *Plessy v. Ferguson,* 163 U.S. 537 (1896).

94. *Missouri ex rel Gaines v. Canada.*(305 U.S. 337); Kluger, *Simple Justice,* 195–204; Mark V. Tushnet, *The NAACP's Legal Strategy Against Segregation, 1925–1950* (Chapel Hill: University of North Carolina Press, 1987).

95. *Sipuel v. Board of Regents of University of Oklahoma* (332 U.S. 631).

96. *V. W. McLaurin v. Oklahoma State Regents for Higher Education et al.,* 339 U.S. 637 (1950).

97. *Sweatt v. Painter*, 339 U.S. 629 (1950); Tushnet, *NAACP's Legal Strategy Against Segregation*.

98. *Sweatt v. Painter* file, Schools Cases, Legal File, Series II, NAACP Papers. Although the JACL had no direct involvement in the schools cases before the conference, A. L. Wirin had argued a case involving the segregation of Mexican American schoolchildren in Texas (in connection with which he borrowed from Thurgood Marshall the lower court transcript in *Sweatt* as a reference), and the JACL brief in *Takahashi* used *Sipuel* as its precedent for a Supreme Court remand to a lower court.

99. Brief of the Japanese American Citizens League as amicus curiae, *V. W. McLaurin v. Oklahoma State Regents for Higher Education et al.*

100. Ibid., 3.

101. Brief for Appellant, *V. W. McLaurin v. Oklahoma State Regents for Higher Education et al.*, 30–34.

102. United States Supreme Court, *McLaurin v. Oklahoma State Regents for Higher Education*, 339 U.S. 637 (1950); *Sweatt v. Painter*, 339 U.S. 629 (1950).

103. *Brown v. Board of Education*, 347 U.S. 483 (1954). See generally Kluger, *Simple Justice*, 543–82.

104. The JACL did not submit an independent brief in *Brown*. Rather, in November 1952 the national JACL joined five other organizations in a consolidated amicus brief, on which Saburo Kido was listed as of counsel. A month later, the JACL's Washington, DC, branch, represented by Rikio Kumagai, joined a separate consolidated amicus brief directed at the District of Columbia school case, *Bolling v. Sharpe*. Internal evidence suggests that the JACL did not take part in the writing of either brief and that the organization's presence in them was simply an expression of solidarity. The two amicus briefs were similar. Both asserted, as the NAACP briefs did, that the Court should apply strict scrutiny and thereby overturn the state and District of Columbia laws at issue, since they made racial distinctions in the absence of grave necessity. Brief of the American Civil Liberties Union, American Ethical Union, American Jewish Committee, Anti-Defamation League of B'nai B'rith, Japanese American Citizens League, and Unitarian Fellowship for Social Justice as amicus curiae, *Brown* (no. 52-8). Brief of the Unitarian Council on Human Rights as amicus curiae, *Bolling* (no. 4).

105. Kluger, *Simple Justice*, 582–616.

106. Earl Warren, *The Memoirs of Chief Justice Earl Warren* (Garden City, NY: Doubleday, 1977), 147–49. On Warren's role in the evacuation and subsequent attitude, see G. Edward White, *Earl Warren: A Public Life* (New York: Oxford University Press, 1982), 67–77.

107. Kluger, *Simple Justice*, 678–99.

108. *Brown v. Board of Education*, 347 U.S. 483 at 495.

109. Brief for Petitioners on Reargument, *Bolling v. Sharpe*, 17–18, 41–42, 60–64.

110. United States Supreme Court, *Bolling v. Sharpe*, 347 U.S. 497.

111. Ibid. at 499.

112. Scott Kurashige, "The Many Facets of *Brown*: Integration in a Multiracial Society," *Journal of American History* 91, no. 1 (June 2004): 56–68.

113. The contemporaneous *Ex parte Endo* decision had much greater immediate ramifications. Patrick O. *Gudridge*, "Remember *Endo*?" *Harvard Law Review* 116 (2003): 1933–70; Robinson, *By Order of the President*, 229–30.

114. Chuman, "Notes on Interview with A. L. Wirin," 3.

12. AN UNEASY ALLIANCE

1. See, for example, Matthew Manuel Briones, "The Unpublished Diaries of Charles Kikuchi: 'Black and Yellow' Through the Eyes of a Progressive Nisei Intellectual," *Prospects* 28 (2003): 429–64.

2. John Howard, *Concentration Camps on the Home Front: Japanese Americans in the House of Jim Crow* (Chicago: University of Chicago Press, 2008).

3. See, for example, Charlotte Brooks, "In the Twilight Zone Between Black and White: Japanese American Resettlement and Community in Chicago, 1942–1945," *Journal of American History* 86, no. 4 (Fall 2000): 1655–87; a more negative view is provided by Jacalyn D. Harden's work *Double Cross: Japanese Americans in Black and White Chicago* (Minneapolis: University of Minnesota Press, 2003).

4. Marie Harlowe Pulley, "Jim Crow Tendencies Among Japanese American Evacuees May Hamper Resettlement," *Pacific Citizen*, January 1, 1944, 3–4.

5. For an early example, see Joe Grant Masaoka, "Colorado Calling," *Pacific Citizen*, August 28, 1943, 6.

6. Mary Oyama [Mittwer], "A Matter of Courage," *Rafu Shimpo*, August 21, 1946.

7. Togo Tanaka, "Editorials of the Times," *Colorado Times*, March 13, 1947.

8. *Pittsburgh Courier*, April 1(?), 1948, cited in *Chicago Shimpo*, April 7, 1948, 1.

9. James Farmer, *Lay Bare the Heart: An Autobiography of the Civil Rights Movement* (New York: Plume, 1985), 105. In his memoirs, Farmer mischaracterized Chino as "half-Chinese and half-Caucasian." In fact, Robert Asahi Chino was a biracial Japanese American. Chino was convicted of draft resistance shortly after the protests, and spent two years in prison before being released to join the 44nd Regimental Combat team, an all-Nisei unit. He was decorated for his wartime service.

10. "Great Basso-Baritone Approves JCCD, Becomes Life Member," *New Canadian*, November 16, 1946, 1.

11. Associated Negro Press Dispatch, June 1, 1946. See also *Pacific Citizen*, June 2, 1946, 1.

12. Larry Tajiri, "Vagaries," *Pacific Citizen*, March 4, 1947, 2.

13. Larry Tajiri, "Nisei and Jim Crow," *Pacific Citizen*, January 1, 1944, 3.

14. Larry Tajiri, "A Film Hits Anti-Nisei Prejudice," *Pacific Citizen*, December 27, 1947, 2.

15. Letter, Mike Masaoka to Walter White, December 7, 1953, Nisei file, NAACP papers.

16. On the Japanese Evacuation Claims Act, see Greg Robinson, *A Tragedy of Democracy: Japanese Confinement in North America* (New York: Columbia University Press, 2009), 274–283. Ironically, the McCarran-Walter Act actually reduced immigration of people of African ancestry by eliminating the previously unlimited immigration from the Western Hemisphere, including Caribbean blacks.

17. "Col. Mashbir Warns Nisei 'Not to Be Used as a Cudgel for Other Groups,'" *Northwest Times*, March 10, 1954.

18. The JACL did propose an amicus curiae brief in the Supreme Court case *NAACP v. Alabama*, in which the state of Alabama used the NAACP refusal to provide its membership list to a legislative investigating committee as a pretext to harass and outlaw NAACP activities in its state, but their participation was vetoed by the opposing side..

19. On Birmingham, see for example Diane McWhorter, *Carry Me Home: Birmingham, Alabama, the Climactic Battle of the Civil Rights Revolution* (New York: Simon & Schuster, 2001). On the civil rights movement more generally, see Taylor Branch, *Parting the Waters: America in the King Years, 1954–1963* (New York: Simon & Schuster, 1989).

20. Yuri Kochiyama, *Passing It On* (Los Angeles: UCLA Asian American Studies Program, 2004), 42–50.. On Kochiyama, see Diane C. Fujino, *Heartbeat of Struggle: The Revolutionary Life of Yuri Kochiyama* (Minneapolis: University of Minnesota Press, 2005).

21. Tooru Kanazawa, "Informal Lines," *Hokubei Shimpo*, April 27, 1961, 1.

22. Daisuke Kitagawa, cited in "Colored People Losing Trust in Christianity, World Council Told," *Chicago Defender*, April 25, 1963, 5.

23. Letter, Nick Iyoya, James Nakamura, and Lloyd Wake, cited in "Three S.F. Nisei Ministers Offer a Human Rights Plea," *New York Nichibei*, June 6, 1963, 1.

24. "More Rights Action Urged by Hayakawa," *New York Times*, August 14, 1963, 26. Hayakawa gave versions of this lecture on several occasions in succeeding months. When the text was serialized in a New York Nisei newspaper, a reader argued that advocating special recruitment of Negro workers was a form of "white guilt" that meant that Negroes were accepted only on the (neurotic) terms of white society. Jeffrey N. Masuda, letter, *New York Nichibei*, May 7, 1964.

25. "Linguist Says Video Pitches Stir 'Equality' Urge in Negro," *Pacific Citizen*, September 4, 1963, 1.

26. Clifford Uyeda, "Rhetorics over Racial Discrimination," *Pacific Citizen*, November 10, 1961, 4. Uyeda was taken to task for his remarks by San Francisco JACL newsletter editor Kiyoshi Matsuo. "Shocked and Surprised," *Pacific Citizen*, December 1, 1961.

27. Samuel A. Boyea, cited in "Drama Critic Says Nisei Should Research, Not Reject, Negro History," *Pacific Citizen*, November 1, 1963.

28. Howard Imazeki, "In Our Voice," editorial, *Hokubei Mainichi*, June 29, 1963, reprinted in *Fresno Bee*, August 30, 1963, 15.

29. Ibid.

30. On African American self-help, see, for example, Joe Allison, "The Angry Man," *San Francisco Call Bulletin*, June 29(?), 1963, cited in "A Negro Voice," *Hokubei Mainichi*, July 3–10, 1963, 2; "Negroes Must Build 'Public Image' Like Japanese Americans After WW2," *Pacific Citizen*, December 4, 1963, 1.

31. Mike Masaoka, "Not Our Voice," *Pacific Citizen*, August 3, 1963, 2.

32. Eddie Fujimoto, letter, "A Fresno Businessman's Woes," *Hokubei Mainichi*, July 29, 1963.

33. Editorial, *Long Beach Independent Press-Telegram*, August 11, 1963; Neil James Jr., "Negroes Hindered," *Chicago Defender*, July 15, 1963, 15.

34. George O. Butler, "Negro leader Asks for Understanding," *Pacific Citizen*, July 26, 1963, 3.

35. Loren Miller, "Wrong Side of His Mouth," *California Eagle*, July 10, 1963, cited in Saburo Kido, "Noted Negro Attorney Who Battled for Civil Rights Answers," *Pacific Citizen*, July 19, 1963, 1–2.

36. Mike Masaoka, "Not Our Voice," *Pacific Citizen*, August 3, 1963, 2; George Aki, "No Man Is an Island," *Christian Science Monitor*, September 5, 1963, 18.

37. Taxie Kusonoki, "An Editorial," *New York Nichibei*, June 20, 1963, 1.

38. Taxie Kusonoki, "Second Thoughts," *New York Nichibei*, November 11, 1963, 1.

39. Bill and Mary Kochiyama, "Rebut SF Editorial That 'Advised' Negroes to Do Some Soul Searching," *New York Nichibei*, September 26, 1963, 1.

40. Ibid., 2.

41. Pat Okura interview, in Bill Hosokawa, *JACL in Quest of Justice* (New York: Morrow, 1982), 317.

42. Saburo Kido, "Direct Action Not Our Course—Says Wartime JACL President," *Shin Nichi Bei*, June 1963, reprinted in *Pacific Citizen*, June 28, 1963, 2.

43. Rev. Gyomay M. Kubose, Joe Sagami, in "Should JACL Demonstrate?" *Pacific Citizen*, July 19, 1963, 3.

44. Clifford Uyeda, "This Is Our Voice," *Pacific Citizen*, July 19, 1963, 3. Ironically, Uyeda, who had escaped confinement during World War II, spent much of the war years in New Orleans.

45. Ibid., July 26, 1963, 3.

46. "National JACL Policy on Civil Rights Is Announced," *New York Nichibei*, August 1, 1963, 2.

47. "Highway 40 Restaurants Start Desegregation, Serve Negroes," *Hokubei Shimpo*, November 30, 1961.

48. Leif Erickson, "Nisei Proved Themselves as Soldiers in American Uniforms," *Hayward Review*, August 2, 1962.

49. "Frank Chuman Chairs Integration Meeting; Seek Avert Violence," *Rafu Shimpo*, June 10, 1963. "Chuman presides over meet to prevent LA 'Birmingham,'" *Kashu Mainichi*, June 7, 1963.

50. "National JACL Policy in Civil Rights Is Announced," *Pacific Citizen*, July 26, 1963, 1.

51. "Orange County JACL to Turn Down 'Seat' on Human Relations Council if Offered," *Pacific Citizen*, August 30, 1963, 3. Following reports of the meeting, chapter members insisted they had discussed ideas and not set official policy, though they did not retract the resolutions formed.

52. Hosokawa, *JACL in Quest of Justice*, 318. One Hawaiian-born Nisei who worked as a congressional aide did sit rather unobtrusively on the podium, in the area reserved for elected officials. See Tom Ige, *Boy from Kahaluu* (Honolulu: Kin Cho Jin Kai, 1989).

53. Rev. Alfred S. Akamatsu, "A Day in a Revolution," *New York Nichibei*, September 12, 1963, 1.

54. Ibid., 2.

55. Letter, Austin Herschel, "The Voice of the People," *Chicago Tribune*, September 9, 1963, 20. Curiously, the person listed as the author disclaimed having written the letter. Austin Herschel, "A Disclaimer," *Chicago Tribune*, October 10, 1963, 20. This raises the question of whether the letter was a prank or provocation, albeit one that had consequences.

56. The oldest continuing black newspaper, the *Baltimore Afro-American*, did not so much as mention Japanese Americans throughout the decade of the 1960s. However, the influential *Chicago Defender*, which had offered sustained support to Japanese Americans during the war, ran scattered articles discussing Japanese Americans and supporting their rights. In 1962, an editorial called on Congress to pass legislation to prevent the Internal Revenue Service from taxing evacuation claims funds. "Japanese Americans," *Chicago Defender*, January 16, 1963, 12. Another editorial three years later called for "justice for the Nisei" whose bank accounts had been seized during the war. *Chicago Defender*, November 4, 1966, 13.

57. Letter, Malcolm Christian, "Minorities," *Chicago Tribune*, September 17, 1963. Christian's focus on the Nisei is shown more prominently by the version of his letter published shortly afterward by the *Chicago Defender*. There Christian softened his argument by distinguishing Asians from white immigrant groups as "dark-skinned," and characterized them somewhat less inaccurately as only "predominantly" foreign-born. Yet the title chosen by the *Defender* ignored Chinese Americans completely and referred only to Japanese Americans, using a word often considered a racial slur. "Asinine Comparison of Negroes, Japs," *Chicago Defender*, October 5, 1963, 7.

58. Letter, Malcolm Christian, "Minorities," *Chicago Tribune*, September 17, 1963.

59. William Marutani, "We Did It; Why Can't They?" *Pacific Citizen*, September 20, 1963.

60. H. Quintus Sakai, letter, "Social Problems Need Collective Action," *Pacific Citizen*, September 13, 1963, 3.

61. In early 1964, Bill and Mary Kochiyama, as part of the Harlem Parents Committee, wrote the Nisei press to build support for a one-day boycott of New York City public schools to protest segregated education. Letter, Bill and Mary Kochiyama, *New York Nichi Bei*, January 30, 1964, 1.

62. "Japanese Americans Hear Civil Rights Plea," *Chicago Defender*, February 17, 1964, 7.

63. "Would the Truth Make Us Free," editorial, *Fresno Bee*, August 16, 1964. See also William J. Raspberry, "Racism in Maryland Surprises Hawaiian," *Washington Post*, August 5, 1964, 9.

64. "Roy Wilkins Bids JACL Help to Implement Rights," *New York Nichibei*, July 16, 1964, 1.

65. Author interview with Barbara Takei, San Francisco, June 2, 2005.

66. Editorial, "All Should Be Concerned," *Pacific Citizen*, October 16, 1964, 2.

67. "California Issei and Nisei Groups Organize to Defeat 'Unfair Housing,'" *New York Nichibei*, August 13, 1964.

68. "I-ye on Proposition 14 Catches On," *New York Nichibei*, October 22, 1964.

69. Mary Ikuta, "Proposition 14 Spurs Housewife Reaction," *Kashu Mainichi*, November 2, 1964.

70. "Prop 14 Opponents Intensify Fight," *New York Nichibei*, October 29, 1964.

71. Jerry Enomoto, "By the Board," *Pacific Citizen*, September 25, 1964, 1.

72. Mary Ikuta, "Proposition 14 Spurs Housewife Reaction," *Kashu Mainichi*, November 2, 1964.

73. Richard A. Iwata, cited in "Chapter and Verse," *New York Nichibei*, October 22, 1964.

74. "For and Against Proposition 14," *Kashu Mainichi*, November 3, 1964.

75. George Yoshinaga, "The Horse's Mouth,"*Kashu Mainichi*, November 1, 1964.

76. "UCLA Student Poll on Fair Housing," *Pacific Citizen*, November 6, 1964, 1. For Mexican Americans and Proposition 14, see "Campaña educacional contre la Proposición 14 en Los Angeles," *La Opinión*, October 11, 1964, 1. See also Celia Heller, "Chicano Is Beautiful," in Joseph Boskin and Robert S. Rosenstone, eds., *Seasons of Rebellion: Protest and Radicalism in Recent America* (New York: Holt, Rinehart, 1972), 81–92.

77. Raymond E. Wolfinger and Fred I. Greenstein, "The Repeal of Fair Housing in California: An Analysis of Referendum Voting," *American Political Science Review* 63, no. 3 (September 1968): 753–69. Charlotte Brooks relies excessively on this methodologically flawed poll in her conclusions on Asian Americans. Brooks, *Alien Neighbors, Foreign Friends: Asian Ameri-*

cans, Housing, and the Transformation of Urban California (Chicago: University of Chicago Press, 2009), 238.

78. In October 1964, George Kanno of the Orange County Goldwater for President Committee and Henry Kanegae of the Republican Central Committee of Orange County appeared together at a public forum on Proposition 14. Although the records of the forum have not survived, anecdotal evidence suggests that they spoke in favor of it. See "JACL Will Debate Initiative, Pro and Con, at Meeting," *Rafu Shimpo*, October 14, 1964, 1.

79. "Japanese May Lose Job over Goldwater Aid," *Los Angeles Times*, October 30, 1964, 5.

80. "Voter Approval of Prop. 14 No Act of Prejudice," *Rafu Shimpo*, November 4, 1963, 1. In the same vein, see "Candidate Raps Foes of Housing Initiative," *Rafu Shimpo*, October 14, 1964, 1.

81. See, for example, Gerald Horne, *Fire This Time: The Watts Uprising and the 1960s* (Charlottesville, VA: University of Virginia Press, 1995).

82. "Claim Nisei Business Loss $1 Million," *New York Nichibei*, August 26, 1965. Hisaye Yamamoto, in her classic 1985 memoir "A Fire in Fontana," describes her own mixed feelings over the riot—fear for her suburban property, but also satisfaction that African Americans were rising up and paying back in kind for the violent discrimination they had suffered. Hisaye Yamamoto, "A Fire in Fontana," in *Seventeen Syllables and Other Stories*, rev. ed. (New Brunswick, NJ: Rutgers University Press, 2001).

83. "JACLer Marches in Alabama," "Calif. Sansei Demonstrating in Montgomery, Ala. Clubbed by Police," *Pacific Citizen*, March 26, 1965; "Hawaii Marchers 'Flabbergast' King," *New York Nichibei*, April 8, 1965.

84. Harry Kitano, *Japanese Americans: The Evolution of a Subculture* (Englewood Cliffs, NJ: Prentice-Hall, 1969); Daniel I. Okimoto, *American in Disguise* (New York: Weatherhill, 1971), 152.

85. In Japanese Americans and intermarriage, see Susan Koshy, *Sexual Naturalization: Asian Americans and Miscegenation* (Stanford, CA: Stanford University Press, 2004).

86. Phyl Newbeck, *Virginia Hasn't Always Been for Lovers: Interracial Marriage Bans and the Case of Richard and Mildred Loving* (Carbondale: Southern Illinois University Press, 2004). Marutani's argument, interestingly, marked the first-ever appearance of a Japanese American attorney before the high court in a civil rights case.

EPILOGUE

1. Edwin O. Reischauer, "Introduction," in Bill Hosokawa, *Nisei: The Quiet Americans* (New York: William Morrow, 1969), xi.

2. William Petersen, "Success Story, Japanese American Style," *New York Times Magazine*, January 9, 1966, 20–43, cited in Hosokawa, *Nisei*, 494–95. See also William Petersen, *Japanese Americans: Oppression and Success*

(New York: Random House, 1971). Petersen's work is generally credited as the first expression of the much-refuted "model minority" thesis. For an accessible critique of "model minority" thinking, see Frank H. Wu, *Yellow: Race in America Beyond Black and White* (New York: Free Press, 2001).,

3. "Morrow to Publish Hosokawa Book," *New York Nichibei*, February 13, 1969; "Hosokawa's Issei Story," *New York Nichibei*, February 27, 1969.

4. Rev. Roy Sano, cited in "Now a Word from Some Un-Quiet Nisei," *Pacific Citizen*, July 8(?), 1969.

5. Raymond Okamura, "letters," *New York Nichibei*, July 10, 1969.

6. Yoshio Kishi, "Neuter Stereotype Image Perpetuated," *New York Nichibei*, February 24, 1971.

7. Mike Masaoka with Bill Hosokawa, *They Call Me Moses Masaoka* (New York: Morrow, 1987), 289.

8. "Frank Discussion Given Area Ethnic Problems," *Los Angeles Times*, October 17, 1965, WS5.

9. James Farmer, cited in Taxie Kusonoki, "Color the Nisei Conservative?" *New York Nichibei*, May 26, 1966.

10. "NAACP Attorney Reveals Store Picketing in Fresno Was Action Not Authorized," *Pacific Citizen*, September 6, 1963, 3.

11. "Negro Weekly Charges Anti-Japanese Sermons Result of $25,000 'Pay-offs,'" *New York Nichibei*, June 17, 1965.

12. "Readers Express Firsthand Views," *Chicago Defender*, February 6, 1967, 12.

13. See, for example, William Wei, *The Asian American Movement* (Philadelphia: Temple University Press, 1995); Daryl J. Maeda, *Chains of Babylon: The Rise of Asian America* (Minneapolis: University of Minnesota Press, 2009).

14. For the redress movement, see Mitchell T. Maki, Harry H. L. Kitano, and S. Megan Berthold, *Achieving the Impossible Dream: How Japanese Americans Obtained Redress* (Urbana: University of Illinois Press, 1999). The law provided an official apology for mass removal and a $20,000 payment to each individual affected.

Index

Acheson, Dean, 200, 210, 290n32
Adams, Ansel, 79
African Americans: artists and musicians, 220–22; education segregation, 211–13, 269n4; employment, 49–51, 149; housing, 51, 57, 62, 65, 93, 204; in-migration, 8, 48, 218; intermarriage, 92, 158; newspapers, 86, 149, 164–65, 172, 191, 220; opinions of Japan, 159; prejudice against "Orientals," 160; reactions to Japanese confinement, 8, 157, 160–61, 164–65, 167–70, 171–73, 221, 245; relations with Japanese Americans, 9, 93, 106, 152, 158–59, 217–23, 260n56; relations with Mexican Americans, 123–26, 137–38, 272n58; relations with Nisei, 8, 88, 149, 158, 171, 196, 217–23, 244; religion, 170–71; response to Imazeki's letter, 228; segregation and Jim Crow, 195; soldiers, 168; voting discrimination, 189–91, 216, 239; women, 167–69. *See also* Legal cases: *Brown v. Board of Education*; Legal cases: *Plessy v. Ferguson*
African Methodist Episcopal Church, 170
Akamatsu, Alfred, 183, 184, 233
Akamine, George, 50

Aki, George, 229
Akiya, Karl, 153, 191
Alameda, CA, 110
Alaska, 32
Alianza Hispano-Americano, 137
Alien land legislation, 9, 48, 54–55, 62, 107, 124, 181, 197–203, 205, 210, 289n15, 290n32, 290n35
Allen, Wayne, 61
Almaguer, Tomas, 109
Amemiya, Yuriko, 59
American Baptist Home Mission Society, 58, 90, 170
American Civil Liberties Union, 90, 131, 137, 161, 166, 177–79, 184, 199–200, 204, 206, 275n90, 286n14, 291n36
American Committee for the Protection of the Foreign Born, 60, 185
American Council on Race Relations, 223
American Federation of Labor, 53
American Friends Service Committee, 63, 167
American Jewish Committee, 24
American Jewish Congress, 106, 130, 137, 148–49, 170, 206
American Journal of Sociology, 83
American Legion, 61, 163, 173, 178

303

Americans of Japanese Ancestry: A Study of Assimilation in the American Community, 38
Americans with Japanese Faces, 242
American Veterans Committee, 223
Ames, James Baer, 172
Anaheim, CA, 115
Anderson, M. Margaret, 76–78, 81–82, 89, 264n27
Angelou, Maya, 160
Ann Arbor, MI, 48, 53
Anti-Semitism. *See* Hayakawa, S. I.; Hitler, Adolf; Japanese Americans; Los Angeles; Nazism; Nisei; Tajiri, Larry
Aoki, Helen, 143
Ariyoshi, Koji, 153
Arizona, 114
Arkansas, 217
Armour Institute of Technology, 95
Arts Council, 188
Asano, Shichinosuke, 199
Asia, 88, 89, 94; *Asia and the Americas*, 147
Assimilation. *See* African Americans; Japanese American Citizens League (JACL); Japanese Americans; LaViolette, Forrest E.; Mexican Americans; Sugihara, Ina; Tajiri, Larry; War Relocation Authority
Avery Normal School, 172

Baja California, 173
Baldwin, Roger, 177, 184, 187, 286n14, 291n36
Baltimore, 158, 172
Baltimore Advocate (*Baltimore Times*), 172
Bandwagon, The, 191
Bass, Charlotta, 123
Beaumont, Campbell E., 179
Bendetsen, Karl, 120
Benjamin, Robert, 59
Berlin Hospital, 143
Berlin Olympics of 1936, 142
Besig, Ernest, 90, 146
Bird, Remsen, 146

Birmingham, AL, 225
Black, Elaine, 152
Black, Hugo, 197, 201–2, 209, 211, 294n89
B'nai Brith, 148
Boas, Franz, 29
Bonesteel, Charles H., 27, 252n35
Booth, G. Raymond, 65
Bowman, Isaiah, 17–18, 21–23
Bowron, Fletcher, 61, 115, 120, 175
Boyea, Samuel A., 227
Bracero Program, 122
Brick Foxhole, The, 150
Briggs Manufacturing Company, 49
British Columbia, 32, 34, 39–42, 93, 94
Bronzeville (Little Tokyo area), 62, 65, 160, 220
Brooklyn Eagle, 16
Broom, Leonard, 148
Brotherhood of Sleeping Car Porters, 166
Brown, George, 174
Brumbaugh, T. T., 50
Buchenwald concentration camp, 81, 82
Buck, Pearl S., 88, 184, 186
Buddhist Church, 46, 50, 55, 236
Bull Moose Party, 172
Butler, George, 228

Calexico, CA, 109
Calgary, AB, 93
California. *See* Alien land legislation; Los Angeles; San Francisco
California Art and Architecture, 71
California Eagle, 123, 168, 272n58
California Institute of Technology, 61
California Real Estate Association, 235
Californio, 111
Camden, NJ, 58
Canada: English and French Canadian relations, 20; fear of Japanese invasion, 116; Hayakawa in, 93–94; immigration policies, 16; wartime removal of Japanese, 35, 38–40, 49, 252n38. *See also* LaViolette, Forrest E.

Canadian Institute of International Affairs, 38, 40
Canadian Japanese and World War II, The, 40
Cannon, J. Alfred, 245
Carrillo, Leo, 111
Carter, John Franklin, 21–23, 25, 28
Carter, Robert, 133
Cary, Miles, 147
Cayton, Horace, 220
CBS, 83
Cecil, William D., 112
Central Avenue, 137, 173–74, 175
Chandrasekhar, Sripati, 23
Chapultec Act of 1945, 173
Chavez, Cesar, 137
Chicago, 48, 91; CORE sit-in of 1942, 221; Hayakawa in, 95–98; Japanese population, 45, 46, 218, 282n8; NAACP Labor Day conference in, 205; race riot of 1919, 159
Chicago Co-Operative News, 96
Chicago Defender, 96, 149, 161, 164, 220, 299n56, 299n57
Chicago Resettlers Committee, 97
Chicago Shimpo, 47, 149
Chicanos, 65, 110, 121, 137
China, 95, 113, 142, 145, 187, 278n31
Chinese Exclusion Act, 189
Chinese Hand Laundry Alliance, 189
Ching, Hung Wai, 26
Chino, Robert, 221, 296n9
Christian Century, 86
Christian, Malcolm, 233–34, 245, 299n57
Christian Institute, 55
Christian Science Monitor, 86, 233
Chrysler Corporation, 49
Chuman, Frank F., 11, 137, 206, 231–32, 236
CINO, 98–99
Cisco Kid, The, 111
Citizen 13660, 6, 69–70, 78–80, 82–84
Citizens' Housing Council, 62
Civil Rights Act of 1866, 208
Civil Rights Congress, 220
Civil Rights Defense Committee, 163

Clark, Kenneth B. and Mamie, 214
Clark, Tom, 206–7, 293n67
Cleveland, 46, 48
Cohn, Al, 175
Cold War, 23, 97, 224, 250n8
Collins, Charles, 188
Colorado. *See* Denver
Colorado Times, 47, 124
Colored American Legion, 163
Columbia University, 54, 56, 78, 80, 109, 150, 151
Committee for Equal Employment, (Kennedy administration), 225
Common Council for American Unity, 60, 76–78, 223
Common Ground, 76, 83, 86, 89
Commonweal, 86, 87
Commonwealth Club of San Francisco, 72
Communist Party USA, 152, 183, 186–87, 191
Community Church, 56
Confinement of Japanese Americans, 1–2; comparison with Nazi camps, 82, 120, 141–44. *See also* African Americans; Executive Order 9066; Japanese American Citizens League (JACL); Japanese American Committee for Democracy (JACD); Japanese Americans; *La Opinión*; *La Prensa*; LaViolette, Forrest E.; Legal cases: *Korematsu v. United States*; Mexican Americans; Nisei; Okubo, Miné; Roosevelt, Franklin D.; WRA camps
Congress of Industrial Organizations, 53, 137
Congressional Record, 228
Congress of Racial Equality (CORE), 65, 91, 221
Coordinating Council for Latin-American Youth, 123–25
Coughlin, Charles, 51
Council for Civic Unity, Los Angeles, 65
Council for Latin-American Youth, 123–25

Cranbrook, BC, 93
Creef, Elena Tajima, 69
Crisis, The, 91, 164, 167
Crisis of the Negro Intellectual, The, 191
Crossroads, 47, 65, 232
Cruse, Harold R., 191
Cummings, Bill and Elisabeth, 165
Czechoslovakia. *See* World War II

Dachau concentration camp, 78, 82, 140
Daniels, Roger, 83
Date, Hideo, 59
Davis, Elmer, 180
Delaplane, Stanton, 113, 118
Delaware, 214
Dellums, C. L., 166
Democracy and the Japanese Americans, 176
Denman, William, 136
Denver, 47–48, 166
Denver Post, 92, 241
Dermaway University, 50
Detroit, 4, 56, 57, 60, 62, 65–66; Japanese Americans in, 48–53; riot of 1943, 51
Detroit Committee to Aid Resettlers of Japanese Ancestry, 50
Detroit Council of Churches, 50, 52
Detroit Free Press, 52
Detroit News, 52
Detroit Resettlement Committee, 50, 51
Deutsch, Monroe, 70, 261n8
Devil's Lake, ND, 31
DeWitt, John, 43, 177–79
Díaz, José, 122
Dickerson, Earl, 189
District of Columbia. *See* Washington, D.C.
Doi, Frank, 50
Doi, Marie, 50
Donner, Frank, 205
Doreski, C.K., 96, 164
Douglas, William O., 202
Dower, John, 152

Du Bois, W. E. B., 65, 159, 162, 283n22
Duus, Masayo, 139–40

Eisenberg, Ellen, 11, 146
El Centro school district, 137
El Monte, CA, 124
El Monte Berry Strike of 1933, 109
Endo, Todd, 239
Endow, Kay Karl, 55
England, 143
Ennis, Edward, 212
Essex Wire Company, 49
Estrada, Ralph, 137
Estrada, Thomas, 126
Etc., 97
Evacuation Claims Act of 1948, 224
Evans, Walker, 78
Evansville, IN, 163
Evergreen Hostel, 63
Evian Conference, 17
Ex-cell-o Company, 49
Executive Order 9066, 8, 25, 43, 56, 96, 113, 115, 118, 121, 146, 161–62, 166–67, 169, 171, 176–78, 185–86, 221

Fair Employment Practices Committee (FEPC), 53, 91, 173, 189, 222
Fair Play Committees, 35, 37, 61, 73, 139, 183
Fair Play United, 151
Farago, Ladislas, 18
Far Eastern Survey, 39
Farmer, James, 91, 221, 246, 296n9
Federal Bureau of Investigation (FBI), 46, 52, 55, 175, 180, 187, 191
Federal Council of Churches, 58, 90, 170
Federal Public Housing Authority, 63
Federation of Hispanic American Voters, 124
Ferguson, Edwin, 201
Field, Henry, 21–24
Field, Marshall, 97
Fields, Alonzo, 178
Fisk University, 163, 172
Foley, Neil, 125

Ford, Gerald R., 28–29, 100
Ford Motor Company, 49
Fort Shelby, MS, 218
Fortune, 74–75, 86, 263n20, 263n23
France, 142
Frase, Robert, 11, 94, 96
Frazier, E. Franklin, 162
Free France, 113
French Canadians, 16, 20, 34
Friends of the American Way, 61
Fujihara, Toge, 55
Fujii, Grace, 50
Fujii, John, 141
Fujii, Sei, 142–43, 174
Fujii, Shuji, 59
Fujioka, Peter, 51
Fujita, Jun, 158–59

Gabaldon, Guy, 111
Gaines, Lloyd, 212
Gallicchio, Marc, 159
Ganbatte, 153
Gandhi, Indira, 24
Garcia, Mario, 125
Garcia, Nellie, 124, 126
Garvey, Marcus, 159, 173
Gar Wood Industries, 49
Geisler, Jerry, 173
Gengo, Kimi, 55
German American Bund, 142
Germany. *See* Hitler, Adolf; Kristallnacht; Nazism; World War II
Goldblatt, Louis, 146
Goldwater, Barry, 235
Goldwater, Julius, 62, 238
Gonzalez, Gilbert, 109
Grace Hospital, 50
Graham, Martha, 59
Granger, Lester, 160, 165
Greater New York Citizens Committee for Japanese-Americans, 59
Greenberg, Cheryl, 167
Greensboro sit-in, 224
Grew, Joseph, 74, 188
Griffith, Thomas L., 166, 180
Grodzins, Morton, 148
Guadalajara, Mexico, 116

Guadalupe, 175
Guthrie, Woody, 188
Guzman, William, 126

Hachimonji, Kumezo, 151, 152
Haines, Charles G., 199
Hamanaka, James, 145–46
Hampton Institute, 158
Harlem, 57, 59, 158, 191, 225
Harlem Parents Committee, 225
Harlem riot of 1943, 59
Harris, Andley, 120
Harris, Erna P., 168
Hart, John, 231
Hartmann, Sadakichi, 54
Harvard University, 172
Hashimoto, Mas, 50
Hatchimonji, Ike, 152
Hawaii, 9, 21, 34, 54, 117–18, 159, 178, 224, 234, 238–39, 250n3, 260n53
Hawaiian-Japanese Civic Association, 112
Hawkins, Augustus, 137
Hayakawa, S. I., 6, 7, 267n14, 267n17, 297n24; after retirement, 99–101; against anti-Semitism, 149; birth and early life, 93–95; on civil rights, 226; columns in the *Chicago Defender*, 165, 220; opposition to ethnic particularism, 95–99; opposition to McCarthyism, 97; relations with Japanese communities, 96–101; relations with the JACL, 97–98; views of Japan, 93–94
Haynes, George, 170
Heco, Joseph, 158
Hepburn, Mitchell, 116
Herschel, Austin, 233
Hibi, Hisako, 59
Hikide, Yasuichi, 159
Hilliard, William A., 165
Himes, Chester, 165, 219
Hirabayashi, Gordon, 166
Hiraoka, Yoichi, 57
Hitler, Adolf, 141–42, 144, 152, 164, 278n31
Hohri, Sam, 86, 87, 145, 220, 278n34

Hokubei Mainichi, 11, 47, 227
Hokubei Shimpo, 47, 82, 149
Holland, Thomas, 50, 96
Holmes, John Haynes, 184
Holmes, Oliver Wendell, 94, 267n17
Hollywood Legion Stadium, 173
Hollzer, Harry, 179
Hood River, OR, 163
Hoover, J. Edgar, 180
Horsky, Charles, 200, 290n32
Hosokawa, Bill, 86, 148, 241–43, 249n2
House Un-American Activities Committee, U.S. (HUAC), 97
Houston, Charles H., 205, 206, 211, 293n65
Howard, Harry Paxton, 164, 167
Howard, John, 218
Howard University, 158, 169, 170
Hrdlicka, Ales, 19–23, 26
Huerta, Delores, 137
Hughes, Langston, 96, 164, 165, 168, 218
Hull, Cordell, 21
Hyde Park, 24–26

Ichioka, Toshio, 115
Ichioka, Tsutayo, 115
Ichioka, Yuji, 115
Ickes, Harold, 26, 27, 75, 82
Iijima, Kazu, 59, 191
Iijima, Tak, 59
Iiyama, Chizu, 11, 190, 191
Iiyama, Ernest, 11, 59, 189
Ikeda, Mary, 82
Imazeki, Howard, 227–31, 233
Immigration Act of 1924, U.S., 160
Indian Bureau, U.S., 206
Inouye, Daniel, 9, 234
Inter-Mountain Cooperative Farmers' Association, 177
International Institute, 51
Iriyama, Howard, 239
Ishigaki, Eitaro, 54, 158
Ishikawa, Samuel, 65, 209
Ishimaru, Kutsu, 49
Ishioka, Masujiro, 50
Italians, 20, 23, 24, 117, 125, 136, 185

Ito, Michio, 54
Ives-Quinn Bill, 58
Iwata, Richard, 237
Iyoya, Nick, 226

JACD Newsletter, 82, 190
James, C. L. R., 164
James, Joseph, 166
Japan, 2, 40, 41, 50, 52, 58, 74, 100, 114, 117, 139, 140, 151, 179, 185, 188, 190, 241, 253n8, 263n19; African American interest in, 159; pro-Japan newspapers and organizations, 55; relations with Japanese Americans, 5, 34, 107, 113, 142, 145, 152, 219, 228; relations with United States, 33–35; war with China, 142, 145, 187, 278. *See also* Alien land legislation; Canada; Hayakawa, S. I.; LaViolette, Forrest E.
Japanese American Association, New York, 55
Japanese American Citizens League (JACL): Anti-Axis Committee, 112; Anti-Discrimination Committee, 9, 92, 97, 98, 209; Assimilation policy, 5–6, 107, 123–24; in Chicago, 97–98; collaboration with Mexican American organizations, 106–7, 124–25, 131–32, 137–38; collaboration with the WRA, 46, 73, 123, 222; cooperation with NAACP, 91–92, 131–32, 138, 195–96, 203–13, 223, 235, 239–40; in Detroit, 51, 234; fight for Nisei citizenship and rights, 123–25, 134, 137–38, 180, 199–213; focus on Issei, 159; internal conflicts, 10; interracial unity, 165–66; in Los Angeles, 65; and Martin Luther King Jr., 100; membership restrictions, 5, 107; in New York, 59, 91; opposition to Proposition 14, 235–37; position toward civil rights, 226–32, 234–35, 239–40; social events, 46–47; support for McCarran-Walter Act of 1952, 97–98

Japanese American Committee for Democracy (JACD), 55, 60, 82, 163, 183–92, 220, 243; approval on Japanese confinement, 183–85, 191–92; conflicting goals, 183, 185–87; encouraging resettlement, 187–88, 190; foundation, 183–84; on interracial unity, 183, 185, 188–92; ties to Communist Party, 183
Japanese American Coordinating Committee, New York, 59
Japanese American Courier, 33, 141, 143–44, 253n8
Japanese American Methodist Church, New York, 56, 183
Japanese American Research Project, 241
Japanese American Review, 55
Japanese Americans, 4, 162–71; anti-Semitism, 139, 141–45, 150–53; in Detroit, 4, 48–53, 66; on the East Coast, 45; exclusion from West Coast, 3, 44–45; in Los Angeles, 4, 60–66, 105; loyalty to United States, 21; in the Midwest, 45; newspapers, 47, 82, 85–90, 110, 124, 141–46, 158; in New York, 4, 53–60, 66; opinions on civil rights, 234; political activism, 10; positions on prewar Japan, 34–35; postwar employment and housing, 45–46, 49; postwar relocation and reintegration, 3, 46, 62–63; reactions to Nazism, 142; relations with African Americans, 6–10, 65, 158, 217–18; relations with Jewish Americans, 7, 139, 148–53; relations with Mexican Americans, 7, 105, 107–10, 123–24, 137–38; and religion, 119; return to West Coast, 4; self-identification, 125–26; stereotypes of African Americans, 158–60; and unions, 53; wartime employment, 25. *See also* Confinement of Japanese Americans; Japan; McCarran-Walter Immigration Act; Legal cases: *Hirabayashi v. United States*; Legal cases: *Takahashi v. California Fish and Game Commission*; Nisei
Japanese Canadian Citizens League, 94
Japanese Canadian Committee for Democracy, 221
Japanese Canadians, 4, 30, 31, 35, 39–42, 49, 250n3, 252n38. *See also* Canada
Japanese Diet, 238
Japanese Fishermen's Association, 114, 208
Japanese Mexicans, 116–18, 270n14
Japanese Peruvians, 116
Japanese Student Christian Association, 54
Japanese Union Church, 65
Japanese Workers Club, 55
Jewish Americans, 4; assimilation, 243; in Los Angeles, 62; promotion of equal and civil rights, 212, 223, 232; in Winnipeg, 93. *See also* American Jewish Congress; Anti-Semitism; Japanese Americans; Nisei; Roosevelt, Franklin D.; Tajiri, Larry
Johns Hopkins University, 17
Johnson, Charles S., 162–63, 220
Johnson, Lyndon B., 234, 238, 239
Jones, Willis, 92, 93
Jordan, Winthrop, 2, 250n5
Journal of Negro Education, 164
Justice Department, 2, 166, 175, 178, 206, 209–10, 212–13, 215, 293n66, 293n70

Kalmer, Joseph, 113
Kanazawa, Tooru, 55, 141, 225
Kanda, Mark, 50
Kashiwagi, Marilyn, 239
Kashu Mainichi, 47, 65, 141, 144, 158, 232, 236
Katayama, Sen, 55
Kawamoto, George, 50
Kearney, Reginald, 159
Kennedy, John F., 225, 232, 234
Kenny, Robert, 130–31, 136, 166, 199

Kido, Saburo, 88, 124, 131–32, 142, 144, 163, 200, 206, 208, 230, 275n92, 295n104
Kikuchi, Charles, 153, 218, 281n69
King, Martin Luther, Jr., 100, 217, 224, 239
Kingsley, Charles, 65, 170
Kishi, Yoshio, 242, 243
Kitagawa, Daisuke, 226
Kitamura, Bill, 49
Kitano, Harry, 239
Kluger, Richard, 133
Knaefler, Tomi Kanazawa, 239
Knight, Rolf, 42
Kobashigawa, Hideo, 59
Kochiyama, Yuri, 225
Kondo, Carl, 59
Konvitz, Milton R., 166–67
Korematsu, Fred, 49
Korematsu, Hi, 25, 49, 177
Korzybski, Alfred, 95
Koyama, Terry, 52
Koyke, Hizi, 54
Kristallnacht, 142–43
Ku Klux Klan, 51
Kuninosuke, Mazumizu, 158
Kuniyoshi, Yasuo, 75, 188
Kurihara, Gilbert, 49
Kuroki, Ben, 74
Kuromiya, Steve Kiyoshi, 239
Kusayanagi, Masako, 63
Kushida, Tets, 124
Kusonoki, Taxie, 229
Kuwahara, Robert (Bob), 59

Lafferty, Nori Ikeda, 59
La Guardia, Fiorello, 57, 167, 187
Lane, Layle, 163
Lange, Dorothea, 78
La Opinión, 111–22
La Prensa, 111–14, 118, 121, 272n40
Latinos. See Mexican Americans
LaViolette, Forrest E., 4, 253n6, 253n8; early academic work, 32–33; early life, 31–32; interest in Japan, 32–33, 253n2; on Japanese assimilation, 33–35, 38; on Japanese confinement and dispossession, 35, 37–42; opposition to racism and deportation, 40–41, 254n19; work at McGill University, 34–36; work at the WRA, 36–37; work at Tulane University, 41
La Violette, Wesley, 31
Lazo, Ralph, 111
Leadbelly, 188
Leadership Conference on Civil Rights (LCCR), 9, 223, 224, 232, 239
League of United Latin American Citizens (LULAC), 106, 109, 124–25, 136–37
League of Nations, 159
Legal cases: *Amer v. Superior Court*, 205; *Bolling v. Sharpe*, 195; *Brown v. Board of Education*, 9, 10, 106, 128, 134, 136, 137, 182, 195, 196, 214–16, 223, 224, 268n2, 295n104; *Corrigan v. Buckley*, 204; *Delgado v. Bastrop*, 136; *Estate of Tetsubumi Yano*, 200; *Hernandez v. State of Texas*, 136; *Hirabayashi v. United States*, 136, 196, 200, 203, 207, 208, 212, 213, 216, 274n80; *Hurd v. Hodge*, 205; *Kim v. Superior Court*, 205; *Korematsu v. United States*, 49, 132, 134, 136, 165, 187, 195–216, 275n92, 288n3, 288n7, 288n10, 290n35, 291n44, 292n58, 293n70; *Loving v. Virginia*, 239–40; *McLaurin v. Oklahoma*, 212; *Méndez v. Westminster School District*, 105, 106, 107, 126–34, 136–38, 200; *Missouri ex rel. Gaines v. Canada*, 212; *Morgan v. Virginia*, 197; *Oyama v. California*, 9, 181, 200, 202, 203, 205, 206, 207, 209, 210, 211, 213, 215, 216; *Ozawa v. United States*, 198; *People v. Hirose*, 181, 199; *People v. Oyama*, 181, 199; *Plessy v. Ferguson*, 127, 130, 132–34; *Porterfield v. Webb*, 198; *Regan v. King*, 166, 180; *Shelley v. Kraemer*,

204–5; *Sipuel v. Board of Regents*, 212; *Skinner v. Oklahoma*, 197; *Sweatt v. Painter*, 212; *Takahashi v. California Fish and Game Commission*, 92, 208–11, 213, 215, 216; *Terrace v. Thompson*, 198; *United States v. Carolene Products Co.*, 197
Liberia, 173, 174, 286n20
Liberty, 86
Library of Congress, 23
Lindbergh, Charles, 146
Little Tokyos, 46, 62, 65, 73, 80, 89, 110, 113, 119, 121, 122, 137, 144, 147, 153, 175, 206, 218, 220, 277n3
Liu, Liang Mo, 186
Los Angeles: anti-Semitism in, 144–49; Boyle Heights, 62, 110, 111, 137, 139, 158; Burbank, 63; Crenshaw District, 246; Hollenbeck Heights, 62; housing, 46, 62; Hugh Macbeth in, 172–75, 180; Japanese American newspapers in, 47, 65, 144–45, 220, 232; Japanese and African American relations in, 157–62, 166, 168, 219–21; Japanese population, 60; Japanese residents and resettlers in, 4, 48, 60–66, 114, 170, 180, 218; Jefferson Park, 63, 174; and mass Japanese removal, 114–15, 119, 161; Mexican American immigration, 107–8, 110; prejudice and discrimination against Japanese in, 61–64, 87; Sawtelle, 63; school segregation in, 107–10; temporary housing, 63; wartime discrimination against Mexicans in, 122–23; Watts, 218, 238–39, 245; West Adam Heights, 204
Los Angeles Citizens' Housing Council, 62
Los Angeles County Human Relations Commission, 231
Los Angeles Herald-Examiner, 61, 232
Los Angeles Times, 61, 147, 168
Los Angeles Tribune, 65, 149, 162, 168, 220
Lozano, Ignacio, 111–12

Macbeth, Gobert, 173, 180
Macbeth, Hugh E., 8, 158, 162, 171–82, 285n1, 285n14, 286n20, 291n36
Macbeth, Hugh, Jr., 11, 172, 174, 180, 181, 285n1, 291n36
Mackenzie King, W. L., 19–20
MacLeish, Archibald, 23
Malcolm X, 225
Manhattan Hostel, 56
Marcantonio, Vito, 189
Marcus, David, 124, 126–27, 129–31, 134, 273n71
Margold, Nathan, 211
Marietta County, GA, 25
Marshall, Thurgood, 92, 97, 106, 133, 162, 195, 206, 209, 211, 214
Marutani, William M., 231, 234, 239–40, 301n86
Masaoka, Joe Grant, 6, 9, 148
Masaoka, Mike, 9, 61, 124, 186, 222, 223, 230, 231, 232, 234
Mashbir, Sidney, 224
Masuoka, Jitsuichi, 163, 220
Matsuda, Minn, 191
Matsui, Haru (Ayako Tanaka Ishigaki), 54
Matsumoto, Taishi, 142
Matsumoto, Teru, 186
Matsumoto, Toru, 54, 59
Matsumoto, Tsuyoshi, 145
Matsushige, Isaac, 231
Maus, 79
Mays, Benjamin, 170
McCarran-Walter Immigration Act, 3, 9, 97–98, 211, 224
McCarthyism, 10, 97, 191, 224, 245
McCloy, John, 43
McClung Lee, Alfred, 81
McCormick, Paul J., 126, 128–29, 135, 137, 274n80
McCullough, Margaret C., 164, 168
McGill University, 31, 34, 35, 36, 40, 93

McGovney, Dudley, 181
McWilliams, Carey, 38, 122, 130, 255n36
Méndez, Gonzalo, 126, 131, 132, 134
Merriam, Frank, 174
Methodist Universal Church, 119
Mexicali, Mexico, 109
Mexican Americans: assimilation, 108; LULAC, 109; postwar struggle for civil rights, 124–27; reactions to Japanese American confinement, 111; relations with Japanese Americans, 7, 105–6, 125–26, 244, 246; segregation, 108; wartime employment, 110; World War II veterans, 126. See also Chicanos; *La Opinión*; *La Prensa*; Legal cases: *Delgado v. Bastrop*; Legal cases: *Méndez v. Westminster School District*
Mexico City, 116
Mikado, The, 94
Miki, 59
Militant, The, 164
Military Intelligence Service (MIS), 52
Miller, Loren, 132, 133, 137, 158, 179, 204–6, 228, 275n90
Miller, William, 235
Mills College, 78
Minidoka Irrigator, 165
Mink, Patsy Takemoto, 238
Mississippi, 225, 239, 246
Miyagawa, Dyke, 59
Miyakawa, Kikuko, 55
Miyakawa, Masuji, 160
Miyakawa, T. Scott, 49, 55, 187
Miyamoto, Frank, 32, 33, 35, 253n2, 253n6
Modell, John, 5
Monthly Summary of Race Relations, 163
Montreal, 2, 31, 34, 36, 93–94
Montreal Committee on Canadian Citizenship, 41
Morehouse College, 170
Mori, Chiye, 59
Mori, Henry, 150
Moriguchi, Eddie, 237

Morimitsu, George, 76
Morton, Jelly Roll, 173
Mosby, Curtis, 173–74
M Project, 4, 15, 17–18, 23–24, 27–28, 250n1
Munson, Curtis B., 21
Murase, Kenny (Kenji), 59
Murphy, Frank, 196–97, 202–3, 211
Murray, Pauli, 130, 222
Myer, Dillon S., 72–74, 80, 82, 96, 179, 187

Nakamura, James, 59, 226
Nakazawa, Yoshio, 113
Nation, 86
National Association for the Advancement of Colored People (NAACP), 125, 297n18; civil rights and opposition to segregation and discrimination, 195–96, 203–6, 209–16, 223; collaboration with Japanese American organizations, 9, 62, 91–92, 106, 131–35, 205–6, 209–16, 222–23, 235, 239–40, 295n104; legal procedures for desegregation in Washington, D.C., 195, 205; legal procedures for law school desegregation, 212; opposition to confinement, 161, 164–67; opposition to Mexican segregation, 131–38; rejection by SNCC, 246
National Baptist Convention, 170
National Council of Negro Women, 167
National Japanese American Student Relocation Council, 45
National Lawyers Guild, 210
National Maritime Union, 188
National Negro Congress, 190
National Organization for Women, 170
National Urban League, 33, 160–61, 165–66
Native Sons of the Golden West, 180
Navy Department, 114
Nazism, 18, 41, 132, 140–43, 148–49, 151. *See also* Hitler, Adolf; World War II

Negro Labor Committee, 188
New Republic, 86
New Sun, The, 79
New World Sun, 142, 146
New York, 49, 88, 113, 167, 226, 233; artists, 74–75; Brooklyn, 57; Brooklyn Heights, 56; comparison with Detroit and West Coast, 4, 48, 56–57, 60, 63, 65–66; Ellis Island, 55; its ethnic concentrations according to FDR, 16, 20; JACD in, 183–92, 220; JACL in, 205, 233; Japanese American community, 53–60, 183–84; Japanese New Yorkers' response to confinement, 113; newspapers, 47, 81–82, 149; Queens, 93; wartime employment discrimination, 57–58
New York City Advisory Committee on Japanese Americans, 59
New York Herald Tribune, 77, 264n33, 265n54
New York Japanese Address Book, 54
New York Nichibei, 100, 229
New York Times, 75–76, 81, 124, 129, 167, 241
New York Times Magazine, 241
New York Unitarian Service Committee, 56
New York University, 23, 56
Nichi-Bei jiho, 55
Nichi Bei Shimbun (San Francisco), 47, 88, 140
Nichi Bei Times (San Francisco), 11, 47
Nippon Club, 55
Nisei: anti-Semitism, 151–53; belief of African American stereotypes, 219, 227–29, 233–34; college students, 44; conflicts within JACL, 235–36; decline of and debates over cooperation with African Americans, 223–27, 230–32, 239–40; in Detroit, 53–60, 66; identity, 5–6, 85–86; leaders, 25; in Los Angeles, 60–66; newspapers, 47; in New York, 48–53, 66; and Proposition 14, 235–38; relations with African Americans, 10, 218–26; relations with Chicanos, 110; soldiers, veterans ,and conscription, 35, 44, 139, 218, 220, 221; in sports, 51; strikebreakers, 109; writings, 86–87. See also Hayakawa, S. I.; Sugihara, Ina; Tajiri, Larry
Nisei: The Pride and the Shame, 83
Nisei: The Quiet Americans, 242
Nisei Weekender, 47, 82, 190
Nisei Writers and Artists Mobilization for Democracy, 162
Nishi, Setsuko Matsunaga, 11, 83, 97, 220
Nishiura, Michi, 59, 148
Nixon, Richard, 151
Noda, Hideo, 54
Noguchi, Hideyo, 54
Noguchi, Isamu, 55, 88, 158, 162
Noguchi, Yone, 54
No-No Boy, 150
Northwest Times, 47
Nyokyu Shimpo, 55

Oakland, 78, 88, 90, 166
Occidental College, 146
O'Connor, J. E. T., 179
Office of War Information (OWI), 23, 74, 180, 184, 187
Ogle, Joel, 127, 129, 274n73
Oka, Dale, 51
Okada, John, 150
Okamoto, Kiyoshi, 139, 151
Okamoto, Yoichi, 54
Okamura, Raymond, 242
Okimoto, Daniel, 239
Okrand, Fred, 137, 146, 178, 200, 206
Okubo, Miné, 5, 6, 59, 86; art exhibitions, 70–72, 75, 261n9; critique and reception of her works, 69–70, 74, 75–76, 78, 80–82, 262n10; leaves confinement for New York, 74–75, 263n20, 265n44; and Margaret Anderson, 76–77, 81–83, 264n27; postwar career, 83–84; relations with the WRA, 70, 74–75, 77–78; wartime influence on

Okubo *(continued)*
  her works, 72, 79–80, 82–83, 261n8, 263n19, 264n33
Okura, K. Patrick, 230–32, 235
Olson, Culbert, 25
Omaha, NE, 231
Omura, Bunji, 54
Omura, James, 142, 151–52
Opler, Morris and Marvin, 153
Oppenheimer, J. Robert, 146
Oregon, 114, 169
Oregon Institute of Technology, 31
Ota, Kenji, 58
Ottawa, ON, 94
Oyabe, Jenichiro, 158
Oyama, Fred, 199, 200
Oyama, Joe, 59, 141, 149, 158
Oyama, Kajiro, 199, 200
Oyama Mittwer, Mary, 6, 65, 86, 140, 165, 219, 277n8, 296n6

Pacific Citizen, 47, 51, 78, 82, 88, 91–92, 124, 147, 149, 165, 205, 218, 222, 230, 234, 236, 238, 242
Palestine, 151
Palmer Company, 53
Palomino, Frank, 126
Paonessa, Alfred E., 124
Park, Robert, 32
Pasadena Junior College, 61
Pauling, Linus, 61
Pearl Harbor (Japanese attack), 5, 21, 43, 55, 57, 61, 76, 88, 95, 114, 118, 146, 150, 162, 168, 175
Pearlman, Philip, 209, 294n84
Pen, The, 147
People's Voice, 163
Perry, Marian Wynn, 205, 209
Peru, 116
Peters, Margedant, 94, 96
Petersen, William, 241, 242, 249n2, 302n2
Philadelphia, PA, 233
Pickett, Clarence, 167
Pilgrim House, 65, 170
Pittsburgh Courier, 220
Point IV Program, 28

Poland. *See* World War II
Poling, Daniel A., 81
Portland, OR, 31–32, 41, 165
Possony, Stefan, 23
Poston News-Courier, 147
Post War World Council, 162, 186
Powell, Adam Clayton, Jr., 163, 170, 186, 287n9
Prejudice, 76
Presbyterian Church, 63
President's Committee on Civil Rights, U.S., 203, 207, 209, 223
Proposition 14, 235–38
Protestant Council of Churches, 50
Protestant Council of New York City, 205
Protestant Welfare Council, 58, 90
Protocols of the Elders of Zion, 139
Pulley, Mary Harlowe, 218
Purcell, James, 199, 200

Rafu Shimpo (Los Angeles), 47, 65, 143, 146, 149–50, 158, 238
Ramirez, Lorenzo, 126
Randolph, A. Philip, 162, 225
Ray, Ann, 176
Redfield, Robert, 32
Reed College, 32
Reischauer, Edwin O., 241
Resettlement. *See* African Americans; Japanese Americans; Los Angeles; Mexican Americans; New York; Nisei; San Francisco; Sugihara, Ina; Tajiri, Larry
Reuther, Walter, 53
Roberts Commission Report, 114
Robeson, Paul, 162, 221
Rochelle, Charles E., 163
Rockii Shimpo, 47
Roosevelt, Eleanor, 16, 25, 73, 74, 146, 167, 169
Roosevelt, Franklin D., 43, 112, 162, 176, 178, 179; creation of the FEPC, 91; death of, 27; on displaced persons, 3–4, 17–23, 28–30; on European immigration, 15–17; on Japanese relocation and ethnic

dispersion, 23–27, 72–73, 167; NNC and JACD reelection support, 190; on racialism, 3–4, 15–17
Roosevelt, Theodore, 130, 172
Rostow, Eugene V., 203
Roth, George Knox, 146, 175, 279n43
Royal Canadian Air Force, 35
Roybal, Edward, 111, 137, 271n22
Rundquist, George, 50
Rustin, Bayard, 163, 220, 222, 225
Ryerson, Edward L., 97

Sacramento, CA, 107
Sakai, Hisoji Quintus, 234
Sakamoto, Chiyoko, 180
Sakamoto, James, 25, 33
Sakamoto, Yasuchi, 114
Sakow, Shawshew, 50
Salt Lake City. *See* Utah
Sanchez, George, 139
Sanchez, Gilbert, 111
San Diego, 46, 108, 109, 181, 199, 289n26
San Fernando Valley Landscape Gardeners Association, 236
San Francisco: Human Rights March in, 226; Japanese American newspapers in, 47; Japanese and African Americans, 158, 160; and Japanese resettlers, 166, 170; Japanese school segregation, 130; Nisei and Chicanos relations in, 110; Proposition 14 in, 237–38; restrictive covenants, 206. *See also* Okubo, Miné
San Francisco Art Association, 71, 262n9
San Francisco Chronicle, 71, 113, 118, 129
San Francisco Museum of Art, 71, 75
San Francisco State University, 93, 98–99
Sano, Ray, 242
Santa Barbara, CA, 174
Santa Fe, NM, 137
Satow, Masao, 205, 231, 236
Saturday Evening Post, 226

Saturday Review, 81, 86
Scene, 47
Schuyler, George, 91, 162, 165, 168, 218, 220, 282n6
Seattle, 33, 35, 47, 78, 158, 162, 166, 253n8
Seeger, Pete, 188
Seeger, Toshi Aline Ohta, 54, 188
Seki, Hozen, 55
Selma, AL, 239
Setsuda, Roy, 50
Shangri-La, 24
Shibutani, Tomatsu (Tom), 40, 147
Shimano, Eddie, 59
Shimoda, Jack, 51
Shin Sekai, 47
Shirai, Jack, 54
Shorter, Fred, 166
Silverstein, Leo, 179
Sinaloa, Mexico, 116
Slaughter, Elizabeth, 173
Sleepy Lagoon Defense Committee, 123
Slocum, Tokie, 55
Smith, Gerald L. K., 51
Smithsonian Institution, 19
Socialist Party, 76, 90, 161, 176, 185
Socialist Workers Party, 164
Society for the Promotion of Japanese-American Civil Rights, 199
Sonoda, Kiyoshi, 50
Southern California League of Cities, 115
Southern California Retail Produce Workers' Union, 145
Soviet Union, 24, 186–87, 190
Spanish-Speaking People's Congress, 123
Spiegelman, Art, 79
Spokane, WS, 31
Spotlight, 160
Squires, George, 166
Stafford, Yoné, 150
Stalin, Joseph, 24
Stars and Stripes, 167, 168
State Department, U.S., 21, 29
Stewart, Tom, 185

Stimson, Henry L., 25, 43
St. Louis, 143
Stone, Harlan, 196, 197, 200, 288n5
Strausz-Hupé, Robert, 18, 23, 28
Struggle for Survival, The, 41
Student Christian Association, 54
Student Nonviolent Coordinating Committee, 225
Suenaga, Richard, 118
Sugahara, Roku, 144
Sugihara, Ina, 6, 11, 59, 85–86; actions in New York, 90–92, 205; on collaboration with African Americans and the FEPC, 91–92, 167, 220; early life, 90; death of, 93; on Nisei dispersion, 87–88; support of Nisei assimilation, 91
Sugimoto, Etsu, 54
Sugimoto, Henry, 59
Sunahara, Ann Gomer, 41
Suzuki, Lewis, 59

Tagami, Jimmie, 50
Tagami, Tom, 50
Tajiri, Larry, 6, 47, 55, 78, 82; on assimilation of Nisei, 90–91; on civil rights, 222; creation of and participation in *Pacific Citizen*, 88, 124; debating with Hayakawa, 98; early life and biography, 88; on Jewish discrimination, 141, 147–49, 151; leaves *Pacific Citizen*, 92; as spokesperson for the Nisei, 76, 86, 88–93
Tajiri, Marion (Guyo), 82
Takagi, Yoshitaka, 184, 186
Takahashi, Satotaka, 159
Takahashi, Torao, 208
Takaki, Ronald, 106
Takamine, Jokichi, 54
Takei, Esther, 61
Takita, Miyeko, 169
Tamagawa, Kathleen, 55
Tamotsu, Chuzo, 54
Tamura, Joe, 190
Tanabe, Shigeo, 50
Tanaka, Hideo, 58

Tanaka, Togo, 98, 143, 145, 149, 219–20
Tatsuni, Alice, 118
Taylor, Christopher, 231
Ten Years in Japan, 188
Terao, Yoshio, 150
Terminal Island, 60, 64, 114–15, 147
Texaco, 93
This World, 71–72, 74
Thomas, Dorothy Swaine, 35
Thomas, Norman, 76, 286n14; conflicts with JACD, 185–86; influence on Sugihara, 90–91; opposition to Japanese confinement, 161–62, 176–78
Thompson, Samuel, 162
Thurman, Howard, 170
Tijuana, Mexico, 109
Time, 78
Tobias, Channing, 162
Togasaki, Jane, 50
Togo, Alice M., 82
Toguri d'Aquino, Iva, 100
Tolan, John, 151, 162, 185
Tolan Committee. See Tolan, John
Toronto, ON, 221
To Secure These Rights, 203
Townsend, Willard, 162
Townshend Harris Society, 187
Tozier, M. M., 80
Traphagan School, 56
Truman, Harry S., 27–28
Tsurutani, James, 143
Tulane University, 41
Tuskegee Institute, 158, 172
Tynes, Richard, 165

Union of Mexican Railroad Workers, 116
United Auto Workers, 53
United Federation of Teachers, 163
United Nations, 130, 187, 210
United Negro Improvement Association (UNIA), 159
United States Congress, 16, 72, 91, 97, 137, 166, 198, 211, 224, 228–30, 234, 238, 239, 245, 299n56

Index / 317

University of California, 35, 70–71, 90, 163–64, 169, 181, 241
University of Chicago, 31, 32, 97
University of Guelph, 41
University of Manitoba, 93
University of Michigan, 48, 49, 52
University of Minnesota, 150
University of Missouri, 212
University of Oklahoma, 212
University of Texas, 212
University of Toronto, 41
University of Washington, 31, 32, 166, 253n8
University of Wisconsin, 93
Uno, Kazumaro "Buddy," 141, 278n35
Utah, 47, 49, 88, 177, 221, 264n33, 284n41, 289n20
Utah Nippo, 47, 124, 131
Utopian Society of America, 174
Uyeda, Clifford, 100, 226, 230–31, 297n26, 298n44
Uyeno, Tad, 110, 144, 278n31

Varzally, Allison, 139
Versailles Peace Conference of 1919, 159
Vietnam War, 29, 99
Vinson, Fred, 201–3, 207, 214
Voorhis, Jerry, 178
Voting Rights Act of 1965, 239
Voyage of the Damned, 143

Waggoner, Joe D., 228
Wakayama, Ernest K. and Toki, 178–79
Wake, Lloyd, 226
Wallace, Henry, 21, 24, 191
Waller, Odell, 169
Walsh, Richard, 88
War Department, 43–44, 73, 188
War Relocation Authority: aid in resettlement, 48–50, 57–58, 62–63; approval of Miné Okubo's works, 70, 72, 77–78, 80; care of Jewish refugees, 149; encourages Japanese assimilation, 85; end of operations, 59, 80, 190; establishment of camps, 25; food and salary discrimination, 44; judgment of impact of Japanese confinement, 73–74; parole system and gradual release, 44–47, 74–75, 160, 188; recruitment of administrators, 36, 96; segregation of disloyal people, 37
Warren, Earl, 48, 128, 136, 179, 214–15
War Worker, The, 165
Washington (state), 32, 48, 50, 114
Washington, Booker T., 173
Washington, D.C., 19, 144, 177, 178, 204–5, 208, 214, 215, 218, 222, 226, 233, 295n104
Washington, March on, 99–100, 225, 230, 232, 246, 286n14, 295n104
Waters, Ethel, 204
Watts riot of 1965, 238–39, 245
Wayne University, 49
Weglyn, Walter, 148
White, Walter, 161, 166–67, 223
White Plains, NY, 93
Wilkins, Roy, 161, 167, 235
Willamette University, 32
Wilson, Emmet, 109
Wilson, Woodrow, 17
Windsor, ON, 49
Winnipeg, MB, 93
Wirin, A. L., 124, 131–32, 137, 146, 148, 179–81, 199–201, 204–6, 208–9, 216, 275n90, 275n92, 289n26, 290n32, 290n35, 291n36, 295n98
Wirth, Louis, 32
Wong, Kei T., 174
World War II, 1, 15, 31, 40, 41, 100, 139, 140, 171, 198, 212; impact on Mexican American communities, 110–11; and Japanese Americans outside the West Coast, 43, 48, 53; Mexican American reactions to Japanese confinement, 105–10; migration and dispersion, 28, 85; Nazi Germany in, 140–43; United States entry, 18. For wartime confinement of Japanese Americans, *see* Confinement of Japanese Americans

WRA camps: Amache, 181; Gila River, 25; Hawthorne, 63; Heart Mountain, 4, 31, 36–37, 150; Jerome, 53, 217; Manzanar, 111, 114, 117–19, 123, 152–53, 179; Owens Valley, 119–20; Pendleton, 29; Perote (Mexico), 116; Pomona, 119; Rohwer, 147, 217; Santa Anita, 83, 117, 120, 178; Tanforan, 70, 72, 264n33; Topaz, 70–71, 72, 79, 169, 264n33; Tulare, 119; Tule Lake, 35, 37, 72, 75, 150, 168
Wright, Pamela Stennes, 69

Yamamoto, Hisaye, 65, 149, 220
Yamamoto, Joe, 150
Yamaoka, George, 55, 59
Yamasaki, Minoru, 49, 55
Yamashita, Sak, 110
Yamuchi, Wakako, 65
Yancey, John, 170
Yashima, Taro and Mitsu (Jun and Mitsu Iwamatsu), 54, 75
Yasui, Minoru, 212, 231
Yasui, Roku, 50
Yasumura, Michi, 33
Yasutake, Anthony, 50
Yoneda, Karl, 152–53
Yoshinaga, George, 237
Yoshino, John, 225
Yoshino, Ruby, 59
Young-Megahy, Consuelo, 167–68
Young Men's Christian Association (YMCA), 46

Text:	10/13 Aldus
Display:	Aldus
Compositor:	Westchester Book Group
Indexer:	Gabriel Séguin
Printer and binder:	IBT Global

www.ingramcontent.com/pod-product-compliance
Lightning Source LLC
Chambersburg PA
CBHW020637230426
43665CB00008B/206